DICKENS STUDIES ANNUAL
Essays on Victorian Fiction

DICKENS STUDIES ANNUAL
Essays on Victorian Fiction

EDITORS

Michael Timko
Fred Kaplan
Edward Guiliano

DICKENS STUDIES ANNUAL

Essays on Victorian Fiction

VOLUME
14

Edited by
Michael Timko, Fred Kaplan,
and Edward Guiliano

AMS PRESS
NEW YORK

DICKENS STUDIES ANNUAL
ISSN 0084-9812

International Standard Book Number
Series: 0-404-18520-7
Vol. 14: 0-404-18534-7

Dickens Studies Annual: Essays on Victorian Fiction welcomes essay and monograph-length contributions on Dickens as well as on other Victorian novelists and on the history or aesthetics of Victorian fiction. All manuscripts should be double-spaced, including footnotes, which should be grouped at the end of the submission, and should be prepared according to the format used in this journal. An editorial decision can usually be reached more quickly if two copies are submitted. The preferred editions for citations from Dickens' works are the Clarendon and the Norton Critical when available, otherwise the Oxford Illustrated Dickens or the Penguin.

Please send submissions to the Editors, *Dickens Studies Annual*, Room 1522, Graduate School and University Center, City University of New York, 33 West 42nd Street, New York, N.Y. 10036; please send subscription inquiries to AMS Press, Inc., 56 East 13th Street, New York, N.Y. 10003.

Contents

List of Illustrations

Contents

vii

Preface

Of the making of prefaces there may be no end, at least as long as *Dickens Studies Annual* continues to flourish. Five of the essays in this volume testify to the fascination of modern readers with *David Copperfield*; the two essays on *Our Mutual Friend* and the essay "What's in a Name" represent both Dickens' and modern critical fascination with language and its variations. As usual, both well-known and less-well-known scholars and critics and a variety of scholarly and critical approaches are represented. While Dickens takes pride of place and frequency, fine essays on Eliza Lynn Linton, George Eliot, and Thomas Hardy, as well as a review article on new work in the study of literature and society in nineteenth-century British fiction, authenticate the subtitle "Essays on Victorian Fiction." All this is, of course, obvious to the attentive reader of the table of contents, and calling the obvious to the attention of readers hardly justifies prefatory paragraphs.

What does justify the making of prefaces is the extending of thanks to those who have assisted us in the creation of this volume and in the ongoing work of *Dickens Studies Annual*. The California Dickens Project has again demonstrated its creativity and value. Particularly to be thanked are Murray Baumgarten and John Jordan of the University of California at Santa Cruz and Edwin Eigner of the University of California at Riverside. The 1984 Conference at Santa Cruz, directed by Murray Baumgarten, provided a stimulating series of talks and papers on *David Copperfield*, and John Jordan and Edwin Eigner have contributed to transforming some of these papers into articles.

Numbers of experts in Victorian fiction have generously contributed their time and energy to help us and our authors by reading and evaluating articles. For such service, we wish particularly to thank Felicia Bonaparte, Edwin Eigner, and Barry Cualls. We continue to enjoy (and to offer our thanks for) the generous support of Presidents Saul Cohen and Harold Proshansky, of Queens College and the Graduate School and University Center respectively; Acting President and Provost William Hamovitch and Dean John H. Reilly of Queens College; Vice President and Provost Steven Cahn and Professor Lillian Feder, Executive Officer of the Ph.D. Program in English, the Graduate School and University Center; Professor Fred Buell, Chairman, Department of English, Queens College; Gabriel Hornstein, President, William B. Long, Editor, and Robert Harris, Copy Editor, AMS Press. Our editorial assistant for this volume, Elizabeth Licata, deserves our thanks for her thoroughness and efficiency.

Notes on Contributors

NANCY F. ANDERSON teaches English History and Women's History at the University of New Orleans. She has published articles on the Victorian family in the *Journal of British Studies* and *Psychohistory Review*, and is completing a biography of Eliza Lynn Linton.

MURRAY BAUMGARTEN is Director of The Dickens Project of the University of California, centered at Santa Cruz. He is also the Editor-in-Chief of the Essential Carlyle Edition, a selected edition of the works of Thomas Carlyle to be published by the University of California Press.

JOEL J. BRATTIN is a Whiting Fellow at Stanford University, and is currently serving as Associate Editor of *The Essential Carlyle*, a selected scholarly edition of Thomas Carlyle's works. He has written extensively on nineteenth-century literary manuscripts, and is the author of *Our Mutual Friend: An Annotated Bibliography* (1984). By the time this volume is in print, he expects to have celebrated the delivery of both his Ph.D. and his first child.

WILLIAM E. BUCKLER is Professor of English at New York University. Long a dedicated student of Victorian literature, his most recent contributions include *Poetry and Truth in Robert Browning's "The Ring and the Book"*, *Man and His Myths: Tennyson's "Idylls of the King" in Critical Context*,

Matthew Arnold's Prose: Three Essays in Literary Enlargement, and *The Poetry of Thomas Hardy: A Study in Art and Ideas*. He is currently at work on Walter Pater.

KAREN CHASE is an associate professor at the University of Virginia and author of *Eros and Psyche: The Representation of Personality in Charlotte Brontë, Charles Dickens and George Eliot*.

RICHARD J. DUNN is Professor and Chairman of English at the University of Washington. He is the author of *Approaches to Teaching Dickens' David Copperfield* (1984) and *David Copperfield: An Annotated Bibliography* (1981), and of numerous essays on Dickens, Carlyle, the Brontës, and others. He has served as secretary-treasurer and president of the Dickens Society. Among present projects he is considering a play based upon the Skimpole-Hunt slander.

EDWIN M. EIGNER is Professor of English and Creative Writing at the University of California, Riverside, and author of *Robert Louis Stevenson and Romantic Tradition* (1966) and *The Metaphysical Novel in England and America: Dickens, Bulwer, Hawthorne, Melville* (1978). He and George J. Worth are currently editing a collection of Victorian Criticism of Fiction.

MICHAEL GREENSTEIN, Associate Professor of English at the University of Sherbrooke, Quebec, has published numerous articles on Canadian literature, and was awarded a Fellowship from the Social Sciences and Humanities Research Council of Canada to complete *The Ghetto and the Garrison: Jewish-Canadian Literature*. Upon completion, he intends to explore further changes in perception from the Romantics to the Victorians.

ROGER B. HENKLE is Professor of English at Brown University, where he co-directs the interdisciplinary Program in Modern Literature and Society. He is the author of *Comedy and Culture: England 1820–1900* (1980), and his articles on nineteenth-century fiction and comedy theory have appeared in *Sewanee Review, Virginia Quarterly Review, Critical Quarterly, Mosaic*, and elsewhere. He is presently working on a book on the use of the imagination to deal with certain social issues in Victorian culture and its effect on literary form.

JOHN O. JORDAN teaches at the University of California at Santa Cruz, where he helps coordinate the Dickens Project.

JOHN KUCICH is Associate Professor of English at the University of Michigan. He has published a book on Dickens and numerous articles on Dickens, George Eliot, and Charlotte Brontë. His book on repression in Victorian fiction will be published by the University of California Press next year.

RICHARD LETTIS, a professor of English Literature at Long Island University, is working on a book on the Dickens aesthetic.

ANNE LOHRLI is Professor Emeritus of English at New Mexico Highlands University. Her publications include numerous articles on Victorian writers and writings, and *Household Words . . . List of Contributors and Their Contributions* (1973).

CAROL HANBERY MACKAY is Assistant Professor of English at the University of Texas at Austin. Besides publishing articles on Dickens, Carlyle, Thackeray, and Hawthorne, she has prepared an extensive introduction to Anne Thackeray Ritchie's Biographical Introductions to the Centenary Edition of Thackeray's Works. Her recently completed study of soliloquy in nineteenth-century fiction has been accepted for publication by Macmillan.

D. A. MILLER teaches English and comparative literature at the University of California, Berkeley. He is the author of *Narrative and its Discontents: Problems of Closure in the Traditional Novel* (1981).

HARRY STONE, Professor of English at California State University, Northridge, is the author of *Charles Dickens' Uncollected Writings from "Household Words"*, *Dickens and the Invisible World*, and many other books and essays on nineteenth- and twentieth-century English literature. His most recent book, just published, is a limited, illustrated edition of *George Silverman's Explanation*. Another book, *Dickens' Working Notes for His Novels*, is now in the press.

David Copperfield
and the
Benevolent Spirit

Edwin M. Eigner

In his recent book *Dickens and Women* Michael Slater calls Betsey Trotwood "the finest flowering of Dickens's concentration on women in his mid-career."[1] Another critic, Sylvère Monod, who is perhaps the most appreciative of *David Copperfield*'s modern readers, notes that David's aunt "has been regarded as the real heroine of the novel." He feels that "she is at any rate its most powerful creation." He goes on to say that Aunt Betsey "is all that the novelist loved most: superficially eccentric and arbitrary, but at bottom generous and sensitive." Her presence in *David Copperfield* is "the supreme achievement of Dickens' art in his autobiographical novel."[2]

A number of critics come close to sharing this high opinion of this relatively minor character, although frequently for reasons which differ from Slater's and Monod's and indeed one another's. Stephen L. Franklin, for instance, one of several critics interested in the elegiac quality of *David Copperfield*, believes that Betsey Trotwood "is at the moral center of the novel," and that she "strikes the keynote" when she says, "it is vain, Trot, to recall the past, unless it works some influence upon the present."[3] Q. D. Leavis values her highly as "a very human case-history" on which Dickens worked "very hard."[4] Gwendolyn Needham, whose seminal article "The Undisciplined Heart of *David Copperfield*" has at least established the terms of debate for most modern discussions of the novel, including my own, sees Aunt Betsey as the first of the characters who succeeds in the necessary business of opening a heart, her own, which a mistaken and crippling marriage had at first closed to all mankind.[5]

Needham and Leavis thus see Betsey as a fully realistic character, subject, like David, to the vicissitudes of experience. Others have seen her in quite a different light. According to G. K. Chesterton, "Dickens writes realism," in the case of Betsey Trotwood "in order to make the incredible credible,"[6] and Shirley Grob, A. O. J. Cockshut, and Harry Stone all mount formidable arguments for seeing Betsey as David Copperfield's fairy godmother, endowed with magical powers both to console and to transform.[7] In direct opposition to Needham's position, Cockshut goes so far as to say—too far, it seems to me—that "she has no human need to conform herself to reality."[8]

Nevertheless, as Mrs. Leavis herself concedes,[9] there is good reason to regard David's aunt as a supernatural character. She appears and disappears abruptly, she is eccentric, and she seems to have the mystical power, twice employed, of projecting herself out of her quietly sitting body and across rooms so that she can console with a touch of the hand. Betsey's power over the Murdstones is also somewhat more than natural, as is the transforming effect on David of her employment of this power.

The scene just referred to, in which Aunt Betsey puts the Murdstones to flight and rescues the hero's psyche, distinguishes *David Copperfield* from the sub-genre of fiction it had appeared up to this point to be imitating. Much of the early material in the story seems influenced—influenced nearly to the point of plagiarism—by incidents from Charlotte Brontë's popular novel of two years earlier, *Jane Eyre*.[10] Both Jane and David are driven to rebellion against a cruel step-parent, and they are both punished, first by a long isolation in a dark room and then by being sent off to a brutal school. Jane must stand on a stool while her new classmates and teachers are informed that she is a liar; David must wear a humiliating sign: "*Take care of him. He bites.*" Both are first comforted by a schoolmate and ultimately vindicated by a kindly and judicious adult. The difference in the two protagonists, and indeed in the two authors' views of human nature, is that Jane is in no real psychical danger, while David most certainly is. The unjust cruelty of adults can hurt Jane, can even put her in danger of her life, but it can't make her into a liar. She has too much integrity for that. In the Dickens world, on the other hand, characters are frequently in the most dreadful danger of becoming whatever they are treated as. David bites when Murdstone beats him like an animal.[11] Later on, "He ordered me like a dog, and I obeyed like a dog" (8.103). Still later, when he is sent to work in the warehouse, he literally loses his social class: "I *became*, at ten years old, a little laboring hind in the service of Murdstone and Grinby" (11.132, emphasis mine). Jane could never forget herself in this way. When Mrs. Reed calls her a liar, she decisively quells her accuser with the savage response: *"You* are deceitful. . . . Deceit is not my fault" (Ch. 4).

And just as the danger is the greater in Dickens, so must the rescue be the more extraordinary. There is plenty of the supernatural elsewhere in *Jane Eyre*, but Charlotte Brontë's Miss Temple investigates the truth of the charge against the heroine by writing a letter to ascertain the facts of the case and as a result is able to exonerate her. Aunt Betsey makes a similar show of judicial prudence, but at the crucial moment she appeals to Mr. Dick as though he were a familiar spirit. Only then, it appears, can she tell Murdstone the story of his deceptions and persecutions as though she herself had witnessed them. Murdstone is thus annihilated from David's psyche, and David can begin a new life with a new name and with his humanity and social position fully restored.

David's new name, which he of course shares with his aunt, gives an insight into the source of the magical power that enables a single lady living on a modest income to rout so consummate a villain as Murdstone. Variations of the name resonate throughout Dickens. Job Trotter of *Pickwick Papers* and Trotty Veck of *The Chimes* are two early examples. More to the point I shall be trying to make, Dame Trot is one of the not very flattering nicknames affectionately bestowed on Esther Summerson, the heroine of the novel Dickens wrote directly after *David Copperfield*.

A trot is an old woman or an old hag, and Dame Trot was a nursery rhyme character, a kind of Mother Hubbard with a comical cat instead of a dog. The two of them, mistress and pet, broke into print, so far as I have been able to discover, around 1800, and while their adventures were numerous, just a few doggerel verses will give one the idea of them:

> She went to the butcher's
> To buy her some meat.
> When she came back
> Puss lay dead at her feet.

> She went to the undertaker's
> For a coffin and shroud.
> When she came back
> Puss sat up and miawed.[12]

So far, and in the rest of the nursery rhymes, all the power belongs to the cat, but things changed when the Dame was adopted as a character in the nineteenth-century Christmas pantomimes and figured there on several occasions as the Benevolent Spirit.[13]

The Regency and early Victorian Pantomime was, as I have argued previously in these pages,[14] a significant influence on both the characterization and structure of Dickens' novels. The genre was a development from the *commedia dell'arte*, in which a typical new comedy love story, involving a girl, her suitable and unsuitable lovers, her mercenary, wrong-headed father, and his clumsy servant, gets converted into a Harlequinade by the magic of a Benevolent Spirit, derived from mythology or the literature of fairy tales and nursery rhymes. The Benevolent Spirit brings about a happy ending for the true lovers by changing not only their natures, but the very genre, and hence the world-view, of the work in which they appear. From as early as *Nicholas Nickleby*, the constellation of characters surrounding most every Dickens heroine may be fruitfully regarded as representing the Pantomime cast involved in the pursuit of Columbine. They are either Harlequins, Dandy Lovers, Pantaloons, Clowns, or Benevolent Spirits. And there is always in the production a crucial and essential genre shift from realism to romance.

The Benevolent Spirit is obviously a powerfully magical figure simply by virtue of his or her literary sources. When the Benevolent Spirit is female, moreover, as in the case of Dame Trot or Mother Goose or Cinderella's Godmother, she takes on an added power because of her ambivalent sexuality. Hers, which is called a dame part, is one of the two transvestite roles in the Pantomime, the other being Harlequin, who was frequently played by the Principal Boy, an actress. I am at a loss to explain why this sexual confusion has always been so hilariously appealing to British audiences or why it confers so much power on the character, but both phenomena are as observable in English theatre and television of today as they were in *Twelfth Night* and *As You Like It*, where, of course, a boy played a girl disguised as a boy. One of the popular and critical triumphs of the 1983 West End season was a revival of *Charley's Aunt*!

Aunt Betsey Trotwood is not only mannish in appearance and behavior; she has a richly ambivalent attitude toward men and toward sex. Michael Slater has noted, for instance, that since Betsey's attempts to educate her servants "to reject the male species" always ended in a marriage, the education could "hardly" have been "of a very serious or determined kind."[15] Q. D. Leavis believes that while it cannot have been meant "as a symbolic threat of murder or castration" at the conscious level, "the chop in the air with her knife" with which Betsey punctuates her first greeting of David—"Go along! No boys here" (13.163)—"is undoubtedly the right gesture to express the attitude . . . [she] has taken up."[16] On the other hand, Mrs. Leavis notes Betsey's kindnesses towards David and Mr. Dick.

Her violence towards donkeys and donkey boys, according to Mrs. Leavis, is also "psychologically right: the aggressiveness belongs to her condition, as the touch of mania against the opposite sex sees the donkey-drivers as suitable objects of her animus against mankind."[17] So put, the mania sounds a bit mysterious—why donkeys, especially?—but it is perhaps worth noting a fact with which Dickens' readers, living in an age without automobiles, might have been familiar through observation: that the erect penis of the donkey is proportionately longer than that of any other mammal.[18]

In any event, as a fairy-tale personage and as a figure of great sexual ambivalence, Aunt Betsey inherits the power of the Benevolent Spirit derived from the pantomime Dame Trot; and if we feel, as many readers *have* felt, that *David Copperfield* almost switches genres, becomes a different kind of novel, after Aunt Betsey changes David, the "little laboring hind," into Trotwood, the scholar gentleman and spritely lover, then we are sensing something similar to what pantomime audiences must have experienced when the Benevolent Spirit transformed the melodrama of the "opening" into a fast-moving Harlequinade. At this point in the pantomime, she faded into the background for a while, but it was only to reappear later when the cheeky Harlequin overplayed his hand and could not get on without her magical assistance. Similarly, after the routing of the Murdstones, Betsey Trotwood seems to subside into a realistic aunt and guardian. This appearance, I shall argue, is equally deceptive.

According to Gwendolyn Needham, whose influential article I noted earlier, Betsey Trotwood is not only the first example of a realistic character who must learn to open her damaged heart, she is also David's mentor in the business of disciplining his own heart, toughening up his character. Needham points out the large debt *David Copperfield* owes to *Tom Jones* and the English novel of development. "Fielding directly warns," she writes, "that Tom's innate goodness is not enough; he must learn prudence."[19] Betsey, whose "object in life," as she says, "is to provide for . . . [David's] being a good, a sensible, and a happy man" (23.296), tells him, in a very much quoted passage:

> But what I want you to be, Trot . . . is, a fine firm fellow. A fine firm fellow with a will of your own. With resolution. . . . With determination. With character, Trot—with strength of character that is not to be influenced, except on good reason, by anybody or by anything.　　　　(19.234–235)

This is indeed the ideal of the English novel of development as established by Fielding, and it is easy to see that David, likable though he is, stands in considerable need of such training. His life has no direction, so that he thinks any career would suit him as long as it is gentlemanly. He is subject to infatuations which lead to dangerous loves and dangerous friendships. More-over, while the critic Robin Gilmour is undoubtedly correct to point out the Wordsworthian regret with which Dickens mourns the passing of this charm-ingly spontaneous David,[20] it is also true that David's reckless softness brings grief to himself and to many of those around him—the servants, whom he lets Dora corrupt; the Peggottys, whom he exposes to the even more undisciplined heart of James Steerforth; and Agnes, whom he weakly abandons to the lustful machinations of Uriah Heep.

Betsey Trotwood tries to help David overcome this immature softness by employing a number of techniques which a judicious guardian might adopt either in the real world or, indeed, in a realistic novel. She sends him to a good school and lets him live away from home. She does not interfere in his life with useless advice or criticism. When he is having a hard time choosing a career, she buys him "a little breathing-time," so that he can look at the question "from a new point of view, and not as a schoolboy" (19.234). And when the breathing-time does not produce the desired results, she steps in without recriminations, finds him a job and sets him up in independent London lodgings. At this point, "my aunt informed me how she confidently trusted that the life I was to lead would make me firm and self-reliant, which was all I wanted" (23.303).

This is, indeed, model behavior, but it is nevertheless appropriate to the realistic novel of development. The same cannot be said, however, of Betsey's next ploy, which is to inform David that she has lost her entire fortune. It is, of course, a lie; she still has two thousand pounds which Heep knew nothing about. Later on, she will justify herself saying, "I wanted to see how you would come out of the trial, Trot" (54.665). Now, characters tell lies in realistic novels, no doubt, and tell them as frequently or more frequently perhaps than they do in romances, but Harry Stone is right when he calls this particular kind of falsehood "a typical folk-tale testing."[21] When such tests or constructed ordeals occur, not only in folk tales but in chivalric romances and elsewhere, the purpose is seldom entirely or even primarily to measure virtue, but more frequently to inculcate it. In David's case the situation of his aunt's supposed poverty, together with his need to become an eligible suitor for Dora, force him to develop at least some of the qualities Aunt Betsey has been aiming at. "You came out nobly," she tells him later, anticipating the praise of Pip, "you acted nobly, my boy," which Magwitch offers as the justification of his fairy godfather gift of a fortune. "I have never forgot it."[22]

In the case of Aunt Betsey Trotwood, nobly means "persevering, self-reliant, self-denying" (54.665). David has already come to the same conclusion about himself:

> I will only add, to what I have already written of my perseverance at this time of my life, and of a patient and continuous energy which then began to be matured within me, and which I know to be the strong part of my character, if it have any strength at all, that there, on looking back, I find the source of my success. (42.517)

Betsey's lie has formed David's character, and while there is nothing unrealistic in the telling of such a lie, the implications of the aesthetics of such an action are highly disturbing to the realist position. The falsehood or fiction she invents for David's good would be out of place, therefore, if *David Copperfield* were a realistic novel of development, because the very notion of education through deception cuts at the heart of the philosophy of realism, which holds that the truth only is good for us and that we learn by confronting it.

Monod writes that "perhaps the essential message [of the novel] lies in *Copperfield*'s insistence on the value of perseverance,"[23] but few readers have felt that David has found his way out of his forest of difficulties when he learns through supposed necessity the value of hard work. Indeed, his new industry looks to be at least as dangerous to himself and others as his old indolence. David's early morning plunges into the Roman Bath have brought him into what he recognizes as "a state of ferocious virtue" (36.447), and a number of critics, including Monod himself,[24] have seen the self-righteously grim face of Mr. Murdstone in the new, energetic David. Arnold Kettle writes that "one of the most revealing moments in the David/Dora story is when David recognizes that he is trying to 'form' Dora's character just as Mr. Murdstone had tried to form his mother's."[25] Aunt Betsey is certainly right when she tells David that both his father and his mother would have "been the better" for firmness (19.235), but we should remember that Dickens' first idea of a name for David's cruel step-father was "Mr. Harden"[26] and that his sister, Jane Murdstone, is proud she belongs "to a family remarkable . . . for some firmness" (26.335).

Nor, although subsequent critics seem to have lost sight of this fact, had Needham herself intended to suggest that Fieldingesque prudence, derived from *Tom Jones*, is all David has to learn. "Dickens' theme of the undisciplined heart," she wrote, "encompasses this truth and goes further; natural goodness plus prudence may win affectionate respect, but one must learn a higher wisdom of the heart if he would achieve inner strength and peace.''[27] It is not Betsey Trotwood, of course, but Annie Strong, who rings the keynote of the theme to which Needham alludes. Annie says in a scene David witnesses:

> If I were thankful to my husband for no more, instead of so much, I should be thankful to him for having saved me from the first mistaken impulse of my undisciplined heart.   (45.564)

Critics, at least since the time of Needham's article, have been trying to explain what Mrs. Strong meant to say exactly and why the phrase, with a different meaning perhaps, keeps echoing in David's consciousness throughout the rest of the novel. Is Annie simply expanding on the theme of prudence and advising against marriages based on youthful passion rather than mature reason? This seems to be the first meaning David perceives, especially when he combines it, as he immediately does, with Mrs. Strong's other memorable statement: "There can be no disparity in marriage like unsuitability of mind and purpose" (45.567). Given this reading of the phrase "undisciplined heart," the novel seems simply to be recommending safe, practical, passionless marriages like the Strongs' and like those between Traddles and Sophy, David and Agnes, Barkis and Peggotty, Martha and the Australian farm laborer. And if we cannot go beyond this reading, then it is easy to sympathize with a critic like Robin Gilmour when he writes that "one can respect the seriousness of Dickens's recommendation of prudence and emotional self-discipline without being convinced that this official subject makes contact with the centres of vitality in the novel."[28]

These "centres of vitality," according to Gilmour, do not spring from Henry Fielding and eighteenth-century rationalism at all, but from Romantic thought and feeling. He locates them specifically in Wordsworth's "Immortality Ode." Gilmour's is an intelligent reading. Wordsworth's autobiographical poem, *The Prelude*, was, of course, published in 1850 while Dickens was writing and publishing his autobiographical novel, and indeed the poet's words echo strongly and frequently in the last chapters of *David Copperfield*. But so do those of a number of other nineteenth-century writers—Tennyson, Byron, Carlyle, Goethe—whose works may have more relevance than Wordsworth's to the problem of the undisciplined heart, a phrase which David repeats frequently in these last pages, but without reference sometimes to the prudence in marriage theme. By the time of Dora's death, for instance, David has certainly learned that there can be no disparity in marriage like unsuitability of mind and purpose, but he still refers to his heart as "undisciplined"

(53.658), as he does later on, after the death of Steerforth: "Listlessness to everything but brooding sorrow was the night that fell on my undisciplined heart" (58.697).

Tennyson is used in the late passages to show how time and human concerns transform devastating grief into purposeful work. "A letter from Agnes," writes Jerome H. Buckley, "helps restore . . . [David's] perspective on the purposes of human life and society, somewhat as the more mystical letters from Hallam in *In Memoriam* [another work of 1850] help affirm the continuity of the living soul. As Tennyson sees the darkness dissolve, so, in reading [the letter], David feels 'the night . . . passing from [his] mind.' Again like Tennyson, who resolves to 'take what fruit may be / Of sorrow under human skies,' he now cultivates 'the human interest' he had shrunk from."[29] Moreover, the chapter in which David and Agnes finally come to understand one another's disciplined hearts begins iambically with an obvious echo from Tennyson's *In Memoriam*: "The year came round to Christmastime" (62.733).

Byron's undisciplined heart is recalled in the tempest scene at Yarmouth and later during David's European exile:

> I roamed from place to place, carrying my burden with me everywhere. . . .
> From city to city, seeking I know not what, and trying to leave I know not what
> behind.   (58.696)

But Byron is opened in *David Copperfield* only that he may be closed, closed first in favor of Carlyle, whose *Sartor Resartus* the just quoted passage also echoes. Ultimately Byron is closed, as I shall be arguing, in favor of Goethe, Carlyle's master, whom Carlyle had recommended, also in *Sartor*, as the proper antidote to Byronic self-pity and self-indulgence.

Richard Dunn has written perceptively that *David Copperfield* can, in fact, "be read as a sequel to *Sartor Resartus*."[30] If so, then Dickens' novel belongs in the tradition of the *Bildungsroman*, the German novel of development, which was visionary where Fielding and the English were experiential, and which was informed frequently with Romantic, anti-rationalistic sentiments. Dunn goes on to say that "nowhere in nineteenth-century literature is the disciplining of heart more obvious than in Carlyle's writing," and that Carlyle meant and Dickens understood the disciplining of heart to be "renunciation of the self (that is, renunciation of selfishness)."[31]

Here is a meaning for Annie Strong's often repeated phrase which goes beyond prudence and which was or should have been implicit in the critical discussion since Needham, who wrote, with Carlyle clearly enough in mind,[32] "the good heart must have no 'alloy of self,' must love humanity as well as persons."[33] So defined, moreover, the list of characters with undisciplined hearts in *David Copperfield* includes not only the good-hearted and sympathetically drawn people of the novel like David, his mother, Dora, young Betsey Trotwood, Little Em'ly, and Murdstone's second wife. These have loved foolishly and therefore unsuitably. But if the root cause of their mistakes can be understood, not as youthful impetuosity, but as egoistical selfishness, then the list can be expanded to take in some of the less charming lovers and would-be lovers of the novel—Murdstone, Steerforth, Rosa Dartle, Littimer, and Heep. Thus David does not miss out with Agnes in the early chapters because he is too blind (Betsey Trotwood's oracular word) to realize that she is the suitable woman for him; he makes his near-tragic mistake because his blindness does not let him see that his love for her, like his love for Steerforth and Dora and Peggotty and all the others, is for his own gratification and to fulfill his own immature psychological needs, not for the sake of the beloved or of the good work for humanity she can help him perform. Indeed, David's selfishness is apparent, as Sylvère Monod has pointed out, at the very moment when he seems to be passing Aunt Betsey's fairy-tale test. "He is distressed by Miss Betsey's loss of her fortune," Monod concedes, "but there is clearly something defensive in his insistence on the non-selfish motives of his feelings: 'I was roused from my amazement, and concern for her—I am sure for her—by her falling on my neck'" (34.425–426).[34] The habits of hard work and persevering self-reliance which issue from this test are admirable and necessary for David's development, but they are ultimately dangerous because David's purpose in the forest of difficulty is unworthy. He is only, as he says, "cutting down trees *until* . . . [he comes] to Dora" (36.444, my emphasis). According to Carlyle, as Richard Dunn interprets him, a person must "renounce the selfish ego, deny imposture, and define his character by diligent work that aims at noble ends. . . . [David] has gone through the motions of seeking identity and has learned not renunciation and certitude but tactics of evasion. Though kindly intended, Betsey Trotwood's benevolence," Dunn believes, "becomes in effect David's summons to join what Carlyle called the 'Dandiacal Body,' those whose 'existence consists in the wearing of clothes'."[35]

Carlyle derived his philosophy of renunciation from the ancestor of the *Bildungsroman*, Goethe's *Wilhelm Meister*, the second part of which is subtitled *Die Entsagenden*, or, as Carlyle translated it, *The Renunciants*. Charles Harrold, the author of *Carlyle and German Thought: 1819–1834*,[36] argues persuasively that Carlyle entirely misunderstood and distorted Goethe's meaning, but this question need not concern us here, since Dickens' Goethe was certainly Carlyle's, and if Dickens knew *Wilhelm Meister*, as I believe he did, it must have been through Carlyle's translation. Moreover, nothing in the text of Goethe's novel itself directly contradicts what Carlyle says. As Harrold points out, "nowhere in the *Wanderjahre* is [the word] *Entsagen* defined or discussed."[37]

It is, however, not in the second part of *Wilhelm Meister*, but in the last chapters of the first part, the *Lehrjahre*, that the topics of renunciation and the disciplined heart are treated in ways that are relevant to *David Copperfield* and may even have influenced it. Here is the incident I have in mind. Wilhelm, after a number of purely impulsive loves, is educated by his friends to the point of proposing marriage to Theresa, a woman of whom his intellect entirely approves. As he explains, and one must excuse the awkwardness of Carlyle's translation, "this resolution, of soliciting Theresa's hand, is probably the first that has proceeded altogether from myself. I had laid my plan considerately; my reason fully joined in it; by the consent of that noble maiden all my hopes were crowned."[38] However, things are never so simple in Goethe. Before she met Wilhelm, Theresa had been about to marry Lothario, Wilhelm's valued friend. The engagement ended when it was discovered that the lovers were apparently brother and sister. Now it is suddenly reported that they are not related, after all. Theresa, who still loves Lothario, nevertheless suspects a trick and presses for an early marriage with Wilhelm. Poor Wilhelm is in a constant state of ill-humor during these chapters because he believes, and with good reason, that people are playing games with his life, perhaps for his own good, perhaps not. In spite of this, he believes that Lothario "well merits every sort of friendship and affection; and, without sacrifices, friendship cannot be imagined. For his sake . . . [Wilhelm concludes] it shall be possible for me to give away the worthiest bride."[39] And he does renounce Theresa—several times, in fact.

Goethe almost certainly intended irony here, for Wilhelm is already beginning to half suspect, when he makes his grand sacrifice, that he is falling in love with another woman. Still, the exercise appears to have aided the hero's development, and the irony may even have been lost on Carlyle and also on Dickens, who in 1846 had written a Christmas Book in which two noble sisters, both in love with the same man, positively outdo one another in the business of renunciation. Even readers who can come to terms with Agnes Wickfield are unable to credit the noble selflessness of Grace and Marion Jeddler, heroines of *The Battle of Life*.

Loving his fellow men selflessly, as Carlyle was urging, was obviously important to Dickens. It was also something he had a relatively easy time doing, just as the kind of "story with a purpose" (58.699) Agnes inspires the grieving David to write was the kind Dickens wrote always. But equally important to him, and much less easy for him to accomplish in his own life, was the ability to love another person without self-gratification, to be happy in the beloved's happiness even when it excluded himself. Agnes and the Jeddler sisters come by this quality naturally: there is no need for them to be instructed. But Dickens seemed to believe that, when it was lacking, the disciplined heart could be attained, that it could be learned and that it could even be taught. Betsey Trotwood is one who learned it, and I think Dickens wanted us to understand that even Dora achieved it at last when, as her deathbed wish, she asked Agnes to take her place with David.

But David himself, like most of the Harlequin-heroes of Dickens, is an exasperatingly difficult case. He understands the necessity of disciplining his heart, right enough, but he cannot for a long time bring himself to do it. He needs both instruction and conversion. Here again his story is like that of Wilhelm Meister. Goethe's hero is surrounded by a numerous society of benevolent friends who patiently manipulate the events of his life until they educate and initiate him into *Bildung*, the harmonious development of maturity. To match this society of well-wishers, David Copperfield has Aunt Betsey, his personal Benevolent Spirit, who rescued his psyche with the staged explosion of the Murdstones when he was a child, and, in his youth, helped him achieve a Fieldingesque kind of maturity with the lie about her own lost fortune. Now, in his manhood, she steps forward with another lie about Agnes's forthcoming marriage in order to bring him the more necessary Goethean *Bildung*.

Actually she has to tell the lie twice before it takes, once in Chapter Sixty and again in Sixty-two. The first attempt, when she tells David she suspects Agnes has an attachment (60.717), very nearly succeeds. David pulls back only at the last moment. "I had sought to lead her [Agnes] to what my aunt had hinted at; for, sharply painful to me as it must be to receive that confidence, I was to discipline my heart, and do my duty to her. I saw, however, that she was uneasy, and I let it pass" (60.719). The next time, after Betsey has said more specifically and emphatically, "I think Agnes is going to be married" (62.735), David finally overcomes what he was pleased to call *Agnes's* uneasiness and comes at last of age with a renunciation like that of Wilhelm Meister:

I must speak plainly. If you have any lingering thought that I could envy the happiness you will confer; that I could not resign you to a dearer protector, of your own choosing; that I could not, from my removed place, be a contented witness of your joy; dismiss it, for I don't deserve it! I have not suffered quite in vain. You have not taught me quite in vain. There is no alloy of self in what I feel for you. (62.737)

Gwendolyn Needham wrote of this incident that "Dickens skillfully contrives a test which, plausibly motivated by his hero's character, dramatizes the novel's last bit of action. . . . Having thus proved his hero's disciplined heart, Dickens rewards him with Agnes' hand and lifelong love."[40] I should prefer to say, of course, that it is Betsey Trotwood who does the contriving and that it is not so much a question of David's proving, as it is of his achieving a disciplined heart. Until he could bring himself actually to speak the words quoted above, David's heart was undisciplined and he remained unworthy of Agnes.

When David reflects on the deception his aunt has practiced on him, he calls it "a pious fraud" (62.740). This is the same term Dickens was to use fifteen years later in his last completed novel to describe the elaborate deception through which Mr. Boffin redeems Bella Wilfer, one of the two heroines of *Our Mutual Friend*. Boffin, by the way, is also connected to the Dame Trot figure, not through his name, but by his invariable means of locomotion; he never walks, he trots, even if it is only to get across the room. And of course Boffin is the most obvious Benevolent Spirit in all the late novels of Dickens.

The device of the "pious fraud" in *Our Mutual Friend* has sparked a lively, sometimes a violent literary discussion. Some critics are outraged because not only Bella Wilfer but even the reader is fooled into believing that money has corrupted Mr. Boffin. Fewer hackles have been raised by the Trotwood deceptions, although they also involve the reader. We are led to believe, along with David, that Betsey has lost all her money and that Agnes is about to marry. My own position, and this is the note on which I should like to conclude, is that in both cases the "pious fraud" stands as an emblem for Dickens' own aesthetic as a novelist. Just as the Benevolent Spirits within the novels deceive the heroes in order to redeem them, so does Dickens, the writer of fictions, after all, deceive his readers. *David Copperfield* is a success, according to this aesthetic, if through reading and believing in it, being taken in by it, our own hearts have been disciplined. And it is this attitude towards his art, I believe, that marks the Pantomimist Dickens as the arch romancer of nineteenth-century fiction and distinguishes him most significantly from his contemporaries among the realists.

NOTES

1. (Stanford, Calif.: Stanford University Press, 1983), p. 274.
2. *Dickens the Novelist* (Norman: University of Oklahoma Press, 1968), pp. 333 and 335.
3. "Dickens and Time: The Clock Without Hands," *Dickens Studies Annual*, 4, Robert B. Partlow, Jr., ed. (Carbondale: Southern Illinois University Press, 1975), pp. 18–19.
4. "Dickens and Tolstoy: The Case for a Serious View of David Copperfield," in *Dickens the Novelist* by F. R. Leavis and Q. D. Leavis (London: Chatto & Windus, 1970), p. 61.
5. *Nineteenth-Century Fiction*, IX (1954), 88.
6. *The Victorian Age in Literature* (New York: H. Holt and Co., 1913), p. 25.
7. "Dickens and Some Motifs of the Fairy Tale," *Texas Studies in Literature and Language*, V (1964), 570–571; *The Imagination of Charles Dickens* (London: Collins, 1961), p. 121; *Dickens and the Invisible World: Fairy-tale, Fantasy and Novel Making* (Bloomington: Indiana University Press, 1979), 197–199.
8. *The Imagination of Charles Dickens*, p. 121.
9. "Dickens and Tolstoy," p. 90.
10. I am aware that there is no extrinsic evidence of Dickens having read *Jane Eyre* and that an anonymous source purporting to summarize Gad's Hill conversations of 1860–61 quotes Dickens as saying that he had not read it. (See Jerome Meckier, "Some Household Words: Two New Accounts of Dickens's Conversation," *The Dickensian*, LXXI [1975], 5.) On the other hand, Charlotte Brontë noted an "affinity . . . now and then" (see her letter to W. S. Williams, September 13, 1849, in Clement Shorter [ed.] *The Brontës: Life and Letters* [New York: Charles Scribner's Sons, 1908], II, 71), and I find myself in agreement with Mrs. Leavis, who concludes from internal evidence that "it seems hard to reject the conclusion that David Copperfield inherits from Jane Eyre" in some respects ("Dickens and Tolstoy," p. 109). I shall be quoting from Jane Jack and Margaret Smith's edition of *Jane Eyre* (London: Oxford University Press, 1975).
11. *David Copperfield*, Nina Burgis, ed., (Oxford: Clarendon Press, 1981), Chap. 4, p. 50. Subsequent citations from *David Copperfield* will be from this edition, indicating chapter and then page thus: 4.50.
12. *The Moving Adventures of Old Dame Trot and Her Comical Cat* (New York: McGraw-Hill, 1972), based on *Old Dame Trot and Her Comical Cat* (London, 1807).
13. I have been able to locate eight pantomimes featuring Dame Trot produced between 1837 and 1883.
14. "The Absent Clown in Great Expectations," *Dickens Studies Annual: Essays on Victorian Fiction*, 11, Michael Timko, Fred Kaplan, and Edward Guiliano, eds. (New York: AMS Press, 1983), pp. 115–133; "Charles Darnay and Revolutionary Identity," *Dickens Studies Annual: Essays on Victorian Fiction*, 12, Michael Timko, Fred Kaplan, and Edward Guiliano, eds. (New York: AMS Press, 1983), pp. 147–159.
15. *Dickens and Women*, p. 272.

16. "Dickens and Tolstoy," p. 62.
17. *Ibid.*, p. 64.
18. My colleague John Jordan has pointed out to me that this donkey hater keeps a servant named Janet and that the diminutive for this name, Jenny, signifies a female donkey. Betsey outwardly repulses Jacks, Jordan suggests, but she keeps a Jenny as bait. This is perhaps a mine worth working. Aunt Betsey also keeps Mr. Dick, who, she tells David, has "a longer name if he chose to use it" (14.172). In the nineteenth century and in David's dialect, a Jack-ass was called a Dick-ass, and a Jenny was sometimes called a Betty.
19. "The Undisciplined Heart of *David Copperfield*," p. 86.
20. "Memory in *David Copperfield*," *The Dickensian*, 71 (1975), 30–42.
21. *Dickens and the Invisible World*, p. 260.
22. *Great Expectations*, Angus Calder, ed. (Harmondsworth: Penguin, 1965), Chap. 39.
23. Monod, p. 365.
24. *Ibid.*, p. 321. See also Richard Dunn, "David Copperfield's Carlylean Retailoring," in *Dickens the Craftsman: Strategies of Presentation*, Robert B. Partlow, Jr., ed. (Carbondale: Southern Illinois University Press, 1970), pp. 105–106, and Michael Black, *The Literature of Fidelity* (New York: Barnes and Noble, 1975), p. 94.
25. "Thoughts on 'David Copperfield'," *Review of English Literature*, n.s. II (July, 1961), 73.
26. See his plan for *David Copperfield*, No. I, *David Copperfield*, Nina Burgis, ed. (Oxford: Clarendon Press, 1981), p. 757.
27. "The Undisciplined Heart of *David Copperfield*," p. 86.
28. "Memory in *David Copperfield*," p. 30.
29. *Season of Youth: The Bildungsroman from Dickens to Golding* (Cambridge, Mass.: Harvard University Press, 1974), p. 41.
30. "David Copperfield's Carlylean Retailoring," p. 97.
31. *Ibid.*, pp. 106 and 111.
32. "The Undisciplined Heart of *David Copperfield*," p. 103.
33. *Ibid.*, p. 86.
34. Monod, p. 325.
35. "David Copperfield's Carlylean Retailoring," p. 101.
36. (New Haven, Conn: Yale University Press, 1934; rpr. New York: AMS Press, 1978), p. 217.
37. *Ibid.*, p. 215.
38. *Wilhelm Meister's Apprenticeship*, Thomas Carlyle, trans. (London, 1824), Book VIII, Chapter 4.
39. *Ibid.*
40. "The Undisciplined Heart of *David Copperfield*," pp. 105–106.

Secret Subjects, Open Secrets

D. A. Miller

I

"And who's this shaver?" said one of the gentlemen, taking hold of me.
"That's Davy," returned Mr Murdstone.
"Davy who?" said the gentleman.[1]

For a moment in *David Copperfield*, the text raises the possibility that David might be any David; for a moment, it so happens, it invites me to imagine that he might be myself. Assuming that autobiographical representation is replete with such narcissistic lures, sites where the reader's own subjectivity comes to be invoked and identified, even without benefit of a namesake, why not begin with myself? Why not begin by recounting the insertion of my own person into a novel which I read and reread as a child, "in those tender years," Virginia Woolf called them, "when fact and fiction merge"? Why not anthologize those all-too-affecting passages in the novel through which David's story—I mean the other one's—became hopelessly entangled with my own? Why not admit, by the way, how readily everything else in this novel flees from my memory—rather, how peremptorily everything else is dismissed from it: much as the other David admits, sitting by the fire, that "there was nothing real in all that I remembered, save my mother, Peggotty, and I" (165)? And why not gloss those figures in the novel who have signified and predicted my sentimental education: from the Mother who fondled me, saying "Davy, my pretty boy! my poor child!" (162); the (step-) Father whose unfeeding hand I rabidly bit; the Friend who, though Mr. Sharp and Mr. Mell were notable personages in my eyes, was to them what the sun was to two stars (144); and the (second) Wife, center and circle of my life, in whom I might have inspired a dearer love (938, 902); down to David himself, cognate and first cognition of myself, who, of a summer evening, the boys at play in the churchyard, sat on my bed, reading as if for life (106)?

But as I eagerly put these questions, in the arrogant rhetorical form that waited for no reply, but already did what it pretended to ask permission for, I was also obliged to recognize why, "subduing my desire to linger yet" (950), I must not pursue such a confession. For we are all well acquainted with those mortifying charges (sentimentality, self-indulgence, narcissism) which our culture is prepared to bring against anyone who dwells in subjectivity longer or more intensely than is necessary to his proper functioning as the agent of socially useful work. (It is bad enough to tell tales out of school, but to tell them in school—or what comes to the same, in a text wholly destined for the academy—would be intolerable.) And those envious charges have at least this much truth in them, that the embarrassing risk of *being too personal* all too often comes to coincide with its opposite in the dismal fate of banality, of *not being personal enough*. Nothing, for instance, is more striking than the disproportion between the embarrassed subject and the occasion of his embarrassment: while the former imagines his subjectivity on conspicuous and defenseless display, the latter has usually been rendered all but invisible by its sheer mundaneness, its cultural or physiological predictability. Rarely does anyone even think to watch the spectacle we assumed we were making of ourselves. We say truly, "I could have died of embarrassment," but nearer than one's fantasized murder at the hands (the eyes, the tongues) of the others is the danger lest such worldly homicide prove embarrassingly unnecessary, the subject who fears extinction having already died out on his own. The painfulness of embarrassment, which at least ought to have guaranteed its subject's vitality, instead betokens a mountainously agitated subjectivity which refuses to acknowledge its mousey stillbirths. Accordingly, what could whatever "embarrassed" revelations I might make about my intimacy with *David Copperfield* amount to, except a particularly cathected paraphrase of an already written text? What could I—presumptively unique, private subject of unique, private desires—finally signify in such revelations, but a character in a novel so familiar that no one, it is said, can even remember reading it for the first time?

Let me not, then, speak of myself, but let my seduction by *David Copperfield* stay a secret. Yet is my secrecy any less paradoxical than the embarrassment that I thereby seem to avoid? It almost goes without saying that, though I conceal the details of this seduction, they would not be very difficult to surmise: no more esoteric, perhaps, than Oedipus and his commonplace complex. For I have had to intimate my secret, if only *not to tell it*; and conversely, in theatrically continuing to keep my secret, I have already rather *given it away*. But if I don't tell my secret, why can't I keep it better?

And if I can't keep it better, why don't I just tell it? I can't quite tell my secret, because then it would be known that there was nothing really special to hide, and no one really special to hide it. But I can't quite keep it either, because then it would not be believed that there *was* something to hide and someone to hide it. It is thus a misleading common sense that finds the necessity of secrecy in the "special" nature of the contents concealed, when all that revelation usually reveals is a widely diffused cultural prescription, a cliché. A character in Oscar Wilde is closer to the truth when he observes of secrecy that "it is the one thing that can make modern life mysterious and marvellous. The commonest thing is delightful if one only hides it."[2] More precisely, secrecy would seem to be a mode whose ultimate meaning lies in the subject's formal insistence that he is radically inaccessible to the culture that would otherwise entirely determine him. I cannot, therefore, resolve the double bind of a secrecy which must always be rigorously maintained in the face of a secret that everybody already knows, since this is the very condition that entitles me to my subjectivity in the first place. But the double bind is not at all the same thing as a dead end, and if I cannot speak of myself without losing myself in the process, I can keep myself secret and—"so to speak"—change the subject: convinced of my indeterminableness in the safety of silence, as I speak of—and seek to determine—somebody or something else. Were not the personal rewards for good behavior in the administered society so readily accepted, it might seem strange that I can best establish myself as a private subject only in the dutiful performance of the professional obligation that it profits nothing to put off any longer: to speak of *David Copperfield*.

We begin, then, not with myself, but with the first paragraph of Dickens' text, which falls in his Preface:

> I do not find it easy to get sufficiently far away from this Book, in the first sensations of having finished it, to refer to it with the composure which this formal heading would seem to require. My interest in it, is so recent and strong; and my mind is so divided between pleasure and regret—pleasure in the achievements of a long design, regret in the separation from many companions—that I am in danger of wearying the reader whom I love, with personal confidences and private emotions. (45)

Strongly hinting at the intimate and specular nature of his relationship to *David Copperfield*, Dickens nonetheless courteously refrains from elaborating on it. Yet it is fair to wonder how "wearying" the personal confidences and private emotions could possibly be, when something very like them has been appetizingly promised on the title page of the very book that Dickens is presenting: "The Personal History, Adventures, Experience, & Observation of David

Copperfield . . . (Which He never meant to be Published on any Account)."
And if we do not fully believe in their wearisomeness, neither can we quite
credit the "love" for the reader on whose account they are suppressed: the
concern for the burdened reader is surely more defensive than protective. In
any event, no sooner is Dickens' subjectivity put before us than it is also put
away: made to vanish in the act of proffering the Book itself: "all that I could
say of the Story, to any purpose, I have endeavoured to say in it." Unwilling
to speak of himself, Dickens instead points to his story of the other, in which
C. D., authorial signature, will be inverted—or rather, extroverted—into D.
C., sign of a character who is also, as though to indicate his purely verbal
existence, sign of a book.

While it may be the usual task of a preface to manage such transitions from
author to text, from subjectivity to its eclipse in the object at hand, here, at any
rate, the business is not just routine. For the gesture made in Dickens' preface
is repeated within the novel by David himself, who regularly and almost
ritually "secretes" his subjectivity at precisely what would appear to be its
determining moments. For example, when David returns home on holiday
from school, he has the more than pleasant surprise of finding his mother alone
nursing her newly delivered child:

> I spoke to her, and she stared, and cried out. But seeing me, she called me
> her dear Davy, her own boy! and coming half across the room to meet me,
> kneeled down upon the ground and kissed me, and laid my head down on her
> bosom near the little creature that was nestling there, and put its hand to my lips.
> I wish I had died. I wish I had died then, with that feeling in my heart! I
> should have been more fit for Heaven than I ever have been since.   (162)

The supreme importance of the incident seems to depend wholly on the
intensity of an affect which, though cited, is never specified. No doubt we
could be more precise than David about the nature of that feeling in his heart,
whose principal component it would not be hard to nominate: the bliss of
recovering the mother in a relationship which has been unexpectedly de-tri-
angulated not only by Murdstone's absence, but also by the presence of the
new sibling, a minorized third who is more David's surrogate at the maternal
breast than his rival. To which one could add: the unholy excitement at seeing
the mother who abandoned him for another abjectly repentant at his feet, along
with the already pitiable infant by whom he might have been supplanted a
second time; and finally the consequent guilt that accedes to conscience only
as the self-satisfied wish to have died in such a state of grace. Yet what matters
more than the availability of these determinations is the fact that, even in this

ample autobiography, intended for no one's eyes but his own (671), David
only alludes to the feeling whose decisiveness he nevertheless advertises. And
much as, in the Preface, Dickens managed his own fraught subjectivity by
introducing the novel in its place, so David, shortly after this episode, finds
himself in his room, "pouring over a book" (171).

The same pattern is enacted in Steerforth's bedroom, to which David
"belongs" (137), at Salem House:

> . . . The greater part of the guests had gone to bed as soon as the eating and
> drinking were over; and we, who had remained whispering and listening
> half-undressed, at last betook ourselves to bed, too.
> "Good night, young Copperfield," said Steerforth. "I'll take care of you."
> "You're very kind," I gratefully returned. "I am very much obliged to you."
> "You haven't got a sister, have you?" said Steerforth yawning.
> "No," I answered.
> "That's a pity," said Steerforth. "If you had had one, I should think she
> would have been a pretty, timid, little, bright-eyed sort of girl. I should have
> liked to know her. Good night, young Copperfield."
> "Good night, sir," I replied.
> I thought of him very much after I went to bed, and raised myself, I recollect,
> to look at him where he lay in the moonlight, with his handsome face turned up,
> and his head reclining easily on his arm. He was a person of great power in my
> eyes; that was, of course, the reason of my mind running on him. No veiled
> future dimly glanced upon him in the moonbeams. There was no shadowy
> picture of his footsteps, in the garden that I dreamed of walking in all night.
>
> (140)

Here again a powerful affect is evoked, but evacuated of any substantial
content. *What* did David think of Steerforth as he looked at him where he lay
in the moonlight, his handsome face turned up? In one sense, the question
scarcely merits an answer, so eloquently here does the love that dare not speak
its name speak its metonyms (the "whispering and listening half-undressed,"
and so on). Yet in another sense, such an answer is positively averted, since
David lapses into distractingly cryptic reverie at just the point where—but for
the veil of "no veiled future . . . "—the classic erotics of the scene would
have become manifest. And once again, the affect is soon displaced in an
experience of fiction: in lieu of the nocturnal sexual episode that—as David
might say, "of course"—does not take place between him and Steerforth,
they organize the institution of bedtime stories, in which David recounts to
Steerforth from memory the novels he has read at home. As in the scene with
his mother, David's reticence here may be largely "unconscious," but the
distinction is secondary to a pattern which is also capable of being rehearsed

quite consciously, as when David is forced to do manual labor at Murdstone and Grinby's warehouse. "I never said, to man or boy, how it was that I came to be there, or gave the least indication that I was sorry I was there. That I suffered in secret, and that I suffered exquisitely, no one ever knew but I. How much I suffered, it is . . . utterly beyond my power to tell" (218). The importance of this secret suffering—not just for David, but for Dickens, too, with his own traumatically secreted *déclassement* in Warren's Blacking Factory as a child—is in no danger of being underrated. It only loses the privilege that we are accustomed to accord to it by displaying the common structure of all such important moments in the novel: first the allusion ("how much I suffered . . . "), then the elision (". . . is beyond my power to tell"), and finally the turn to the novelistic, as David attempts to entertain his fellow-workers "with some results of the old readings."

The pattern which thus recurs in David's life, however, finds its most extensive embodiment in his life-story. We notice, for instance, that the gestures of secretiveness are made, not just then, at the time of the narrative ("That I suffered in secret, no one ever knew"), but now as well, at the time of its narration ("How much I suffered, it is beyond my power to tell"). The diffidence of this narration obviously perpetuates the same fears of discipline that inhibited David with the Murdstones, at Salem House (even Steerforth is likened to a magistrate [136]), and in the warehouse. But the narration of this diffidence also perpetuates that turn to (reading, recounting, writing) stories which was David's regular escape from these fears. The manuscript to which, in his own phrase, he *commits his secrets* (713), is precisely that: the place where he encrypts them. The manuscript to which, in his own phrase, he commits his secrets, *if he knows them* (713), is rather the place where he encrypts them so as neither to know them nor to make them known.[3] Writing the self, then, would be consistently ruled by the paradoxical proposition that the self is most itself at the moment when its defining inwardness is most secret, most withheld from writing—with the equally paradoxical consequence that autobiography is most successful only where *it has been abandoned for the Novel*. The paradoxes determine not only David, who intimates his subjectivity only to displace it into various modes of experiencing the Novel, but also Dickens, who, just as he abandoned what thus remained an autobiographical fragment to write *David Copperfield* in the first place, strikes, and then strikes out, the personal note in his Preface. And what had been, it seemed, my own personal note would now prove no less impersonal than a faithful reproduction of these same paradoxes. Even at the moment of its annunciation, my subjectivity had already been annulled as a mere effect of its object. Or alternatively: I have been able to be a subject in the only way this object-text allows: by pointing to the Novel, where one's own secret will be kept because somebody else's will be revealed. In the knowledge, then, that at least where *David Copperfield* is concerned autobiography can *only* be an "autobiographical fragment," let us again change the subject.

II

Characters in *David Copperfield* are frequently coupled with boxes: bags, parcels, luggage. Betsey Trotwood can be accurately identified by David, who has never seen her, through the fact that she "carries a bag . . . with a great deal of room in it," and which seems a ready accessory to her "coming down upon you, sharp" (245). Miss Murdstone, who embellishes herself in numerous steel fetters, brings with her to the Rookery "two uncompromising hard black boxes, with her initials on the lids in hard brass nails," and the boxes "were never seen open or known to be left unlocked" (97, 98). Mr. Barkis, himself a carrier of boxes, also has his own, full of money and hidden under his bed, "which he pretended was only full of coats and trousers" (205). So close is the connection between the miser and his box that on his death bed Barkis becomes "as mute and senseless as the box, from which his form derived the only expression it had" (506). As these examples suggest, characters come with boxes because characters come in boxes, as boxes. Some characters in *David Copperfield* run the risk of being put away, in the asylum with which Mr. Dick is threatened or the prison in which Uriah Heep and Littimer are actually incarcerated, and others encounter the fate of being sent away, like David to his room or to school, or even like Jack Maldon, Mr. Mell, the Micawber family, Mr. Peggotty, and Emily, to the colonies, but a far greater number—anticipating and attempting to avert these fates—have simply put themselves away, in boxes that safeguard within their precious subjectivity. Familiar to us as their eccentricities seem to make them, the characters in *David Copperfield* (as though the real function of eccentricity were to render the eccentric a private person, inaccessible to the general) typically manage to be *arcane*—even when they do not literally inhabit, like Daniel Peggotty, an ark.

How do they box themselves in, seal themselves off? At the molecular level of gesture, they may stop up their ears like Betsey Trotwood and Dora, or suck in their cheeks like Uriah Heep, or, like Betsey Trotwood again and Mrs. Markleham, retire behind their fans. At the molar level of deportment, they may take refuge in a militant bearing. The "firmness" recommended and practiced by the Murdstones is not confined to them: it shows up as well in Betsey's "fell rigidity of figure and composure of countenance" (52), in the "atmosphere of respectability" with which Littimer surrounds himself (356), and in "the outward restraints" that Uriah Heep "puts upon himself" (848). Alternatively, they may pursue a thoroughgoing self-effacement, like Mr. Chillip, who sidles in and out of a room, to take up the less space (58), or Ham with his "sheepish look" (78), or the "mild" Mr. Mell (147). Even their dress participates in their self-sequestration. Betsey ties her head up in a handkerchief, and Peggotty throws her apron over her face. Ham wears a pair of such very stiff trousers that they would have stood quite as well alone (78), and Traddles wears a tight sky-blue suit that made his arms and legs like German sausages (143). Uriah Heep, like Mr. Spenlow, is "buttoned up to the throat" (275). And when these characters speak, they rarely speak their mind, but more often only its screen: Littimer's composed courtesy, Uriah Heep's hypocritical humility, Betsey's gruff understatement. At the extreme, they protect their subjectivity by refusing to assume it even grammatically: by refusing to say "I," like Markham, who says "a man" instead (419), or Barkis, who designates himself and his desires in the third person—what, more simply and strictly, Emile Benveniste calls the "non-person."[4]

Thoroughly encased in such diverse armor, the characters in *David Copperfield* prepare to do battle with the outside world. But the battle, fundamentally dubious, has already been lost in the very preparations for it. It is as though the ravages feared from the others have been assumed by the self in its own name, and that the costs of social discipline have been averted only in an equally expensive self-discipline. Part of the expense, surely, is paid out of the moral category which, though frequently and often hysterically invoked by Dickens to differentiate his characters into good ones and bad, proves absolutely irrelevant to the structural uniformity of their self-concealment. No doubt, Uriah Heep's "umbleness" hides only a vaulting ambition and cankering resentment, while Ham's "sheepishness" masks a heroically good nature; and Betsey Trotwood with her bag and her fell rigidity of figure is a quite different moral type from Miss Murdstone with her two black boxes and her firmness. But the obvious moral distinctions here simply overlay a formal similarity of character which they have not determined and are powerless to affect. It is as if Heep and Ham, Betsey Trotwood and Jane Murdstone, however much the ethical content of their inwardness might differ, agreed on the paranoid perception that the social world is a dangerous place to exhibit it, and on the aggressive precautions that must be taken to protect it from exposure. To be good, to be bad are merely variants on the primordial condition which either presupposes: to be *in camera*. Thus, the practical social consequences of goodness, on which Dickens puts strong ideological pressure, are of necessity extremely limited, since the good can only be good, do good, in secret. And the text holds a worse irony in store for the good as well: that in defending against the outrages of socialization, they unwittingly beat them to the punch. Either, to protect themselves against "outside" aggressions, they need to commit them, like Betsey Trotwood stuffing cotton in her ears and then stuffing Ham's ears as well, "as if she confounded them with her own" (59), or later with the donkeys. Or, fearful of the consequences of their aggression, they take it out on themselves, like Mr. Mell, who "would talk to himself sometimes, and grin, and clench his fist, and grind his teeth, and pull his hair in an unaccountable manner" (133). Despite the thin skins in which they are all enveloped (even Murdstone's firm hand can be humiliatingly bitten), characters add to the rough-and-tumble social buffetting from which they would withdraw. Still, if their elaborate defenses finally amount to no more than the fact that they have made their social necessity into their personal choice, this perhaps suffices for a subject who can thus continue to affirm his subjectivity *as a form* even where it no longer has a content of its own.

This is not, of course, the whole story. Such defenses may be indistinguishable from that which they defend against, and thus reduce the subjectivity that mobilizes them to a purely formal category. But they can surely continue to be opposed to that which they defend: the hidden innerness that like the miser's hoard must never see the light of day. Just as we can say of this hoard in a capitalist economy that it is *worth nothing* as soon as it has been removed from circulation and exchange, so we might wonder what value can be put upon an innerness that is never recognized in inter-subjectivity. And the epistemological questions inevitably brought forward in such cases are not far away: if the secret subjective content is so well-concealed, how do we know it is there? How does the concealing subject know it is there? What could the content of a subjectivity that is never substantiated possibly be? Accordingly, at the same time as the characters in *David Copperfield* embox their subjectivity, they find oblique means and occasions to take the lid off. Peggotty's tendency to burst her buttons, Mr. Mell's pouring what seems like "his whole being" into his doleful flute-playing (132), the wasting fire within Rosa Dartle finding vent in her gaunt eyes (350): these are only a few examples of the odd compromises that characters strike, like Freudian hysterics, between expression and repression. In some sense, therefore, the secret subject is always an open secret.

Sometimes, certainly, this open secret is actively *opened*. The dramatic heights of Dickens' fiction are customarily reached when a secret is explosively let out, as at Uriah Heep's unmasking, or when two boxed-in, buttoned-up subjects find release in one another, like David and Peggotty whispering and kissing through the keyhole of his locked room on the last night of his "restraint." Yet even such moments as these only explicate as "information" what had been previously available to characters as "intuition." Though David seems to know Betsey Trotwood only as a legendary dragon, if he nonetheless risks throwing himself on her mercy, sight unseen, it is because he has always known more than this: hadn't his mother told him that "she had a fancy that she felt Miss Betsey touch her hair, and that with no ungentle hand" (53)? Far more often, however, dramatic revelation even of this order is superfluous. Barkis's box might be taken for an emblem of those many secrets in the novel to which everyone is privy: David's "secret" attachment to Dora, which even the drunken dimness of Mrs. Crupp is capable of penetrating; the "secret" of Uriah Heep's interest in Agnes, which he asks others to keep so as to keep them from interfering; Mr. Wickfield's alcoholism, the secret that everyone hides because everyone holds; Miss Murdstone's fetters, "suggesting on the outside, to all beholders, what was to be expected within" (453); and so on. The radical emptiness of secrecy in the novel is most forcefully (if all unconsciously) argued by Miss Mills, whose "love of the romantic and mysterious" (619) fabricates trivial secrets on the same popular romance principles that make them so easily divined.

Even when a character's subjectivity may be successfully concealed from other characters, for us, readers of the novel, the secret is always out. Like David, we have suspected the good nature that underlies Betsey Trotwood's decided and inflexible exterior, and, long before him, we have detected the "secret" of Agnes's attachment. Similarly, we never doubt that Mr. Mell, mild or unmelodious as a social presence, has the milk of human kindness within; that the Murdstones, despite their firmness, are ultimately purposeless creatures; that Uriah Heep lies through his professions of humility; or that Peggotty is dear and loving for all her comic inarticulateness. The hermeneutic problem put to characters by the discrepancy between outside and inside (such that the former can never be counted on to represent the latter, which it is rather constituted to disguise) is never a problem for us, for whom the outside, riven with expressive vents, quite adequately designates the nature of the subject it thus fails to conceal. For us, all the camouflage that characters devise to deceive one another gives way to readerly transparency, as, no less immediately, their secrets become our sure knowledge.

Yet, curiously enough, the fact the secret is always known—and, in some obscure sense, known to be known—never interferes with the incessant activity of keeping it. The contradiction does not merely affect characters. We too inevitably surrender our privileged position as readers to whom all secrets are open by "forgetting" our knowledge for the pleasures of suspense and surprise. (Even a first reading, if there is one, is shaped by this obliviscence, which a second makes impossible to doubt.) In this light, it becomes clear that the social function of secrecy—isomorphic with its novelistic function—is not to conceal knowledge, so much as to conceal the knowledge of the knowledge. No doubt an analysis of the kinds of knowledge that it is felt needful to cover in secrecy would tell us much about a given culture or historical period—though in the case of *David Copperfield* the results of such an analysis would be banal in the extreme: sex, drink, and (for the middle-class subject) work are the taboo categories they more or less remain today. But when the game of secrecy is played beyond those contexts that obviously call for suppression, it is evident that the need to "keep secret" takes precedence over whatever social exigencies exist for keeping one or another secret in particular. Instead of the question, "What does secrecy cover?," we had better ask "What covers secrecy?" What, that is, takes secrecy for its field of operations? In a world where the explicit exposure of the subject would manifest how thoroughly he has been inscribed within a socially given totality, secrecy would be the spiritual exercise by which the subject is allowed to conceive of himself as a resistance: a friction in the smooth functioning of the social order, a margin to which its far-reaching discourse does not reach. Secrecy would thus be the subjective practice in which the oppositions of private/public, inside/outside, subject/object are established, and the sanctity of their first term kept inviolate. And the phenomenon of the "open secret" does not, as one might think, bring about the collapse of these binarisms and their ideological effects, but rather attests to their fantasmatic recovery. In a mechanism reminiscent of Freudian disavowal, we know perfectly well that the secret is known, but nonetheless we must persist, however ineptly, in guarding it. The paradox of the open secret registers the subject's accommodation to a totalizing system which has obliterated the difference he would make—the difference he does make, in the imaginary denial of this system "even so."

III

It remains, therefore, an odd fact that readers have traditionally found the Dickens character, particularly in *David Copperfield*, a source of great "charm." What charm, we may ask, is there in the spectacle of such pathetically reduced beings, maimed by their own defense mechanisms, and whose undoubtedly immense energy can only be expended to fix them all the more irremovably in a total social system? How is it that such grotesques are not perceived as the appalling evidence of what T. W. Adorno, speaking of the fate of the subject in such a system, calls "damaged life," but instead as the complacently enjoyed proof of our own unimpaired ability to love them? The charm we allow to Dickens' characters, I submit, is ultimately no more than the debt of gratitude we pay to their fixity for giving us, in contrast, our freedom. We condescend to praise these characters as "inimitable" because they make manifest how safe we are from the possibility of actually imitating them. The reduced model of the subject which they exemplify is refuted or transcended automatically in any reader's experience. For one thing, the consciousness of this reader, effortlessly capable of disarming their self-be-traying defenses and penetrating their well-known secrets, must always thereby exceed that of the characters, both individually and severally. Indeed, this "inclusive" consciousness is part of what contributes to the sense that the characters are boxed in. For another, the novel-reading subject can never resemble Dickens' characters, conspicuously encased yet so transparent that they are always inside-out, because the novel-reading subject as such has no outside. However much this subject inclusively sees, he is never seen in turn, being invisible both to himself (he is reading a novel) and to others (he is reading it in private). The boxed-in characters, already so reified that they are easily and frequently likened to things (boxes great, like rooms and houses, as well as small), thus come to play object to the (faceless, solitary, secreted) reading subject, whose structural position and the comparison that reinforces it both release *him* from the conditions that determine *them*.

The reader's comparative freedom vis-à-vis the constraints of character is, of course, a general effect in the nineteenth-century novel. For if the Novel is the genre of "secret singularity,"[5] it becomes so less by providing us with an intimate glimpse of a character's inner life than by determining this life in such a way that its limitations must forcibly contrast with our own less specified, less violated inwardness. The contrast is inscribed within the nineteenth-century novel as one between the character and the narrator, our readerly surrogate and point of view, who is in general so shadowy and indeterminate a figure that it scarcely seems right to call him a person at all. But Dickens' fiction is particularly relevant to the problematics of modern subjectivity, because his novels pose such a sharp contrast in the extreme difference and distance between the character, who is so thoroughly extroverted that his inner life seems exiguous, and the narrator, who is so completely defaced that, even when he bears a name like David Copperfield, Phiz hardly knows what "phiz" to give him.

As early as the *Sketches by Boz*, these problematics are already rehearsed, though in ways that *David Copperfield* will modify substantially. Formally speaking, the narrative in the *Sketches* is skimpy, fragmentary, never more than anecdotal: stories either never get off the ground, or if they do, terminate in the arrested development characteristic of the "short story." Thematically speaking, the deficiency of narrative in the text corresponds to the lack of adventure, even as a possibility, in the world the text represents. On one hand, a viable agent of adventure cannot really emerge from among the dwarfed and emaciated subjects (typically too small or too thin) who populate the metropolis and who are far too much like the objects that overwhelm them there. And like the diverse articles inventoried in the various junkshops Boz visits— human products divorced from human production or use—these short, foreshortened subjects are serially juxtaposed to one another without ever forming a cohesive "community." On the other hand, even if a properly qualified agent of adventure did appear—and several characters at least attempt to qualify for the role—his adventure could only be played out as parody in a world which has routinized even the opportunities for breaking routine. (In "Making a Night of It," for example, the carnivalesque release from clerical chores is as regular as the quarterly pay for doing them.) And should routine fail to meet the case, there would always be the police to close it: the police who appear to stand on every London streetcorner and whose function, like that of their many surrogates in the *Sketches*, is to return adventure to the confinement from which it all too briefly emerged.

Yet every dreary characteristic of the world that Boz represents has been overcome in his representation. Though this world is bound in stasis, Boz is demonstrably the free-ranging *flâneur*, and to him, in his casual meanderings, befall the adventurous possibilities denied to the characters. Though the world of objects is mute, Boz has wit enough to overcome its alienation and make it speak once more to and of human subjects. And though the faces Boz gazes upon are horribly precise in the deformations by which they reveal class, profession, and the general scars of city-dwelling, Boz himself, faceless, shows none of them. Even the characters' lack of community is negated by

Boz's confident use of the plural first-personal pronoun, as though here were a subject who could count on allies. Altogether, it is as if the problems or constraints arising from the dull urbanism of the *Sketches* found their solution or release in the lively urbanity of the sketching.

The very disparity between problem and solution, however, means that the latter must engender certain problems of its own. Insofar as the subject (Boz) and the object (the world he sketches, including its reified subjects) are merely juxtaposed, each pole retaining its own distinctness, the "solution" borne in the narration has no bearing on the "problem" it would solve—except, no doubt, to offer further evidence of it in the mere contiguity of terms that otherwise remain mutually unrecognizable and unrelated. The lack of any interactive or dialectical connection between subject and object thus becomes registered as the fragmentary form of the sketches themselves, which not only bespeaks the inability of the subject to master his materials, whose abiding heterogeneity can be grasped only in bits and pieces, but also casts into the shadow of a doubt the continuity of that very subject, whose freedom is purchased at the price of his intermittence, his utter ungroundedness. The interest of *David Copperfield* in this light is that the two models of subjectivity which the *Sketches* never reconcile—the one objectified in the character, the other abstracted in the narrator—are here linked and mediated in the actual story, in which a character becomes his own narrator. As Copperfield the narrator recounts the life (really, the death) of David the character, we witness an abstracted, all-embracing subjectivity telling the story of its own genesis, of how, and against what odds and with what at stake, it came to be. Implicitly, the process submits the whole category of the "social" to radical revision. It is not that the phenomenology which (as in *Boz*) locates the social outside the subject is ever abandoned, but rather that, instead of being taken for granted, it now has to be produced. No longer a mere content whose oppressions or determinations are confined to the second term of a rigid opposition between self and other (or between subject and object, or narrator and character), the social now appears as the very field in which these oppositions are strategically constituted.

IV

We need, then, to consider the story of this autobiography, whose essential drama stems from David's desperate attempt not to be boxed in, or confounded with a box, like the other characters. "Master Copperfield's box there!'' says Miss Murdstone, as the wheels of Barkis's cart are heard at the Rookery gates (112). Her words, as always, are ominous, and at the coaching inn not long afterwards, David has the anxious experience of being abandoned among boxes, as he waits on the luggage scale for someone from Salem House to claim him:

> Here, as I sat looking at the parcels, packages, and books . . . a procession of most tremendous considerations began to march through my mind. Supposing nobody should ever fetch me, how long would they consent to keep me there? Would they keep me long enough to spend seven shillings? Should I sleep at night in one of those wooden bins, with the other luggage, and wash myself at the pump in the yard in the morning; or should I be turned out every night, and expected to come again to be left till called for, when the office opened next day? Supposing there was no mistake in the case, and Mr Murdstone had devised this plan to get rid of me, what should I do? . . . These thoughts, and a hundred other such thoughts, turned me burning hot, and made me giddy with apprehension and dismay. I was in the height of my fever when a man entered and whispered to the clerk, who presently slanted me off the scale, and pushed me over to him, as if I were weighted, bought, delivered, and paid for.   (124)

David has more grounds for panic than he knows. Already Mr. Murdstone has locked him up for five days in his room, where, already starting to internalize his confinement, he has been ''ashamed'' to show himself at the window, lest the boys playing in the churchyard should know that he was ''a prisoner'' (109). Even when he is no longer in prison, but down in the parlor, he has retained ''a sensitive consciousness of always appearing constrained'' (170). But a more awful fate awaits him at Salem House—''a square brick building with wings'' (129)—where Murdstone's discipline will be institutionalized. The placard David is there made to carry—''*Take care of him. He bites*'' (130)—imposes on him the forfeiture of even linguistic subjectivity, its reduction to the pronoun of the non-person. (Indicatively, when David inquires about the dog, Mr. Mell replies, ''that's not a dog—that's a boy,'' not ''that's you.'') David is thus linked to the closed, ''close'' character in the novel par excellence: ''Barkis is willin''' is no worse than ''he bites.'' It is, in fact, rather better, for Barkis has at least taken charge of his self-annulment, whereas David, obliged to wear the placard—on his back, where he can't see it—must submit to his.

> What I suffered from that placard, nobody can imagine. Whether it was possible for people to see me or not, I always fancied that somebody was reading it. It was no relief to turn around and find nobody; for wherever my back was, there I imagined somebody always to be. . . . I knew that the servants read it,

and the butcher read it, and the baker read it; that everybody, in a word, who
came backwards and forwards to the house, of a morning when I was ordered
to walk there, read that I was to be taken care of, for I bit.   (130–131)

As the subject of readerly perusal unable to *look back*, David assumes the very
ontology of a character in fiction. This dog's life is only trivially metamor-
phosed when, again under Murdstone's compulsion, he becomes ''a little
labouring hind in the service of Murdstone and Grinby'' (208). There his
confinement is symbolized daily and in detail by the tasks he must perform.
''When the empty bottles [to be rinsed, washed, examined for flaws] ran
short, there were labels to be pasted on full ones, or corks to be fitted to them,
or seals to be put upon the corks, or finished bottles to be packed in casks. All
this work was my work'' (209). And, as though these operations were being
simultaneously practiced on himself: ''I mingled my tears with the water in
which I was washing the bottles; and sobbed as if there were a flaw in my own
breast, and it were in danger of bursting'' (210). Finally, when David forms
his ''great resolution'' to run away to Dover, even his own box threatens to
turn him into one—the kind the long legged man calls ''a pollis case'' (234).
If David has ''hardly breath enough to cry for the loss of [his] box'' (235), this
is because, quite apart from the fact that he is exhausted from running, the box
ultimately doesn't deserve his tears. All things considered, it is not a bad thing
that he takes very little more out of the world, towards the retreat of his aunt,
than he had brought into it.[6]

     We have already glanced at what David calls ''my only and my constant
comfort'' (106) throughout all this: the experience of the Novel. It begins
when he happens to read the small collection of novels left by his father and
impersonates his favorite characters in them, and is resumed when he recounts
these novels to Steerforth at Salem House and to the other boys at Murdstone
and Grinby's. It takes a still more active turn when, dejectedly lounging in
obscure London streets, David fits the old books to his altered life, and makes
stories for himself, out of the streets, and out of men and women. ''Some
points in the character I shall unconsciously develop, I suppose, in writing my
life, were gradually forming all this while'' (224). From here it is an orderly
progression: first to the fearful and tremulous novice who writes a little
something ''in secret'' and sends it to a magazine (692); then to the writer
who, Dora rightly fears, forgets her, ''full of silent fancies'' (715); and
finally, to ''the eminent author,'' as Micawber calls him, who, though
''familiar to the imaginations of a considerable portion of the civilized world''
(945), nevertheless modestly occults himself in the same gesture that we saw
Dickens make in the Preface:

. . . I do not enter on the aspirations, the delights, anxieties and triumphs of my art. That I truly devoted myself to it with my strongest earnestness, I have already said. If the books I have written be of any worth, they will supply the rest. I shall otherwise have written to poor purpose, and the rest will be of interest to no one. (917)

To the last, the experience of the novel provides David's subjectivity with a secret refuge: a free, liberalizing space in which he comes into his own, a critical space in which he takes his distance from the world's carceral oppressions. Yet if, more than anything else, this secret refuge is responsible for forming David into "the liberal subject," this is paradoxically because, in a sense, *he is not there*. Certainly, as Miss Murdstone might well have complained, David hides behind his books—but as Clara might have fondly observed, he loses himself in them as well. What has often been considered an artistic flaw in Dickens' novel—David's rather matte and colorless personality—is rather what makes the novel possible, as David's own artistic performance. Far from an aesthetic defect, the vacuity is the psychological desideratum of one whose ambition, from the time he first impersonated his favorite characters in his father's books, has always been *to be vicarious*. It is as though the only way to underwrite the self, in the sense of insuring it, were to under-write the self, in the sense of merely implying it. The Novel protects subjectivity not by locking it in, in the manner of a box, but by locking it out, since the story always determines the destiny of *somebody else*. And what goes for the subject of *David Copperfield* goes in a different dimension for the subject who reads it. He too defines his subjectivity in absentia. Entirely given over to the inner life and its meditations, constantly made to exceed the readerly determinations he both receives and practices, this subject finds himself not where he reads, but—between the lines, in the margins, outside the covers—where he does not. (Another open secret which everyone knows and no one wants to: the immense amount of day-dreaming that accompanies the ordinary reading of a novel.) In this sense, the novel would be the very genre of the liberal subject, both as cause and effect: the genre that produces him, the genre to which, as its effect, he returns for "recreation."

What, then, are we to make of the fact that the experience of the Novel, alleged to take its subject out of a box, takes place in one (the "little room" at the Rookery, the "little closet" in Mr. Chillip's surgery, and so on)? The connection between the book and the box is always far closer than their effective polarity suggests. At the coaching inn, for instance, David looks at "parcels, packages, and books," and this reminds us that the book, read in a box, has the visible, palpable shape of one too. But perhaps what best "betrays" the secret consubstantiality of box and book—better than their phonetic alliteration, better than their etymological affinity (both, in a sense, coming from branches of the same *tree*[7])—is the article of furniture combining a chest of drawers and a writing desk that we call a bureau. At Peggotty's new home, really Barkis's old one, David is "impressed" by "a certain old bureau of dark wood in the parlour . . . with a retreating top which opened, let down, and became a desk, within which was a large quarto edition of Foxe's *Book of Martyrs*" (203). Instead of straightforwardly ascending from box to book, the image suggests rather that one descends *en abyme* within the box through a smaller box to reach the smallest box of all, the book, where the subject at last finds himself, but only in a martyred state. What Barkis's bureau thus opens is the possibility that the book quite simply belongs to the box, as its "property" or one of its "effects."

All this is to say, in other terms, that the story of David's liberation runs parallel to the story of his submission: the chastening of what, with an ambiguous wistfulness, he calls an "undisciplined heart." The discipline from which he has escaped to become the "subject of the Novel" reappears as his own self-discipline. "What I had to do," he says of the time he labored to win Dora, "was to turn the painful discipline of my early years to account, by going to work with a steady and resolute heart" (582). Mr. Murdstone's firmness and Mr. Creakle's unspared rod were not, it would appear, total losses. They stand behind David's victories in a succession of trials (Betsey Trotwood's "ruin," the winning of Dora, the losing of Dora) concluded and rewarded by the marriage to Agnes, the woman whom Micawber aptly calls an "appealing monitor" (820). But what seems to ensure this self-discipline most of all is writing itself. "I could never have done what I have done, without the habits of punctuality, order, and diligence, without the determination to concentrate myself on one object at a time, no matter how quickly its successor should come upon its heels, which I then formed" (671). Though David is not recalling here his service at Murdstone and Grinby's, but rather his apprenticeship in shorthand, he might as well be: minus the value judgments, the habits required are quite the same. It is clear as well that the discipline of writing does not lie in merely technical skills. As David's apology on the next page for the importance of being earnest confirms, these skills are immediately raised to high moral values—and these values, though differently valorized, are the very ones which help the characters to box themselves in. Paradoxically, writing is thus offered to us in *David Copperfield* as a socializing order from which the written self, always subject to omission, is separated, but with which the writing self, inevitably the agent of such omission, comes to be entirely identified.

What difference, then, is there finally between this book-loving subject and the box-like characters he would transcend? We see how ambiguous and complicated an answer to this question must be if, by way of conclusion, we consider the rather unmotivated visit that David pays to a prison at the end of the novel. With Mr. Creakle as administrator, and Uriah Heep and Mr. Littimer as model prisoners up to their old tricks, the prison scene makes some familiar points in Dickens' representation of the carceral. That the former Master of Salem House is now the magistrate in charge of a prison, as though he had merely been transferred, bears out the systemic coherence of an institutional network which fabricates the very subjects who then require its discipline. It is true that Uriah Heep's incorrigible hypocrisy would seem to be a manner of resisting the institution that seeks to restrain him, and thus of saving from discipline the subject who "puts restraints upon himself." But this secret resistance only perfects the thoroughgoing accommodation which it camouflages. Small wonder the prison has no effect in reforming Uriah, when in another, earlier version (as the "foundation school" where he and his father were raised) it has formed him in the first place. In this sense, Uriah's extravagant encomia on the prison-system—"It would be better for everybody, if they got took up, and was brought here" (928)—belie their obvious resentment to bespeak truly the weird erotic attraction between a subject and an institution "made for each other."

The spurious opposition between Uriah and the prison is no sooner displayed, however, than it is displaced into the more authentic-seeming opposition between David and the prison. If the carceral is abruptly brought on stage at the end of the novel, when David is a respected, "untouchable" author, this is to dramatize and celebrate his distance from it: a distance that can be measured in the detached tones—and even the critical ones—of his response. David can afford irony and indignation here because, as the pure observer, he is as free to go as he was curious to come: "We left them to their system and themselves, and went home wondering" (930). Still, much as Uriah, the carceral subject, was fated to be matched with the prison, so David, the liberal subject, must also ensure his status with an institutional match. Not by accident is the prison scene framed, on one side, by David's realization that he loves Agnes as more than a sister, and on the other, by the actual declaration of his love to her, which prompts her to reveal her well-guarded, well-known "secret." Uriah humbly kowtows to the prison authorities; David modestly asks to be "guided" (916) by the "appealing monitor without" (to use Micawber's distinction) who will reinforce "the silent monitor within." We can't even say that the discipline that merely befalls Uriah is David's voluntary choice, since Uriah too has chosen self-discipline, just as David has turned to account the painful discipline of his early years. Faced with the abundance of resemblances between the liberal subject and his carceral double, the home and the prison-house, how can we significantly differentiate them?

Only, I think, according to the logic of their effects, by the ways in which the two modes of discipline are played off against one another in a single system of social control. If only from the *roman noir* (but not only from it[8]), we know that the police interrogate in teams of two. While one agent brutally attacks the suspect's body, the other more humanely appeals to his soul. The suspect is so afraid that the one will beat the guts out of him that he spills them anyway to the other. Likewise, one withdraws from the discipline of step-fathers and their institutional extensions only by turning that discipline to account, "by going to work with a steady and resolute heart." David is ultimately no different from the boxed-in characters he seeks to transcend, just as they are ultimately no different from the processes of disciplinary social-ization they seek to avoid; yet in both cases, one becomes no different from the others only by, like them, assuming the effect of a difference which thus continues to operate. *David Copperfield* everywhere intimates a dreary pattern in which the subject constitutes himself against discipline by assuming that discipline in his own name. The pattern can hardly be broadcast in the novel, which requires the functioning of the difference to structure its own plot. But neither does the pattern go unbroached in the novel, whose discreet analogies remove the bar of the difference on which its very *Bildung* depends. The fact that the difference between liberal and carceral camps is not substantive, but only effective, has thus the status of a secret—that is to say, inevitably, an open secret. Accordingly, the novel must both keep this secret and give it away. Keep it, because the liberal/carceral opposition is the foundation of the liberal subject as well as the basis of the novel's own role in producing him. Give it away, because this opposition is effectively maintained by seeming always in need of maintenance—as though an impending "deconstruction" were required to inspire the anxious and incessant work of reconstructing a social order that thus keeps everyone on his toes, including the figure of the novelist who writes "far into the night" (950). Can the game of secrecy ever be thrown in? It is not likely so long as the play remains profitable—not just to the subject whom the play allows to establish his subjectivity, but also to the social order which, playing on the play, establishes his subjection. Listen to the different voices of the police, as David does them: "That I suffered in secret, and that I suffered exquisitely, no one ever knew but I. How much I suffered, it is . . . utterly beyond my power to tell. But I kept my counsel, and I did my work" (218).[9]

NOTES

1. Charles Dickens, *David Copperfield* [1849–50] (Harmondsworth: Penguin Books, 1966), p. 72. Further page references to this edition will be made parenthetically in the text.
2. Oscar Wilde, *The Picture of Dorian Gray* [1890], in *The Portable Oscar Wilde* (Harmondsworth: Penguin Books, 1977), chapter 1, p. 143. Appropriately, the character in question, Basil Hallward, affirms the value of secrecy in virtually the same breath as he violates it, in telling Lord Henry what he didn't intend to tell him: the name of Dorian Gray.
3. For several obvious reasons, it cannot here be a question of undertaking David's psychoanalysis. But for a psychoanalytic account of the "crypt" as a "false unconscious," see Nicolas Abraham and Maria Torok, *Cryptomanie: Le Verbier de l'homme aux loups* (Paris: Flammarion, 1976); and for a more-or-less psychoanalytic account of the account, Jacques Derrida, "Fors," the introductory essay to the same volume, pp. 7–73.
4. That the third person is not a person at all, but rather the form whose function is to express the non-person, Benveniste argues in "Relationships of Person in the Verb" and "The Nature of Pronouns," both collected in his *Problems in General Linguistics*, trans. Mary Elizabeth Meek (Coral Gables, Florida: University of Miami Press, 1971). Even apter are Roland Barthes's reflections on the "possible affinity of paranoia and distancing" in the use of the third person: "'he' is wicked: the nastiest word in the language: pronoun of the non-person, it annuls and mortifies its referent; it cannot be applied without uneasiness to someone one loves; saying 'he' about someone, I always envision a kind of murder by language." (*Roland Barthes by Roland Barthes*, trans. Richard Howard [New York: Hill and Wang, 1977], p. 169).
5. "And if from the early Middle Ages to the present day the 'adventure' is an account of individuality, the passage from the epic to the novel, from the noble deed to the secret singularity, from long exiles to the internal search for childhood, from combats to phantasies, is also inscribed in the formation of a disciplinary society" (Michel Foucault, *Discipline and Punish*, trans. Alan Sheridan [New York: Pantheon, 1977], p. 193 [translation modified]).
6. For the ultimate mortifying box, of course, is the oblong kind made at Mr. Omer's establishment. It is from Mr. Omer's that David is conveyed to his mother's funeral along with her coffin. Though he is accompanied in the "half chaise-cart, half pianoforte-van" by Omer, Minnie, and Joram, he seems almost grieved to note that "there was plenty of room for us all" (183).

7. "Book" from OE *bōc*, beech; "box" from Gk *pyxos*, boxtree.

8. In the *Miranda* decision, the U. S. Supreme Court cites actual manuals of police interrogation to describe the ploy known as the "friendly-unfriendly" or the "Mutt and Jeff" act:

> " ' . . . In this technique, two agents are employed. Mutt, the relentless investigator, who knows the subject is guilty and is not going to waste any time. He's sent a dozen men away for this crime and he's going to send the subject away for the full term. Jeff, on the other hand, is obviously a kindhearted man. He has a family himself. He has a brother who was involved in a little scrape like this. He disapproves of Mutt and his tactics and will arrange to get him off the case if the subject will cooperate. He can't hold Mutt off for very long. The subject would be wise to make a quick decision. The technique is applied by having both investigators present while Mutt acts out his role. Jeff may stand by quietly and demur at some of Mutt's tactics. When Jeff makes his plea for cooperation, Mutt is not present in the room' " (*Miranda v. Arizona*, 384 U. S. 436, 452 [1966]).

9. Happily, not alone. I thank the following secret sharers: Marston Anderson, Mitchell Breitwieser, Joel Fineman, Lizbeth Hasse, Audrey Jaffe, Caroline Newman, Robert Newsom, and David Suchoff.

Writing and *David Copperfield*

Murray Baumgarten

At one time or another most of the characters in *David Copperfield* commit their thoughts to paper. Little Em'ly, Steerforth, Agnes, and Aunt Betsey all send and receive letters. Doctor Strong compiles a dictionary. Jack Maldon reads the newspaper. Even Omer & Joram have enough schooling to bury the body and memorialize the name. And however umble Heep is, writing and reading are the central instruments by which he intends to join the ''writhing'' class. In this novel only Daniel Peggotty and Ham are analphabetic.

From Barkis's scratched message to the newspaper account of Australian life written by Micawber, much of this novel is taken up with the re-presentation of writing. Presenting characters who are writers and displaying the products of their work as well, *David Copperfield* explores some of the meanings of writing for its time. Its many writers and their writing are both framed by and mirrored in the novel's narrator, himself not only a writer of fiction but engaged in the narrative present of the novel in recalling and inscribing his autobiography.

In 1849, when *David Copperfield* was published, the state of English education was emerging as a major cultural issue, dealt with in the relevant parts of the great political reform of 1832 and the 1840 Grammar Schools Act, and later in the second reform bill of 1867 and the Education Act of 1870. Thus the novel articulates relationships between literacy and social success, writing and heroism, literature and love. To read *David Copperfield* is to deal with the meanings of writing.

Three of the major characters focus our attention upon writing, bringing it into the novel's foreground: David Copperfield, the narrator as writer; Mr. Micawber, who addresses letter-writing with the same verve as he does the punchbowl; and Mr. Dick, constantly interrupted in his Memorial by King Charles' Head. Their pursuit of this characteristic function invites reflection upon both the near ubiquity of writing in the novel and its varying effects and purposes. What is impossible for Mr. Dick to get on with, what threatens Mr. Micawber in the form of unpaid bills, and what makes David successful, famous, and, as Agnes says, increases his power for doing good—writing— for each of these characters constitutes his fictional ambience as in a larger sense it defines this novelistic realm.

The vividness of David's recollections and the power of his observations endow the novel with the realistic edge of autobiographical narrative. Nevertheless, its framing storyteller-as-narrator serves to remind us that it is fiction we are reading. The novel thus focuses on the interplay of the lyric present and past tense narration. The range of classes David encounters echoes the Brechtian social epic of *Nicholas Nickleby*, but the novel does not edge over into the carnival spectacle of *A Tale of Two Cities*. Instead, we have the memorial reverie of Wordsworth presented in a Victorian rhetoric of retrospection and recording. The act of remembering is the reverie which both constructs the tableau of the past and, bringing it forward through the use of the present tense of recollection, makes possible the gesture of deciphering at the moment of encoding. We read *David Copperfield* like our own dream at the moment of awakening—at the instant of writing it down. Sitting with the novel's narrator at the writing table—not so long before Dickens' time still called an escritoire—we are both imaginer and secretary at once.

We therefore tend to sympathize with the writers in and of this tale and learn from their literary struggles. Mr. Dick's constant endeavor to get on with his Memorial makes David realize (as the reader does with him) that once engaged in, writing is an unending enterprise. A series of repetitions of strokes and combinations of characters, writing is a self-defining, self-perpetuating process, whose purpose tends to become enclosed completely within its own enactment. Writing for writing's sake, we might call it, though if asked why it is so important we would also hasten to add various reasons of utility. Implicit in our response would be our understanding that writing changes us.[1]

As readers and writers, we bear the sign of our literate status. The code which makes it possible for us to avail ourselves of the technology of the modern world and turn its resources to our purposes transforms us. Medium, cultural frame, matrix, and force-field, writing irrevocably shapes our personalities. Like Mr. Dick, who is defined, even consumed by his writing, and David, who is marked by the writing he bears on his back at Creakle's school, we gain our sense of self from the consumption and production of the written word.

The complexity of the novel is then the complication of its writing. In it, writing serves as the ritual act of Mr. Dick, the theatrical performance played out by Micawber, and the memorial and newspaper which David, the narrator, enacts in the process of his novel writing. Pleading for help in paying emotional creditors, David's narration is his version of a Micawber letter as well as of Mr. Dick's petition for the restoration of rights. Like his Shakespearean model, David encompasses the powers of all his guides. Similarly, the novel dramatizes the range of meanings of its culture's constitutive act.

In this literate universe, our abilities as readers and writers become the measure of our value as human beings, the worth of our status. This, as David realizes, is one of the reasons Mr. Dick cannot relinquish the writing of his Memorial. ''I found him still driving at it with a long pen, and his head almost laid upon the paper. He was so intent upon it, that I had ample leisure to observe the large paper kite in a corner, the confusion of bundles of manuscript, the number of pens, and, above all, the quantity of ink (which he seemed to have in, in half-gallon jars by the dozen,) before he observed my being present'' (Chapter 14, p. 257).[2]

A culturally binding action, writing also has potentially recuperative powers. To write is to overcome the barriers distance places on face to face encounters. As Jack Goody points out, ''alphabetic literacy'' makes possible ''the scrutiny of discourse'' because it gives oral communication a ''semi-permanent form.'' Spreading discourse before the eyes, writing increases ''the potentiality for cumulative knowledge, especially of an abstract kind.'' Changing the nature of communication from ''face-to-face contact,'' and changing as well ''the system for the storage of information,'' it makes available ''a wider range of 'thought'.'' These qualities of writing make it possible for Mr. Dick to hope his Memorial will change his situation. The written text will tell the truth over and against changeable oral discourse.

For writing, as Goody indicates, initiates long-lasting changes in culture. ''No longer did the problem of memory storage dominate man's intellectual life; the human mind was freed to study static 'text' (rather than be limited by participation in the dynamic 'utterance')—a process that enabled man to stand back from his creation and examine it in a more abstract, generalized, and 'rational' way. By making it possible to scan the communications of mankind over a much wider time span, literacy encouraged at the very same time criticism and commentary on the one hand and the orthodoxy of the book on the other.''[3] Abstract rather than personal, writing thus yields the possibility of rescuing the individual from the consequences of familial interaction. Mr. Dick's Memorial is a petition for the restoration of rights taken away from him by his blood relatives due to his supposed insanity. It is as well a release of pent-up emotion. Mr. Dick's writing—how close to Dickens own?—occupies him without allowing him to conclude it. His Memorial will not become the finished petition that, as writing, might serve to gain him legal redress. And Mr. Dick cannot abandon it for a face to face encounter with his relatives to demand his rights in person. Inconclusive and inadequate as writing, his Memorial represents the moment and standpoint of his transition from oral to literate culture. The comedy of his role lies in his inability to move forward totally into writing or backward away from it. As such it teases us into comparisons with Dickens' own obsessive writing and his equally obsessive preoccupation with theatrical modes of self-presentation, including the public performance of his novels that literally took over the last decade of his life. Like Mr. Dick's, Dickens' may be seen as ritual and ritualistic acts.

Part of the reason Mr. Dick cannot end his writing lies in the wish central to its purpose. As petition, his writing proposes the hope of redress. Constantly interrupted, it never reaches its putative recipient. Repeating the writing, Mr. Dick does not complete the communication, while constantly reiterating its intention. What he wants is to affirm his writer's rather than his family name—to be Mr. Dick and not Richard Babley. (As the pun makes clear, his hope lies in his writerly rather than his familial name, which locates him in a deprecated oral tradition.) Thereby, Mr. Dick asserts his new status in his new domicile. Near the beginning of this chapter in which David meditates upon the meanings of Mr. Dick's writing, Aunt Betsey informs her nephew that though "the gentleman's true name" is "Babley—Mr. Richard Babley"—in her house "and everywhere else, now—if he ever went anywhere else," his name is Mr. Dick. "So take care, child, you don't call him anything but Mr. Dick." In parallel fashion, as Chapter 14 ends David acquires not only Mr. Dick and Aunt Betsey as his guardians but a new name, Trotwood, for himself.

Like Mr. Dick's, David's two names make his present status ambiguous. (The multiplication of nicknames which he receives in the course of the narrative will further complicate his identity.) Just as Mr. Dick's family name will infect his effort to make a new one for himself by his writing, which has the nonsense qualities of babbling implicit in his old name, so Copperfield will resist the efforts of Aunt Betsey to turn David into a Trotwood. Like much else in the novel that shifts between past and desired future, the present of the narration is a crossing point of oppositions. While David will become the industrious, "firm, fine fellow" Aunt Betsey admonishes him to turn out when she sends him off to Doctor Strong's school in Canterbury, he will also continue to be his parents' soft, emotional, hero-worshipping son. The problems of identity are here focused in the relationship of writing and naming.

In the world of this novel differential access to writing expresses class differences. One of the central ways the class system makes its presence felt in *David Copperfield* is through the conflict of literate and illiterate or almost literate characters—between oral and written cultures. That is one aspect of the encounter of Little Em'ly and Steerforth, Murdstone and Clara, Daniel Peggotty and David. Consider the letter that Em'ly leaves behind when she runs off with Steerforth. Her explanation for her act takes the form of a vow and wish for upward mobility: "it will be never to come back, unless he brings me back a lady" (31.513). In its letter form it expresses Em'ly's yearning to climb the social ladder. As writing, it defines the tension that articulates her desire, just as David's recounting of "The Personal History, Adventures, Experience, & Observation of DAVID COPPERFIELD the Younger of Blunderstone Rookery" engages us in the expression of his.[4]

Writing is a learned act so central to modern culture that like a name it is mostly taken for granted. Only when its meaning is challenged do we become aware of its importance in defining our social and cultural identity. In this novel, the same phenomena disturb naming and writing. To resolve one, the other must also be resolved.

Names in *David Copperfield* are not only sounds characters are called by but writing that marks their desire and their station. Through Barkis's scratched characters we discover that he wants Clara Peggotty to become C. P. Barkis. Similarly it is in and through the narrator's writing that the finality of the transformation of Clara Copperfield into Murdstone is expressed for us and for him. Dora becomes a Copperfield, as does Agnes, rather than a Heep, though neither Rosa Dartle nor Em'ly becomes Steerforth's. These names are not just uttered but have resonance in the novel by being written down in various forms. As writing, they inscribe characters into their class.

The numerous letters that pass between the characters of this novel and advance the action of plot and pattern are always addressed and signed. They are directed messages, identifying recipient and sender, by means of written characters—akin to the "written character, as large as a proclamation" of David and Dora's servant, "Paragon" (44.701).

It is worth noting that like much of the writing with which this book is concerned, the character of this Paragon turns out to be if not a forgery at the very least highly misleading. Her character is a Rorschach test. Hope and desire lead David and Dora to project meanings rather than accurately delineate the meaning of the available markings.

What David will have to do is learn how to read correctly. Here David's encounter with Agnes is representative. As Sylvia Manning notes, it ''is developed emphatically as a sequence of signs—tears, phrases—that David must read and from which he must infer her feelings. When he does so correctly and breaks a three years' silence, the novel can conclude."[5] The process of learning leads David to distinguish between the abstract marks of writing and the physical presence of utterance. Discovering how to make a text of both, he learns how to decipher their meanings. As a writer, he shifts between the unstable recall of the present tense evocation of memory and the sequential recounting of past tense narration.[6] Like Wordsworth and other Romantics, Dickens in this novel charts the collision of utterance and literature.

In the world of this novel, signature authority is the mark of possession, be it of women or property. This holds not only for Wickfield and Uriah Heep, the forger, but for Emma, who never will desert Mr. Micawber, for Wilkins Micawber himself, the glad signator of reluctant I.O.U.'s, and for David, the maker of fictions. Not only the definer of personal identity, signature here is the mark of cultural value, the deed attesting to the ongoing existence and reality of the social order. Especially in the form of paper money, defined in 1844 in the Bank of England Act, which provided for a national paper currency, the written name promises true exchange value.

This condition of writing, which makes its witnessing power so great and enables it to function to shape the future, also makes it peculiarly liable to deception. Like Em'ly's written phrase, "unless he brings me back a lady," this writing too is often an expression of desire, presented in the subjunctive mood. Instead of bodily presence, whose solidity and vitality make it difficult to impersonate, writing (especially as money) offers only the abstract code of alphabetic characters. Fixed in denotative function, the individual units yet are inherently indeterminate—at the same time that their abstractness (by contrast with the calligraphic qualities of hieroglyphics) endows alphabetic writing like paper money with enormous power.

Like other culturally constitutive acts, writing and monetary exchange become problematic in their absence. It is worth noting how they are brought together in Micawber's famous speech about happiness and misery, when the difference between the two is seen as a matter of accounting. Writing like money is a sign of the value-making power of symbolic forms. Especially for the three central writers in this novel, what counts is not the content but the act. That is one reason David does not dwell on the subjects of his tales. What is important is the rite of writing itself.

Focusing on writing in this way, *David Copperfield* defines one of "the active centers of the social order" which serves to concentrate its most serious acts and locate them "in the point or points in a society where its leading ideas come together with its leading institutions to create an arena in which the events that most vitally affect its members' lives take place."[7] To write, then, for everyone in this novel is fateful. Thus when she leaves a note to direct Daniel Peggotty to her rooms, where he will find Em'ly, Martha initiates the concluding movement of the novel that will change the lives of all the characters.

As they write, the characters in this novel articulate their desired social status, and thus identify the value they hope to find, make, and hold in their world. Here currency and writing are interchangeable. Both function as evidence of class status as well as promissory notes. For in the world of this novel (as well as ours) genuine writers are valuable human beings. Martha's note proves her true worth in the novel's moral economy. After that it is only a matter of time, despite her prostitute's past, before she will be redeemed.

The characters of *David Copperfield* reveal who they truly are in the ways in which they conduct themselves in the crucial modern ritual of literacy. Performing the act of writing, each character is epitomized in the process of his or her characteristic production of moral and social value. As they write, these characters contact the central arenas of their culture and participate in "the momentous events" that take place in them. They are makers of value, like Dickens himself. Their obverse, of course, is Heep, the forger, trying to pass falsified documents for true. So too he is the counterfeit hero of this novel, the simulacrum who points us to the real thing.

We recognize the novel's true heroes in their writing—"a sign, not of popular appeal or inventive craziness, but of being near the heart of things." In this novel, writing marks the heroic impulse. A charismatic act, it stamps the effort of its characters to create new values for the self as well as the social order.[8]

As readers, we are implicated in their efforts to be the heroes of this tale— that is, in their attempts at charismatic self-definition. To translate Weberian language back into one of its sources familiar to Dickens, we participate in their heroism and their hero-worshipping. These terms of course are from Carlyle—Dickens' friend and literary colleague. For him, the social order is constituted by hero-worship. "Tell me who your heroes are and I will tell you who you are." Heroes are the guarantee of a society's value(s). They attest to its realities. They stand by its promises, as they fight to ensure the worth of its currency, proving it with their persons. False heroes, as we know by observing Murdstone and Heep, are not worth the promises they make. Like bad writers, they cheat us of the value we had hoped to find in paying for their work.

From its first sentence *David Copperfield* is filled with comments about writing. However, there is no extended discussion of its function to gather various meanings together and yield a comprehensive definition. Writing as topos remains indeterminate. The questions raised by the theme of writing are displaced onto the problems of heroism central to the novel.[9] Who after all is the novel's hero? That role and station "these pages must show." From the first page the narrator engages us in helping him discover "whether I shall turn out to be the hero of my own life"—a finding to be revealed on paper, that is by writing. Displaced from self to aspect, heroism thus becomes in this book a question not of character but of writing.[10]

In *David Copperfield*, belief is compelled by writing. True writing is charismatic, providing real exchange value, and makes hero-worshippers of us all. As Dickens commented in the 1850 Preface, in a sentence whose convoluted syntax emphasizes the centrality of writing for this novel, "Yet, I have nothing else to tell; unless, indeed, I were to confess (which might be of less moment still) that no one can ever believe this Narrative, in the reading, more than I have believed it in the writing" (p. 45).

In this novel, Micawber, Dick, and David encompass its range. Despite David's prominence as character and narrative voice, his view of writing is not the only one in the novel. We are not allowed to accept his while treating the others merely as way stations on the road to his conclusion. Believing in writing, we confirm their importance; the power of Micawber and Dick carries over into their writing. Just as he imbibes their values, David partakes of their views of writing.

It is worth noting that the displacement which begins the novel is paralleled in many of Micawber's letters.

> "SIR—for I dare not say my dear Copperfield,
> "It is expedient that I should inform you that the undersigned is Crushed. Some flickering efforts to spare you the premature knowledge of his calamitous position, you may observe in him this day; but hope has sunk beneath the horizon, and the undersigned is Crushed."

Here too the subject is turned into an object, connected to the speaker by the genitive case. "I" becomes "he." [11] Writing makes possible the objectification of personality as it enables the reification of statement. "The present communication is penned within the personal range (I cannot call it the society) of an individual, in a state closely bordering on intoxication, employed by a broker. That individual is in legal possession of the premises, under a distress for rent." The speaking voice of the narrator of the letter engages us in his role-playing. "If any drop of gloom were wanting in the overflowing cup, which is now 'commended' (in the language of an immortal Writer) to the lips of the undersigned, it would be found in the fact, that a friendly acceptance granted to the undersigned, by the before-mentioned Mr. Thomas Traddles, for the sum of £23 4s. 9 1/2d. is over due, and is NOT provided for."

Micawber's letter moves theatrically through the changes of costume which are gathered together in the orotund signature of the undersigned. The phrasing of the salutatory clause combines logic and tragic gesture; we are in the presence of a consummate actor. Even as he waits for something to turn up, he has his part to play on the stage of this life. " 'After premising thus much, it would be a work of supererogation to add, that dust and ashes are for ever scattered

On

The

Head

Of

WILKINS MICAWBER '.' '

In large type, this signature collects all the displacements and representations, all the roles he has split himself into, and gathers them into the actor's self. He has played his part for his audience. Now he awaits his due.

For Micawber writing is promise of payment, and expectation with him is as good as culmination. Writing is an I.O.U. owed to him—the bill of theatrical role-playing, executed in the punning multiplication of words that would make him rich were language coin of the realm. He is a usurer of words,[12] the Falstaff of a novel in which David is to play Prince Hal, and thus destined to banish not only the soul of wit but the cause of it in other men.

What is effortless in Micawber is painful for Mr. Dick. His Memorial is constantly interrupted by King Charles' Head. Ultimately Babbly Dick outwits his traumatized historical and cultural memory, attaching the sheets of the interrupted Memorial, which he will never complete, to the kite that launches his writing into the air.[13] Then his words are free almost as birds (like money fluttering up to heaven and down from the sky). Kite-flying for Mr. Dick is an act of great joy, in which David joins, sharing in this liberation of language as he joins in Micawber's theatrical energy and linguistic glee.

Mr. Dick and Micawber are at the very least avuncular figures for David, legal guardians serving *in loco parentis*, if not surrogate fathers. He is implicated in their familial as well as their writing practice. Indeed, through their writing (as well as their affection) both help to rescue David, Mr. Dick by earning money as a copyist and Micawber by taking notes that will eventually substantiate Heep's forgeries. Their ways of writing prepare us to assess David's, and the emotions which they enact in their writing focus the central issues of his life and narrative recounting.

While writing terrorizes both Micawber and Mr. Dick, it also makes possible their freedom and childish joy. As code it threatens both with imprisonment. As calligraphic flourish, it makes possible their impudence and spontaneity. That is the blessing they render David, the socially and fictionally validated writer of this tale.

The one character of this novel who remembers everything without relying upon the promptings of written memory is Peggotty. It is worth noting that after he has been reunited with Em'ly he visits David to tell him how she escaped from Littimer. David, the narrator, recollects the event, describing how Peggotty in reviewing the past is preparing for "the beginning of a longer journey"—the forthcoming emigration to Australia. The title of Chapter 51, which begins monthly number XVII, this phrase also signals one of the concluding themes of the novel.

David's phrasing reminds us that he is writing down the record of events which Peggotty narrated to him from memory. David emphasizes the effect the oral narration has had upon him and thus defines the power of oral as distinguished from written memory. "He saw everything he related. It passed before him, as he spoke, so vividly, that, in the intensity of his earnestness, he presented what he described to me, with greater distinctness than I can express." It is a power writing strives for but cannot hope to achieve because it lacks the immediacy and bodily presence of oral narration.

In having David, the character, make this statement, Dickens inclines the reader to respond to David's narrating voice as if he, like Peggotty to him, were present to us in an act not of writing but oral recitation. Paradoxically, then, David's further response points to the power of oral memory in such a way as to lead us almost into its presence, despite the impossibility of reproducing it in written characters. "I can hardly believe, writing now long afterwards, but that I was actually present in these scenes; they are impressed upon me with such an astonishing air of fidelity" (51.793). To have heard Peggotty tell the story is to have participated in the recounted events. David, and through him the reader of the novel, become witness to them as much as

Peggotty has been, attesting as he did to their veracity. Writing thereby acquires some of the qualities of oral recitation.

Peggotty's recounting is also a description of the representational force of the indirect speech of the narration—so theatrical, dramatic, and realistically rendered—that has just preceded it. We too assent to the truth of the story it has made visible to us. "'Ever so fur she run, and there was fire afore her eyes, and roarings in her ears. Of a sudden—or so she thowt, you unnerstand—the day broke, wet and windy, and she was lying b'low a heap of stone upon the shore, and a woman was a-speaking to her, saying, in the language of that country, what was it as had gone so much amiss?'" Here Peggotty functions, as Carl Dawson notes, as "in Wordsworth's terms," a silent poet— "someone with sympathies and the eyes of a poet, though nothing of a writer."[14]

As if to make sure we know that Peggotty is illiterate, his inability to read is made explicit the last time he appears in the novel. When he visits David he brings the newspaper account of Australian life with him but must point to the appropriate passages, which David then reads aloud. And he makes sure that David copies the inscription on Ham's gravestone for him to take to Em'ly (63.945, 947). As he is illiterate, so too is Daniel Peggotty uncorrupted by abstraction, whether of writing or of money. Remember too how he refuses to touch the pound notes Steerforth has given Em'ly.

His fidelity to Em'ly, his devotion to Ham, his enduring friendship with David—in all these as well as his touching naïveté, Peggotty embodies the values of the pre-industrial world of his origins. A character of and from the folk, he speaks always of events that succeed each other in a continuous present. When at the end of the novel he intrudes upon the literate world of David, Agnes, and their children, he appears as someone out of the fairy-tale world of the Arabian Nights. And the children hide as if he were an ogre.

David begins this final chapter by reminding us that "what I have purposed to record is nearly finished; but there is yet an incident conspicuous in my memory, on which it often rests with delight, and without which one thread in the web I have spun, would have a ravelled end" (63.939). The image echoes the world of oral narration though it has a self-consciously literary and written quality. By contrast with David, Daniel Peggotty sees both future and past and is faithful to his witnessing without recourse to pen and ink. What David writes, Mr. Peggotty lives.

Unlike David, the older man is in touch with his instincts—the Wordsworthian and natural sources of his being. This is attested to by the verbal richness of his speech—for example, by his ability to turn the ejaculation of gorming into an endless variety of words. David writes the story of his loss, trying to recover the lost innocence Peggotty embodies.

It is worth remembering that in introducing Steerforth to Em'ly David has participated in the crime against hospitality which his friend perpetrated. Peggotty's encounter with David is a reconciliation thus of unacknowledged enemies and repressed enmity. Forgiveness is implicit in the loving detail with which Peggotty narrates the story of the lives of the Australian pioneers (that David retells to us).

In the dialectical interplay of present reverie and narrative recounting, David, the writer, seeks to recover, record, and memorialize his cultural as well as his psychic past. Given the nature of his effort, the best he can hope for is written testimony of the existence of that vivid life. Writing his memory, he cannot relive it. By contrast, as we read the novel we recover both the writerly ideology, which drives David to his work of writing, and the meandering of his (fantasy) life, which informs the subject-matter at its core.

Of all the characters in this novel who grow up, go to school, get older and perhaps even wiser, it is only David whom we see in the act of learning to read and write. He is initiated into literacy by his mother; perhaps that is why writing for him has the ease we associate with the mother tongue. David suffers under the glaring eyes of the Murdstones (we will meet their educational method again in Gradgrind), and endures Creakle's academy, to which he is introduced as a dog-like creature bearing the badge "He Bites" upon his back. Later, in Canterbury at Doctor Strong's school, and with the presence of Agnes to encourage him, he becomes a scholar and accomplished writer, a skill that serves him well in his apprenticeship at Doctors' Commons.

Writing replaces living for the young David. Like many other Romantic heroes and heroines, novels become his guides to life. This occurs first when he reads "as if for life," and then when it is possible for him to entertain Steerforth at bedtime with the stories he has acquired in his desperate reading. His beloved novels help him enact the role of Scheherezade, for whom the production and recitation of fictional tales is life preserving. Here literature is not a matter of "as if" but a game played for life itself.[15]

Hero-worship and literacy intersect at this point in the novel. David's assessment of Steerforth will be in writing. It comes at the very beginning of the eleventh monthly number, thus immediately after Em'ly has run away with Steerforth. "What is natural in me," David begins Chapter 32, "is natural in many other men, I infer, and so I am not afraid to write that I never had loved Steerforth better than when the ties that bound me to him were broken." Attempting to preserve Steerforth in written memory as the loved one, David is also attempting to evade the blame that might be laid at his feet for introducing him into the Peggotty household. The justification of natural behavior is for David as well an effort to share his guilt with other males. What is particularly interesting is how for him the act of writing is so much a part of this natural behavior.

In the rest of the paragraph David is able to use the distancing effect of writing to screen out Steerforth's unworthiness and write a paean of hero-worship. "In the keen distress of the discovery of his unworthiness, I thought more of all that was brilliant in him, I softened more towards all that was good in him, I did more justice to the qualities that might have made him a man of a noble nature and a great name, than ever I had done in the height of my devotion to him." This is not simply self-delusion on David's part, or self-justification. The abstractness of writing and its apparent rationality as a medium of logic embodied in a literary text, as Jack Goody points out,[16] make it possible for David—and with him the reader—to magnify Steerforth's merits. As a result, David is able to imagine him purified, even were they to meet face to face. "Deeply as I felt my own unconscious part in his pollution of an honest home, I believed that if I had been brought face to face with him, I could not have uttered one reproach. I should have loved him so well still—though he fascinated me no longer—I should have held in so much tenderness the memory of my affection for him, that I think I should have been as weak as a spirit-wounded child, in all but the entertainment of a thought that we could ever be re-united. That thought I never had."

Recalled not to life but to the mind through the process of writing, Steerforth is now as one dead—that is, to be spoken about only in the terms of a eulogy. "I felt, as he had felt, that all was at an end between us. What his remembrances of me were, I have never known—they were light enough, perhaps, and easily dismissed—but mine of him were as the remembrances of a cherished friend, who was dead" (p. 516). Writing here functions as a kind of moral accounting. Since Steerforth is no longer a face to face actor, David's putatively balanced and rational weighing of his friend's merits can proceed. Writing makes it possible for David to maintain his abstract image of Steerforth as a hero—and not have to repudiate that own part of his psyche implicated in his friend's actions and misdeeds.

Writing has drawn the sting from the potential blame between individuals, which has now been displaced to the next world. It makes possible the enshrining of Steerforth as hero. "Yes, Steerforth, long removed from the scenes of this poor history! My sorrow may bear involuntary witness against you at the Judgment Throne; but my angry thoughts or my reproaches never will, I know!'' (p. 517). David's tone is sorrowful—and also worshipful.

As long as writing exists, heroes can. Like the reader, David the writer knows that once there were heroes but they are gone now. All that can be done is to write (and read) about them. Though no longer living, they can yet be represented. The charisma of the hero, like desire, is an eternal absence, reminding us here of the potential only of presence. Writing's ideological function makes it possible to evade the natural blame we would heap on our cherished models and heroes were we dealing with them in a face to face culture. Here, writing reinforces the effect of the class system. David's writing is not a revolutionary unmasking but a conservative excusing and justification by someone eager to join his hero's social class.[17] It is no accident that writing is the vehicle of David's ultimate success, bringing him fame and fortune. It is also the means which rescues him from the collapse of his expectations, in Aunt Betsey's ruin and Mr. Spenlow's failure.

The most extended discussion of the acquisition of literacy comes when David tells us how he learned shorthand. Chapter 38, which begins monthly number XIII, describes how David learned to master the hieroglyphic art of stenography. It concludes with David perusing Julia Mills's journal, written in a version of shorthand, which his love makes him eager to decipher. ''Miss Mills and her journal were my sole consolation at this period. To see her, who had seen Dora but a little while before—to trace the initial letter of Dora's name through her sympathetic pages—to be made more and more miserable by her—were my only comforts. I felt as if I had been living in a palace of cards, which had tumbled down, leaving only Miss Mills and me among the ruins. I felt as if some grim enchanter had drawn a magic circle round the innocent goddess of my heart, which nothing indeed but those same strong pinions, capable of carrying so many people over so much, would enable me to enter!'' (p. 625). Like Pip, who invests the letters of his dead parents' names with the emotional energy that would make absence into presence, David treats writing here as calligraphic mystery and power. It alone will provide the answer to the spell, the force and ''open sesame'' that will undo the magic circle of captivity drawn round the innocent goddess of his heart.

In this novel, the grim enchanter will turn into the fairy godmother. This good side of writing will lead David to his brilliant recording of Parliamentary Debates and then to his successful writer's career. Dickens draws upon his own experience here, just as he did in the Murdstone & Grinby's episode, though the fact of similarity does not entitle us to claim that the novel is therefore autobiography. Instead, it is important to note that writing functions to help the prince rescue the captive princess as if "life was more like a great fairy story, which I was just about to begin to read, than anything else" (19.330). How very different—how much more genteel—this is than poor Em'ly's escape from her enchanter, Steerforth, which depends upon her desperate resolve not to marry Littimer and her willingness to confront the truth about her degraded state, in which she cannot ever again even hope or fantasize that she will be a lady.

Em'ly will depend upon her strength and agility and will be bruised by the sand and cut by the rocks. David's labor will be mental. Note also how writing as calligraphic power opens the doors closed to David by the grim enchanter in a brilliant melding of fairy-tale imagery, as well as sexual and social possibilities, but at a level of abstraction not available to Em'ly. For David, unlike other characters in this remarkable multi-faceted novel, everything depends upon the ability to master the calligraphic forms of the stenographic code.

David's auto-didacticism is presented in a marvelous comedy of persistence and perseverance at learning how to read and write—consume and produce—the code that will enable him to reproduce and re-present oral speech in written form. It is an act that will fix oral value in abstract shapes and therefore make David, the stenographer and reporter, a man of value and social standing. It will repair his fallen station. It will make him worthy of Dora. In order to achieve all this he must become the naturalized citizen of this new realm. It will require the work of reading and writing, the consumption and production of symbolic and symbol-making meaning and value.

He has to master the "changes that were rung upon dots, which in such a position meant such a thing, and in such another position something else, entirely different; the wonderful vagaries that were played by circles; the unaccountable consequences that resulted from marks like flies' legs; the tremendous effects of a curve in a wrong place." The effort "not only troubled my waking hours, but reappeared before me in my sleep." We have a description that fits all learning to read and write. Shorthand stands here for all the codes of writing.

David is learning to do what we are doing as readers of this novel, which after all is just another kind of shorthand. *David Copperfield*, which we are deciphering, presents the act of learning what constitutes a code very similar, though comically exaggerated, to the one to which we are responding. "When I had groped my way, blindly, through these difficulties, and had mastered the alphabet, which was an Egyptian Temple in itself, there then appeared a procession of new horrors, called arbitrary characters; the most despotic characters I have ever known; who insisted, for instance, that a thing like the beginning of a cobweb, meant expectation, and that a pen-and-ink skyrocket stood for disadvantageous. When I had fixed these wretches in my mind, I found that they had driven everything else out of it; then, beginning again, I forgot them; while I was picking them up, I dropped the other fragments of the system; in short, it was almost heart-breaking'' (pp. 608-609). We are in the presence of a description of a fundamental aspect of modern experience. Its difficulties are our difficulties in learning to be writers and readers, whose costs we have probably repressed as the price of being good at reading and writing, and which we recover only when trying to learn a radically new form of reading and writing, say a non-Indo-European one. Or shorthand.

How difficult it is to acquire these skills—to become literate—comes clear in David's comments. ''It might have been quite heart-breaking, but for Dora, who was the stay and anchor of my tempest-driven bark'' in its voyage upon the ''sea of perplexity'' of writing (pp. 608–609). We see the power of literacy at the end of the chapter, when the stenographic notations of Julia's journal reinforce David's love and keep it alive. In making him a new person, with the hope of amatory and financial advancement along with upward social mobility, writing saves David.

It also imprisons him. He gains habits of industriousness that will help him make his way in the world. If his love for Dora drives him to acquire shorthand, the resulting discipline will also keep him from loving her with the naïveté and simplicity of his youthful fantasies. Once they are married he will demand that she keep accounts and no longer consider a book a place for Jip's meanderings or her own. At least where it concerns money, David expects Dora to give up, as he has, the childish love of meandering—a theme presented at the beginning of his narrative by the purchaser of his caul.[18] Since she is his wife, David expects Dora to participate with him in the ''privileg-ing'' of writing that is central to middle-class life in its expansive phase. She too is to be an instrumental rather than an expressive being. His home life, like his work world, commits David to the ideology of writing, which does not allow meandering. Instead, it demands the kind of focused attention Mr. Dick gains when, abandoning his Memorial (which parallels though on a larger scale Dora's account book even to ink spots), he becomes a responsible copyist earning his keep and then some. The fairy-tale world of success, love, and romance David desires is to be achieved not through luck or grace (nothing will turn up) but through hard work, in which the act of writing is at once frame, model, and context.

At the beginning of the concluding double number of the novel the narrator reminds us of the literary convention he is enacting, in which the writer narrates his life story. This novel he tells us is his "written memory." It is not only that fiction is presented as autobiography. The phrase links the function of memory in oral culture and the ways in which writing in this world replaces the classic mnemonic training of oral rhetoric.

To call the novel he is writing his "written memory" is to place it at the fulcrum of transition between these two cultural ways. As Carl Dawson notes, "the association of retrospective literature with artificial memory may help to suggest . . . the widespread emphasis on memory as imagination . . . [as well as] the survival of a mnemonic art." It also helps to place the novel in its historical and cultural milieu, for Dickens' age was a time "when memory was emphasized in educational theory, when politicians . . . used trained memories to great effect, and when a large amount of literature employed devices of memory. . . ." It is worth recalling that the young Dickens was regarded as the fastest and most accurate transcriber of political speeches and was specifically requested by Lord Grey to take down some of his campaign utterances. "Written memory" also serves further to link *David Copperfield* and Wordsworth's "Tintern Abbey," which Dawson points out "could almost serve as an illustration of how the artificial memory works, the enumerated objects of the Wye scene prompting certain remembered emotions while the scene as a whole evokes a complete retrospective vision."[19] Wordsworth also shapes the novel's concern with writing. For this, like Wordsworth's *Prelude*, is a text articulating the writer's coming to consciousness of his vocation, and is art made of prolegomena.

In the terms of literary history, David the narrator—the artist dramatized— also points us to Stephen Daedalus. The grace of art contrasted to the failures of experience, the endings of *Portrait of the Artist as a Young Man* and *David Copperfield* launch our heroes into a mythic realm. The young artificer soars free of Ireland's nets in order to forge its uncreated conscience, while the Victorian writer embraces Agnes as the reality and sign of his participation in the community of human sympathy,[20] which acknowledges "the thoughts that lie too deep for tears."

In this novel, as in much else of Dickens' work, Wordsworth is an abiding influence, as nature heals the restless, striving heart, preparing it for the acceptance of obligation and responsibility that stamps its now ripened condition. Like Wordsworth's characters—leechgatherer and solitary reaper—Peggotty and the other "orflings" of *David Copperfield*, including

Agnes, bear the marks of their origins and in the act of remembrance tend to fuse with them.

At the beginning of the concluding number of the novel, David proceeds to recount how "Nature, never sought in vain" helps heal his heart, "and I admitted to my breast the human interest I had lately shrunk from." The Byronic tour which Steerforth took with Em'ly David has made into a Wordsworthian pilgrimage. "Close thy Byron, Open thy Goethe," Carlyle intones in *Sartor,* and Dickens follows his advice in having David turn to the healing natural world of the English Goethe.

Under its influence David begins to write again. "My health, severely impaired when I left England, was quite restored." Then he pauses and defines the ontological status of his autobiographical recollections. "I have now recalled all that I think it needful to recall here, of this term of absence—with one reservation. I have made it, thus far, with no purpose of suppressing any of my thoughts; for, as I have elsewhere said, this narrative is my written memory" (58.889). Here Dickens' novel functions as the crossing point of classic high culture and democratic popular culture. Written memory echoes more than Wordsworth's usage. Recalling Carlyle's view of modern literature as nothing more than a newspaper, and the function of the newspaper in and for Joyce's *Ulysses,* it is not too far off to view *David Copperfield* as a text embedded in a similar universe of discourse. Perhaps one reason for its enormous popularity lies in this function of its ontological status.[21] The newspaper after all was where Dickens learned to write—just as it trained the masses to read fiction. Furthermore, his serial fiction shared many qualities with the newspapers of his day, among them relative brevity, chronological completeness, and low cost. Both were of course addictive and became interleaved with everyday life in such a way as to inform and change the ways in which their readers perceived their world. And the widespread availability of both is one of the defining phenomena of the Victorian era.

As "written memory," *David Copperfield* serves as a memorial. Like the ruins of Tintern Abbey or Bury St. Edmunds, it is a physical presence, with weight and volume, that serves to stir the memory and link the past and future of the speaker (and reader) in such a way as to define his present. In cultural terms, it serves to legitimate David's role and rank as writer, linking it not with Heep the upstart (whose red-hair and writhing remind us of medieval legends of the Jew as devil), but with the gentleman's world which has brought so many in this novel so much sorrow, and the capitalist's world of Dickens' own practice of the production of meaning, commodities, and money. And, of course, this novel is then the successful Memorial that Mr. Dick has been unable to write because King Charles' Head keeps intruding (it is the two-hundredth anniversary of Charles's beheading on which Dickens wrote *David Copperfield*).

The O.E.D. lists three entries in which the word "Memorial" is used in this sense in Victorian literature. In 1849, just as *David Copperfield* appeared, Macaulay, in his *History of England*, uses the word to refer to historical artifacts of battle; in 1853 Newman makes it a form of writing ("the memorials of the rule of the Pharaohs are still engraved on the rocks of Libya"); and in 1857 Ruskin brings artifact and the witness of writing together in lamenting how "every day renders the destruction of historical memorials more complete in Europe."[22]

The text as memorial is not only a petition or legal evidence, a word parallel to our use of "memorandum" or "memo" and thus a jogging of the memory to bring about an action (or more often to bury it in paper, as alas we all know too well), but also an historical artifact. Writing thereby serves as evidence— it is a legal witnessing of the real existence of the past as well as of its contemporary power and meaning. This text is a proof of the existence of the self—a Victorian articulation of a Romantic view of the nature of identity. As a memorial, the novel is an invitation to reverie as well as an act of meditation itself. Just as a newspaper publically records the events of the day, so in similar democratic form available to all this book charts the popular meaning of the Romantic exploration of self articulated by the high culture that preceded the Victorian age.

NOTES

1. See J. Goody and I. P. Watt, "The Consequences of Literacy," *Comparative Studies in Society and History*, 5 (1963), 304–345.
2. Page numbers following the quotations refer to the Penguin edition, edited by Trevor Blount.
3. Jack Goody, "Literacy, Criticism, and the Growth of Knowledge," in *Culture and Its Creators: Essays in Honor of Edward Shils*, eds. Joseph Ben-David and Terry Nichols Clark (Chicago, Ill. and London: University of Chicago Press, 1977), pp. 227–228.
4. Part of my understanding of the privileging of writing in this novel I owe to Chris Vanden Bossche. See his essay, "Cookery, not Rookery: Family and Class in *David Copperfield*," forthcoming in *Dickens Studies Annual: Essays on Victorian Fiction*, volume 15.

5. Sylvia Manning, "David Copperfield and Scheherezada: The Necessity of Narrative," *Studies in the Novel*, volume 14, n. 4 (Winter 1982), 331.
6. Structurally, as Manning points out, this encounter leads to the necessity of narrative and the stabilization of meaning into the disciplined heart of sequence.
7. Clifford Geertz, "Centers, Kings, and Charisma: Reflections on the Symbolics of Power," in *Culture and Its Creators, op. cit.*, p. 151.
8. *Ibid.*
9. Robert L. Patten argues from similar premises, though he reads the novel more completely as a Bildungsroman. "Thus, in his own act of writing, David/ Dickens himself creates the world of his desire and discovers for himself and us its design and meaning. He unfolds the hero from his indeterminacy, discloses the writer in the name." Robert L. Patten, "Autobiography into Autobiography: The Evolution of *David Copperfield*," in *Approaches to Victorian Autobiography*, ed. George P. Landow (Athens, Ohio: Ohio University Press, 1979), p. 287.
10. For a somewhat different view, see Bert G. Hornback, "The Hero Self," *Dickens Studies Annual*, vol. 7, ed. Robert B. Partlow, Jr. (Carbondale: Southern Illinois University Press, 1978), p. 152.
11. I owe this formulation to David A. Miller. See his essay, "Secret Subjects, Open Secrets," in this volume.
12. Catherine Gallagher has articulated the meanings of this image in a talk delivered at the Dickens Universe gathering, University of California, Santa Cruz, 7 August 1983, and in different form presented at the English Institute at Harvard in September. See her essay, "George Eliot, *Daniel Deronda*, and the Jewish Question," in *Proceedings of the English Institute, 1983*, for a full development of its importance in a related Victorian context.
13. I owe this insight to John O. Jordan.
14. Carl Dawson, *Victorian Noon: English Literature in 1850* (Baltimore, Md. and London: Johns Hopkins University Press, 1979), pp. 140–141. For further discussion of Wordsworth's influence, see Robin Gilmour, "Memory in *David Copperfield*," *The Dickensian*, 71, n. 375 (Winter, January 1975), 33–43.
15. I owe this insight to Edwin M. Eigner. See his essay, "*David Copperfield* and the Benevolent Spirit" in this volume. Also see Sylvia Manning, "David Copperfield and Scheherezada: The Necessity of Narrative," *Studies in the Novel*, volume 14, n. 4 (Winter 1982), 327–336.
16. "Literacy, Criticism, and the Growth of Knowledge," in *Culture and Its Creators, op. cit.*, p. 228.
17. See John O. Jordan, "The Social Sub-text of *David Copperfield*," in this volume.
18. "'Let us have no meandering,'" she emphatically states (1.50).
19. Carl Dawson, *Victorian Noon: English Literature in 1850, op. cit.*, p. 127.
20. I owe the phrase to Karen Reifel.
21. See John M. Ellis, *The Theory of Literary Criticism: A Logical Analysis* (Berkeley: University of California Press, 1974), especially Chapters 5 and 8.

22. *Oxford English Dictionary*, from "Memorial," entry 3: "**1849** MACAULAY, *History of England*, I, 613, 'The plough and the spade have not seldom turned up ghastly memorials of the slaughter.' **1853** J. H. NEWMAN, *Historical Sketches* (1873), II, 168, 'The memorials of the rule of the Pharaohs are still engraved on the rocks of Libya.' **1857** Ruskin, *Arrows of Chace* (1880), I, 44, 'Every day renders the destruction of historical memorials more complete in Europe'."

The Social Sub-text
of *David Copperfield*

John O. Jordan

David Copperfield has not been a particularly fruitful text for critics interested in tracing Dickens' development as a social novelist. Unlike *Dombey and Son* and *Bleak House*, the novels that immediately precede and follow it, *Copperfield* does not attempt to analyze Victorian England as a totality of social and economic relations. Rather, it seems to be essentially a domestic novel. Its focus is more narrow and personal, partly as a result of the first-person narrative perspective and partly as a result of David's absorption in the process of retrospective fantasy.

The book is more concerned with David's inner experiences, with the growth of his consciousness and the disciplining of his heart, than it is with outer realities. History, in the immediate sense of public events and controversies, intrudes very little into David's narrative. For example, the only reference in the book to industrial unrest in the North comes not from David but from a most unlikely source, Jack Maldon. Similarly, although David works as a Parliamentary reporter for a morning newspaper he remains silent about this aspect of his life. He tells us at length about the domestic problems of his marriage to Dora, but says nothing about the Parliamentary debates that he attends or about the social issues that Parliament seeks, unsuccessfully in his opinion, to address. In his ability to keep separate the world of work from his life at home, David here seems every bit as successful as that other commuter to the office, Wemmick, in *Great Expectations*.

What social criticism the novel does contain seems rather mild by comparison with Dickens' other novels. The satire on Doctors' Commons, for instance, does not deeply engage David's imagination or elicit from him the angry social voice that we hear from the omniscient narrators of *Bleak House* and *Little Dorrit* when confronted by similar institutions. Time and distance, plus the generalized nostalgia that David tends to adopt toward the past, combine to soften his memory of these and other social abuses. Thus, he is irritated but not indignant when he recalls the aristocratic pretensions of Mrs. Henry Spiker and the Waterbrooks or the parasitism of Mrs. Markleham and her nephew. His more spirited attack on the model prisons in Chapter 61 therefore comes as something of a surprise, but here David's social criticism may be partly motivated by his personal dislike of Littimer and Heep, the two prisoners who benefit most from what David considers the laxity and high living of the Middlesex penal experiment.

Indeed, David's anger in the book seems reserved almost exclusively for Uriah Heep, whom he dreams of skewering with a poker and whom he actually strikes on the face in one memorable scene. Moreover, David abuses Uriah throughout the book from his position as narrator by emphasizing Heep's repellent physical appearance and by comparing him constantly to a variety of sub-human creatures: snakes, frogs, snails, etc.[1] David's excessive hatred of Uriah will require further consideration; for the moment, however, it is sufficient to point out the apparent surplus of personal, as opposed to social, anger in David's narrative.

Critics have tended to explain the relative lack of emphasis on social themes in *David Copperfield* by stressing the novel's autobiographical origin. In *Copperfield*, they argue, Dickens was writing not about the world but about himself—about some of the most intimate experiences from his own past, notably the humiliating episode at Warren's Blacking Factory. The novel is thus seen as a working out of private conflicts and concerns in fictional disguise. In order to examine these personal themes and come to terms with them, Dickens presumably felt obliged to narrow the focus of his book. As a result, he took a holiday, so it seems, from the insistent public and social concerns that animate his other novels of the 1840s and 1850s.

There is ample evidence to support a biographical interpretation of *Copperfield*: the reversal of the initials CD/DC, for example, as well as the inclusion in the novel of several passages taken word for word from Dickens' own unfinished autobiographical narrative. Biographical critics such as Edgar Johnson have detailed many other parallels between David's life and that of his creator.[2] The danger of such interpretations, however, is that by aligning novelist and character so closely they risk blurring the differences between them. In particular, biographical readings of *Copperfield* may prevent us from taking a critical perspective on David's actions as a character and, more importantly, on his conduct as narrator.

Recent interpretations of *Copperfield* have tended to play down its connections to Dickens' life and, at the same time, have begun to voice dissatisfaction with the tone of the novel's ending, especially David's self-congratulatory display of prudence and restraint and his elevation of Agnes to secular sainthood as the angel in his house. Increasingly, revisionist critics resist the moral pattern that David seeks to impose on the events of his life. Instead, they find a deep division in the novel between its official morality of the disciplined heart and some other, more subversive force, such as memory or comedy, wherein the authentic life of the book is said to lie.[3]

My own reading of the novel is in sympathy with such attempts to resist the value system that David espouses, but it seeks to go beyond them in locating a social basis for the contradictions that other critics have noted in David's character and in the book as a whole. In particular, I shall argue that anxiety about social class infects David's narrative and produces significant distortions, displacements, and omissions in his self-presentation and in his accounts of other people. I want, in other words, to recuperate a social sub-text for the novel and, in so doing, to claim for *Copperfield* the important place that it deserves in Dickens' development as a social novelist. *Copperfield*, in my view, is a work where social themes and History are not absent but have been repressed.[4]

My account of the work will necessarily be selective and will focus on those points in the text where I find the distortions and displacements most strongly in evidence. These include David's version of his relations with Steerforth and with the Peggotty household, as well as what he tells us about Uriah Heep. These, of course, are the two main subplots that flank the narrative of David's progress toward domestic happiness and worldly success. Class anxieties, less evident in David's own story after his escape to Dover in Chapter 13, typically reemerge in other parts of his narrative.

Steerforth and Heep are particularly significant in this respect. I view them not only as psychological "doubles" who act out David's sexual fantasies toward two of the women whom he desires, thereby allowing him to remain passive and innocent, but also as boundary figures in the class system, indicating respectively the class affiliation that David wishes to strengthen and the class entanglement he most strongly seeks to avoid. The Peggottys play a somewhat different role in David's fantasy life. Ostensibly a happy, working-class family, they are in fact neither a family nor happy, and as the story progresses, they suffer an additional loss on top of those already endured. Steerforth's seduction of Emily is both a sexual crime and a crime across class boundaries. David faithfully records some of the traumatic consequences of this event, but he evades others in order to keep from facing his own involvement in the deed and in order to preserve a myth of social deference centered in the Peggotty home.

The evasions and distortions of reality in the novel belong to the narrator, not the author, and it is thus David rather than Dickens on whom I wish to focus. The extent to which Dickens also is implicated in these evasions is a question I find difficult to answer. There is evidence external to the text of *Copperfield* that Dickens shared David's anxieties about social class. I believe, however, that Dickens was more aware of these anxieties than David, or at least was more open in his writing to the contradictions that they produce, and therefore that he was able to expose the limitations and self-deceptions of David's perspective. Whether Dickens deliberately intended an ironic view of David is impossible to say. Certainly he took an indulgent view of the novel, calling it his "favorite child." But neither this fact nor anything else that we can learn about authorial intention should deter us from looking closely at the play of textual effects that undermines David's narrative authority.[5] These textual effects, taken as symptoms of David's social malaise, are finally more important, I believe, than the problem of where to situate Dickens with respect to David's text.

I

Anxieties about social class are evident from the very beginning of the novel, both in its title and in its opening sentence. Consider first the famous sentence with which David begins his narrative: "Whether I shall turn out to be the hero of my own life, or whether that station will be held by anybody else, these pages must show" (1.1).[6] The problematic word in the sentence is of course "hero." Many pages have been written on the meaning of this term, both for Dickens and for David, as well as on the larger question that the sentence raises concerning heroism in the book as a whole.[7] In all the speculation about what David means by the term "hero," no one has stopped to look at the evidence most closely at hand, the noun that he puts in apposition to "hero" within his opening sentence.

At first glance, the word "station" does not seem to carry any particular weight. It is a neutral term meaning place, position, or location. In the nineteenth century, however, before being replaced by the modern all-purpose term "class," "station" frequently designated a person's social standing or rank, particularly as acquired by birth, and it is almost exclusively in this sense that the word is used in *Copperfield*. " 'We know our station and are thankful in it,'" says Mrs. Heep of Uriah and herself (17.219). "'He found himself the monarch of the place,'" explains Mrs. Steerforth of her son's experience at Mr. Creakle's school, "'and he haughtily determined to be worthy of his station. It was like himself'" (20.253). "'Then she should have kept to her own station in life, father,'" retorts Minnie, the undertaker's daughter, referring to Emily (21.260). David too uses the word to describe his former childhood sweetheart: "'She is engaged to be married to a most worthy and deserving man in her own station of life'" (22.284). "'Have you considered my daughter's station in life, the projects I may contemplate for her advancement?'" demands Mr. Spenlow indignantly when David announces that he loves Dora (38.470). And finally, Uriah himself: "'But how little you think of the rightful umbleness of a person in my station, Master Copperfield!'" (39.490).

What all of these statements have in common is the assumption of a stable social hierarchy in which persons should not seek to change their position through marriage or any other means of advancement. The essence of social "station" is to be stationary, inalterable. *Copperfield* of course contains several characters who challenge this assumption, notably Emily and Uriah Heep, as well as David himself. To return to the novel's opening sentence, let me suggest that part of the difficulty David has in knowing whether he is the hero of his own life has to do with his uncertainty about the relation between heroism and social station. David does not know whether heroes are born, like Steerforth, or whether they can make themselves through industry and earnestness, as he himself tries to do. If he is confused about these questions, it is partly because he does not see or think clearly about social class.

Questions about social class are also implicit in the novel's title. The full title of David's narrative is *The Personal History, Adventures, Experience, & Observation of David Copperfield the Younger of Blunderstone Rookery (Which He Never Meant to be Published on any Account)*. Whether we take this title as the invention of an omniscient narrator or as David's own third-person introduction to himself does not matter. In either case, it reveals important things about his character that are borne out subsequently in his own narration. First, there is the question of how we come to be reading David's autobiography at all, if he never meant for it to be published. David himself reiterates this intention when he says of his manuscript that it is "intended for no eyes but mine" (42.517). Later, he explains the fact of his writing the autobiography as a result of "the compact I have made with myself, to reflect my mind on this paper" (48.594–595). David's language here is sternly protestant and invokes the tradition of moral self-scrutiny as one of the duties of every religious person. Writing the story of his life is thus a spiritual exercise, a means of disciplining his heart, and as such it aims at no readership beyond the self (except perhaps God). But David is also a novelist who enjoys his new-found fame as well as the financial rewards that accompany it, and it is presumably these more worldly motives that overcome his initial reluctance to publish.

But why the reluctance to publish in the first place? Not, I think, out of any wish to avoid the sin of pride. On the contrary, David appears quite pleased with the shape his life has taken and, like other successful entrepreneurs in the protestant tradition, he seems to be telling the story of his life as a moral example to others of how hard work and self-discipline lead to material success and to the sign of divine approval—in his case, marriage to the angelic Agnes. The source of David's reluctance to publish his autobiography lies neither in modesty nor in piety, I believe, but in a sense of social shame. Included in the story of his life are not only episodes of intemperance and imprudence, such as getting drunk and going to the play or marrying Dora, but the account of his experience at Murdstone and Grinby's, when through no fault of his own he fell out of the genteel class into which he was born and, briefly, into the working class.

The passage describing David's reaction to this event is well-known.

> The deep remembrance of the sense I had, of being utterly without hope now; of the shame I felt in my position; of the misery it was to my young heart to believe that day by day what I had learned, and thought, and delighted in, and raised my fancy and my emulation up by, would pass away from me, little by little, never to be brought back any more; cannot be written.   (11.133)

It cannot be written because the pain and humiliation are greater than David believes he or perhaps any words can express. It cannot be written also because to write it down is to preserve a record of the event, and this David does not wish to do. But in this case, David's compact with himself is stronger than his sense of shame. Words elude the social censor and the shameful social secret does get written down. David's reluctance to publish his autobiography comes from his knowledge that to do so is to make his secret public.

A second trace of class anxiety in the novel's title appears in David's name. He is not "David Copperfield, Author, of London," but David Copperfield the Younger of Blunderstone Rookery. The name that identifies the autobiographical subject is not the destination of his narrative, that which he becomes at the end of the book, but his origin, the point where he begins. Moreover, it is not simply a name; it is a title with pretensions to gentility acquired through birth. Rather than stress the middle-class occupation of novelist that David has earned through his own labor, the title emphasizes that he is well-born, that he has a father whose name he is proud to bear, and that he has an estate with a rather grand-sounding name. The hollowness in all these claims to gentility is soon evident in the book. David's father dies before his son is born and leaves the boy no patrimony other than his name. There are no rooks at Blunderstone Rookery, and the estate, far from belonging to David, is acquired by a shrewd commercial entrepreneur, Murdstone, who makes a practice of marrying rich young widows and who sells the house to someone who uses it as an asylum for a "poor lunatic gentleman" who sits at the window of David's room and looks down into the churchyard where David's parents are buried. Nevertheless, David persists in returning to Blunderstone whenever he is down at Yarmouth, and spends his days there wandering among the graves and mooning about his early hopes, "the figure I was to make in life, and the distinguished things I was to do" (22.272). This lingering over the past obviously satisfies a psychological need for David, but it also betrays the extent to which he attempts to ground his social identity, his "station," in the family estate and in the class expectations that derive from it.[8]

A further irony in the novel's title emerges in the phrase "David Copperfield the Younger." In addition to indicating David's position as the bearer of a supposedly distinguished patronym, the phrase alludes to his persistent problem of being taken advantage of on account of his youth and innocence. Much of the comedy in this novel of growing up comes in scenes where David is the victim of someone older than himself, usually someone from a lower social class. Encounters with waiters, beginning with the one he meets in Yarmouth on his way to London, are particularly troublesome in this regard. As David grows up, however, the problem of being younger (i.e., literally a child) shifts to the problem of feeling younger—that is, not being treated with respect by his social inferiors: coachmen, landlady, more waiters, and finally his own domestic servants, who commit innumerable petty thefts upon him and Dora and conspire with the tradesmen to perpetrate still more. If ever anyone had a servant problem, it is David Copperfield.

The focus of this problem, however, is Littimer: with Littimer we can see that David's anxiety about feeling younger has more to do with social class than with psychological maturity or simply inexperience in the world. To David, Littimer is "a pattern of respectability" (21.255) before whom he feels himself "the greenest and most inexperienced of mortals" (21.256). Littimer's power over David derives, however, from something deeper than his incarnation of respectability, something that David does not know how to name and that he conceals by saying that he feels "young." Littimer is a gentleman's body servant, and from his privileged position close to but not inside the upper class he sees things that others cannot and that understandably make a young social climber like David extremely nervous.

For one thing, Littimer can tell a true gentleman from a pretender. At the very least, he can see that David has no knowledge of the aristocratic sports in which Steerforth instructs his eager young friend. Although David has been to Doctor Strong's Academy and hopes to become a proctor, there is still an enormous social gap between him and an "Oxford man" like Steerforth. Littimer's withering look is a constant reminder to David that this gap exists, but David says only that Littimer makes him feel "young."

Littimer also understands the true nature of patronage in a class society, something that David is unwilling to face since he is so deeply implicated in it. Thus, Littimer can see the self-serving economic transaction that underlies David's boyish admiration for Steerforth. What David seeks in this friendship is the protection and sponsorship of a gentleman and hence, ultimately, confirmation that he too is acceptable in Steerforth's social class. In return for this patronage, David supplies the uncritical adulation that feeds Steerforth's narcissism. But the patronage system never involves an equal exchange. David gives more than he gets. Steerforth withholds the ultimate boon, recognition of David as a social equal. To him, David is always "young Copperfield" or "Daisy" or "little Copperfield," terms of condescending familiarity. Thus, Steerforth too makes David feel "younger," but David loves it, for he thinks that it means acceptance into Steerforth's intimate circle. Littimer, standing outside the patronage system, knows what his master really thinks of David. Having nothing himself to gain or lose from the relationship, he hardly bothers to mask his contempt, and so inevitably makes young David feel uneasy.

David's infatuation with Steerforth begins at Mr. Creakle's school, as does his willingness to betray members of the lower class in exchange for patronage and class solidarity from Steerforth. The incident with Mr. Mell not only foreshadows the role that David will play as an accomplice in the seduction of Emily, but also anticipates his evasion of responsibility in narrating the event. David feels contrition and self-reproach about Mell's dismissal, but suppresses his feelings lest Steerforth regard them as "unfriendly—or, I should rather say, . . . undutiful" (7.86). Traddles, with his stronger sense of justice, is discovered in tears and predictably gets beaten for this offense. David, the mature narrator, recounts the incident without a word of condemnation for Steerforth and without treating his own breach of Mell's confidence as more than an innocent lapse in judgment.

Readers who have sensed an erotic dimension in David's attraction to Steerforth are not entirely wrong, but it is useful, I think, to view their relationship in terms of social as well as sexual dominance and submission. If David is feminized in the relationship, it is largely a result of the inequality in social power between them. The sexual transactions between Steerforth and David are mediated by an exchange of women. David renounces his sexual interest in Emily and, instead, "gives" her to Steerforth in return for Steerforth's friendship. Emily is the object of exchange in a male economy, the "sister" given by one man to his friend as confirmation of a social bond.

Because David wants to believe that Steerforth treats him as a social equal, he expects that the sexual exchange of "sisters" will be mutual. During David's first visit to Steerforth's home, there is a remarkable sequence of events. First, David invites Steerforth to accompany him to visit the Peggotty family in Yarmouth, mentioning that Mr. Peggotty "has a very pretty little niece too" (20.251). Then David inquires about the history of Rosa Dartle, whom he has just met for the first time, and listens to Steerforth's explanation of the remarkable scar on her lip. Then the following dialogue takes place:

> "And I have no doubt she loves you like a brother," said I.
> "Humph!" retorted Steerforth looking at the fire. "Some brothers are not loved over much; and some love—but help yourself, Copperfield!" (20.252)

Steerforth breaks off his sentence to propose that he and David drink a toast to "the daisies of the field, in compliment to you," but his invitation to "help yourself, Copperfield" is ambiguous and finds David all too ready to hear it as an invitation to help himself sexually to Rosa Dartle. The chapter concludes with David undressing in his bedroom before a picture of Rosa Dartle, imagining the scar coming and going on her lip where the portrait painter has left it out. Finally, he falls asleep, only to dream of Rosa throughout the night.

Not surprisingly, David soon thereafter feels himself falling a little in love with Miss Dartle. He does so not because she has shown any romantic interest in him, but because he imagines that Steerforth has made him a gift of this passionate woman who carries the mark of Steerforth's sexual violence on her mouth. David's romantic fantasy, of course, does not lead anywhere, but this is the point. David deceives himself into imagining a reciprocity of sexual exchange with Steerforth, based on an assumption of social equality, but here again the exchange is unequal. Not only does David give more than he gets, but by introducing Steerforth into the Peggotty home with the implicit

understanding that Emily is sexually available to him, David thereby betrays
his friendship with the entire Peggotty household and makes himself an
accomplice in the crime that Steerforth commits. David's prolonged absences
during the stay at Yarmouth implicate him still further. They give Steerforth
time to carry out the seduction while keeping David ignorant and thus
technically guiltless of the deed, though he may unconsciously take vicarious
pleasure in it.

It is important to emphasize that almost never in his narrative does David
face up to the possibility of his involvement in Steerforth's action.[9] Thus, to
the extent that he is complicitous in the crime (and this judgment will vary for
different readers), he is also, as the narrator of these events, "blind, blind,
blind" to the motives for his actions as well as to the evasions in his
retrospective account of them. Moreover, he explicitly refuses to condemn
Steerforth, preferring instead to cherish the idealized memory of him as a
boyhood hero. If David refuses to judge Steerforth, the reader, I think, must,
and in so doing must also question David's narrative authority. The play of
David's text exposes gaps and distortions in his story and points to repressed
motives, notably the wish for a class alliance with Steerforth, that persist
throughout his narrative, up to and including the time of writing.

II

The climax of the Steerforth-Emily seduction plot comes midway through
the novel in Chapter 31. Before considering this important scene, however,
we must look more closely at some aspects of David's relationship to the
Peggottys. Here, too, questions of social class are of utmost importance, and
it is necessary to distinguish carefully between what David tells us about the
Peggottys and what their life is really like, as best we can determine this from
the evidence David supplies.

Our introduction to the Peggotty household comes in Chapter 3 when David
describes his initial visit to Yarmouth. David's expectations about the Peggottys are shaped to some extent by their relationship to his own beloved
Peggotty, who nursed him from the time he was a baby. Since Peggotty is
virtually a mother to David,[10] he enters the Yarmouth houseboat on a footing
of immediate intimacy, almost as a member of the family. Since his own
family unit is incomplete, he is delighted to find what he takes to be a happy,
intact nuclear family with a father, a mother, a sibling of each sex, and a little
room just waiting to accept him as the latest addition to the group. He is, of

course, sadly mistaken about the real nature of this "family," and his initial error in perception should alert us to the possibility that David will continue to misperceive the Peggottys in other, perhaps less obvious ways.

David's delight in the houseboat itself is immense and contributes to the fairy tale charm of his narrative. "If it had been Aladdin's palace, roc's egg and all, I suppose I could not have been more charmed with the romantic idea of living in it" (3.25). The houseboat epitomizes a particular snugness that one finds often in Dickens, usually associated with a womb-like security, and it is in this way that David wants to remember it. Charming as they are, however, we should not let David's romantic fantasies about the house blind us to its material and social realities. Consider the distribution and allocation of physical space, for example. The houseboat has three rooms: a central living and eating area with two small sleeping quarters at either end. There are six people to be lodged: the four regular occupants plus David and Peggotty. David is the only one with a room to himself. Ham and Mr. Peggotty sleep in hammocks suspended from the ceiling in the main room, while the two women and Emily are crowded into a space the size of David's.

These facts are all available to David. Indeed, they are in his narrative, but he fails to notice them as significant either at the time of his visit or later in his adult retelling of it. He takes it for granted, in both instances, that he will have a room to himself, and he refers thereafter to the room with the oyster-shell mirror as "my bedroom." At no point does he ever ask himself who had to be displaced in order for him to have the room. (The height of the mirror indicates that it belonged to Emily. Taking her room is thus David's first offense, though a relatively trivial one, against her.) He appears to assume that the room was vacant and simply waiting for him to occupy it.

It is the same with food. "By and by," David says, "when we had dined in a sumptuous manner off boiled dabs, melted butter, and potatoes, with a chop for me, a hairy man with a very good-natured face came home" (3.27). If David is a member of the family, he also receives special treatment as befits his social station. From the outset, class differences in the houseboat are carefully observed. David, though only a boy, is regularly addressed as "sir." Despite his youth, he confidently initiates conversations with adults. David never feels "young" in the Peggotty home. If anything, he feels and acts more adult among them. But just as feeling young is often an indication of David's class insecurity, so feeling mature among the Peggottys reflects his sense of social superiority.

Remembering his first visit to the houseboat, David as narrator constructs a myth of timeless childhood innocence around it. In his memory, social distinctions have no place since the boat exists outside of time and history. "As to any sense of inequality, or youthfulness, or other difficulty in our way, little Em'ly and I had no such trouble, because we had no future" (3.32). However, the chapter contains many signs and premonitions of the difficulties resulting from "inequality,"[11] and to his credit, David as narrator does recognize some of them: the wind howling out at sea, Emily's dangerous fantasy of becoming a lady, and the vision of her running along a jagged timber over the deep water. In retrospect, this final image remains a vivid portent for David of what he knows will happen. Although he anticipates the outcome of Emily's story and thus in hindsight can recognize danger signs in their first encounter, David as narrator still does not understand the role that he has played in encouraging her fantasies or the extent to which social class is a factor in their supposedly pure and "innocent" love.

David's desire to incorporate the Peggotty home into his myth of childhood innocence leads him to remember it as a place where everyone, except of course Mrs. Gummidge, is happy. However, this myth of happiness is as much a misperception on David's part as his belief that the Peggottys are a nuclear family. Despite their smiling faces ("Mr. Peggotty smiled at us from behind his pipe, and Ham grinned all the evening and did nothing else" [3.32]), the Peggottys are in pain through much of the book. When David first meets them, he learns of the tragic losses that mark the family history: two sets of parents, a husband, two brothers, and a business partner. These losses, it should be noted, are a result of the hard working conditions faced by people who make their living from the sea. And yet the Peggottys seem to bear up under these losses with remarkable fortitude. Only Mrs. Gummidge complains from time to time, and the others tolerate her outbreaks of misery with stoic forbearance.

In fact, Mrs. Gummidge plays a crucial role in the family, and she is often misunderstood by readers of the novel as well as by David, who finds her irritating when she moans about being "a lone lorn creetur'." Rather than take her at face value as the only complaining member of an otherwise happy home, I think it is more accurate to see her as the vehicle of authentic feeling for a family that does not know how to grieve and that has difficulty expressing negative emotion of any kind. Mrs. Gummidge carries and periodically gives voice to the repressed unhappiness that everyone in the houseboat is feeling. "'I feel more than other people do,'" she says, "'and I show it more. It's my misfortun'" (3.34). The others therefore tolerate her, for she functions as a kind of safety valve for negative feelings that allows them to remain "happy." As her name suggests, she holds the group together, providing the adhesive element that keeps the Peggotty family system precariously intact.

She also presumably does the housework, for there is no one else to do it. Emily is too small, and the men are away fishing until evening. When David first enters the houseboat, he notes that it "was beautifully clean inside, and as tidy as possible" (3.26). Typically, however, he does not notice that anyone ever works to keep the house clean, since that labor is performed by servants at Blunderstone Rookery. (David learns more about housework when he is married to Dora.) The remarkable transformation that Mrs. Gummidge undergoes in the second half of the book should not surprise us, therefore, as much as it does David. When she announces that henceforth she will "keep a Beein" for Mr. Peggotty while he is away in search of Emily, it is only an affirmation that she will continue to do what she has done for the family all along. The only difference now is that she is relieved of the need to be unhappy for other people, since that role has been assumed by Emily and the unhappiness is more equally distributed among the other family members.

Both as individuals and as a group, the Peggottys are much more complicated than David generally gives them credit for being. True, he does not go to the extreme of Steerforth in denying their humanity and in regarding them as animals who "have not very fine natures" and who are "not easily wounded" (20.251). But he does sentimentalize them as hearty, simple folk, and this sentimental vision becomes a way, if not of denying their humanity, then at least of reducing it to a form that suits his own psychological and social needs. The version of the Peggottys that David gives us confirms his myth of Edenic childhood. It also confirms his middle-class social myth of the common people as deferential toward their superiors and as happy in their social station. Every time David tells us that the Peggotty men smile and call him "Mas'r Davy," he reinforces a comforting social stereotype of the poor created by the middle class. This stereotype has a familiar American counterpart in the image of black slaves as smiling darkies who love their "Massah." Let me reemphasize, however, that it is David and not Dickens, who gives us this sentimental picture of the working class. The contradictions and omissions in David's account force us to recognize his middle-class perspective and to look beyond it at the more complex facts of working-class life.

Perhaps the saddest thing about the Peggotty household is the extent to which its members internalize their own class oppression and thus conform to the middle-class stereotype. This is especially true in the case of Ham and Mr. Peggotty, who spend their time grinning insufferably in an effort to repress their class resentment and anger. After Emily's elopement, Ham finds it almost impossible to express his anger at her and at Steerforth. Outwardly he remains the same sweet, good-natured fellow that he was before, and devotes himself to a life of serving others. Such sweetness is difficult to believe. If we look more closely at Ham, we can recognize him as a terribly depressed person who has internalized his anger and directed it against himself. On the day following Emily's departure, David finds Ham staring out to sea and has ''a frightful thought . . . —not that his face was angry, for it was not; I recall nothing but an expression of stern determination in it—that if ever he encountered Steerforth, he would kill him'' (32.389). However, when he asks Ham what is on his mind, Ham replies, '' 'I doen't rightly know how 'tis, but from over yon there seemed to me to come—the end of it like' '' (32.390). Already, though he may not know it, Ham is thinking of suicide. Ham's death contains all these elements. It is at once an attempt to rescue and to kill the man he hates, but it is also clearly an act of self-destruction.

Mr. Peggotty's anger, though also repressed, lies closer to the surface. It emerges in his constant roaring and ''horroaring,'' in the powerful good-natured blows he gives Ham on the chest and back, and in David's references to his ''sledge-hammer'' arm (7.89). When David first meets him, he learns of Mr. Peggotty's infrequent fits of violent temper and his use of the ''terrible verb passive to be gormed'' (3.29). The important thing about this verb is the way in which the passive form suspends, without negating, its violent potential. The target of Mr. Peggotty's anger is seldom specified. Indeed, he usually seems unaware that he is angry at all. There are moments, however, when the class basis of his unconscious anger becomes apparent in his language. Thus, when the ''two gent'lmen'' walk in on the scene of Ham and Emily's betrothal, Mr. Peggotty explains to his niece (quite unnecessarily, of course) who the unknown stranger is.

> ''There's the gent'lman as you've heerd on, Em'ly. He comes to see you, along with Mas'r Davy, on the brightest night of your uncle's life as ever was or will be, Gorm the t'other one, and horroar for it!''   (21.266)

Apparently uttered in welcome, this speech is also a roar of pain and anger at the class intrusion on his moment of joy. The ''t'other one'' whom he gorms is the devil, but it is of course also Steerforth, who carries many Luciferian associations in the novel. The speech is also darkly prophetic, for it proclaims this night the brightest ''as ever was or will be.'' Even the final ''horroar'' portends doom. The phonetic spelling in the text makes it cognate with ''horror.''

To read this scene as a foreshadowing of Mr. Peggotty's class anger at Steerforth is perhaps obvious. Less apparent, however, is the way in which it anticipates Mr. Peggotty's anger at David too. If Steerforth is "the t'other one," then David is the one who came first and after whom Steerforth is the second. Steerforth alone receives the terrible "Gorm" from Mr. Peggotty here. However, we should be prepared for David to receive his share of the anger as well, since he is the one who brings Steerforth to Yarmouth in the first place.

The inclusion of David as a target of the Peggottys' social anger takes place in the climactic Chapter 31. The chapter is entitled "A Greater Loss," following upon Chapter 30, "A Loss," in which the death of Barkis is described. The ambiguity of David's chapter title indicates the extent of his divided class loyalties: his uncertainty about which is greater, the loss of Emily or his own loss of Steerforth. The scene leading up to the revelation of Emily's elopement is full of painful contradictions. Mrs. Gummidge, ever the voice of true feeling, groans about being "lone and lorn." Mr. Peggotty tries in vain to cheer her up, shaking his head at the same time as if to negate his own false cheer. He roars with inappropriate laughter, smites his hands together, and says, "I'm—I'm Gormed" with sudden emphasis (31.384).

Finally, Ham arrives and invites David to step outside for a minute. David records their conversation as follows:

> "Ham! What's the matter?"
> "Mas'r Davy!—" Oh, for his broken heart, how dreadfully he wept!
> I was paralyzed by the sight of such grief. I don't know what I thought, or what I dreaded. I could only look at him.
> "Ham! Poor good fellow! For Heaven's sake, tell me what's the matter!"
> "My love, Mas'r Davy—the pride and hope of my 'art—her that I'd have died for, and would die for now—she's gone!"
> "Gone!"
> "Em'ly's run away! Oh, Mas'r Davy, think *how* she's run away, when I pray my good and gracious God to kill her (her that is so dear above all things) sooner than let her come to ruin and disgrace!"   (31.385)

The syntax in this passage is brilliantly arranged to expose registers of feeling unacknowledged by either speaker. We recognize Ham's despair (his readiness to die for Emily "now") as well as his unconscious anger at her (he calls on God to kill her). More surprising, however, is Ham's apparent anger at David. Twice David asks what's the matter, and twice Ham's grief-stricken voice breaks off after saying "Mas'r Davy" and "My love, Mas'r Davy." Despite what Ham knows and David fears, Ham's language accuses David, not Steerforth. David's paralysis and dread reflect his own unconscious guilt. Fearing that an accusation may soon follow, he tries to regain control of the situation by reminding Ham of their relative social stations, calling him "poor good fellow."

A similar syntactical displacement occurs a few minutes later when Mr. Peggotty demands the name of Emily's seducer.

> "Who's the man? I want to know his name."
> Ham glanced at me, and suddenly I felt a shock that struck me back.
> "There's a man suspected," said Mr. Peggotty. "Who is it?"
> "Mas'r Davy," implored Ham. "Go out a bit, and let me tell him what I must. You doen't ought to hear it, sir."
> I felt the shock again. I sank down in a chair, and tried to utter some reply; but my tongue was fettered, and my sight was weak.   (31.386)

David's sight here is indeed weak. Throughout the rest of the scene, syntax and suspended quotations[12] shift the blame from Steerforth to David or else make the two gentlemen indistinguishable. Finally, Mr. Peggotty's anger erupts into the open and he announces his plan to seek Emily after first staving in the boat. The explicit class basis of his anger is apparent, and it comes dangerously close to being unleashed upon David, who, we recall, has sunk down in a chair. "'As he sat afore me,' [Mr. Peggotty] said, wildly, holding out his clenched right hand, 'as he sat afore me, face to face, strike me down dead, but I'd have drownded him, and thought it right!'" (31.387).

The imminent class violence that seethes through these exchanges subsides at last, and David as narrator brings his chapter to a close. His concluding paragraph shows only a partial understanding of what he has just described.

> [Mr. Peggotty] was quite passive now; and when I heard him crying, the impulse that had been upon me to go down upon my knees, and ask their pardon for the desolation I had caused, and curse Steerforth, yielded to a better feeling. My overcharged heart found the same relief, and I cried too.   (31.388)

Tears of self-pity, tears that express his sorrow at the "greater loss" of his male friend, take the place of his impulse to curse Steerforth and to ask forgiveness from the Peggottys. Most damning of all is the phrase that David uses to describe his tears. To call them "a better feeling" shows that he as narrator still remains blinded by class loyalties and thus unaware of his culpability, no matter how much it threatens to explode from within his own narrative.

III

The loss of David's aristocratic patron at this point effectively puts an end to his fantasies of entry into the highest levels of society. It does not prevent him, however, from remaining loyal to Steerforth's memory. Significantly, it is Steerforth's body, not Ham's, that David honors with his presence following the double drowning. David also retains many of the values of Steerforth's class. For example, he seems to want very much to move into the well-to-do suburbs. When he and Dora marry, they rent a cottage in Highgate, the same fashionable district where Mrs. Steerforth lives.

A second and perhaps ultimately more important blow to David's social aspirations follows closely upon the elopement of Steerforth and Emily. The failure of Betsey Trotwood's business investments removes her from the position of David's benefactor and in effect throws David into the world to make his way on his own. This point marks the beginning of David's progress into the middle class. With increasing emphasis from here on, David's narrative will stress the virtues of hard work, earnestness, and self-discipline that lead to his eventual worldly success.

Aunt Betsey's failure not only requires that David cancel his articles at Doctors' Commons, it also jeopardizes his relationship with Dora. Such at any rate is the burden of the comic nightmare that David dreams, in which he appears first as a ragged boy selling matches to Dora, next at the office dressed in his nightgown and remonstrated with by Mr. Spenlow, then "hungrily picking up the crumbs that fell from old Tiffey's daily biscuit," and finally as a suitor at Doctors' Commons, "hopelessly endeavoring to get a license to marry Dora, having nothing but one of Uriah Heep's gloves to offer in exchange" (35.431). As the dream makes clear, David's courtship of Dora has important class implications.

David conducts his courtship of Dora according to the sentimental conventions of romantic love. From his later position as the practical, self-disciplined husband of Agnes, David can expose the foolishness of his youthful infatuation, while at the same time relishing its narrative re-creation. From neither perspective, however, does he recognize that his falling in love with Dora is motivated, initially at least, by a desire to improve his social station. Dora, after all, is the daughter of his apparently wealthy employer, and David becomes infatuated with her only after Mr. Spenlow has explained in detail the social and economic advantages of membership in Doctors' Commons. David readily submits to Mr. Spenlow's class ideology: "*I* was not the man to touch the Commons, and bring down the country" (26.333). He then drives down to Norwood in Mr. Spenlow's phaeton, looks over the beautiful grounds and house of the estate, and proceeds to fall in love.

Again, David's psychological and social needs converge. Dora is not only a replacement for the youthful mother of his childhood; she also lives in an estate whose grandeur equals or surpasses that of Blunderstone Rookery. The tragedy of Dora is that she has been brought up to be a luxury consumer object (like Jip) in a world of genteel refinement and wealth. When Aunt Betsey fails and when Mr. Spenlow dies insolvent, David is able to adjust himself to a middle-class way of life, but Dora unfortunately cannot.

David's nightmare of appearing before Dora as a ragged boy selling matches shows the extent of his class anxiety in this relationship. He fears that Aunt Betsey's financial ruin will make him ineligible as Dora's suitor. In the dream David reverts not to the Murdstone and Grinby period of his life but to the waking nightmare of his journey to Dover, when he was in fact ragged, hungry, and forced to sell his clothes, and when he experienced in all its terror the violent hostility of the poor toward members of the upper class.

David's brief identification with Uriah Heep in the dream points to another important aspect of class relations in the novel. David and Uriah are in fact alike in many ways. Both are social climbers. Both aspire to improve their station in life by an advantageous marriage to the daughter of their employer. Both seek the friendship of an upper-class male—Steerforth in David's case, David himself in Uriah's. Both desire the same woman, though David is slow to recognize this fact and comes to love Agnes only after Uriah has aroused his jealousy. Finally, both adopt a program of hard work and self-discipline in order to achieve their goals in life. Here again, Uriah shows David the way; if Steerforth is David's role model during the first half of the book, Uriah, curiously enough, teaches him how to become middle-class. Mastering the art of shorthand is the equivalent for David of Uriah's studying Tidd's *Practice*.[13]

In view of these similarities, it is not surprising that David feels himself drawn to Uriah, "attracted to him in very repulsion" (25.328), as he says. It is the repulsion more than the attraction, however, that one feels most strongly in David's narrative. Both as a character and as a narrator, David tends to disavow his social ambition and aggression. Instead, he projects them onto Uriah and condemns them, meanwhile pursuing his own parallel course under the cover of moral superiority.

There are many reasons for David to dislike Uriah; he finds him both morally and physically repugnant. Perhaps the real reason for David's loathing is the one suggested by George Orwell long ago. According to Orwell, Dickens could not tolerate the thought of Agnes's going to bed with a man who drops his Hs.[14] Orwell's remark is pertinent, but he is wrong in attributing the class hatred of Uriah to Dickens. It is David, not Dickens, who detests Uriah for his class origins. With Uriah, then, as with the Peggottys, we must recognize the class bias in David's perspective and look beyond it if we are to begin seeing Uriah in a fuller and more complex way.

It is important to keep in mind that everything we know about Uriah is filtered through the consciousness of a narrator steadfastly committed to the values and moral superiority of the middle class. Under the pressure of David's moralizing rhetoric, the second half of the novel takes shape almost as a social allegory, a kind of Whig history of class relations, narrated by a middle-class subject. The aristocracy has abandoned its role of national leadership, having corrupted the innocent working class and led the minor gentry astray. In the leadership vacuum created by the aristocracy's departure, a new class emerges into prominence—a class of earnest, hard-working individuals to whom the future of the nation should be entrusted.

The problem with this social fable is that, like so much of the narration from which it derives, it is transparently self-serving and tends to conceal the ways in which the middle class reproduces similar patterns of domination and power to those created by the aristocracy. David's abuse of Uriah is a form of class oppression. Whenever he calls Uriah a fox or Aunt Betsey tells him not to be "galvanic" like an eel, they are treating someone from a lower social class like an animal, much as Steerforth did to the Peggottys. Every dropped H in the narrative is the mark of a significant social distinction made by the middle-class narrator for his presumably middle-class audience. Verisimilitude in representing Heep's accent thus supports David's program of legitimizing middle-class superiority.

Heep becomes a very useful figure for the middle-class characters to have nearby as they consolidate their power at the end of David's narrative. By ganging up on him and treating him as a scapegoat, they assert his difference from themselves (despite evidence to the contrary) and reaffirm their class solidarity. Heep is in this way a victim of the ruling class, just as his Biblical namesake, Uriah, was for King David.

To present Heep only as a victim is of course to overstate the case. He does commit crimes—forgery, fraud, and conspiracy—and his punishment is well-deserved. Still, there is something excessive in the abuse that he receives from David and the others. Traddles provides a corrective and typically fair-minded view of the case, anticipating his future career as a judge. When Aunt Betsey calls Heep "a monster of meanness," Traddles objects. "'Really, I don't know about that,' observed Traddles thoughtfully. 'Many people

can be very mean, when they give their minds to it'" (54.667). Traddles's
comment serves as a useful reminder that although Heep may be a criminal he
is not the inhuman stereotype that David's biased perspective makes him out
to be. Indeed, others, including perhaps David himself, are just as capable of
meanness as Uriah.

If we attempt to remove Heep from David's distorting narrative perspective,
a somewhat clearer view of his role in the novel becomes possible. The son
of a sexton, he belongs by birth to the lower middle class, a cut above Mealy
Potatoes (whose father was a waterman) but not by much. Indeed, David's
hatred of Uriah may derive in part from a wish not to be associated with
someone who reminds him of his own lower-class connections at the warehouse.[15] Clever and ambitious, Uriah determines to advance into the middle
class, using the pretense of ''umbleness'' as a cover for his devious manipulations behind the scenes.

Like Littimer, Heep's marginal position within the class system gives him
insight into its operations and thus makes him potentially a subversive figure
with respect to the unstable hierarchies on which the system rests. Heep's
social ambition threatens the idea of ''station'' as something inalterable from
birth. At the same time, his professions of ''umbleness'' parody the more
genuine social deference of the Peggottys. The Peggottys have no word for
humbleness; they simply *are* humble without calling attention to it, and this
is part of what David likes about them. Heep's reiteration of his humbleness
has an aggressive, hostile edge that makes David uncomfortable, even angry.
It keeps the inequalities of the class system constantly in view, rather than
letting them operate invisibly as David and the middle class prefer. There is
a world of difference between the Peggottys' reassuring ''Mas'r Davy'' and
Uriah's taunting ''Master Copperfield,'' in which insolence and familiarity
are joined with the merest pretense of class deference, and in which David's
role as master is constantly thrown in his face.

Uriah is thus a dangerous fellow to set loose in a class society, for he
understands it too well and too cynically. At some level, David recognizes this
danger. He has a dream about Uriah, the first of many, in which ''he had
launched Mr. Peggotty's house on a piratical expedition, with a black flag at
the masthead, bearing the inscription 'Tidd's Practice,' under which diabolical
ensign he was carrying me and little Em'ly to the Spanish Main, to be
drowned'' (16.202). The dream condenses several fears into a single image,
but among them is the frightening possibility that Uriah might lead a working-class insurrection that would include even the Peggotty household in an
attack on bourgeois society.[16] One of the reassuring things about the Peggotty

home for David is that, although a boat, it does not move. Heep has one other association with insurrection in David's narrative, his "Guy Fawkes pair of gloves" (25.322). These call attention to the lanky, skeletal hands that Uriah is forever writhing, but they also suggest Uriah's potential as the leader of a dangerous political conspiracy.

If David dimly recognizes Uriah's class hatred and insurrectionist potential, this provides a further basis for the loathing that he feels toward him. It may also help to explain David's desire to keep both him and Littimer under stricter institutional surveillance at the end of the book. Chapter 61 has often been considered a blemish on the novel's ending and an unwarranted intrusion of Dickens' own social concerns into David's "personal history." If we think of the novel's ending as having to do with the consolidation of social power in the hands of the middle class, then David's visit to the prison makes better sense. Now a successful novelist, he is invited to inspect one of the chief institutions by which the bourgeoisie exercises control over dangerous elements in the lower classes.

Mr. Creakle, we learn, has retired from schoolmastering to become a magistrate, but in his new position he remains as sensitive as ever to questions of prestige and power. He recognizes David as an influential member of the new ruling class and treats him with the same respect that previously he had given to Mrs. Steerforth and her son. It is ironic that, whereas David found Mr. Creakle to be a tyrant when he ran the school, he sees him as too lenient toward the inmates of his present institution. No doubt this changed perception on David's part owes something to his own more comfortable circumstances. Certainly it has to do with his wish to keep those two dangerous characters, Littimer and Heep, more firmly in check. In any event, the principal irony of the situation lies in the fact that Littimer and Heep have learned how to manipulate the prison system to their own advantage and appear headed toward a successful reentry into David's middle-class world. What becomes of them after the end of the novel we do not know, of course, but I for one strongly suspect that Heep emigrates to America, changes his name to Snopes, and pursues a successful business career in a small town in Mississippi.

IV

One principal group of characters remains to be considered in the sorting out of class relations that takes place in the second half of the novel. These, of course, are the Peggottys. Their role is in some ways less prominent than in the early parts of the book, for the obvious reason that they are dispersed. David can no longer go down to Yarmouth in expectation of finding a snug haven of innocence in their home. Mr. Peggotty wanders the earth in search of his niece, and Ham now lives alone. Only Mrs. Gummidge remains in the houseboat to keep the candle lit and waiting in the window for Emily's return.

The breaking up of the Peggotty household has considerable symbolic importance in the book. Their houseboat is one of the foundations of the social system. In its humble way, it is the ship of state. For it to founder means that the old stable hierarchy of classes, perhaps even the nation itself, has begun to collapse. Thus, when Mr. Peggotty announces his decision to go in search of Emily, David inquires, " 'Will you desert the old boat?' " Mr. Peggotty's reply is darkly foreboding:

> "My station, Mas'r Davy," he returned, "ain't there no longer; and if ever a boat foundered, since there was darkness on the face of the deep, that one's gone down." (32.389)

Mr. Peggotty's reply anticipates his decision to emigrate at the end of the book. His "station" is no longer "there" in the "old boat" of England. For him, that boat's "gone down." His "station" is no longer there in another sense as well. Steerforth's seduction of Emily violates the bond of mutual trust between him and the Peggottys, with its associations of feudal obligation between lord and peasant. Once the seduction has occurred, the exploitative nature of the feudal relationship begins to be exposed, and along with it the falsity of ideas like deference and station.

The transformation that Mr. Peggotty undergoes in the second half of the book marks the beginning of a movement toward class consciousness. No longer content in his "station," he wanders the continent of Europe in pursuit of Emily and Steerforth, driven by the wish to rescue her and by the sense of his own class injury. When he returns to England he no longer remains in Yarmouth, but takes up residence in London and restlessly wanders the city streets at night.[17] His appearance changes dramatically. David notes that his hair is long and ragged; he is grayer and has deep lines in his face and forehead. From the simple, hearty sailor whom David knew in Yarmouth, he is changed into a type of restless, alienated, modern man. We can perhaps appreciate the nature of his transformation better if we compare him to the innocent Sol Gills in *Dombey and Son*, who goes off in search of his nephew Walter but who returns unchanged by his wanderings to resume his happy existence in the Wooden Midshipman, the snug little nautical shop that is the counterpart in that novel of the Peggotty houseboat. In *Copperfield*, however, the little pocket of pastoral innocence is no longer safe from the storms of social inequality. The change in Mr. Peggotty marks his growing awareness of what it means for people like him and Emily to live in a class society.

The understanding of class relations that Mr. Peggotty develops is obviously limited in many ways. He makes no demands for equality, and outwardly at least he retains his deferential manner toward the upper classes. He continues to call David "Mas'r Davy," for example, and in his interview with Mrs. Steerforth, he still seems to believe that Steerforth can make a lady of Emily by marrying her. When Mrs. Steerforth explains that such a marriage is impossible (" 'you cannot fail to know that she is far below him' "), Mr. Peggotty's blunt reply is " 'Raise her up!' " (32.400). When she offers to pay him in compensation for the loss of his niece, however, he responds with eloquent indignation.

For the most part, Mr. Peggotty's social anger does not surface in the second half of the novel. It is perhaps displaced into his wandering and his anxiety about Emily's welfare. Significantly, however, there is none of the false cheer and "horroaring" that masked his anger in the early chapters. In their place, a more mature and sober determination appears that even David can recognize. The class hostility that threatened to erupt against David in Chapter 31 never returns (though there is of course some doubt whether David could recognize it if it did). One faint trace only of middle-class anxiety about working-class violence remains at the end of David's narrative. When Mr. Peggotty returns from Australia in Chapter 63, Agnes's and David's children think that the mysterious stranger at the door is "a wicked old Fairy in a cloak who hated everybody" (63.741), but it is only good Mr. Peggotty with his happy story of resettlement to tell. The threat of class violence is displaced to the realm of childish fairy tale. Dickens waited until *Great Expectations* and the scene of Magwitch's return to take up the more sinister implications of this fantasy.

To the end, David remains convinced that he can see into the depths of Mr. Peggotty's soul. "I believe his honest heart was transparent to me" (50.609), he says, but this too may be another of David's reassuring middle-class fantasies. As a storyteller also, David likes to think that he understands his characters completely, for then he can control them, keep them in their place in his narrative. As we have seen, Heep and Littimer pose more of a problem for David in this respect than does Mr. Peggotty, who conveniently decides to emigrate rather than remain in England where he might cause David trouble.

The character whom David has most difficulty keeping under narrative control, however, is Emily. Her curious absence from the second half of the book has less to do with Dickens' problems in portraying a fallen woman than with David's inability to look at her directly lest she accuse him of betraying her and being Steerforth's accomplice in her seduction.[18] The omissions and distortions in David's portrayal of Emily are thus symptomatic of his unconscious guilt over his part in the central social crime of the novel.

From early on, beginning with his inability to see that he has displaced her from the little room, there is a pattern in David's narrative of failures or evasions of vision with respect to Emily. In Chapter 10, describing his second visit to Yarmouth, David comes closer than he ever does again to noticing this pattern. He goes out to meet Emily on her way home from school and sees her approaching in the distance. But as she draws closer and he notices her blue eyes, dimpled face, and pretty figure, David does something very strange:

> A curious feeling came over me that made me pretend not to know her, and pass by as if I were looking at something a long way off. I have done such a thing since in later life, or I am mistaken.   (10.121)

This refusal to look at Emily or to confront her face to face is typical of David's subsequent encounters with her. In Chapter 21, on his next return to Yarmouth, David goes to Mr. Omer's, where Emily is apprenticed. He peeps in on her at her work, but when Mr. Omer invites him to step in, he declines, pleading bashfulness. ''I was afraid of confusing her, and I was no less afraid of confusing myself'' (21.261). Another telling refusal to meet with Emily face to face occurs when Ham asks David to deliver a final message to her before she departs for Australia.

> ''Mas'r Davy, shall you see her, d'ye think?''
> ''It would be too painful to her, perhaps,'' said I.
> ''I have thowt of that,'' he replied. ''So 'twould, sir, so 'twould.''
> ''But, Ham,'' said I, gently, ''if there is anything that I could write to her, for you, in case I could not tell it; if there is anything you would wish to make known to her through me; I should consider it a sacred trust.''   (51.630)

David's generous offer conceals the fact that a meeting with Emily might be more painful to him than to her. Writing, as opposed to speaking, thus becomes another of David's means of keeping her at a distance.

The most important and the most damning of David's evasions with respect to Emily occurs in the one scene during the second half of the novel where she appears before him in person. This is the scene in which David follows Martha Endell to the house in Golden Square. There, from an adjoining room, he watches and listens as Rosa Dartle pours out her venomous class hatred on the helpless Emily, urging her to marry Littimer or else to kill herself and vowing to pursue her without remorse unless she withdraws from Rosa's reach or drops her ''pretty mask'' (50.618). Finally, Mr. Peggotty arrives to rescue his ''darling'' and carries her away unconscious down the stairs. The question of why David remains passive, looking on from another room just as he had done at Mr. Omer's, is of crucial importance in evaluating his moral authority both as character and as narrator. He explains himself thus:

> I did not know what to do. Much as I desired to put an end to the interview, I felt that I had no right to present myself; that it was for Mr. Peggotty alone to see her and recover her. Would he never come? I thought impatiently.
>
> (50.613)

David's refusal to intervene makes him complicit in Rosa Dartle's savage attack and thus constitutes a second betrayal of Emily, worse even than the first, because it occurs before his eyes in a situation he could stop. Faced with a choice between loyalty to Emily and loyalty to Steerforth, here represented by Rosa Dartle, the middle-class character sides with the upper class against the poor, deceiving himself about the true nature of his choice. The middle-class narrator, moreover, repeats the self-deception and tacitly approves the failure to act.

David remains untrue to Emily to the end. His account of the Peggottys' departure for Australia is a masterpiece of narrative duplicity. He describes the scene in great detail, turning it into an occasion for displaying his talent as a painter of low-life settings and even naming, somewhat pretentiously, the painter whose work he takes as his model: ''I seemed to stand in a picture by OSTADE'' (57.694). The below-decks setting reminds us of the Peggotty houseboat, only now there are many families instead of one. With a skill that befits his profession as a novelist, he vividly evokes the pre-departure scurry and bustle. His eye takes in every detail—except one.

> As my eye glanced round this place, I thought I saw sitting, by an open port, with one of the Micawber children near her, a figure like Emily's; it first attracted my attention, by another figure parting from it with a kiss; and as it glided calmly away through the disorder, reminding me of—Agnes! But in the rapid motion and confusion, and in the unsettlement of my own thoughts, I lost it again; and only knew that the time was come when all visitors were being warned to leave the ship.
>
> (57.694)

Again, David avoids focusing on Emily. His eye finds her, but slips away ''in the unsettlement of my own thoughts.'' And although he bids Mr. Peggotty a last farewell, he makes no effort to address the sweetheart of his youth.

He leaves the ship and watches as it sails away. Then and only then, with a safe distance between them, is he able to bring her into focus. David concludes his chapter thus:

> Then, I saw her, at her uncle's side, and trembling on his shoulder. He pointed to us with an eager hand; and she saw us and waved her last good-bye to me. Aye, Emily, beautiful and drooping, cling to him with the utmost trust of thy bruised heart; for he has clung to thee, with all the might of his great love!
> Surrounded by the rosy light, and standing high upon the deck, apart together, she clinging to him, and he holding her, they solemnly passed away. The night had fallen on the Kentish hills when we were rowed ashore—and fallen darkly upon me.   (57.695)

The narrative duplicity of this passage is remarkable. On the one hand, it is an accomplished piece of writing on David's part. Like the earlier below-decks genre scene, it is a set piece of nineteenth-century art: the sentimental farewell. (As a "farewell to England," it invites comparison specifically with Ford Maddox Brown's *The Last of England*, painted in 1852–55.) The aureole of rosy light around the two figures, their spatial positioning "high upon the deck," and phrases like "the might of his great love," "apart together," and "passed away" all have religious overtones and help transform the scene into a secular equivalent of the Ascension of the Virgin.

And yet there is something dreadfully wrong, for me at least, in David's narrative handling of this sequence. All of his elaborate scene-painting serves his purpose of keeping Emily under control. Turning her into a sentimental religious icon helps him to avoid addressing her as a woman, all the while enabling him to appear loyal and sympathetic to her. We must not forget that David has just avoided speaking to Emily, and moreover that he has not communicated with her other than in writing since Chapter 22, when she begs him " 'for the sake of old times' " to try and help her, a plea he apparently ignores. And yet, now that she is gone, David feels free to call her by name: "Aye, Emily, beautiful and drooping, cling to him with the utmost trust of thy bruised heart." The duplicity of this sentimental apostrophe lies in the fact that it is not really addressed to Emily at all. It is a rhetorical trope, again in writing, rather than a mode of direct address. When David writes that "they solemnly passed away," his language suggests transfiguration but also death. David as narrator here executes Rosa Dartle's threat. Rather than confront his guilt, David prefers Emily absent from his narrative—in other words, dead. The figurative death at the end of the scene, however, may belong more to David than to the Peggottys. As they sail away into the sunset to begin a new life, night falls on the Kentish hills, and "darkly" upon David as well.

Once the duplicity of his narrative has been exposed, we are in a better position to see what happens to the Peggottys at the end of the novel, free from the distortions of David's middle-class perspective. Rather than stress what *happens to* the Peggottys, however, it is more useful to examine what the Peggottys *do for themselves* to cope with the hardships in their lives. In drawing this distinction, I am mindful of the emphasis that E. P. Thompson gives in his monumental study, *The Making of the English Working Class.* In the preface to his book, Thompson explains the use of the word "making" in his title:

> *Making,* because it is a study in an active process, which owes as much to agency as to conditioning. The working class did not rise like the sun at an appointed time. It was present at its own making.[19]

In *David Copperfield,* the Peggottys very clearly *make* their own solution to the problems that follow Emily's seduction, and in so doing they begin to become aware of themselves as part of a *class*—the other functional word in Thompson's title.

The concluding movement of the novel begins with Emily's return to England. The confrontation scene between Emily and Rosa Dartle shows not only the continuing mistreatment of the working class by the aristocracy but also the refusal of the middle class to intervene and end such class abuse. The resolution of the painful scene comes only with the arrival of Mr. Peggotty, who carries Emily away to safety. The pattern established in this scene is repeated several times toward the end of the book. For example, as Mr. Peggotty's narrative in Chapter 51 makes clear, when Emily escapes from Littimer she is saved by members of her own class, an Italian fishing family who call her "Fisherman's daughter" instead of "Pretty lady" as they did at first (51.622). Again, when Emily makes her way back to England it is another member of her own class, Martha, who saves her from falling into prostitution and who writes the note that brings Mr. Peggotty to the rescue.

The absence in the book of any middle-class philanthropic organizations may at first seem surprising, especially in view of Dickens' own involvement with such programs as the home for fallen women established by Miss Coutts at Urania Cottage and his outspoken support in the pages of *Household Words* for Mrs. Caroline Chisholm's Family Colonization Loan Society, which helped provide funds for poor families seeking to resettle in Australia.[20] Yet nothing like either organization appears at the end of the book.

The absence of middle-class charity for the poor is in fact significant. In *David Copperfield,* the working class solves its own problems, without depending on the middle class either for ideas or for financial support. The idea of emigration comes from Mr. Peggotty himself, not from David or from any middle-class reformer. Even the money for resettlement has a working-class origin—the legacy of old Barkis, the carrier. Mr. Peggotty proudly refuses the money that Mrs. Steerforth offers him, and he repays everything that Emily had forwarded to the family during her time with Steerforth. It is instructive to compare the Peggottys' proud independence about money with Micawber's endless borrowing and with David's increased willingness to pay off Micawber's debts in order to get him out of the country. In this way, David effectively rids himself of the chief witness to his laboring-class connections at the warehouse.

The Peggottys' success in Australia thus comes as the result of a series of efforts by working-class characters to help other members of their own class. The Peggottys embrace the general Victorian virtues of hard work and self-help, but give them a specific class emphasis. Resettlement in Australia becomes a way not only of enabling Emily to lead a life free from the social stigma of being a fallen woman but also of removing the entire household (without Ham but now including Martha) from England's class society. Australia offers the promise of a working-class utopia, where social station matters less than the willingness to work.[21] The Peggottys thus reestablish the supportive communal life of the houseboat, but on a firmer foundation. They are now less innocent and less vulnerable to class injury. The inclusion of Mrs. Gummidge in the new community is crucial, for she continues to be a binding force by her industry and selfless devotion.

The fact that Emily does not marry in Australia is often taken as a sign that Dickens remained uneasy about her sexuality and felt the need to punish it by withholding from her the ultimate sanctity of marriage. This interpretation is neither necessary nor persuasive, however. Martha marries, and Emily has many opportunities to do so, but deliberately refrains. To argue that she is thereby excluded from domestic happiness is to deny the legitimacy of her decision to remain a single woman and to adopt a conventional middle-class view (David's view, in fact) of what woman's happiness entails. The choice that Agnes makes is not necessarily the right choice for Emily as well. In choosing to remain unmarried, she elects a life of service to the wider community, while remaining committed to the only family she has ever known.

If there is a threat at the end of the book to the vision of Australia as a working-class utopia, it appears not in the exclusion of Emily from marital bliss but in the person of Micawber, now Wilkins Micawber, Esquire, Port

Middlebay District Magistrate. For all the delightfulness of its outrageous comic rhetoric, the newspaper report that David reads about the dinner in honor of Micawber is in fact a description of the emergence into power of a new colonial elite, seizing control of social institutions such as government, the newspaper, and the schools, and consolidating its power through marital alliances. Micawber calls them "the beauty, fashion, and exclusiveness of Port Middlebay" (63.745). By whatever name they go, they are the ruling class, and their appearance in Australia shows that the colony has not delayed long in reproducing the class structure of the mother country.

V

By way of conclusion, let me return to the problem that David poses in his opening sentence about the relation between heroism and social station. There are, I believe, three different answers to the question David asks in this sentence, and therefore three possible endings to the novel. These correspond, in turn, to the three different social classes that David's narrative represents. First, an aristocratic reading of the novel might argue that Steerforth is the hero of David's life. Certainly, he looks and acts the part. His noble birth and valiant death meet the traditional literary criteria for heroism. His body lies in state, covered by a flag, and he is mourned by two women, fiercely devoted to preserving their memory of him as a superior being. David's narrative preserves many traces of his earlier worshipful attitude toward Steerforth and thus lends support to the view that Steerforth alone, of all the people David has known, is worthy to be called a hero. To accept such a view, however, requires an understanding of heroism that divorces it entirely from questions of honor and virtue, something that David at times seems quite ready to do.

A middle-class reading of the novel would argue that "these pages" have shown David rather than Steerforth to be the hero of his life. The criteria for middle-class heroism, of course, are quite different from those of traditional heroic literature. Hard work, earnestness, self-discipline, piety, material success, and a virtuous domestic life count for more than either birth or valiant deeds. David's narrative fully demonstrates that he meets the criteria for middle-class heroism, and although he does not apply this term to himself, his claim to it is implicit in the tone of his ending. To understand the novel in this way is relatively easy, though for many readers it proves somewhat dissatisfying. All it requires is that we accept David's version of his life and along with it the values of his middle-class viewpoint. It also requires, however, that we collaborate with David in overlooking his betrayals of Emily and that we blind ourselves to the self-serving omissions and distortions in his narrative perspective.

The reading of *Copperfield* that I have proposed in this paper attempts to point out the class biases in David's perspective and to look beyond them at what I have called the social sub-text of the novel. In this reading, there is no hero in the book, but there is heroism—the collective heroism of the Peggottys, who remain loyal to each other and who make their lives anew in Australia. Emigration to the colonies is no solution to the problems of class conflict within England, but for the Peggottys at least it is an answer.

One's preference among these three readings will depend on one's own values, including those of class. In this way the novel reads us, as well as we it. I hope to have made clear my reasons for preferring the third reading. It was the genius of Dickens, writing in the wake of his sympathetic reaction to the revolutions of 1848 and to some aspects even of Chartism, to have written in *Copperfield* not only a powerful social novel but one that understood the heroism of the working class.[22]

NOTES

1. Elsewhere, I have called this kind of retrospective abuse ''narrative revenge.'' See ''The Medium of *Great Expectations*,'' *Dickens Studies Annual: Essays on Victorian Fiction*, 11, Michael Timko, Fred Kaplan, and Edward Guiliano, eds. (New York: AMS Press, 1983), pp. 73–88.

2. *Charles Dickens: His Tragedy and Triumph*, 2 vols. (New York: Simon and Schuster, 1952), 677–700.

3. Two important essays along these lines are Robin Gilmour, ''Memory in David Copperfield,'' *The Dickensian*, 71 (1975), 30–42, and James Kincaid, ''*David Copperfield*: Laughter and Point of View,'' in *Dickens and the Rhetoric of Laughter* (Oxford: Clarendon Press, 1971), pp. 162–191.

4. For a more fully developed theory of textual repression, to which my reading of *Copperfield* is indebted, see Fredric Jameson, *The Political Unconscious: Narrative as a Socially Symbolic Act* (Ithaca, N. Y.: Cornell University Press, 1981), pp. 48–49 and 81–85.

5. William T. Lankford, in ''The Deep of Time: Narrative Order in *David Copperfield*,'' *ELH*, 46 (1979), 452–467, makes a similar observation about David's authority as narrator. Lankford attributes the instability in David's narrative perspective to ''a continuing vacillation between the incompatible values associated with innocence and discipline'' (461). Although he does not explore the social basis for this instability, Lankford anticipates some of the questions I wish to raise about David's role as narrator.

6. *David Copperfield*, ed. Nina Burgis (Oxford: Clarendon Press, 1981). Subsequent references, indicating chapter and page number, are to this edition and will be noted parenthetically in the text.

7. The critical literature on heroism in *David Copperfield* is extensive. The best discussion of the question, in my opinion, is that of Pearl Chesler Solomon, *Dickens and Melville in Their Time* (New York: Columbia University Press, 1975), pp. 134–153. Solomon's analysis of David's social position anticipates my own in several respects, but places greater emphasis on psychological factors and on the similarities between David's experience and Dickens' own.

8. For a view of David's attitudes toward family and social class that in many ways complements my own, see Chris R. Vanden Bossche, "Cookery, not Rookery: Family and Class in *David Copperfield*," forthcoming in *Dickens Studies Annual: Essays on Victorian Fiction*, Volume 15.

9. For a brief moment at the beginning of Chapter 32, David acknowledges his "unconscious part in [Steerforth's] pollution of an honest home," but he immediately goes on to mourn the loss of Steerforth and to say that he "could not have uttered one reproach" against him (32.388).

10. Her first name, Clara, is the same as David's mother's. Moreover, David associates her throughout the book with physical qualities and objects that suggest the maternal breast and nipple: her "cheeks and arms so hard and red that I wondered the birds didn't peck her in preference to apples"; her workbox "with a view of St. Paul's Cathedral (with a pink dome) painted on the top"; "the little bit of wax-candle she kept for her thread—how old it looked, being so wrinkled in all directions"; and finally, the buttons on the back of her gown that explode whenever she hugs him and that he imagines he could use to track his way home, "like the boy in the fairy tale," if ever he were lost.

11. Less obvious as a premonition of danger is the tea-tray that David sees upon first entering the Peggotty home. It is a tray "with a painting on it of a lady with a parasol, taking a walk with a military-looking child who was trundling a hoop. The tray was kept from tumbling down, by a bible; and the tray, if it had tumbled down, would have smashed a quantity of cups and saucers and a teapot that were grouped around the book" (3.26). Coded into this bit of descriptive detail is both the source of Emily's social fantasies and a hint about the destructive consequences that her dream will have on the Peggotty household.

12. Dickens' use of this technique is discussed in Mark Lambert, *Dickens and the Suspended Quotation* (New Haven, Conn.: Yale University Press, 1981). Lambert's emphasis on interruption as evidence of "authorial jealousy" keeps him from recognizing the ways in which suspended quotations create semantic ambiguity, as in the *Copperfield* passage under consideration.

13. For a useful discussion of writing, with reference to both David and Heep, see Murray Baumgarten, "Writing and *David Copperfield*" in this volume.

14. George Orwell, *Dickens, Dali, and Others* (New York: Reynal and Hitchcock, 1946), p. 41.

15. Uriah not only reminds David of a time in his life that he would sooner forget, he actually knows about it through Micawber and therefore can expose the shameful

secret of David's past. " 'I never was in the streets either, as you were, according to Micawber,' " Uriah blurts out at David in the exposure scene (52.641).

16. In addition to its conventional associations with piracy, the black flag was also an emblem of working-class insurrection. Among the standards carried at Peterloo, for example, was a black ensign. That Dickens himself saw the connection between piracy and the threat of working-class rebellion is evident in the burlesque letter that he sent to his friend Augustus Tracey on April 8, 1848. "My Dear Admiral," writes Dickens,

> Keep your weather eye on that there Lion figurehead o' yourn, o' Monday, for in case I hoist my pennant aboard o' the Chartist flagship, I'm damned if I don't pour in a broadside (in answer to your'n) and rake you fore and aft, you swab. (*The Letters of Charles Dickens*, volume 5, 1847–1849, eds. Graham Storey and K. J. Fielding. Oxford: The Clarendon Press, 1981, p. 273.)

The letter was written two days before the large Chartist assembly on Kensington Common, where 150,000 were expected to march on the House of Commons with a petition bearing more than five million signatures. Dickens knew that Tracey, a prison governor, was hardly a Chartist sympathizer. For more information on Dickens' attitude toward Chartism, see N. C. Peyrouten, "Charles Dickens and the Chartists," *The Dickensian*, 60 (1964), 78–88 and 152–161.

17. Critics interested in biographical interpretations of *Copperfield* might do well to notice this similarity between Mr. Peggotty and Dickens.

18. He may also fear her violence. We should not forget that when Steerforth leaves her, Emily takes a knife and has to be restrained from using it against Littimer or herself.

19. *The Making of the English Working Class* (New York: Vintage, 1966), p. 9.

20. Together with Mrs. Chisholm, Dickens wrote an article on Australia for the first issue of his new weekly journal: "A Bundle of Emigrants' Letters," *Household Words*, 1 (March 30, 1850), 19–24. Four more articles on the same topic appeared in subsequent issues between April and August, 1850.

21. For a valuable discussion of Australia as the symbol of a working-class utopia, see Coral Lansbury, *Arcady in Australia: The Evocation of Australia in Nineteenth-Century English Literature* (Melbourne: Melbourne University Press, 1970). Lansbury's discussion of *Copperfield* is extremely useful, but gives more attention to the Micawbers than to the Peggottys.

22. For their valuable comments on an earlier draft of this essay, I am grateful to my colleagues Murray Baumgarten, Al Hutter, Helene Moglen, and Chris Vanden Bossche.

Dickens and Art

Richard Lettis

I

Studies of Dickens' experience with painting and related art have been limited to cursory summaries of his activities and to still shorter comments by his biographers on the quality of his critical pronouncements. Most of the latter have been disparaging, though a few in recent years have expressed limited, at times almost grudging, approval. [1] The present examination of Dickens and art will not so much attempt to assess the quality of his art criticism as to provide a full record of his activity in the world of painting, and to define the aesthetic principles he applied. Still, it may be well to begin with a brief assessment of previous commentary.

Attackers and defenders of Dickens' opinions on art are not as sharply divided as they at first appear to be; the difference between them is rather of degree than of kind. And those who minimize his critical ability err not so much in the specific points they make, which are often correct, as in the impression they leave with the reader that Dickens' understanding of art is negligible. Despite the defects, it is not. We need neither Dickens' daughter nor his biographer to tell us, as they have, [2] that he had no training in art; he tells us so himself. "I am not mechanically acquainted with the art of painting," he says quite simply in *Pictures from Italy*. [3] But then, he had little if any formal training in anything else, yet managed to write great novels, to read widely in the areas of his interest, to become the foremost parliamentary reporter of his time and one of the best editors, and to establish a reputation for greater knowledge of the theater than any other man of his age. Certainly his immersion in the world of art—through friendships, attendance of art exhibitions, acquisition of paintings by gift and by purchase, writing on art for his journals and editing of such writing by others, and most of all through his intense involvement with the artists who illustrated his novels—must have

93

been very nearly the equivalent of a formal education. If he lived as intimately as he seems to have done among the artists of his time and still could manage nothing more than the commonplace opinions which some critics find in him, Dickens must stand convicted of limited aesthetic ability indeed.

Dickens knew most of the artists of any repute in his time—knew them as men, whatever limitations may have existed in his knowledge of their work. "Since I first entered the public lists," he said in a speech at the Royal Academy Banquet, "a very young man indeed, it has been my constant fortune to number amongst my nearest and dearest friends members of the Royal Academy who have been its grace and pride."[4] Dickens, indeed, had more artists than writers as friends: the first, his daughter tells us, was David Wilkie;[5] another early acquaintance was George Cruikshank.[6] One of his lifelong friends was the Irish painter Daniel Maclise; others more or less within the Dickens circle were Ary Scheffer, George Cattermole, W. P. Frith, Clarkson Stanfield, John Leech, Hablôt Knight Browne, Frank Stone (and his son, Marcus), Augustus Egg, and Charles Collins (who became the first husband of Dickens' daughter, Kate, herself an accomplished amateur painter). The names of dozens of other artists are to be found in his letters and minor writings: Turner, Richard Doyle, William Oliver, Samuel Palmer, William Mulready, Benjamin Robert Haydon, Charles Robert Leslie, Thomas Webster, Canaletto, Samuel Tovey, John Tenniel, Francis Topham, Robert Scanlon, John Branvard, Edward Ward, Benjamin West, Thomas Sully, David Roberts, William Boxall, Hogarth, Godfrey Kneller, Reynolds, Gainsborough, Watteau, Washington Alston, Francis Alexander, Robert and Fanny M'Ian, and Bamfylde Moore Carew, not to mention such amateur artists as Mrs. Shipton, Count D'Orsay, George Putnam, and Mrs. Richard Watson.[7] A number of these were also acquaintances of Dickens. Wherever he went he seems to have sought out artists. Forster says that during his stay in Paris in 1855, "Dickens's life was passed among artists. . . . His associations were with writers, painters, actors, or musicians. . . ."[8] And several of his other friends, like Wilkie Collins and John Forster, were known for their knowledge and appreciation of art.

Curiously, Dickens' constant contact with artists never led to an inclusion of them in his novels. As Kate Perugini said, "in the numerous volumes which contain my father's writings . . . never once has he introduced an artist as one of his important leading characters." But if Dickens did not allow artists into his world, he very actively entered into theirs. Kate spoke of "the hours he passed in [the] studios" of artists.[9] His letters show him to have attended exhibitions fairly frequently: he wrote to his friend Stanfield that, even in the midst of a hectic reading tour, he hoped "to look up your latest triumphs on the day of the Academy Dinner. Of course as yet I have had no opportunity of even hearing of what anyone has done."[10] He thanked another friend, Angela Burdett Coutts, for tickets to an exhibition of "Old Masters and English School paintings" at the British Institution.[11] He wrote to the American painter John Branvard to express his pleasure at the latter's three-mile-long painting of the Mississippi valley which he had seen in an exhibition at the Egyptian Hall in Piccadilly.[12] From Paris, he informed his friend John Forster that he had been an interested observer of the international exhibition of paintings there in 1855.[13] *Pictures from Italy*, of course, gives ample evidence of his careful attention to the art of Italy, but even in *American Notes*, which makes no pretense of treating the culture of the United States, references to painting are not infrequently made.

Evidence of Dickens' constant exposure to art can also be found outside of his own writing. For example, his actor-friend William Charles Macready records in his diary that he and Dickens went to the Royal Academy Exhibit on May 2, 1846.[14] And there is considerable evidence that Dickens not only observed but actively participated in the world of art. Twice he chaired Artist Benevolent Fund anniversary festivals, once in 1858 and again in 1862. He attended several of the Royal Academy Banquets, the last on April 4, 1870, just two months before his death, and was a successful speaker at such functions. He seems also to have provided financial assistance to painters: his daughter Kate says that "his earnest desire to help the younger and poorer [artist] is well known. . . ."[15] Only once, at least in writing, did Dickens refuse to help an artist, for the same reason he declined at times to assist writers: his influence with those who employed artists was, he said, limited, and he could not gain access to employment where the artist's talent had not. Even here Dickens was kind; he complimented the unknown artist's "studies from nature" as "excellent observations of nature, in a loving and healthy spirit."[16] But that opinion, he added, would not influence experts on art.

We can trace Dickens' interest in art back as early as his childhood. In an 1859 piece for *Household Words* he says that among his childhood posses-sions were "some coloured engravings of Bamfylde Moore Carew, Mrs. Shipton, and others, in a florid state of art. . . ."[17] It has been argued from a reading of *Sketches by Boz* that Dickens remembered the plates in many of his childhood books more vividly than the texts.[18] This continuing interest, many believe, exerted an important influence upon his fiction.[19] The most important evidence of such continuing interest is obviously his close work with the illustrators of his novels, but there is ample evidence too in the many illustrated books found in his library at his death, and in numerous gifts of such books, as well as paintings, which he received throughout his life.[20]

Dickens was also a purchaser of art. He perpetrated a "pious fraud" upon his friend Maclise in order to buy a picture the artist would otherwise have given him, and there is record of his acquiring several other works—e.g., from Francis Topham and Samuel Tovey.[21] As the catalog of his library shows, many paintings and drawings were in his possession at the time of his death. It is hardly the work of a connoisseur: one gets the impression of a casually acquired rather than carefully selected gallery. Nevertheless, it is a substantial collection.

There is even evidence of some interest by Dickens in the developing art of photography during his later years, though hardly any of his comments on it add to our understanding of his aesthetic. Perhaps he was attracted to the new art form because he found in it that exact likeness which Johnson says he made a principal tenet of his criteria for portraiture. In June of 1859 he wrote to his daughter Mamie, of a photo of her and Kate, "it is not a very pleasant or cheerful presentation of my daughters, but is wonderfully like for all that, and in some details remarkably good."[22] He could even forgive the photo for being ugly, as long as it was true. But the new art form seems never to have been of more than passing interest to Dickens. There is no mention of it in his novels, and his comments, with the single exception of his preference for "likeness," add nothing to our understanding of his aesthetic, though they do help to demonstrate his range of interest.

Frequent contact with art is no proof of ability to understand it, but it seems clear that Dickens, whatever his limitations in technical training, did learn from his constant association with artists and their work. He was au courant with at least some of the artistic movements of his time, as his strong opposition to the Pre-Raphaelite School shows. And he was familiar with the styles of several artists, as is demonstrated by his allusions to them in his letters. He knew and detested the style of Alfred and John Chalon, and told Forster he was glad their friend Maclise had escaped "the maudlin taint of the sweet Chalon school of silk and ermine. . . ."[23] When another friend, Mrs. Gore, wrote a satire on a series of engravings by Chalon and others entitled *Portraits of the Nobility*, he wrote to congratulate her. "Those books," he said of the collected engravings, "are the gall and bitterness of my life. I vow to God they make me wretched, and taint the freshness of every new year. Your satire is most admirable, and to pluck the peacock's feathers from such daws is worthy of you."[24]

Occasionally Dickens uses an allusion to an artist as a part of his description of a person or scene, thereby demonstrating his familiarity with the style, quality, or characteristic subject matter of the painter. In a piece in *Household Words* he mentions a police sergeant who "might have sat to Wilkie for the Soldier in the Reading of the Will."[25] A room in Avignon looks to his eye "exactly like a picture by Ostade."[26] Paintings on the wall of an Italian church have the same quality as woodcuts in old books, and the artist strikes him as being "like the painter of the Primrose family."[27] In writing about Branvard's Mississippi painting he says that "it is not [comparable to] those delicate and beautiful pictures by Mr. Stanfield. . . ."[28] A letter to Maclise from Italy comments upon the artist's use of color:

> Apropos of blue. In a certain picture, called "The Serenade," you painted a sky. If you ever have occasion to paint the Mediterranean, let it be exactly of that colour. . . .
> I hardly think you allow for the great brightness and brilliancy of colour which is commonly achieved on the Continent, in that same fresco painting. I saw some—by a French artist and his pupil—in progress at the cathedral at Avignon, which was as bright and airy as anything can be,—nothing dull or dead about it; and I have observed quite fierce and glaring colours elsewhere.[29]

Writing to Macready from a site two miles above Niagara, Dickens said that "Turner's most imaginative drawing in his finest day has nothing in it so ethereal, so gorgeous in fancy, so celestial."[30] In a letter written in 1841 to Washington Irving, a friend of Leslie's, Dickens remarked on that painter's "great abilities and uncommon gift of humour, with his pencil. . . ."[31] And in a published piece in which he discussed a scene acted by Macready, he observed that "we seemed to be looking on a picture by Leslie. It was just such a figure as that excellent artist, in his fine appreciation of the finest humour, might have delighted to produce."[32]

Gladys Storey tells of an incident related to her by the artist Fred Roe that dramatically conveys Dickens' ability to recognize the style of a painter.

> One morning this gentleman happened to be in the vicinity of Seven Dials. Looking into the window of an old junk-shop, which displayed a miscellaneous collection of odds and ends, he noticed among them a water-colour drawing which, even through the grime of the window-glass, appeared to be very good. He entered the shop. Over the counter lolled a stout female who, upon request, unconcernedly extracted the work of art from amongst old lamps, walking-sticks, fire-irons and the rest, with the tips of her none-too-clean fingers.
> "How much do you want for it?" inquired the prospective purchaser.
> "Oh—five shillin's" she ventured.
> Inspecting the water-colour closely, then holding it at arm's length, he said he would take it.

"May I look at the drawing?" said a voice.

"Certainly," returned the purchaser: when to his surprise he discovered that the request had come from none other than Charles Dickens, who was sitting unobtrusively, notebook in hand, in the corner of the shop. After scanning the water-colour for some moments, he handed it back to the owner, observing:

"T" (meaning Turner).

"Yes," replied Roe.

"I congratulate you," said Dickens.[33]

It should be noted that even in the small sampling of commentary we have observed, we are encountering references to color, light, and shade—aspects of painting which critics have said Dickens refers to infrequently, if at all. There are, indeed, not many references to color throughout Dickens' writing, but there are enough to indicate that he was aware of its importance. His confession that he was "not mechanically acquainted" with art is followed by a description of his "means of judging a picture," and this includes the appreciation of "graceful combinations of form and colors."[34] Color is commented upon occasionally: Dickens praised the Branvard painting of the Mississippi but objected to "the colour of its water";[35] he also deplored the "horrible combinations of color"[36] in the Duke of Wellington's funeral car. He noted that the artist who painted the "votive offerings" on the walls of an Italian church "had not been sparing of his colors."[37] In paintings by Giulio Romano in the Palazzo Te in Mantua he found that "the coloring is harsh and disagreeable. . . . "[38] He lamented that *The Last Supper* had lost "its original coloring, . . . because of damp, decay, and neglect, & because inferior painters have disastrously retouched it."[39] Writing a review of Maclise's *The Spirit of Chivalry*, he spoke of "the prodigious force and *colour* which so separate this work from all the rest exhibited. . . . "[40] In one instance, Dickens even described color for an illustration for *Martin Chuzzlewit*, though the picture was to appear in black and white: "Jinkins . . . wears a white favor in his buttonhole. . . . The bride wears a bonnet with an orange flower."[41]

It is hardly possible to decide from such statements whether Dickens' judgment of color was good or bad, but an incident with the painter John Leech suggests that in at least one instance it was better than the artist's. When Leech was upset by the quality of the printed colors in the four plates he did for *A Christmas Carol*, Dickens reassured him: "You can't think how much better they will look in a neat book, than you suppose."[42] Jane R. Cohen says that the critics sided with Dickens: the *Illustrated London News* found the pictures "tastefully coloured. . . . "[43] In fairness to Leech, it was probably Dickens' experience with plates for books that enabled him to make his better judgment.

Dickens also commented upon details of composition to some extent. He spoke of the "beautiful composition and arrangement"[44] of *The Last Supper*; he complained of a painting in which "a little figure on a mountain has a head-dress bigger than the temple in the foreground, or adjacent miles of landscape."[45] He praised the composition of Tintoretto's *Assembly of the Blest*, "with all the lines in it tending majestically and dutifully to Almighty God in the Centre,"[46] though it is disappointing that he had nothing to say about the vivid contrasts of color which are characteristic of that artist. In the same letter Dickens commented upon another painting, "in which the surprising art that presents the generals to your eye, so that it is almost impossible you can miss them in a crowd though they are in the thick of it, is very pleasant to dwell upon."[47]

Other comments show that Dickens was aware of how conditions of publication or location can affect the reception of a work of art. A series of drawings by John Leech, originally published in *Punch* and reproduced as *The Rising Generation*, Dickens described as showing "to infinitely greater advantage in the present enlarged and separate form of publication."[48] Examining Italian art, he thought that "in the private palaces, pictures are seen to the best advantage."[49] And of the Egyptian Room in the Vatican he wrote:

> There is a fine collection of Egyptian antiquities, in the Vatican; and the ceilings of the rooms in which they are arranged, are painted to represent a starlight sky in the Desert. It may seem an odd idea, but it is very effective. The grim, half-human monsters from the temples, look more grim and monstrous underneath the deep dark blue; it sheds a strange uncertain gloomy air on everything—a mystery adapted to the objects; and you leave them, as you find them, shrouded in a solemn night.[50]

There are also a few indications that Dickens understood at least some technical aspects of painting and the care of paintings. In October of 1852 he went to Fulham to get a "copy" by an "ancient artist" named Mrs. Brayne for Miss Burdett Coutts. Dickens decided that it would be injured by light, and so would need a case; he also advised his friend on the size of a frame and on "another slight alteration"[51] which has not been identified. At another time we find him writing to Mrs. Richard Watson that his "baby collection" of pictures looks better at Gad's Hill—"in country light and air"[52]—than in London.

In a comment upon Maclise's painting, *Hamlet*, which he thought "a *tremendous* production," Dickens noted the artist's use of light and shade; the artist, he said, "so manages the lights in this picture, that on the scene behind, is an enormous shadow of this groupe—as if the real murder were being done again by phantoms! And what a carrying-out of the prevailing idea, it is, to paint the very proscenium of the little stage with stories of Sin and Blood. . . ."[53] Dickens may not have noticed this on his own: Thackeray, who was among other things a professional art critic, had made much the same comment in an article in *Ainsworth's Magazine* the preceding month. But Dickens' comments on Maclise's *The Spirit of Chivalry*, in his own article published in *Douglas Jerrold's Shilling Magazine* in 1845, are not derived from any known source, and are probably his own.

II

Obviously that art form with which Dickens was most familiar, and from which he learned much if not most about art, is the illustration of books. His participation in the work of putting pictures into his novels brought him into a close working relationship with many of the major English artists of his day, and developed to a high level his ability to select subjects, decide upon the kind of face and figure characters should have, choose the props and scenery most appropriate for a picture, offer directions upon composition and spatial arrangement, understand methods of printing pictures, and make decisions about locating them in the text. If, as several scholars have remarked, Dickens' fiction was significantly influenced by this experience, it is also true that his understanding of art was improved, as well. He worked with the most important English artists of his day. Three—Landseer, Maclise, and Stanfield—were members of the Royal Academy of Art, and several others are important figures in the history of Victorian art, quite apart from their work for Dickens.

Much of the work Dickens did with his illustrators gives evidence of his mastery of technical aspects of art. He was familiar with the several methods of reproducing pictures, and was particularly knowledgeable about engraving. We find him at the age of twenty-five confidently passing judgment upon an engraver, W. C. Walker, who engraved the frontispiece to W. L. Rede's *The Peregrinations of Pickwick*. Walker was ". . . a line engraver of great promise,"[54] the young author confided in a letter to his much older publisher, Bentley. In another judgment, rendered to Leopold C. Martin, the engraver (along with one Corbould) of seven of the sixteen illustrations of *The Haunted Man*, Dickens showed himself aware of the different quality of proof and final print in a book: "I am much obliged to you for the proofs you had the kindness to send me, yesterday. The drawings of course appear to greater advantage in such a form, but I think—all things considered—that they have been *very well* rendered in the book, and especially in the frontispiece."[55] Another comment upon an engraving shows Dickens with a sharp eye for what can be lost when something is omitted from the original picture. In the second volume of Forster's biography of Landor, he wrote,

> is an engraving from a portrait of the remarkable man when seventy-seven years of age, by Boxall. . . . The original picture is a singularly good likeness, the result of close and subtle observation on the part of the painter; but, for this very reason, the engraving gives a most inadequate idea of the merit of the picture and the character of the man.
>
> From the engraving, the arms and hands are omitted. In the picture, they are, as they were in nature, indispensable to a correct reading of the vigorous face. The arms were very peculiar. They were rather short, and were curiously restrained and checked in their action at the elbows; in the action of the hands, even when separately clenched, there was the same kind of pause, and a noticeable tendency to relaxation on the part of the thumb. Let the face be never so intense or fierce, there was a commentary of gentleness in the hands, essential to be taken along with it.[56]

It has been alleged that Dickens did not see with the eye of an artist. Sometimes he did not; he was too busy seeing paintings with the eye of a novelist. But the two kinds of seeing are not mutually exclusive—Dickens could see some art as well as any painter.

But Dickens' work with his illustrators also reveals limitations in his understanding of art. Although Jane R. Cohen highly values his overall contribution to the quality of the pictures which appear in his works, she also notes instances in which his interference hurt. Several of these instances are owing to Dickens' pressuring his artist to do more than art can do. In his instructions to Browne about the "Paul and Mrs. Pipchin" picture for Chapter 8 of *Dombey and Son*, for example, Professor Cohen points out that had Browne taken his instructions about placing Paul "in the fireplace corner, with his gaze shadowed by the black drapery as the text specified, the problems of composition and light would have been almost insuperable."[57] Occasionally he seemed unaware of how much an illustration could contain, and would give an artist much more than he could put into his drawing (Dickens almost always chose subjects for his illustrators, and usually described what he wanted in considerable detail). On Dickens' letter to Browne concerning the "second subject" for *Martin Chuzzlewit*, Browne wrote "I can't get all this perspective in—unless you will allow of a long subject—something less than a mile."[58] There is much more than perspective in

Dickens' instructions that the most conscientious artist could never get in. There is movement: for a scene in *Martin Chuzzlewit* Dickens advised his artist to draw a picture in which "Mr. Pecksniff hastens in. . . . The old man in a transport of burning indignation, rises from his chair, and uplifting his stick, knocks the good Pecksniff down. . . ."[59] Dickens' instructions even include the cessation or absence of activity: "Kit . . . stops for a moment. . . ."[60]; or "a subject representing Master Humphrey's clock as stopped. . . ."[61] (How in the world does a picture show a clock as having stopped?) It is clear that Dickens wants cinema, not stills—or that he would, if he could, endow his pictures with all the powers of his narrative. Yet not even his narrative could accomplish some things his instructions detail: in a carriage scene in *Barnaby Rudge* a character is required to turn on the driver's seat and look into the carriage while menacing with his cudgel someone running beside the carriage.

Obviously Dickens did not intend his artists to get all that he mentioned in his instructions into their pictures. Much of the information is supplied to assist their imagination, to prepare them for the still life they are to draw, to help them acquire a sense of mood, of feeling. But if this much is clear, it is equally clear that he wished they *could* "get it all in." Could they have done so, could Dickens have had motion pictures, each illustration would have invested his story with more life than even his gifted pen could bring to it; the characters would have lived more completely than even his prose could make them live.

It is this, one suspects, that attracted Dickens so strongly to art: he felt in it the potential to create life beyond the limits of his own genre. His fascination with drama is surely of a similar nature; his perceptive comments on the dramatic in painting show how close he thought the two arts to be. In one such comment he drew a distinction between *dramatic* and *theatrical*: "in the former case a story is strikingly told, without apparent consciousness of a spectator, and . . . in the latter case the groups are obtrusively dressed up, and doing (or not doing) certain things with an eye to the spectator, and not for the sake of the story. . . ."[62] "For the sake of the story"—certainly everywhere in his work with his illustrators, Dickens' first concern is that. The fault in an illustration which provoked his stongest reaction was the artist's failure to follow the narrative. The worst such instance occurred when John Leech put the wrong character in a scene near the end of Part II of *The Battle of Life*. Dickens wrote Forster:

> When I first saw it, it was with a horror and agony not to be expressed. Of course
> I need not tell *you*, my dear fellow, Warden had no business in the elopement

scene. *He* was never there! In the first hot sweat of this surprise and novelty, I was going to implore the printing of that sheet to be stopped, and the figure taken out of the block. But when I thought of the pain this might give to our kind-hearted Leech; and that what is such a monstrous enormity to me, as having never entered my brain, may not so present itself to others, I became more composed; though the fact is wonderful to me.[63]

Important facets of the critical Dickens are to be found here, perhaps the most important being that no criticism, not even of the most devastating flaw of which Dickens can conceive, is worth giving offense to a friend; in the above letter, he recovered from his anguish enough to go on to praise the work Leech had done for *The Battle of Life*. But almost equally important is the fact that a picture drawn contrary to his story is a "monstrous enormity," almost a kind of threat to the imagined reality that the story is as it existed within his brain. It is "wonderful" to Dickens that anything contrary to that imagined reality could exist; he has to convince himself that others will not find it monstrous too. It is almost like science fiction, in which some departure from cosmic law may threaten existence itself.

There is no doubt that Dickens felt a powerful connection between his illustrations and his stories. He did not spend time on them simply because he wanted the finished book to be as good as it could be, though that was no doubt an important consideration. He labored over them as exhaustingly as he did because they lived for him exactly as his fiction did, and he felt the integrity of the second threatened by any lapses in the first. Seeing so much, one understands far more clearly than before such a statement as Dickens wrote into a speech for Frank Stone, to be delivered at the Manchester Athenaeum on October, 1845, in which he said that painting was "an art which had ever been allowed to possess a kindred, nay, sisterly relation, to the spirit of literature. . . ."[64] Siamese sisters, one might add.

I think no one has quite understood the mortal intensity of this linkage before, though several have noticed the influence of drawing upon Dickens' writing.[65] Jane R. Cohen suggests that working with artists both helped to form Dickens' vision of his world and taught him ways of conveying it to his readers through details of character and setting.[66] Others have commented upon the similarity between Dickens' prose and the technique of painting. Van Gogh, from Dickens' own century, said that "there is no writer, in my opinion, who is so much a painter and black-and-white artist as Dickens."[67] Dickens himself said, "I don't invent it—really do not—*but see it*, and write it down."[68]

But if drawing influenced Dickens' writing, it was all too often simply in terms of his writing that he viewed the drawings of his illustrators: they are not so much to be judged on their own terms as art as they were merely another kind of writing. Though they turned out to be among the best of their kind, it was not their excellence as art that he concentrated on, but their fidelity to his story and their support of his characters. His letters sometimes show a nervous fear, not that an illustrator may draw an artistically poor figure, but that he may not catch the idea of the character which Dickens felt the need to present. (Certainly quality and accuracy often overlapped: a drawing that captured Dickens' conception was for that reason a good piece of art.)

> The points for illustration, [he wrote to Forster, who often helped him with all aspects of his novels] and the enormous care required, make me anxious. The man for Dombey, if Browne could see him, the class man to a T, is Sir A——— E——— of D———'s. Great pains will be necessary with Miss Tox. The Toodle family should not be too much caricatured, because of Polly.[69]

Forster says that Dickens "expressed his anxiety about Browne's illustrations for Dombey, with a nervous dread of caricature in the face of Mr. Dombey. 'I do wish he could get a glimpse of A, for he is the very Dombey.'"[70] But Browne could not get his glimpse, and so Dickens required him to supply a "sheetful" of "actual heads as well as fancied ones,"[71] so that he might select the face most like that of his imagined reality.

Just a few months later, Dickens was upset by Browne's handling of other characters in *Dombey & Son*; he wrote Forster that the illustration of Paul and Mrs. Pipchin was "frightfully and wildly wide of the mark. Good Heaven: in the commonest and most literal construction of the text, it is all wrong. . . . I can't say what pain and vexation it is to be so utterly misrepresented."[72] Again, one has the sense that Dickens' imagined characters are as real to him as any actual being; to be "utterly mispresented" is not only damaging to them, as a poor photograph in a magazine might be to a public person, but to their creator, as though some of nature's journeymen had made a man and not made him well, and thereby had offended the image in the creator's mind. If his most severe criticism is leveled against those who got the story wrong, his highest praise is given not to those who drew the finest pictures but to those who managed what Dickens told John Leech he had done in his drawings for *Master Humphrey's Clock*: "this is the very first time any designs for what I have written have touched and moved me, and caused me to feel that they expressed the idea I had in my mind."[73] When Cattermole sent him watercolors of two of his illustrations for *The Old Curiosity Shop*—one of Little Nell's grave, and one of the interior of the shop—Dickens expressed similar satisfaction:

It is impossible for me to tell you how greatly I am charmed with those beautiful pictures, in which the whole feeling and thought and expression of the little story is rendered to the gratification of my inmost heart; . . . [74]

And when W. P. Frith, after doing a picture of Dolly Varden for *Barnaby Rudge*, later painted Dolly again, and also Kate Nickleby, Dickens is reported to have said, "All I can say is, they are exactly what I meant." [75] "The idea I had in my mind," "the whole feeling and thought and expression of the little story," "exactly what I meant"—it is this, more than artistic excellence, that Dickens looked for in the illustrations of his novels. Rarely did his letters mention such matters as composition, shading, or spacing.

Some of his critical commentary, however, was directed to the improvement of a picture as picture, not simply to strengthening its fidelity to his novel. Dickens called for better representation of a detail, or suggested additions or deletions that would improve the illustration. [76] One plate drawn by George Cruikshank displeased him so much that he immediately brought the older man to account:

With reference to the last plate—Rose Maylie and Oliver. Without entering into the question of great haste or any other cause which may have led to its being what it is—I am quite sure there can be little difference of opinion between us with respect to the result—

and Dickens asked Cruikshank to do the plate "afresh and . . . *at once*," [77] which is about as imperious as he ever got with any of his illustrators.

Perhaps Dickens came to realize that too much domination of his artists (particularly his less famous ones—he always allowed the established artist more leeway) could hurt their work; he gave them freer reign (though never final say) as the years went by. Professor Cohen says that "as Dickens's instructions to Browne became more suggestive and less imperative, the artist responded with increased creativity." [78] As early as *Martin Chuzzlewit* we find him asking Browne to do the frontispiece of Tom Pinch playing the organ, with "any little indications of his history rising out of it, and floating about it, that you please." [79] In a very few instances, Dickens even solicited the artists' opinions about the nature of an illustration; as time passed, he would on occasion give them the option of selecting detail, locations—sometimes even the subject, out of a number of the novel. To the end, though, he would remind them that their work was subject to "correction, alteration, revision, and all other ations and isions connected with the Fine Arts." [80]

The extent to which Dickens' work with his illustrators improved his knowledge of and taste in art cannot be fully assessed, but it seems likely that both were materially improved. If the experience did nothing else, it brought him into intimacy with artists at work, and probably prompted him to undertake the fairly ambitious commentary on some of them which he attempted in later years. If this later commentary is not always superior, some of it is very good, and much of it demonstrates a competence for which he has not often been given credit.

The illustrator-artists upon whom Dickens wrote at length were George Cruikshank, John Leech, Daniel Maclise, and Clarkson Stanfield, all of whom he greatly admired. Cruikshank, in fact, was the only one he criticized, though most of his objection was to the content, not the artistry, of the great caricaturist. His first reference, to an unidentified drawing (perhaps for Barber's "Nights at Sea" in *Bentley's Miscellany*, No. 6, 12/37, which Dickens was then editing), professed that he was "delighted with the drawing, which is most admirable."[81] A few months later, he was even more enthusiastic about an illustration for another piece in the *Miscellany*: "I've seen Cruikshank this morning, and he has left me in transports with his Mudfog association subject."[82] And Cruikshank's first book, consisting of eleven illustrations for the artist's version of the popular poem *Lord Bateman*, earned high praise from Dickens. "You never did anything like those etchings— ever."[83] A subsequent work brought less enthusiastic approval: of *George Cruikshank's Omnibus*, edited by Laman Blanchard and illustrated by Cruikshank, Dickens wrote to Harrison Ainsworth that "there seems to me to be too much whisker for a shilling, but that's a matter of taste."[84] Cruikshank, of course, was bearded. The *Omnibus* was successful for a time, but perhaps the public too at last found it too hairy: the publication expired with its ninth number.

Characteristically, Dickens' letter to Cruikshank about the "Buss" carried no hint of adverse criticism: "It is wery light, wery easy on the springs, well horsed, driv in a slap up style, and altogether an uncommon spicy con-sarn," he said. The same kindness appears in his next comment on and to Cruikshank: writing to him about his *Cruikshank's Almanac* for 1844, he said "you are prodigious,"[85] though actually he may not have liked the work.

Despite his customary refusal to criticize the work of his friends, Dickens could not refrain from adverse comment on several of Cruikshank's later works—not on their artistry, but on their ideas. The first of these was a collection of eight plates entitled *The Bottle*, of which Dickens wrote to Forster:

> I think it very powerful indeed; the two last plates most admirable, except that
> the boy and girl in the very last are too young, and the girl more like a

circus-phenomenon than that no-phenomenon she is intended to represent. I question, however, whether anybody else living could have done it so well. There is a woman in the last plate but one, garrulous about the murder, with a child in her arms, that is as good as Hogarth. Also the man who is stooping down, looking at the body.[86]

Elsewhere Forster gives us more of Dickens' praise of *The Bottle*:

I think the power of that closing scene quite extraordinary. It haunts the remembrance like an awful reality. It is full of passion and terror, and I doubt very much whether any hand but his could so have rendered it. There are other fine things too. The death-bed scene on board the hulks; the convict who is composing the face, and the other who is drawing the screen round the bed's head; seem to me masterpieces worthy of the greatest painter. The reality of the place, and the fidelity with which every minute object illustrative of it is presented, are surprising. . . . In the trial scene at the Old Bailey, the eye may wander round the court, and observe everything that is a part of the place. The very light and atmosphere are faithfully reproduced. So, in the gin-shop and the barber-shop. An inferior hand would indicate a fragment of the fact, and slur it over; but here every shred is honestly made out. The man behind the bar in the gin-shop, is as real as the convicts at the hulks, or the barristers round the table in the Old Bailey. . . . [87]

But though he admired the artistry of *The Bottle*, Dickens did not like its philosophy. He followed his praise of it with this: "But it only makes more exasperating to me the one-sidedness of the thing,"[88] and added an explanation of why people drink. "The drinking should have begun in sorrow, or poverty, or ignorance—the three things in which, in its awful aspect, it *does* begin."[89] Hogarth, he added, did not undertake a "Drunkard's Progress" because he knew there were too many causes of drunkenness to depict. Cruikshank, who in earlier years had been a hard drinker but had now become a teetotaler, thought drinking produced misery; Dickens saw it the other way around. But though he disliked the message of Cruikshank's art (and was on occasion angered by his rude objections to drinking at private parties), Dickens could appreciate his artistry. If we cannot base upon this single instance an argument against those who claim that Dickens' emphasis upon content influenced his artistic judgment, at least we can note that there were exceptions.

Upon two other occasions Dickens was to render homage to Cruikshank's art while raising objection to its content. One of these was in connection with a work similar in subject and intention to *The Bottle* called *The Drunkard's Children*. "Few men have a better right to erect themselves into teachers of the people than Mr. George Cruikshank," Dickens wrote in his commentary upon the work. "Few men have observed the people as he has done, or known them better; . . . and there are very, very few artists, in England or abroad, who can approach him in his peculiar and remarkable power."[90] But then Dickens objected again to the idea that social ills can be so easily attributed to drink.

But Dickens' most important disagreement with Cruikshank, one which widened the already perceptible gap between them as friends, came in response to the artist's work entitled *Hop-o'-my-Thumb*. Here Cruikshank had mixed together the kind of literature Dickens loved most—fairy tales, children's literature—and the kind he most hated, dry moral tales aimed at improving children. Dickens had already written a tract against such stuff in his *The Uncommercial Traveller*: the title of the piece, "Mr. Barlow," was taken from a character in the novel *Sandford and Merton* (1713), by Thomas Day. Mr. Barlow relentlessly draws a moral from every event in the lives of the two young protagonists of the story, and in his article Dickens recorded his distaste for such stuff. Now, in a piece entitled "Frauds on the Fairies," he enters the same objection against Cruikshank's moral pictures. "It was just the kind of pervasive didacticism that Dickens had always regarded as dreary and deadening," Harry Stone says, "the antithesis of fancy and imagination."

> . . . The child would enter the storybook world only to find that it contained
> the same prosing precepts that nagged at him from the pages of his insufferable
> copy books or his improving moral tracts. To Dickens, Cruikshank's text was
> a fraud. It would turn children away from the fount of fancy and imagination at
> the very source.[91]

In a letter to his subeditor Wills, Dickens said "I mean to protest most strongly against alteration, for any purpose, of the beautiful little stories which are so tenderly and humanly useful to us in these times, when the world is too much with us, early and late. . . ."[92] Cruikshank is a "great artist," but he must be criticized for misusing fancy, a fault that is hard to understand in him because "in his own art he understands it so perfectly, and illustrates it so beautifully, so humorously, so wisely. . . ."[93] Dickens did not believe in criticizing his friends in print, but Cruikshank in *Hop-o'-my-Thumb* was striking at one of his fundamental aesthetic principles, and though he worded his criticism as gently as he could, he could not let even a friend get away with it. (It is also interesting to notice this attack upon a kind of morality in a work of art by the man everybody accuses of placing morality above art, though of course here it is fancy, not art itself, that he elevates.)

Dickens also commented at length upon the work of John Leech, another close friend and illustrator of his novels. Leech was one of the best-known artists of his day, and Dickens found several occasions to praise him. In a speech at the Newsvendor's Benevolent Institution in January of 1852, he referred to "the great popular artist of the time, whose humour was so delicate, so nice, and so discriminating, and whose pencil like his observation was so graceful and so informed with the sense of beauty that it was mere disparagement to call his works 'caricatures'. . . ."[94]

Dickens' longest and most careful criticism of Leech extended this consideration of him as caricaturist. Forster asked him to write for the *Examiner* a review of a series of twelve drawings on stone called *The Rising Generation*, taken by Leech from his designs done for "Mr. Punch's Gallery" in *Punch* magazine. Dickens called the work "a careful reproduction by Mr. Leech, in a very graceful and cheerful manner, of one of his best series of designs. . . . It shows to infinitely greater advantage in the present enlarged and separate form of publication." He called Leech

> the very first English caricaturist (we use the word for want of a better) who has considered beauty as being perfectly compatible with his art. He almost always introduces into his graphic sketches some beautiful forms or agreeable forms; and in striking out this course and setting this example, we really believe he does a great deal to refine and elevate that popular branch of art.

In the works of such caricaturists as Rowlandson or Gilray, Dickens said, the great humor displayed was often

> rendered wearisome and unpleasant by a vast amount of personal ugliness. Now, besides that it is a poor device to represent what is satirised as being necessarily ugly—which is but the resource of an angry child or a jealous woman—it serves no purpose but to produce a disagreeable result. There is no reason why the farmer's daughter in the old caricature who is squalling at the harpsichord (to the intense delight, by the by, of her worthy father, whom it is her duty to please) should be squat and hideous. The satire on the manner of her education, if there be any in the thing at all, would be just as good if she were pretty. Mr. Leech would have made her so. The average of farmer's daughters in England are not impossible lumps of fat. One is quite as likely to find a pretty girl in a farmhouse, as to find an ugly one; and we think, with Mr. Leech, that the business of this style of art is with the pretty one. She is not only a pleasanter object in our portfolio, but we have more interest in her. We care more about what does become her, and does not become her.

Dickens cites another illustration by Leech

> representing certain delicate creatures with bewitching countenances, encased in several varieties of that amazing garment, the ladies' paletot. Formerly these fair

creatures would have been made as ugly and ungainly as possible, and there the point would have been lost, and the spectator, with a laugh at the absurdity of the whole group, would not have cared one farthing how such uncouth creatures disguised themselves, or how ridiculous they became.

But to represent female beauty as Mr. Leech represents it, an artist must have a most delicate perception of it; and the gift of being able to realize it to us with two or three slight, sure touches of his pencil. This power Mr. Leech possesses in an extraordinary degree.

After registering his "protest against those of the 'Rising Generation' who are precociously in love, being made the subject of merriment by a pitiless and unsympathetic world," Dickens commented on the accurate observation and depiction in the twelve drawings, concluding:

> In all his drawings, whatever Mr. Leech desires to do, he does. The expression indicated, though indicated by the simplest means, is exactly the natural expression, and is recognised as such immediately. His wit is good-natured, and always the wit of a true gentleman. He has a becoming sense of responsibility and self-restraint; he delights in pleasant things; he imparts some pleasant air of his own to things not pleasant in themselves; he is suggestive and full of matter; and he is always improving. Into the tone, as well as into the execution of what he does, he has brought a certain elegance which is altogether new, without involving any compromise of what is true. This is an acquisition to popular art in England. . . . [95]

Here are several of the major tenets of the Dickensian canon of art. Where it reasonably can, art should be beautiful; it should find a way of lending pleasantness to "things not pleasant in themselves." It should tell a story, offering characters who can be read, and whose expressions are natural. The work should improve its viewer. Art, in short, should be as close as possible to Dickens' kind of story-telling, though "slight, sure touches of [the] pencil" must replace the written word. Dickens is aware that there are differences between the two disciplines, but he is little interested in them; his first and often only interest is in the extent to which art can do what fiction does.

The only other artist among Dickens' illustrators upon whom he commented at any length was his close friend, Daniel Maclise, the Scotch-Irish painter. Maclise and the Landseer brothers were the only artist members of the famous Portwiners, a group that included Dickens, Forster, Thackeray, and the actor Macready. If Maclise did relatively little as illustrator for Dickens, it was not for want of respect, as Dickens' comments on Maclise's own work show. But curiously, in an exchange of letters with his American friend Felton, Dickens showed a surprising reluctance to characterize Maclise's art: Maclise was, he said, "'such a discursive devil,' (as he says of himself) and flies off at such odd tangents that I feel it difficult to convey . . . any general notion of his purpose."[96] Apparently Felton asked again for a description of the character of Maclise's work, for a few months later Dickens wrote him again, in almost the same words:

> He is such a discursive fellow, and so eccentric in his might, that on a mental review of his pictures I can hardly tell you of them as leading to any one strong purpose. But the Annual Exhibition at the Royal Academy comes off in May, and then I will endeavor to give you some notion of him. He is a tremendous creature, and might do anything. But like all tremendous creatures, he takes his own way, and flies off at unexpected breaches in the conventional wall.[97]

If Dickens kept his promise to give Felton a "notion," it has not been preserved. His reluctance to describe his friend's art, with which he must have been as familiar as with the work of any other man, is perhaps partly understandable: Maclise was eclectic in his selection of subjects, as Professor Cohen notes,[98] and Felton seems to have been asking rather about content than form. But one would think Dickens could at least have called attention to his friend's partiality for dramatic subjects, which was his main attraction for Dickens, rather than settling for the description "tremendous creature." "Maclise is painting wonderful pictures,"[99] he had written to another correspondent shortly before his first response to Felton; but now, with an opportunity to explain in detail just what was so wonderful about paintings like *A Girl in a Waterfall* and perhaps *The Actor's Reception of the Author* and *Scene from Gil Blas*, Dickens is found with very little to say. Still once more, in September of 1843, he had the opportunity of describing Maclise to Felton, but once again evaded the task: "He is such a wayward fellow in his subject, that it would be next to impossible to write such an article as you were thinking of, about him. . . ."[100]

On all other occasions, though, Dickens showed no reluctance to speak about his friend's art. His comments indicate that of all the painters who worked for him Maclise was the most admired. Their close friendship was no doubt part of the reason for his preference—a cool objectivity was rarely part of Dickens' character. But there were other important reasons. Maclise was famed for two qualities which are at the heart of the Dickens aesthetic: beauty and story. Dickens also liked, Kate Perugini tells us, "the extraordinary facility of his work. He painted rapidly. . . ."[101] The speed with which Dickens himself wrote has been greatly exaggerated, but a writer capable of the amazing amount of work he produced would obviously admire an artist who could do a great deal in a short time. Dickens seems also to have approved of the ability of Maclise to visualize his subject. "What an eye you have," he wrote him in 1842, and though there is some reason to believe this was part of an old joke between them,[102] subsequent letters in the same year offer ample evidence that he meant it. "Nothing is to be said of [Maclise's painting] Hamlet, but wonderful. You know what I honestly think of your extraordinary powers; and how much in earnest I am when I say that it amazed, even me."[103] To Charles Sumner, Dickens wrote, "Maclise's picture from Hamlet is a tremendous production. There are things in it, which in their powerful thought, exceed anything I ever beheld in painting."[104]

Before the end of the year, Dickens wrote to Maclise that his *A Girl at a Waterfall*, a work in progress, was "charming";[105] he later acquired this painting by means of the "pious fraud" we have mentioned. And he wrote to Mrs. De La Rue that Maclise's *Superstition of the Ordeal by Touch* was "very fine indeed."[106] Thackeray liked the painting, too, calling it "perhaps the best and greatest of the artist's works. . . ."[107] Dickens and Thackeray also liked Maclise's portrait of Dickens, but George Eliot called it "that keepsaking, impossible face."[108] She probably would have thought little of Dickens' advice to Maclise to put "dreaming expressions" on the faces of figures in his *The Sleeping Beauty*, saying that they would be "Beautiful! Very beautiful!"[109] Maclise did not use the suggestion.

An incident between Maclise and the Fine Arts Commission elicited from Dickens that volcanic indignation with which he reacted to any fancied or real slight to the Arts. In July, the Commission had named subjects for frescoes to be done in the six arched compartments of the new House of Lords, and had invited six artists to submit, for exhibition in 1845, cartoons, colored sketches, and speciments of fresco. The six were Richard Redgrave, W. C. Thomas, C. W. Cope, J. C. Horley, William Dyer, and Maclise—in that order. In addition, other artists were allowed to compete, and no guarantees were given to the six named painters. "I am disgusted with the Fine Arts Commission," Dickens wrote D'Orsay,

> . . . and think their putting Maclise anywhere but at the very head and front of the Competition, abominable. And I think the terms on which their designs are to be sent in, are disgraceful to the Commissioners as gentlemen—disgraceful to the selected artists, as men of talent—and disgraceful to the country in which the paltry huckstering piece of power is exercised.

D'Orsay agreed: "It is an insult to a man of [Maclise's] talent to be put in competition with such wretched daubers."[110]

But it is in his written review of Maclise's *The Spirit of Chivalry* that

Dickens finally gave the thorough description of his friend's art that shows he could indeed say something. The review is too long to be quoted in full, but much of it is worthy of careful attention. Dickens called the painting

> a composition of such marvellous beauty, of such infinite variety, of such masterly design, of such vigorous and skilful drawing, of such thought and fancy, of such surprising and delicate accuracy of detail, subserving one grand harmony, and one plain purpose, that it may be questioned whether the Fine Arts in any period of their history, have known a more remarkable performance.

He remarked upon the difficulty of the work: its size, proportion, subject, even title all ordered by the Fine Arts Commission. The subject he thought particularly challenging:

> That the treatment of such an abstraction, for the purposes of Art, involved great and peculiar difficulties, no one who considers the subject for a moment can doubt. That nothing is easier [than] to render it absurd and monstrous, is a position as little capable of dispute by anybody who has beheld another cartoon on the same subject in the same hall, representing a Ghoule in a state of raving madness, dancing on a body in a very high wind, to the great astonishment of John the Baptist's head, which is looking on from a corner.

Maclise's handling of the subject had been studied by all kinds of viewers, Dickens said: students of art, people accustomed to viewing the great paintings of the world, and "ignorant, unlettered, drudging men, mere hewers and drawers, [who] have gathered in a knot about it . . . and read it, in their homely language, as it were a Book. In minds, the roughest and the most refined, it has alike found quick response. . . ." Reading it himself, Dickens found in it the inspiration which comes from love of woman, of glory, of poetry, both in the "spirit" and in other figures of the painting. There was an appeal to the aged in the older figures clustering around the spirit, which were "of the very highest order of Art, and wonderfully serve the purpose of the picture. There is not one among its three and twenty heads of which the same remark might not be made." Dickens mentioned "the prodigious force and *colour* which so separate this work from all the rest exhibited . . ." and defended it against the charge that it was "too elaborately finished: too complete in its several parts" by pointing out that it "is a design, intended to be afterwards copied and painted in fresco," and therefore had to be more finished than the usual cartoon.

> Great misapprehension on this head seems to have been engendered in the minds of some observers, by the famous cartoons of Raphael; but they forget

that these were never intended as designs for fresco painting. They were designed for tapestry-work, which is susceptible of only certain broad and general effects, as no one better knew than the Great Master. Utterly detestable and vile as the tapestry is, compared with the immortal Cartoons from which it is worked, it is impossible for any man who casts his eyes upon it where it hangs at Rome, not to see, immediately, the special adaptation of the drawings to that end, and for that purpose. The aim of these Cartoons being wholly different, Mr. Maclise's object, if we understand it, was to show precisely what he meant to do, and knew he could perform, in fresco, on a wall. And here his meaning is; worked out; without a compromise of any difficulty; without the avoidance of any disconcerting truth; expressed in all its beauty, strength, and power.[111]

Though the review is something less than a finished piece of art criticism, it is rather better than most published comments on Dickens' ability to judge art would lead us to expect. True, we have in it again the Dickens who wants story in his paintings, to be read "as it were a Book." True, much of the comment is upon content rather than form. But Dickens does recognize the difficulty the painting offered, does speak of the grouping and general harmony, comments upon the color, and shows some knowledge of technical aspects of painting in his distinction between cartoons designed for fresco and those for tapestry, "which is susceptible of only certain broad and general effects. . . . " And some knowledge of Raphael is demonstrated. The opening effusion is embarrassing, but the rest supports Professor Cohen's contention that Dickens' criticism was "often judicious."

Dickens seems to have had but one reservation concerning Maclise's artistry—only one that he voiced—and that was not in regard to the quality of his work but to the energy of the worker. "If he has a care, he will leave his mark,"[112] he had written to Felton in 1843, and again in 1845 he voiced the concern: "if he will only give his magnificent Genius fair play, there is not enough of Cant and Dulness . . . to keep the Giant down, an hour."[113] Dickens' daughter Kate wrote that Maclise was "incorrigibly idle," and that her father "would gently remonstrate or more often merely joke and tease" in an effort "to rouse him from a kind of moral apathy. . . ."[114] It is characteristic of Dickens that even in his private correspondence he made but these two slightly veiled references to the laziness of his friend, whom he knew to be given to severe seizures of depression.

Dickens had much less to say about his remaining illustrators. Among these was another close friend, Clarkson Stanfield. Also a painter of established reputation, Stanfield was one of several whose talents Dickens managed to enlist not only for his books but also for the amateur dramatic productions of which he was so fond. Stanfield and others painted scenes for Dickens (one of which decorated his home for years), and sometimes acted in his plays. Early in their acquaintance Stanfield seems to have sent Dickens pieces of his work: one of Dickens' first letters to him thanks him for two, probably the watercolors *Land's End* and *The Logan Rock*, done during their trip into Cornwall with Maclise and Forster. "Most beautiful," Dickens called them, and wrote to his American friend Felton that on the trip the two artists "made such sketches . . . that you would have sworn we had the Spirit of Beauty with us, as well as the Spirit of Fun." Just a few months later he wrote to Stanfield praising "your immortal scenery," and in a letter from Albaro told him that "the approach to Genoa, by sea from Marseilles, constitutes a picture which you ought to paint, for nobody else can ever do it!" During this same European trip, after seeing Venice, Dickens wrote that Stanfield and Canaletto were "miraculous in their truth"[115] in painting that city.

Subsequent comments continued to express admiration. Stanfield's *Victory* was a "noble painting"; his paintings at the Royal Academy exhibit were (by anticipation) his "latest triumphs."[116] At Stanfield's death, Dickens described him as a "great marine painter" with "wonderful gifts" whose "grand pictures proclaim his powers . . . "[117]—though the eulogy typically concentrated upon the noble nature of the artist rather than upon his artistic gifts. Only in the letter to Forster about the Paris Exhibit of 1855, one of the very few places in all his writing about painters in which Dickens let go, did he comment adversely upon Stanfield, saying that his piece in the exhibit "is too much like a set scene."[118]

The strong control Dickens exercised over his artists—mitigated here and there among the most famous, but never entirely absent—supports the conclusion that, however limited his artistic training might be, he had considerable confidence in his ability to work in the the world of painting and drawing. Though he allowed some artists latitude in selection of detail or even of subject, his custom was to present them with everything, usually supplying more detail, more background, history, and emotion for characters, action, and arrangement of props, than they could possibly use, so intense was his sense of the picture. Indeed, rarely does he comment on the aesthetic value of a picture, except in general terms of approval or dislike. Few comments are made upon composition, use of light and shade, color, arrangement, or design. Specific criticism, when it is offered, usually concentrates upon whether the artist, in illustrations for the stories, caught what Dickens *meant* when he wrote the scene from which the illustration is taken.

But there are strengths to balance the weaknesses. Good, careful, and—considering their context—relatively thorough judgments are rendered about several artists, especially Cruikshank, Leech, and Maclise. In at least one instance—the discussion with Leech about the colors of the illustrations for *A Christmas Carol*—Dickens' judgment proved better than the artist's. In places, he does pay attention to questions of color, arrangement, composition, light and shade. His essay on Leech's *The Rising Generation* makes a valid distinction between the ugliness of early caricature and the new style of beauty—showing in the process a knowledge of recent art history—and demonstrates considerable ability to read a painting and represent what is there. And in his long study of Maclise's *The Spirit of Chivalry* he at last dispels our doubts about his ability to comment on the art of his friend; he shows an understanding of the difficulties a subject can offer an artist (we remember the criticism that he never seemed to think from the artist's point of view), comments upon the figures and the use of color, and again demonstrates some knowledge of art history. There is enough in all this to support Professor Cohen's summary of Dickens' ability in art:

> The author had no pretension about his ability as an art critic. Yet it must be recalled that he not only reflected the tastes of his time, but often helped to mould them. Today, many still share Dickens's assessment of his own illustrators and other artist friends.[119]

But the strongest impression one carries away from a reading of Dickens' correspondence with and about his illustrators is the tremendous sense of what his ruling passion in art, as in most other things, was. Dickens loved a good dramatic tale. Though other things about painting certainly attracted him, it was to the story the picture told that he was inevitably drawn—if it did not tell a story, he was rarely drawn at all. Nothing else in his aesthetic world ever came close to his interest in people and what happened to them; his most discriminating criticism of art is of this kind. One of his most revealing comments is to be found in a little-quoted speech made at the ceremony of a presentation to him at Birmingham:

> . . . it is not now the province of art in painting to hold itself in monastic seclusion. . . . It cannot hope to rest on a single foundation for its great temple—on the mere classic pose of a figure, or the folds of a drapery—but . . . it must be imbued with human passions and action, informed with human right and wrong. . . .[120]

This is the heart of Dickens' ethic of art, and though it includes the moral sense, its larger concern is drama.

III

Dickens' comments upon other and lesser artists are not often helpful; too frequently he merely expresses approval or dislike, without explaining why. But patient reading of them does demonstrate how constantly—and confidently—the author offered opinions about artists. (He assured a correspondent that the reputable painter Robert Benjamin Haydon was "most unquestionably . . . a very bad painter. . . . There was one picture—Nero entertaining himself with a Musical Performance while Rome was burning—quite marvelous in its badness. It was difficult to look at it with a composed and decent face. There is no doubt, on the other hand, that in the theory of his art, he was very clever. . . ."[121]) And here and there clues to his aesthetic convictions are to be glimpsed. His simple eulogy on Sir David Wilkie, for example, contains several of his favorite aesthetic words—*true, beautiful, elevating, nature*—and offers another of his fundamental beliefs about art: it has an obligation to all, including the poor.[122]

Even in his commentary on so humble an artist as John Banvard, Dickens revealed his taste. He wrote that Banvard's three-mile-long painting of the Mississippi River (rolled from one large cylinder to another in an exhibition at the Egyptian Hall, Piccadilly)

> is not a refined work of art (nor does it claim to be, in Mr. Banvard's modest description); it is not remarkable for accuracy of drawing, or for brilliancy of colour, or subtle effects of light and shade, or for any approach to any of the qualities of those delicate and beautiful pictures by Mr. Stanfield which used, once upon a time, to pass before our eyes in like manner. It is not very skillfully set off by the disposition of the artificial light; it is not assisted by anything but a pianoforte and a seraphine.
>
> But it is a picture three miles long, which occupies two hours in its passage before the audience. It is a picture . . . irresistibly impressing the spectator with a conviction of its plain and simple truthfulness . . . except, we believe, in the colour of its water. . . . The picture itself, as an indisputably true and faithful representation of a wonderful region . . . is replete with interest throughout.[123]

Dickens reveals himself far more, however, in his remarks on Hogarth, in a study which John Forster called "a masterly criticism of that great Englishman."[124] Unlike Cruikshank, Hogarth never tried a "Drunkard's Progress" because he knew he could not properly show all the causes as well as effects of such a life. "It was never in his plan," Dickens says,

> to be content with only showing the effect. In the death of the miser-follower, his shoes new-soled with the binding of his Bible, before the young Rake begins

his career; in the worldly father, listless daughter, impoverished young lord, and crafty lawyer, of the first plate of Marriage-a-la-mode; in the detestable advances through the stages of cruelty; and in the progress downward of Thomas Idle; you see the effects indeed, but also the causes. [In the Rake's] immortal journey down Gin Lane, [he] exhibits drunkenness in the most appalling forms, [but] also forces on attention a most neglected wretched neighborhood, and an unwholesome, indecent abject condition of life. . . . I have always myself thought the purpose of this fine piece to be not adequately stated even by Charles Lamb. 'The very houses seem absolutely reeling'; it is true; but beside that wonderful picture of what follows intoxication, we have indication quite as powerful of what leads to it among the neglected classes. There is no evidence that any of the actors in the dreary scene have ever been much better than we see them there. The best are pawning the commonest necessaries, and tools of their trades; and the worst are homeless vagrants who give us no clue to their having been otherwise in bygone days. All are living and dying miserably. Nobody is interfering for prevention or cure, in the generation going out before us, or the generation coming in. The beadle is the only sober man in the composition except the pawnbroker, and he is mightily indifferent to the orphan-child crying beside its parent's coffin. The little children are not so well taught or looked after, but that they can take to dram-drinking already. The church indeed is very prominent and handsome; but as, quite passive in the picture, it coldly surveys these things in progress under shadow of its tower . . . I am confirmed in my suspicion that Hogarth had many meanings which have not grown absolute in a century.[125]

Here we see Dickens in his own critical wheelhouse, whether in painting or any other art: reading the story and idea with keen penetration, with a clear and exact understanding of what is before him. If the work to be examined has even the slightest dramatic aspect, Dickens will seize upon it and devote most of his attention to it; the greater that aspect in the work, the surer and more valuable will be his criticism. In the commentary on Hogarth, the reader must be impressed not only with Dickens' seeing all there is to see, but with his ability to note and interpret what there is *not* to see.

IV

The only other body of Dickensian commentary on artists and their work consists of his well-known pronouncements on Italian painting, found in his letters and in *Pictures from Italy*. If Dickens saw the United States as a place where money ruled, and so entitled his book on it *American Notes for Circulation*, obviously he felt Italy to be best approached through art, both that which he found there and that which he would use to describe it. As Forster has reminded us, Dickens came to Italy with no formal training in painting. At the same time, it is true that he did come to Italy with a certain amount of informal experience with art behind him, acquired in the manner we have seen. But little that Dickens learned from Stanfield, Maclise, or Cruikshank (especially up to 1844) could have prepared him for the experiences of Raphael or Da Vinci; it took those experiences and ten more years of contact with English painters to lead him to the realization of the smallness of English art, of its insular conviction that anything in art not done in the English way could not be very good. The Dickens of 1844 must have brought something of that same British narrowness with him to Italy; it is difficult to see how he could have avoided it.

Dickens apparently had but one guide in his tour of Italian art: Louis Simond's "charming book on Italy," *A Tour in Italy and Sicily* (1828), which he said

> charms me more and more by its boldness, and its frank exhibition of that rare and admirable quality which enables a man to form opinions for himself without a miserable and slavish reference to the pretended opinions of other people. His notices of the leading pictures enchant me. They are so perfectly just and faithful, and so whimsically shrewd.[126]

Instead of opening Dickens' narrowed Anglican view and preparing him for the greater art world he was about to enter, Simond seems to have encouraged him only to exercise the judgment he brought with him.

Another source of weakness in Dickens' criticism of Italian art was his strong prejudice against Roman Catholicism. For all his fairness in *Barnaby Rudge* about persecuted Catholics in England, Dickens shared the English prejudice against the "Romish" European church, and felt that it had a baleful influence upon Italian art. He complains of the Italian masters that

> these great men, who were of necessity very much in the hands of the monks and priests, painted monks and priests a vast deal too often. I constantly see, in pictures of tremendous power, heads quite below the story and the painter; and I invariably observe that those heads are of the convent stamp, and have their counterparts, exactly, in the convent inmates of this hour.[127]

Elsewhere in a letter to Forster, he complained of "legions of whining friars and waxy holy families, whole orchestras of earthly angels, and whole groves of St. Sebastians stuck as full of arrows according to pattern as a lying-in pin cushion is stuck with pins."[128] Here, though, one may notice that it is not Catholicism Dickens objects to, but the conventionalizing of art. It is the business of art, Dickens feels, as it is the business of the play, to hold the mirror up to nature, and the mirror has no business—not for religion or anything else—to show arrows carefully arranged in a corpse as though the archers had design and not death in their aim.

Dickens' first mention of art in his letters from Italy, even before he has entered a museum, reflects his determination to make independent and unawed judgment. "Ask me a question or two about fresco, will you be so good?" he wrote to Daniel Maclise from Genoa. "All the houses are painted in fresco, hereabout—the outside walls I mean. . . . Sometimes (but not often) I can make out a Virgin with a mildewed Glory round her head; holding nothing, in an indiscernible lap, with invisible arms; and occasionally the leg, or arm, or what Marryat would call the arthe of a cherub. But it is very melancholy and dim."[129] That was written in July of 1844; it was not until November that comments on art began to appear in his letters, which suggests either that he was slow to get to see the great art, or not quite so prepared to speak about it as his first letter, inviting an artist to solicit his opinion about art, seems to indicate. In any case, by November the comments began to flow. After seeing Venice, he called "Canaletto and Stanny [Stanfield] miraculous in their truth" (in their paintings of the city), and spoke of "those silent speaking faces of Titian and Tintoretto. . . ." This was quickly followed by a longer and more ambitious criticism:

> I have never seen any praise of Titian's great picture of the Assumption of the Virgin at Venice, which soared half as high as the beautiful and amazing reality. It is perfection. Tintoretto's picture too, of the Assembly of the Blest at Venice also, with all the lines in it (it is of immense size and the figures are countless) tending majestically and dutifully to Almighty God in the centre, is grand and noble in the extreme. There are some wonderful portraits there, besides; and some confused and hurried, and slaughterous battle pieces, in which the surprising art that presents the generals to your eye, so that it is almost impossible you can miss them in a crowd though they are in the thick of it, is very pleasant to dwell upon. I have seen some delightful pictures; and some (at Verona and Mantua) really too absurd and ridiculous even to laugh at. . . ."[130]

Since we are not told what the absurd and ridiculous paintings are, or what makes them so, we cannot judge Dickens' judgment in the last sentence; it is tempting to think that he tacked it on just to show that he was not indiscriminately praising everything. But as his first lengthy comment upon Italian art, the rest of this makes no bad start. It deals in part with the qualities of line and grouping, the absence of which Johnson laments in other Dickensian commentary, and it shows sound and independent judgment. Titian's *Assumption* was generally regarded as a masterpiece in Dickens' time, but Dickens anticipated Ruskin in praising Tintoretto's *Assembly of the Blessed*. On a trip to Italy nine years later, he praised the painting even more highly, in a letter to Forster:

There are pictures by Tintoretto in Venice more delightful and masterly than it is possible sufficiently to express. His Assembly of the Blest I do believe to be, take it all in all, the most wonderful and charming picture ever painted. Your guide-book writer, representing the general swarming of humbugs, rather patronizes Tintoretto as a man of some sort of merit; and (bound to follow Eustace, Forsyth, and all the rest of them) directs you, on pain of being broke for want of gentility in appreciation, to go into ecstacies with things that have neither imagination, nature, proportion, possibility, nor anything else in them.[131]

Writing to Forster in March of 1845, Dickens echoed something of Simond's criticism of Raphael, and added his own liking for the Master's pupil, Marco-Antonio Raimondi:

The most famous of the oil paintings in the Vatican you know through the medium of the finest line-engravings in the world; and as to some of them I much doubt, if you had seen them with me, whether you might not think you had lost little in having only known them hitherto in that translation. Where the drawing is poor and meagre, or alloyed by time—it is so, and it must be, often: though no doubt it is a heresy to hint at such a thing,—the engraving presents the forms and the idea to you, in a simple majesty which such defects impair. Where this is not the case, and all is stately and harmonious, still it is somehow in the very grain and nature of a delicate engraving to suggest to you (I think) the utmost delicacy, finish, and refinement, as belonging to the original. Therefore, though the Picture in this latter case will greatly charm and interest you, it does not take you by surprise. You are quite prepared beforehand for the fullest excellence of which it is capable.

According to Forster, this view had at the time of Dickens' writing "eloquent reinforcement from critics of undeniable authority."[132] Later in the same letter Dickens offered his opinion of other artists:

There are portraits innumerable by Titian, Rubens, Rembrandt and Vandyke; heads by Guido, and Domenichino, and Carlo Dolci; subjects by Raphael, and Corregio, and Murillo, and Paul Veronese, and Salvator; which it would be difficult indeed to praise too highly or to praise enough. It is a happiness to me to think that they cannot be felt, as they should be felt, by the profound connoisseurs who fall into fits upon the longest notice and the most unreasonable terms. Such tenderness and grace, such noble elevation, purity, and beauty, so shine upon me from some well-remembered spots in the walls of these galleries, as to relieve my tortured memory from legions of whining friars and waxy holy families. I forgive, from the bottom of my soul, whole orchestras of earthly

angels, . . . and I am in no humour to quarrel even with that priestly infatuation, or priestly doggedness of purpose, which persists in reducing every
mystery of our religion to some literal development in paint and canvas, equally
repugnant to the reason and sentiment of any thinking man.[133]

But after this, Dickens confined his letters to brief statements of like and
dislike, with very little indication of what had helped to form his opinions.
Thus *Il Putto Bianca* in the Durazzo Palace is "a noble painting," and "the
Venuses . . . [are] all bad . . . and like anything but women. . . ."[134] Nor do
we find much more in *Pictures from Italy* than such statements as that in the
palaces of Genoa he found "masterpieces by Vandyke. . . ."[135]

The materials of the Italian experience, however, are less important as a
record of Dickens' unformed critical judgment than they are as a means
whereby we may learn about other aspects of his experience of art. A brief
humorous incident in Mantua demonstrates again his desire to think
independently, and also shows familiarity with an important treatise on art.
Going into a picture gallery, he was surrounded by geese whose quacking
he interpreted as advice not to go in. Having seen the paintings, he
said of the geese, "I would take their opinion on a question of art, in preference to the discourses of Sir Joshua Reynolds."[136] Another comment, on
the art found in the cathedral at Parma, suggests that he was capable of
looking on painting, if not "with the eyes of an artist," then at least with
the eyes of a fellow-artist: "The decayed and mutilated paintings with
which this church is covered, have, to my thinking, a remarkably mournful
and depressing influence. It is miserable to see great works of art—something of the Souls of Painters—perishing and fading away, like human
forms."[137]

Dickens' comments on Italian art tend to be frustratingly incomplete.
Only in a few instances is there enough to help us understand at least a little. A section of *Pictures from Italy* on art in Rome begins with the usual
generalization: in the Vatican "many most noble statues, and wonderful pictures, are there; nor is it heresy to say that there is a considerable amount of
rubbish there, too." But a few pages later Dickens gets down to specific
judgment:

> The portrait of Beatrice di Cenci, in the Palazzo Berebini, is a picture almost
> impossible to be forgotten. Through the transcendent sweetness and beauty of
> the face, there is a something shining out, that haunts me. . . . She has turned
> suddenly toward you; and there is an expression in the eyes—although they are
> very tender and gentle—as if the wildness of a momentary terror or distraction,
> had been struggled with and overcome, that instant; and nothing but a celestial

hope, and a beautiful sorrow, and a desolate earthly helplessness remained. . . .
The history of her unhappy life, is written in the Painting; written in the dying
girl's face, by Nature's own hand![138]

No one who remembers Little Nell will miss what attracts Dickens here, in
addition to the usual dramatic interest: a young female dying, a situation
including wildness and terror, the overcoming of earthly ills, and the finding
of comfort in expectation of a better world. But there is also appreciation
of the artistry in Dickens' sense that the figure "has turned suddenly": the
painting has conveyed motion to him, just as he wanted some of his illustrations to do. And the reading of the expression of the eyes is sensitive and perceptive; we note too the appreciation for anything that seems
natural.

A comment on Giulio Romano is also interesting. The Palazzo Te is
singular for those

> unaccountable nightmares with which its interior had been decorated by Giulio
> Romano. There . . . are . . . Giants . . . so inconceivably ugly and grotesque,
> that it is marvellous how any man can have imagined such creatures. . . . The
> figures are immensely large, and exaggerated to the utmost pitch of uncouth-
> ness; the coloring is harsh and disagreeable; and the whole effect more like (I
> should imagine) a violent rush of blood to the head of the spectator, than any real
> picture set before him by the hand of an artist.[139]

The passage reflects, I believe, the difficulty Dickens had before art which
intentionally violated his favorite precept of beauty. The greatest imaginer
in the English language cannot understand how any one could imagine such
things, and though the paintings undoubtedly get to Dickens, he can hardly
attribute their effect to human effort; such works are like manifestations of
physical illness rather than like art. A similar feeling can be sensed in his
reaction to the paintings on the walls of St. Stefano Rotondo, a church on
the outskirts of Rome. The pictures there of martyred saints he found

> hideous . . . such a panorama of horror and butchery no man could imagine
> in his sleep, though he were to eat a whole pig raw, for supper. Gray-bearded
> men being boiled, fried, grilled, crimped, singed, eaten by wild beasts, wor-
> ried by dogs, buried alive, torn asunder by horses, chopped up small with
> hatchets: women having their breasts torn with iron pincers, their tongues cut
> out, their ears screwed off, their jaws broken, their bodies stretched upon the
> rack, or skinned upon the stake, or cracked up and melted in the
> fire. . . ."[140]

Dickens seems unable to conceive of why anybody would want to paint such
things.

V

Certainly no great case for Dickens as critic can be made from his reactions to Italian art. Nor can it be claimed that any sudden upsurge in critical acumen occurs upon his return to England: the letters reveal no immediate enlargement of understanding nor deepening of judgment, and in some things Dickens remained limited to the end. But eventually there are, as Johnson says, "strides in his development,"[141] and it is not far-fetched to believe that in part these strides are owing to his exposure to the greatness of Italian art.

Some of the effects of that exposure are certainly doubtful or mixed in their value, it is true. The determination to walk apart, with a developing concurrent inclination to view as "cant" all pronouncements that smacked of the common path, probably both helped and hurt him. This inclination developed early in his Italian trip. "I am already brim-full of cant about pictures," he wrote in 1844, and the following year wrote to D'Orsay that

> there is such an extensive amount of humbug afloat on these matters; and people are so strangely disposed to take what they have heard or read for granted and not use their own intellects and sense, that whenever I go into a Gallery I hang out 'No Trust' in legible white letters on a black ground—like an English Turnpike.

That same year he spoke in a letter of "the Criticism of Art; from which Sterne prayed kind Heaven to defend him, as 'the worst of all the Cants continuously canted in this Canting world . . . '" and asked, "is not our motto Truth for ever, and Cant be damned?"[142]

When he returned to Italy in 1853, Dickens wrote to Forster about what he considered to be canting praise of the famous.

> Egg's honest amazement and consternation when he saw some of the most trumpeted things was what the Americans call a "caution." In the very same hour and minute there were scores of people falling into conventional raptures with that very poor Apollo, and passing over the most beautiful little figures and heads in the whole Vatican because they were not expressly set up to be worshipped.

An earlier part of the same letter reads almost like a credo:

> I am more than ever confirmed in my conviction that one of the great uses of travelling is to encourage a man to think for himself, to be bold enough always to declare without offense that he *does* think for himself, and to overcome the villainous meanness of professing what other people have professed when he knows (if he has capacity to originate an opinion) that his profession is untrue.

The intolerable nonsense against which genteel taste and subserviency are afraid to rise, in connection with art, is astounding.[143]

Certainly Dickens' desire not to mouth accepted judgments is laudable, but he seems to have developed along with this desire the conviction that almost any discussion of art which employed terminology, such as color or line, was equally culpable, as another letter from Italy in 1853, while travelling with Collins and Egg, suggests:

The Fine Arts afford a subject which I never approach; always appearing to fall into a profound reverie when it is discussed. Neither do I ever go into any gallery with them. To hear Collins learnedly holding forth to Egg (who has as little of that gammon as an artist *can* have) about reds, and greens, and things "coming well" with other things, and lines being wrong, and lines being right, is far beyond the bounds of all caricature. I shall never forget it.[144]

Of course Dickens may be responding to pretentiousness on the part of Collins here, but similar criticisms of others suggest that Dickens was beginning to think of all technical discussion as affectation. If this is true, we have another reason for the widely-cited scarcity of such discussion in Dickens' writing: perhaps it was owing not so much to inability as to his desire to avoid what he considered to be cant. Kate Perugini, herself an artist, wrote of her father that "the talk of 'vehicles,' 'flat tones,' 'ciaro-scuro,' 'carnations,' and other mysteries about which artists are apt to grow eloquent, became sometimes a little wearisome to one who was extremely reticent concerning his own work, and who seldom . . . allowed himself to talk 'shop.'"[145] Dickens' letters show that he found such talk more than a little wearisome; "I keep out of the way when pictures are in question and go my own path,"[146] he wrote his wife, and kept to that path for much of the rest of his life.

In painting as in his own art, Dickens felt that a work should speak for itself, and that any discussion of its method, technique, or message by the artist or anybody else was better left unsaid. Artists, he told his daughter Kate, should have "the art to hide the art," and he found little profit or pleasure, and much pretentiousness, in laboring to expose what they had worked to conceal. A number of his letters show him refusing to be drawn into long disquisitions on color and composition.[147] Dickens' refusal to engage in technical discussion is obviously no proof that he could have if he had wanted to, but it does suggest a reason other than ignorance for his frequent silences.

Dickens' rejection of cantish admiration of painting, and of appreciation according to rules, was accompanied by a distaste for artists who, in his judgment, painted by rule. Again it is his experience in Italy that seems to have developed this dislike—at least it is then that he begins to write that the rules of art are too much slavishly followed; making it a pain to you, when you go into galleries day after day, to be so very precisely sure where this figure will be turning round, and that figure will be lying down, and that other will have a great lot of drapery twined about him, and so forth. This becomes a perfect nightmare.[148]

This dislike of the predictable may be seen as one more result of Dickens' love of the dramatic in art. As a story or play loses its appeal when its action is easily anticipated, so a painting must be poor if one knows beforehand what the position of a figure or the nature of his apparel will be. (We find the same dislike of the predictable in Dickens' reaction to drama and to prose fiction.) In any art form, he enjoyed that which could evoke a fresh and untrammeled emotional response; among his favorite words are *striking*, *brilliancy*, and *interest*. His daughter Kate said he called this quality *force*: "He admired more than any other quality great breadth and force in the conception and treatment of a subject, but looked for a certain delicacy and refinement of finish. . . ."[149] And he rejected anything that tended toward uninspiring formula, such as conventional poses or situations, hackneyed props, and the repeated use of the same models. He made fun of conventional backgrounds in portraits: a piece in *Sketches by Boz* speaks of one in which a figure is represented "with a curtain over his head, six large books in the background, and an open country in the distance. . . ."[150] In a piece for *Household Words* entitled "The Ghost of Art," he made serious fun of the conventional in art, first criticizing such standard props as "a high backed chair with a red cushion, and a table with twisted legs," and (in the words of the model in the piece) "warses of flowers, and any number of table-kivers, and antique cabinets, and warious gammon." He also suggested that Royal Academy artists made "monsters" by joining parts of different models to each other. The Ghost of Art is one such model, who links Dickens' feelings about models and about rules by stating "I revere the Royal Academy. I stand by its forty Academical articles almost as firmly as I stand by the thirty-nine Articles of the Church of England." The model has grown a beard in order to meet the "German taste," and has managed, simply by changing its length or shape, to represent "Society!," "Benevolence," "death!," "Adoration, or a vow of vengeance," and "Romantic character," among others. "The beard did everything." The beard haunts the author of the article "from the walls of the Royal Academy (except when Maclise subdues it with his genius) . . . eternally working the passions in hair."[151] If Dickens never actually suffered from such a protean beard, he certainly did endure the stultifying use by artists of stock casts of models, each all too effortlessly representing a standard character, quality, or emotion. It was not that he objected to models: as some of his correspondence with his own illustrators shows,[152] he realized the value to an artist of a living form. But professional models troubled him: when Mark Lemon suggested that actors serve as models for pictures in his novels, he was horrified.

In a letter to Coutts, Dickens wrote from Rome laughing at Italian artists for using professional models who gathered each day on the Spanish Steps, and lamented that "men should go on copying these people elaborately time after time, and find nothing fresh or suggestive in the actual world about them." To his friend Cound Alfred D'Orsay he wrote a longer version of the same experience, claiming that "it is a good illustration of the Student system that young men should go on, batch after batch, reproducing these people: and finding nothing fresh or stirring in the active real world about them."[153] So impassioned was he about the subject that he wrote it out a third time in *Pictures from Italy*,[154] and repeated it in 1856 in his article "Insularities," in which he connects his distaste for models with his ruling passion, the use of art for dramatic purposes. The reason for getting rid of all models, he says, is to "reduce our men of genius, who paint pictures, to the shameful necessity of wresting their great art to the telling of stories and conveying of ideas. . . ."[155] In another article, "His Brown Paper Parcel," he even poked fun at the need for artists to *look* like artists.[156]

Despite his admiration for painters like Frith, Dickens at his best repudiated the art of setting and costume, and looked for the evocation of emotion in the viewer by a fresh perception of the actions, passions, and suffering of men and women. To confine onself to no more than this in art is to miss much, and Dickens did. But his concentration upon the dramatic in painting was not— as most have assumed—owing to a mere taste for the theatrical: it was the consequence of his belief that art should penetrate to an inner truth as seen by the artist.

It has been thought that by *truth* Dickens meant little more than fidelity to nature. Certainly this is part of what he did mean in certain moods or in relation to certain kinds of art—though even then the possibility exists of his meaning something more. In portraiture, for example, Dickens has been held to be exclusively concerned with the accurate, photograph-like reproduction of the subject's face: Count D'Orsay's sketch of Daniel Maclise is "excellent" because "I should have recognized it instantly, though I had seen it pasted on the wooden leg of a Greenwich Pensioner or in any other equally unexpected place."[157] But even in portraiture Dickens seems at times uncomfortable with the mere "likeness" of a face, as though a painter could do no more than a camera. A series of comments upon Ary Scheffer's portrait of him shows Dickens uneasily attempting to reconcile his respect for the painter with his feeling that the picture was not successful. The first of his reactions, written to Forster, sets the pattern:

> Scheffer finished yesterday, and [Wilkie] Collins, who has a good eye for pictures, says that there is no man living who could do the painting about the eyes. As a work of art I see in it spirit combined with perfect ease, and yet I don't see myself. So I come to the conclusion that I never *do* see myself.[158]

In another comment on the portrait, Dickens said that Scheffer "is a great painter, and of course it has great merit," but added "I doubt if I should know it, myself . . . ," and concluded "it is always possible that I may know other people's faces pretty well, without knowing my own."[159] And still again, to Forster, he wrote, "It is a fine spirited head, painted at his very best, and with a very easy and natural appearance in it. But it does not look to me at all like, nor does it strike me that if I saw it in a gallery I should suppose myself to be the original."[160]

When Scheffer later confessed to Dickens that *he* was not satisfied with the portrait, Dickens crowed in relief to Forster, "My own impression of it, you remember?"[161] Still, a feeling that the failure was somehow not Scheffer's but his own seems to have persisted: five years later, writing to a photographer who had experienced difficulty in getting a good picture of him, Dickens said

> I feel I owe you an apology for being (innocently) a difficult subject. When I once excused myself to Ary Scheffer while sitting to him, he received the apology as strictly his due, and said with a vexed air: "at the moment, *mon cher* Dickens, you look more like a Dutch admiral than anything else;" for which I apologized again.[162]

Kate agreed that her father "was exceedingly difficult to represent adequately upon canvas . . . for the features which in repose looked at times so grave and preoccupied completely changed in expression when he was interested or aroused. . . ."[163] The Dickens of one mood, that is, might change in mid-painting to become the Dickens of another, leaving the painter in doubt which he was to attempt to catch. If this fact occurred to Dickens as it did to his daughter, it must also have occurred to him that portraiture was not simply capturing a likeness—for a face might have more than one likeness to catch—but of representing something in the subject that was deeper than the moment's mood.

There is no letter in which Dickens expresses such a thought, but there are several which suggest he may have had it. His final comment upon the

Scheffer portrait, written to his wife, admitted "that nobody could mistake whom it was meant for," but still objected "that it has something disappointing in it. . . ."[164] The painting, he was at last ready to concede, did look like him, yet there was something missing. Simple likeness, it seemed, was not enough.

Even in portraiture, then, where all have agreed that Dickens was concerned only with a recognizable representation of the subject, it is possible that he may have looked for something more, a something which in other kinds of painting I believe he called *truth*. There is another comment on a portrait which conveys a similar sense. Writing to Lewis Gaylord Clark about a picture of him which he had seen in *Knickerbocker* (No. XXIV, facing page one), Dickens started with his usual criterion—"I think [it] . . . might be more like"—but then tried to say what was wrong with it, only to end by confessing that it was a good likeness: "It looks to me the likeness of a testy, contradictory fellow—which I am sure you are not. It is still like the original, too, which is an aggravating kind of merit."[165] It is aggravating, obviously, because it meets what Dickens thought of as a sufficient standard for portraiture, yet does not produce a good portrait: something is missing.[166]

Perhaps we cannot know what the "something" was that Dickens missed in such paintings; if he himself ever knew, he never expressed it in writing. But some things his daughter tells us about him help us to take an informed guess. First, she says that her father "was naturally an excellent judge of a portrait," though "generally very modest in expressing an opinion." We may be grateful that she was not equally modest, and in view of her own ability as portrait painter lend some credence to the opinion she offers, while noting Dickens' modesty as a further possible restraint upon his commentary on art. But if Dickens was an excellent or even a merely good judge of portraiture, why did he have trouble deciding what he did not like about some portraits? Kate provides a possible answer, though she is talking about all painting, not just portraits. Dickens did not like some paintings, she says, because of the "excessive realism of his mental vision": "he always *saw* what he had read or heard about . . . thus the picture in his own mind of any subject which attracted him was often so vivid as to preclude the possibility of its being conceived in any other way. . . ."[167] "Realism of mental vision" exactly describes the overriding concern Dickens had for his illustrations—that they should be not merely good drawings, but should convey precisely "what I meant."

But how may this mental vision apply to portraits, in which the faces are real, not imagined? The answer, I believe, is that Dickens "saw" in human faces much more than surface likeness; like a true Wordsworthian, he half-perceived and half-created, and it was the "excessive realism" of his creative "mental vision" that missed something in the portraits of Clark and of himself, despite their accurate rendering of mere faces. The object of his mental vision could be called the soul or inner nature of the subject, the something that passeth show, that makes the character what he or she is in any mood or expression—that which we all know to be within ourselves that the physical cannot convey. Again, Dickens' word for this in faces or in anything he saw was, I believe, *truth*, and it was this that he thought art should try to capture.

Granted, he did not always use the word with such deep meaning; often he simply meant fidelity to nature, as in his comment upon the "rubbish" he found in the Vatican:

> I unreservedly confess, for myself, that I cannot leave my natural perception of what is natural and true, at a palace door, in Italy or elsewhere, as I should leave my shoes if I were travelling in the East. I cannot forget that there are certain expressions of face, natural to certain passions, and as unchangeable in their nature as the gait of a lion, or the flight of an eagle. I cannot dismiss from my certain knowledge, such commonplace facts as the ordinary proportion of man's arms, and legs, and heads; and when I meet with performances that do violence to these experiences and recollections, no matter where they may be, I cannot honestly admire them, and think it best to say so.[168]

Here *truth* and *nature* are identical, but elsewhere a certain distinction is to be found. Kate remarks that

> he was intuitively an excellent judge of a portrait, remembering with distinctiveness any face he may have seen for however short a time, and although always insisting on the slightest peculiarity of individual character or on the little difference in symmetry of features which sometimes occur and upon which so much of the expression of a head depends, he was quick to note the smallest exaggeration into which the artist might have been tempted to fall in order to enforce the likeness.[169]

This suggests that likeness was not enough for Dickens, at least not a likeness that depended upon such tricks as exaggeration. The true artist must capture not only the "symmetry of features" but "the slightest peculiarity of individual character."

It seems possible that truth in portraiture and in painting in general was for Dickens comparable to what he strove for in the illustrations of his fictional characters: he looked in pictures for what he saw in his mind's eye, and it did not matter whether there was a real or an imagined face to begin with. Dickens was not so much concerned with what was there as with what he saw. Perhaps he felt portraiture to have the same magical power over real people that he felt it did over his fictional characters. When W. P. Frith asked him about a portrait of him begun some time ago, Dickens answered, "well, the truth is, I sat for it a great many times. At first the picture bore a striking resemblance to Ben Carent, then it changed into somebody else, and at last I thought it was time to give it up. I had sat there and looked at the thing till I felt I was growing like it."[170] Dickens' insistence upon "truth" in portraiture may have been something more than a mere liking of likeness, may even have been more than a search for the truth of the inner eye; it may have been akin to the savage's refusal to have his picture taken.

In any case, there is no doubt that in other kinds of painting he looked, as Jane R. Cohen puts it, for "the kind of truth that elevated a subject and its associations."[171] This almost Emersonian desire to thrust through the appearance of an object to some higher meaning he found within it provides a far better explanation than is given by Angus Wilson of why Dickens, the lover of verisimilitude, could attack the Pre-Raphaelite painters, especially Millais, as fiercely as he did. Assuming that Dickens uniformly insisted upon surface reality in painting, Wilson finds it "surprising" that Dickens objected to "everyday models in sacred subjects," and quotes from a Dickens letter:

> You know all the Pictures and Statues I have seen—and how many of them are really good, and how many really bad. I am guilty of all sorts of heresies in these respects; and when I see a Jolly Young Waterman representing a cherubim, or a Barclay and Perkins's Drayman depicted as an Evangelist, am obliged to confess that it is not exactly my idea of either character. Neither am I partial to angels who play on Genuine Cremonas and brazen bassoons, for the edification of sprawling monks apparently in liquor—nor to Josephs surveying Nativities, from shiny backgrounds, in a state of considerable mystification—nor to Saint Sebastians, of whom I wouldn't have a specimen on any terms, notwithstanding the extreme rarity of the subject. All this kind of High Art is out of my reach, I acknowledge. Not the less so, because I have the purest and most enduring delight in those achievements of the pencil which are truly great and grand, and worthy of their theme.[172]

But Dickens' distaste for models is not limited to religious subjects, as Wilson suggests; his assumption that Dickens would like them anywhere else shows he does not fully understand Dickens' idea of reality in art—the idea that reality, slavishly copied, destroys creativity. Wilson concludes that it is Dickens' insistence upon the "elevated" in art that made him frown on commonplace models in religious paintings and that set him against the

Pre-Raphaelites. But it is Dickens' belief that *all* painting, of whatever subject, should seek to elevate its material, that caused him to object to such a painting as Millais's *The Carpenter*. Dickens was indeed a devout Christian, but his objection to Millais's painting is not on sacred grounds—at least not on those grounds alone. He disliked *any* painting that did not attempt to move through surface realism to a deeper truth—the truth, I believe, that he missed in the accurate portraits which he criticized. As Dolores Lehr points out, "Dickens had long complained of the absence of idealized beauty in pictures";[173] it is the absence of this beauty, and the ugliness substituted for it, that he complains of in his review of *The Carpenter* in *Household Words*. First, in a passage that compensates for any slight he gave to Raphael in his Italian letters, Dickens offers that painter as the originator of beauty in painting (since the article is satirical, his admiration is couched in the negative):

> Raphael . . . [was a painter] with a ridiculous power of etherealizing, and exalting to the very Heavens, what was most sublime and lovely in the expression of the human face divine on Earth—with the truly contemptible conceit of finding in poor humanity the fallen likeness of the angels of God, and raising it up again to their pure spiritual condition. This very fantastic whim effected a low revolution in Art, in this wise, that Beauty came to be regarded as one of its indispensable elements. In this very poor delusion, Artists have continued until this present nineteenth century, when it was reserved for some bold aspirants to 'put it down.'

The "bold aspirants" are, of course, the Pre-Raphaelites, whom Dickens attacks in a long description of *The Carpenter*:

> You behold the interior of a carpenter's shop. In the foreground of that carpenter's shop is a hideous, wry-necked, blubbering, red-headed boy, in a bed-gown; who appears to have received a poke in the hand, from the stick of another boy with whom he has been playing in an adjacent gutter, and to be holding it for the contemplation of a kneeling woman, so horrible in her ugliness, that (supposing it were possible for any human creature to exist for a moment with that dislocated throat) she would stand out from the rest of the company a monster, in the vilest cabaret in France, or the lowest gin-shop in England. Two almost naked carpenters, master and journeyman, worthy companions of this agreeable female, are working at their trade; a boy, with some small flavor of humanity in him, is entering with a vessel of water; and nobody is paying any attention to a snuffy old woman who seems to have mistaken that shop for the tobacconists's next door, and to be hopelessly waiting at the counter to be served with half an ounce of her favourite mixture. Wherever it is possible to express ugliness of feature, limb, or attitude, you have it expressed. Such men as the carpenters might be undressed in any hospital where dirty drunkards, in

a high state of varicose veins, are received. Their very toes have walked out of St. Giles's.[174]

This is probably one of the passages Humphrey House had in mind when he said that Dickens "recoiled in almost neurotic horror from all the most vigorous and original work that aimed to bring colour and form back into art and religion"; in the same paragraph, House specifically mentions the Pre-Raphaelites as "targets for his scorn."[175] At the least, this is overstated. In "Old Lamps for New," Dickens does recoil, but it is aesthetic principle rather than neurosis that makes him do so. And it is not the originality of the painting to which he objects, but, as his title indicates, his belief that the Pre-Raphaelites have taken art backward to mere reality instead of forward to greater inner beauty. Dickens, if he had a neurotic horror, had it of the past; his objection to Millais and his school was that he thought, along with most of the people of his time, that they intended to abandon all of the advantages of modern art and return painting to the qualities it had before Raphael. For Dickens and for many others the greatest virtue of Raphael and those who followed him was that they attempted, as Ruskin put it, "to paint fair pictures"[176]—that is, to elevate their subject above the realistic level into a higher beauty. It is the refusal of Millais to do this that Dickens finds most objectionable in his review—just as the *Times* reviewer, who found the painting "disgusting" and "revolting," did. But in another article upon the Pre-Raphaelites in 1851, the *Times* also argued that they lacked "truth" in their work, speaking of their "strange disorder of the mind or the eyes," and arguing that they had "an absolute contempt for perspective and the known laws of light and shade. . . ."[177] Except for the woman with the "dislocated throat" and one other brief comment later in his article, Dickens does not attack Millais on this ground—a ground which Ruskin refuted in his letter to the *Times*. Dickens is not interested in fidelity but in what he considers another kind of truth: the "fair picture" of the carpenter's shop as a holy place (or, to put it less devoutly but no less accurately, the representation of the carpenter's shop which would enable the viewer to see it with the inner eye). And just as we have seen in some of his animadversions on Italian art, he feels that the painting has failed to capture that fair picture because it has held too closely to a low (one could almost say a distorting) reality—has made its figures as real as those in a French cabaret, an English gin-shop, a London hospital, or St. Giles's. For the *Times* "truth" may consist of perspective and light and shade, of fidelity to nature, but for Dickens it seems to require something more.

Ruskin's letter presents the Pre-Raphaelites in terms that, were Dickens the mere advocate of superficial verisimilitude he is often thought of as being, would have made them most congenial to him. Ruskin says that Millais and his colleagues "draw either what they see, or what they suppose might have been the actual facts of the scene they desire to represent. . . ." They intend, he says, not to return to "archaic *art*" but to "archaic *honesty*," which may rescue art from the "acknowledged decadence"[179] it has been in ever since Raphael. If Dickens' "truth" is mere external realism, how much all this ought to have made him admire the Pre-Raphaelite School. But clearly his definition of truth extends beyond such a conception to a higher, inner truth which he thought Millais missed. His response to Millais may have been, as it has been called, "unfortunate,"[180] but it is consistent with the most fundamental principle of his art.

But Dickens was by no means an inveterate enemy of the Pre-Raphaelite painters. As Edgar Johnson has pointed out, he "later became an admiring friend of Millais and of Holman Hunt."[181] Johnson could have added that Millais used Kate Perugini as a model for his *The Black Brunswicker*; indeed, he became a close friend of Mr. and Mrs. Perugini—a "dear fellow" to them. In her article on her father and art, Kate speaks of his judgment on *The Carpenter's Shop* as "a criticism that I have reason to believe he regretted having published in later years."[182] Does this mean Dickens came to accept the Pre-Raphaelite principles? Kate does not say, but I think it more likely that it was the publication rather than the criticism that Dickens came to regret; once again he probably found friendship more important than criticism, and wished that he had held his tongue. In any case, the friendship between Dickens and Millais seems to have survived the criticism. It was Millais, apparently, who recommended Luke Fildes to Dickens as an illustrator for *The Mystery of Edwin Drood*.[183] By that time, it should be noted, Millais had abandoned his Pre-Raphaelite work, and had turned to more conventional painting.

We have seen two *truths* in Dickens, one consisting of fidelity to nature and one of commitment to the inner eye. And we have noted Dickens' conviction that art best conveys the inner vision when it works to find beauty in the passions and suffering of men and women. But were these things all that art ever meant to the great novelist—nothing more than a kind of ur-photography and a showing forth of truth through beauty and dramatic passion? If so, he remains far from the least of the great men of his time in terms of response to art. But there remains one more Dickensian reflection on art, to my knowledge not examined by anyone who has judged his aesthetic, which may demonstrate a wider vision. The reflection comes in a piece written twelve years after the letter he wrote from Italy in which he refused to "leave my natural perception of what is natural and true, at a Palace door, as I should leave my shoes if I were travelling in the East." Now, writing of his wandering through the rooms of Hampton Palace in England, he substitutes for the shoes an umbrella which he had been asked to leave at the door, and speculates upon what else the art would require him to abandon, too:

> Form, colour, size, proportion, distance, individuality, the true perception of every object on the face of the earth or the face of the Heavens. . . . And now I find the moon to be really made of green cheese; the sun to be a yellow wafer or a little round blister; the deep wild sea to be a shallow series of slate-coloured festoons turned upside down; the human face Divine to be a smear; the whole material and immaterial universe to be sticky with treacle and polished up with blacking. Conceive what I must be, through all the rest of my life, if the policeman should make off with my umbrella and never restore it!
>
> Of all the Powers that get your umbrella from you, Taste is the most encroaching and insatiate. Please to put into your umbrella, to be deposited in the hall until you come out again, all your powers of comparison, all your experience, all your individual opinions. Please to accept with this ticket for your umbrella the individual opinions of some other personage whose name is Somebody, or Nobody, or Anybody, and to swallow the same without a word of demur. Be so good as to leave your eyes with your umbrellas, gentlemen, and to deliver up your private judgment with your walking-sticks. Apply this ointment, compounded by the learned dervish, and you shall see no end of camels going with the greatest ease through needles' eyes. Leave your umbrella-full of property which is not by any means to be poked at this collection, with the police, and you shall acknowledge, whether you will or no, this hideous porcelain-ware to be beautiful, these wearisomely stiff and unimaginative forms to be graceful, these coarse daubs to be masterpieces. Leave your umbrella and take up your gentility. Taste proclaims to you what is the genteel thing; receive it and be genteel![184]

There are no "tremendous strides" of development in these paragraphs; here is the same insistence upon independent judgment, the same disgust with conventional tastes, the same demand that art conform to nature that he voiced twelve years earlier. That a painter might deviate from reality for some good purpose—to shock, to force a new way of seeing, to make clear how the artist saw—does not seem to have occurred to this Dickens. But an earlier paragraph in the article sounds quite a different note. After looking at the paintings he wanders outside to the gardens, only to see them "with court-suits on." Adopting the style of *A Sentimental Journey*, he says,

> I wonder, Yorick, whether, with this little reason in my bosom, I should ever want to get out of these same interminable suites of rooms, and return to noise

and bustle! It seems to me that I could stay here very well until the grisly phantom on the pale horse came at a gallop up the staircase, seeking me. My little reason should make of these queer dingy closet-rooms, these little corner chimney-pieces tier above tier, this old blue china of squat shapes, these dreary old state bedsteads with attenuated posts, nay dear Yorick, . . . should make, even of these very works of art, an encompassing universe of beauty and happiness. The fountain in the staid red and white courtyard without . . . would never fall too monotonously on my ear, the four chilled sparrows now fluttering on the brink of its basin would never chirp a wish for change of weather; no bargeman on the rain-speckled river, no wayfarer rain-belated under the leafless trees in the park would ever come into my fancy as examining in despair those swollen clouds, and vainly peering for a ray of sunshine. I and my little reason, Yorick, would keep house here, all our lives, in perfect contentment; and when we died, our ghosts should make of this dull Palace the first building ever haunted happily![185]

Though Dickens probably expects his reader to deprecate to some extent the happiness he and Yorick would experience were they confined forever within Hampton Palace, there is also a distinct sense of the genuine pleasure such imprisonment would give. There is a definite impression of the lure of the unreal—even the unnatural—art-world, of the attractions that make it in some ways superior to those of nature which the later paragraphs insist it should copy. For a moment, at least, he seems to have left behind his insistence upon the superiority of the natural world.

Not long before, Dickens had written another piece for *Household Words* in which he also expressed his sense of the contrast between art and life. Coming out of an exhibition of paintings, he said, "I was much impressed by the contrast between the polite bearing of the Fine Arts, and the rudeness of real life." Inside he was an important person, recognized, deferred to, assisted; outside he was a matter of complete indifference to those around him. The outside had a

barbarous tendency to reality, to change and movement, and to the knowledge of the Present as a something of interest sprung out of the Past and melting into the Future . . . insomuch that the passing from the inside of the gallery to the outside was like the transition from Madame Tussaud's waxwork, or a tawdry fancy ball in the Sleeping Beauty's palace during the hundred years of enchantment, to a windy mountain or the rolling sea. I understand now, what I had never understood before, why there were two sentries at the exhibition door. These are . . . allegorical personages, stationed there . . . to keep out Purpose, and to mount guard over the lassitude of the Fine Arts, laid up in the lavender of other ages.[186]

Again the weight of the passage is on the side of reality over art, yet there is something of fascination, of attraction, in the gallery. Overtly the comparisons all reflect the writer's preference for the outside, however barbarous; still, the inside has its "enchantment"—no doubt with its original meaning of being entrapped, but also carrying something of the modern meaning of delight—and the "lassitude" and "lavender" are not entirely objectionable. We have seen in his criticism of Cruikshank's *Hop-o'-my-Thumb* Dickens' love of the fairy tale; his reference here to the palace of the Sleeping Beauty cannot be perfectly pejorative. And though the passage clearly prefers nature to Madame Tussaud's waxwork, we cannot forget that in his own life Dickens was far more attracted to a good show of any kind than he was to the greatest beauties a country setting had to offer. In these two passages art is neither tied to nature nor required to transcend it; its value rests entirely within itself.

VI

In 1855, in his comments upon the Paris Exhibition and in related reflections on English art, Dickens demonstrated his ability to speak perceptively about painting. It is significant that his criticism here is directed against that same English art which in earlier years had been a part of his own training, and that several of the English artists he criticizes are those whom he had admired before. English art "seemed to him small, shrunken, insignificant, 'niggling,'" Forster tells us. "He thought the general absence of ideas horribly apparent." "And even when one comes to Mulready," Dickens wrote,

and sees two old men talking over a much-too-prominent table-cloth, and reads the French explanation of their proceedings, "La discussion sur les principes de Docteur Whiston," one is dissatisfied. Somehow or other they don't tell. Even Leslie's Sancho wants go, and Stanny is too much like a set scene. It is of no use disguising the fact that what we know to be wanting in the men is wanting in their works—character, fire, purpose, and the power of using the vehicle and the model as mere means to an end. There is a horrid respectability about most of the best of them—a little, finite, systematic routine in them, strangely expressive to me of the state of England itself. . . . There are no end of bad pictures among the French, but Lord! the goodness also!—the fearlessness of them; the bold drawing; the dashing conception; the passion and action in them! The Belgian department is full of merit. It has the best landscape in it, the best portrait, and the best scene of homely life, to be found in the building. Don't think it a part of my despondency about public affairs, and my fear that our national glory is on the decline, when I say that mere form and conventionalities usurp, in English art, as in English government and social relations, the place of living force and truth.

Forster summarizes Dickens' conversation with English artists about the French:

> French nature is all wrong, said the English artists whom Dickens talked to; but surely not because it is French, was his reply. The English point of view is not the only one to take men and women from. The French pictures are "theatrical" was the rejoinder. But the French themselves are a demonstrative and gesticulating people, was Dickens's retort; and what thus is rendered by their artists is the truth through an immense part of the world.[187]

It was in the year after the Paris Exhibition that Dickens wrote the article entitled "Insularities," in which he more fully described the way in which English narrowness inhibited the English perception of art:

> One of our most remarkable Insularities is a tendency to be firmly persuaded that what is not English is not natural. In the Fine Arts department of the French Exhibition, recently closed, we repeatedly hear, even from the more educated and reflective of our countrymen, that certain pictures which appeared to possess great merit—of which not the lowest item was, that they possessed the merit of a vigorous and bold Idea—were all very well, but were "theatrical." Conceiving the difference between a dramatic picture and a theatrical picture, to be, that in the former case a story is strikingly told, without apparent consciousness of a spectator, and that in the latter case the groups are obtrusively conscious of a spectator, and are obviously dressed up, and doing (or not doing) certain things with an eye to the spectator, and not for the sake of the story, we sought in vain for this defect. Taking further pains then, to find out what was meant by the term theatrical, we found that the actions and gestures of the figures were not English. That is to say,—the figures expressing themselves in the vivacious manner natural in a greater or less degree to the whole great continent of Europe, were overcharged and out of the truth, because they did not express themselves in the manner of our little Island—which is so very exceptional, that it always places an Englishman at a disadvantage, out of his own country, until his fine sterling qualities shine through his external formality and constraint. Surely nothing can be more unreasonable, say, than that we should require a Frenchman of the days of Robespierre, to be taken out of his jail to the guillotine with the calmness of Clapham or the respectability of Richmond Hill, after a trial at the Central Criminal Court in eighteen hundred and fifty-six. And yet this exactly illustrates the requirement of the particular insularity under consideration.[188]

Perhaps the public reaction to his criticism in *Pictures from Italy* deterred Dickens from more private and published criticism of art in his later years. Perhaps his own illustrators escaped criticism on the principle that, as he wrote to Forster, "friendship is better than criticism, and I shall steadily hold my tongue."[189]

But as we have seen, in his lifetime he said more than a little. If he was not a skilled student of the discipline, he was by no means ordinary. Though he admitted that he had no training in the fundamentals of art, he was too modest to add that through active and intelligent observation, and through extended and close work with some of the best artists of his time and place, he had learned a great deal and had come to hold definite ideas about painting. He believed that it should be useful, and that the best way for it to convey a moral to its viewer was to offer a dramatic situation, presented in as lifelike a manner as possible. If his comments show relatively little skill in judging form and color, they also record his awareness of the importance of such things, and suggest that he might have spoken more astutely about them if he had not desired so doggedly to avoid the appearance of speaking cant. But he said enough to show how much he valued that art which moved the viewer—which was striking, which evoked powerful emotion, which elevated the subject by seeing in it something more than its outward appearance. By 1855, his judgment had sharpened to the point that he was capable of repudiating the lifeless art of his own English friends in favor of the depth and vigor of European painting. As his father said of him, he had indeed "educated himself," and had acquired an understanding of the visual arts which not only distinguished him from his formally educated contemporaries but contributed to the practice of his own art as well.

Key To Abbreviations

Sources cited more than once are identified by the following abbreviations.

AN—*American Notes for General Circulation*. John S. Whitley and Arnold Goldman, eds. Baltimore: Penguin Books, 1972.

AYR—*All the Year Round*. Edited by Charles Dickens.

BC—*Letters of Charles Dickens to the Baroness Burdett-Coutts*. Charles C. Osborne, ed. London: John Murray, 1931.

CJ—Cohen, Jane R. *Charles Dickens and His Original Illustrators*. Columbus: Ohio State University Press, 1980.

CP—*Collected Papers*. Arthur Waugh, Hugh Walpole, Walter Dexter, and Thomas Hatton, eds. 2 vols. Bloomsbury [London]: Nonesuch Press, 1932.

DG—Dolby, George. *Charles Dickens as I Knew Him*. 1885. Rpr. London: Everett & Company, 1912.

F—Forster, John. *The Life of Charles Dickens*. Intro. by G. K. Chesterton. 2 vols.

London: J. M. Dent; New York: E. P. Dutton, 1927. The work is divided into twelve books; citations here give book, chapter, and page numbers.

HCD—Johnson, Edgar. *The Heart of Charles Dickens*. Boston: Little, Brown and Company, 1952.

HH—House, Humphrey. *The Dickens World*. London: Oxford University Press, 1941.

HW—*Household Words*. Edited by Charles Dickens.

JE—Johnson, Edgar. *Charles Dickens: His Tragedy and Triumph*. 2 vols. New York: Simon and Schuster, 1952.

LC—*Letters of Charles Dickens*. Edited by Georgiana Hogarth and Mary Dickens. 2 vols. 1879.

LD—*The Letters of Charles Dickens*. Pilgrim Edition. Oxford: Clarendon Press. 5 vols. Vol. I, Madeline House and Graham Storey, eds., 1965. Vol. II, Madeline House and Graham Storey, eds., 1969. Vol. III, Madeline House, Graham Storey, and Kathleen Tillotson, eds., 1974. Vol. IV, Kathleen Tillotson, ed., 1977. Vol. V, Graham Storey and K. J. Fielding, eds., 1981.

LE—Lehr, Dolores. *Charles Dickens and the Arts*. Unpublished doctoral dissertation. Temple University, 1979. University Microfilm Reprints, Ann Arbor, Mich., 1979.

MR—*Mr. and Mrs. Charles Dickens: His Letters to Her*. Walter Dexter, ed. London: Constable & Co. Ltd., 1935.

NL—*Nonesuch Letters. The Collected Papers of Charles Dickens*. Arthur Waugh, ed. 2 vols. Bloomsbury [London]: Nonesuch Press, 1937.

PI—*Pictures from Italy. Pictures from Italy and American Notes*, in *The Complete Works of Charles Dickens*. Vol. II. New York: Harper, n.d.

PK—Perugini, Kate. "Charles Dickens as a Lover of Art and Artists," *Magazine of Art* XXVII (1/1903), 125–130; (2/1903), 164–169.

S—Storey, Gladys. *Dickens and Daughter*. London: Frederick Muller, 1939.

SB—*Sketches by Boz. The Works of Charles Dickens*. Introduction, Critical Comments, and Notes by Andrew Lang, Charles Dickens the Younger, John Forster, Adolphus Wm. Ward, and others. New York: P. F. Collier, 1911.

SD—*Speeches of Charles Dickens*. K. J. Fielding, ed. Oxford: Clarendon Press, 1960.

UT—*The Uncommercial Traveller*, in *The Uncommercial Traveller and Reprinted Pieces, Etc.* London: Oxford University Press, 1964.

WA—Wilson, Angus. *The World of Charles Dickens*. New York: The Viking Press, 1970.

NOTES

The reader should remember that, unless otherwise noted, all dates are in the nineteenth century.

1. See, *e.g.*: JE, I:561–562; WA, p. 94; HH, p. 129; F, IV:vi,348; CJ, p. 7; Tillotson, LD, IV:xi; LE, p. 74.
2. JE, I:561; PK, 129.

3. PI, 98.
4. SD, 421 (4/30/70).
5. PK, 164.
6. CJ, p. 38.
7. If we add names mentioned in *Pictures from Italy* and elsewhere, we find a total of nearly seventy artists mentioned, including Titian, Tintoretto, Raphael, Marco-Antonio Raimondi, Rubens, Rembrandt, Van Dyke, Guido, Domenichino, Carlo Dolci, Correggio, Murillo, Paul Veronese, Salvator Rosa, Adriaen Van Ostade, the Carraccis, Spagnoletto, Guilio Romano, William Etty, Sir Charles Eastlake, Francis Danby (or perhaps one of his sons, James or Thomas), Thomas Creswick, William Lee, John Rogers Herbert, William Dyce, Charles West Cope, and the Chalon brothers.
8. F, VII:v,159.
9. PK, 125. Dickens did, of course, include artists in minor roles in his novels: Henry Gowan in *Little Dorrit* is an artist of sorts, as is Miss La Creevy in *Nicholas Nickleby*; and there are artists in his minor writings, *e.g.* the sidewalk artist in "His Brown Paper Parcel."
10. LC, II:335 (4/18/67).
11. LD, V:556 (6/21/49).
12. LD, V:458 (12/16/48).
13. F, VII:iii,172.
14. *The Diaries of William Charles Macready*, William Toynbee, ed. 2 vols. (New York and London: Benjamin Blom, 1969). First pub. 1912. II:336.
15. PK, 130. For evidence supporting this, see LD, V:375 (7/23/48); 480 (1/27/49).
16. LC, II:161–162 (1/19/61).
17. "New Year's Day," HW (1/1/59), in CP, I:712.
18. See, *e.g.*, J. Hillis Miller, "The Fiction of Realism: *Sketches by Boz, Oliver Twist*, and George Cruikshank's Illustrations," *Dickens Centennial Essays*, Ada Nesbet and Blake Nevius, eds. (Berkeley: University of California Press, 1971), p. 127.
19. See, *e.g.*, CJ, p. 3: "Dickens's books reveal his exposure and his debt to prints, particularly to those of Hogarth."
20. See for example LD, III:90–91 (2/25/42); LC, I:248 (1/3/50); LD, IV:351 (8/10/45).
21. LD, V:442 (11/19/48); 207 (12/10/47).
22. LC, II:111 (6/11/59).
23. F, II:xii,164. The Chalon brothers were popular for their watercolors, which they often exhibited at the Royal Academy; Alfred was also a fashionable painter of ladies' portraits.
24. LD, II:201 (1/31/41).
25. "A Detective Police Party," HW (7/27/50) I:409.
26. PI, 25.
27. PI, 18–19.
28. "Banvard's Geographical Panorama of the Mississippi and Missouri Rivers," *Examiner* (12/16/48), in CP, I:182.
29. LD, IV:159 (7/22/44).

30. LC, II:436 (3/21/68).
31. LD, II:395 (9/28/41).
32. "Macready as Benedick," *Examiner* (3/4/43), in CP, I:145.
33. S, p. 116.
34. PI, 98.
35. See note 28, above.
36. BC, 117 (11/19/52).
37. PI, 19.
38. PI, 96.
39. PI, 99.
40. *Douglas Jerrold's Shilling Magazine* (8/45), in CP, I:37.
41. LD, IV:141 (6?/44).
42. LD, III:608 (12/14/43).
43. CJ, p. 143.
44. PI, 44.
45. PI, 139.
46. LD IV:220 (11/17–18/44).
47. *Ibid.*
48. "The Rising Generation," *Examiner* (12/30/48), in CP, I:190.
49. PI, 152.
50. *Ibid.*
51. HCD, 210 (10/30/52).
52. LC, II:171 (7/8/61).
53. LD, III:299 (7/31/42).
54. LD, I:378 (2/22/38).
55. LD, V:468 (1/3/49).
56. AYR (7/24/69), in CP, II:48.
57. CJ, p. 94.
58. LD, III:543n (8/15–18?/43).
59. LD, IV:141 (6?/44).
60. LD, II:378 (9/12/41).
61. LD, II:361 (8/19/41).
62. "Insularities," HW (1/19/56), 626.
63. LD, IV:679 (12/12/46).
64. LD, IV:700.
65. Except perhaps Monroe Engel; see "Dickens on Art," *Modern Philology*, 53 (1955), 25–38.
66. CJ, p. 4.
67. *The Complete Letters of Vincent Van Gogh* (Greenwich, Conn.: New York Graphic Society, 1958; rpr. 1978) 3:374; from letter to Rappard (3/83), p. 5.
68. CJ, p. 5; quoted from Forster, *Life of Dickens*, J. W. T. Ley, ed. (London: Cecil Palmer, 1928), 720.
69. LD, IV:586 (7/18/46). Sir A———E——— has not been identified. Forster says that the man was not used as a model for Dombey, and Kathleen Tillotson suggests that the man was probably only a physical, not a character, study for Dombey.

70. LD, IV:596 (8/2/46).
71. F, VI:ii,471.
72. LD, IV:671 (11–12/46).
73. LD, II:199 (1/30/41).
74. LD, III:397 (12/20/42).
75. LD, III:373n4.
76. See, *e.g.*, LD, II:38 (3/6 or 7/40).
77. LD, I:450–451 (11/9/38). A letter from Forster to Bentley supporting Dickens' opinion of the offending plate is quoted in part in LD (I:451n).
78. CJ, p. 96.
79. LD, III:140 (6?/44).
80. LD, II:115 (8/13/40).
81. LD, I:333 (11?/37).
82. LD, I:450–451 (7/19/38). The piece was "Automaton Police Office, and Real Offenders. From the Model Exhibition before Section B. of the Mud Fog Association," *Miscellany*, IV (1838), facing p. 209.
83. LD, I:559 (7/3/39).
84. LD, II:275 (4/29/41).
85. LD, II:276 (5/2/41); III:601 (11/21/43). The Pilgrim Edition *Letters* speculates that Dickens liked the pieces in the almanac, but not Cruikshank's pictures.
86. LD, V:156 (9/2/47).
87. F, VI:iii,40.
88. *Ibid.*
89. *Ibid.*
90. *Examiner* (7/8/48), in CP, I:157.
91. *Dickens and the Invisible World* (Bloomington and London: Indiana University Press, 1979), p. 11.
92. LC, I:359 (7/27/53).
93. "Frauds on the Fairies," HW (10/1/53) VIII:97.
94. SD, 136 (1/27/52).
95. *Examiner* (12/30/48), in CP, I:190–193. A part of the review is given by Forster (VI:iii,43–45), but he alters phrasing in several places.
96. LD, III:417 (12/31/42).
97. LD, III:453 (3/2/43).
98. CJ, p. 159.
99. LD, III:409 (12/22/42).
100. LD, III:549 (9/1/43).
101. PK, 129.
102. LD, III:94 (2/27/42); 156n.
103. LD, I:558 (6/28/39). *Hamlet* is Maclise's painting.
104. LD, III:299 (7/31/42).
105. LD, III:383 (11/26/42).
106. LD, IV:535 (4/17/46).
107. *Contributions to the Morning Chronicle*, Gordon N. Ray, ed., pp. 145–146. Quoted in LD, IV:535n.

108. LD, I:558 (6/28/39); *George Eliot's Life*, J. W. Cross, ed. (1885), iii, 145; *Frazer's Magazine*, XXII (1840), 113; quoted in LD, I:558n.
109. LD, II:157 (11/25/40).
110. LD, IV:168–169 and note. (8/7/44).
111. *Douglas Jerrold's Shilling Magazine* (8/45), in CP, I:34–39.
112. LD, III:550 (9/1/43).
113. LD, IV:304 (5/9/45).
114. PK, 129.
115. LD, III:418 (1842?); III:415 (12/31/42); III:483 (5/5/43); IV:184 (8/24/44); IV:217 (11/12/44).
116. SD, p. 164 (speech at the Royal Academy Banquet [4/30/53]); LC, II:335 (4/18/67).
117. "The Late Mr. Stanfield," AYR (6/1/67), 537; CP, II:46.
118. F, VII:v,172.
119. CJ, p. 7.
120. SD, p. 157 (1/6/53).
121. LD, IV:576 (7/3/46).
122. SD, pp. 13–14 (1/2/52).
123. "Banvard's Geographical Panorama of the Mississippi and Missouri Rivers," *Examiner* (12/16/48), in CP, I:182–184.
124. F, VI:iii,41.
125. F, VI:iii,41–42. Lamb wrote "On the Genius and Character of Hogarth," *The Complete Works and Letters of Charles Lamb* (New York: Random House, 1935). The passage Dickens refers to is ". . . the very houses, as I heard a friend of mine express it, tumbling all about in various directions, seem drunk. . . ." (p. 312).
126. LD, IV:276 (3/9/45).
127. LD, IV:220 (11/17 and 18/44).
128. NL, I:666.
129. LD, IV:160 (7/22/44).
130. LD, IV:217 (11/12/44); IV:220 (11/17–18/44).
131. F, VII:iii,142.
132. See LD, V:277n.
133. LD, IV:276–277 (3/9/45).
134. LD, IV:305, 307 (5/9/45).
135. PI, 40.
136. PI, 95.
137. PI, 69.
138. PI, 149, 152.
139. PI, 96.
140. PI, 141.
141. JE, II:1131.
142. LD, IV:220 (11/17 and 18/44); IV:284 (3/18/45); IV:304, 307 (5/9/45). The reference to Sterne, slightly distorted, is to *Tristram Shandy*, Book III, Chapter 12.
143. F, VII:iii,141–142.

144. MR, p. 216 (11/21/53).
145. PK, 126.
146. MR, p. 212 (11/14/53).
147. PK, 164. Kate's statement that "my father was passionately fond of colour" supports the possibility that his infrequent references to color are owing neither to indifference nor to ignorance, but to his distaste for technical "jargon."
148. LD, IV:221. (11/17 and 18/49). The passage is also found in PI, 150.
149. PK, 164.
150. SB, p. 237.
151. "The Ghost of Art," UT, p. 439.
152. See, *e.g.*, LD, IV:586 (7/18/46).
153. LD, IV:281 (3/18/45); IV:283 (3/18/45).
154. PI, 186–187.
155. "An Idea of Mine," HW (3/13/58); CP, I:703.
156. CP, II:351, 355.
157. LD, III:401–402 (12/26/42).
158. F, VII:v,174. Dickens' praise of Collins here adds to the possibility that his professed contempt for his friend's technical discussions of art (see above) was directed at such discussion, not at Collins.
159. BC, p. 161 (1/10/56).
160. F, VII: v, 173–174. Forster agreed with Dickens that "the eyes and the mouth" of the portrait gave "the sense of a general unlikeness."
161. *Ibid.*
162. LC, II:174 (9/28/61).
163. *Ibid.*, 127.
164. MR, p. 247 (5/5/56).
165. LD, V:630 (10/22/49).
166. The editors of the Pilgrim *Letters* affirm that there is nothing "testy" or "contradictory" in the portrait of Clark; Dickens is trying to find a way of expressing his dissatisfaction with mere surface fidelity, and not succeeding.
167. PK, 129.
168. PI, 150.
169. PK, 129.
170. PK, 126.
171. CJ, p. 7.
172. WA, p. 194; LD, IV:283–284 (3/18/45).
173. LE, p. 83.
174. "Old Lamps for New," HW (6/15/50), 265–266.
175. HH, p. 126.
176. Letter to the *Times* (May 1851), reprinted in *Realism and Tradition in Art, 1848–1900*, Linda Nochlin, ed., Sources and Documents in the History of Art Series, H. W. Janson, ed. (Englewood Cliffs, N. J.: Prentice-Hall, 1966), p. 119.
177. *Times* editorial (1851), reprinted in book of preceding note, p. 119.
178. See note 176.
179. *Ibid.*, p. 119.

180. Michael Hollington, "Dickens the Flaneur," *Dickensian*, LXXVII:394 (1981), 79.
181. JE, II:1131.
182. PK, 166.
183. S, pp. 104, 130.
184. "Please to Leave Your Umbrella," HW (5/1/58), in CP, I:705–706.
185. Pp. 704–705.
186. "An Idea of Mine," HW (3/13/58), 699–704; in CP, I:699–700.
187. F, VII:iii,172.
188. "Insularities," HW (1/19/56), in CP, I:626–627.
189. F, VII:v,172.

Dickens' Creation
of Bradley Headstone

Joel Brattin

An examination of the holograph manuscript of *Our Mutual Friend* provides
a fascinating view of Dickens' creative methods, particularly in regard to the
creation of Bradley Headstone. Though the manuscript pages are often
difficult to decipher, they are also very rich, filled with many deletions and
interlinear additions. The manuscript[1] and the number plans[2] read together
reveal Dickens' imagination in the process of creating a complex, hauntingly
memorable character.

Bradley first appears in Book II, Chapter 1, "Of an Educational Character," and Dickens' plans for the sixth number reveal his earliest conceptions
of Bradley's nature.[3] On the left side of the sheet, Dickens asks himself "Any
new character?" and answers "Yes. Schoolmaster," underlining the answer
twice. He adds the names of "Miss Pitcher" (later changed to Peecher) and
her favorite pupil "Mary Anne" beneath this, but does not underline them; it
is evident even here that Dickens plans to focus attention on the still unnamed
schoolmaster. On the right side of the sheet, Dickens again writes "The
Schoolmaster," doubly underlined, and then tries out the names "Amos
Headstone," "Amos Deadstone," and "Bradley Deadstone," before arriving
at "Bradley Headstone."[4] Dickens writes "selfish boy," referring to Charley
Hexam, and "and selfish Schoolmaster" beneath it, stressing that Charley and
Bradley are related by selfishness. He then writes "Very particular with
him," and underlines this phrase three times, implying that Bradley is to be
an important figure in the novel, worth drawing with "particular" care.

Dickens evinces this care in the manuscript itself, carefully revising his
presentation of Headstone. Before the schoolmaster is even named, Dickens'
revisions begin to reveal his character. Bradley's first line of dialogue
originally read "So you want to go and see your sister, Charley?" (2/265), but

Dickens replaces "Charley" with the more formal "Hexam,"[5] emphasizing Bradley's consistently restrained and professional behavior in the presence of his student. A few lines below this, on the same manuscript page, Dickens names and renames the schoolmaster, substituting "Bradley" for "Amos," and "Headstone" for "Deadstone." The change from "Amos" to "Bradley" is a felicitous one, as "Bradley" has the same last syllable as "Charley," and thereby reflects the selfishness they share.[6] "Deadstone" and "Headstone" are both revealing names, but "Headstone" is the better one because of its macabre, punning humor.

Also on this page of the manuscript, Dickens characterizes Headstone as "decent," applying that adjective to him no less than seven times in a single sentence (2/266). Part of this sentence appears thus in the manuscript:

decent formal
decent white shirt and ∧necktie, and decent
decent black coat and waistcoat, and ∧pantaloons

Here Dickens actually revises his revisions, intentionally building the anaphora in order to emphasize Bradley's superficial "decency."

From this point in the manuscript, the schoolmaster's name appears as "Bradley," without revision. Though the "Deadstone"/"Headstone" alteration is still evident, "Amos" has been rejected finally.

Dickens takes great care in his presentation of Bradley's behavior and manners. He originally describes the behavior as having "a certain peculiarity," but by substituting "stiffness" for the last word he makes that peculiarity concrete (2/266). The line "as if there were a want of adaptation between him and it [his clothes]," which illustrates Bradley's "stiffness" of manner, is an interlinear addition to the manuscript. It is this "want of adaptation" which recalls "mechanics in their holiday clothes," and the manuscript, again in an interlinear addition, tells us that Bradley "so far belonged to the order [of mechanics] as that he" acquired his store of knowledge "mechanically" (2/266). This addition, which does not appear in the proofs,[7] may have been overlooked by the compositor and has remained unpublished. Headstone's arrangement of his mind as "a place of mechanical stowage" (3/266) has resulted in a suspicious manner, or "a manner that would better be described as one of lying in wait" (3/267). The struggle for this last phrase, which describes the external manifestations of Bradley's barely repressed passions and in fact foreshadows his violent attack on Eugene Wrayburn, cost Dickens much creative energy; he adds a phrase a third of a line long, deletes it, adds another phrase of five or six words interlinearly, deletes that, and finally scrawls the quoted phrase, in a tiny hand, down the right-hand side of the folio. Though Dickens writes, on this same page, that "there was enough of what was animal still visible" in Headstone to suggest courage, it is the interlinear addition of the phrase "and of what was fiery, though smouldering" which suggests repressed passion as well (3/267).

Dickens often sharpens his criticism of Headstone in his revisions. Summing up Bradley's attitude towards his own poor past, Dickens writes that he

was proud, ∧and desired it to be forgotten.

(3/267)

(with interlineation above the line: "moody, and sullen, desiring" and "and desired" struck through)

(Here and subsequently, I strike through the words Dickens cancels in the manuscript.) Substituting the interlinear phrase for "and desired" makes this description more pointed, and more critical. Dickens writes that "Mr. Bradley Headstone walked forth" on the bottom half of the same manuscript page (3/268). Dickens found the name that sounded right, and from here on the schoolmaster's name takes this form without revision. On the next page, when Bradley first addresses the schoolmistress, Dickens originally wrote "'A fine evening, Miss Pitcher,' said Bradley" (4/269). Crossing out "Bradley," Dickens adds "the Master," underlining the "M" twice, and emphasizing the power relationship between the two in a way the original expression does not.

Later in the chapter, when Headstone first meets Lizzie Hexam, Dickens takes great care to show Bradley's attraction—and his discomfort. Dickens mentions that Lizzie's "eyes met those of the schoolmaster" (7/275), but it is only in an interlinear addition that we learn that Bradley "had evidently expected to see a very different person." Bradley is surprised that Lizzie is so attractive; Dickens writes "the schoolmaster was not at his ease." The next line appeared in the manuscript originally as "But he rarely was" (7/275); Dickens changes "rarely" to "never," amplifying our sense of Headstone's social awkwardness. The modifying word "quite," which does not appear in the manuscript, concludes the sentence in the proofs and in the published text. Dickens takes pains to present Headstone's awkwardness with precision. When Charley exclaims to his sister "How well you look!," Jenny Wren's response "Ah! Don't she, don't she?" follows immediately in the manuscript. After beginning the next paragraph, Dickens interlines the brilliant short paragraph "Bradley seemed to think so" (7/275), which through its brevity says much about Bradley. Bradley is confused when Lizzie asks him whether or not she should visit Charley; he is attracted to her, wants to see her again, but does not know what to do. Dickens, in beginning Bradley's response, originally wrote "Bradley Headstone paused." Deleting "paused," and adding and rejecting two other words, Dickens finally finds the word "stammered," which effectively conveys both Headstone's urgency, and his hesitancy (7/276). When Bradley prepares to leave Lizzie, Dickens tells us that "he stiffly offered her his arm" (9/279). The adverb "stiffly" suggests that Bradley is repressing emotion, but it is the prepositional phrase "with his cumbrous and uneasy action," added interlinearly to the manuscript, which really emphasizes Bradley's awkwardness.

Many of the most interesting changes in the manuscript involve the presentation or representation of emotion through gesture, making interior feelings known through external actions. On those comparatively rare occasions where Dickens revises dialogue, he frequently does so for gesture-like purposes, as when Bradley speaks to Charley about Lizzie. Dickens revises the beginning of one of Bradley's lines like this:

$$\text{"I suppose}_{\wedge}\underset{\text{, Hexam, your sister has received.}}{\overset{\text{—your sister—'' with a curious break}}{}} \qquad (10/281)$$

As Dickens knows, there is a vital difference between "your sister" and "—your sister—''; Bradley cannot mention Lizzie without feeling and forcing himself to repress powerful emotions, and the "curious break both before and after the words" is the manifestation of that feeling. Headstone repeats this same verbal mannerism in his next speech, and here again "—your sister—" is an interlinear addition to the manuscript (10/281).

In the course of revising the manuscript Dickens frequently deletes words so heavily that they are completely illegible, but even in these cases the revisions can be revealing. (In quoting these passages, I give empty brackets, struck through with a single line, to indicate an illegible deleted word or phrase.) On the same folio as the last-cited examples, Dickens has Bradley begin to express his feelings for Lizzie to young Hexam. Bradley speaks of how "Some man who had worked his way might come to admire—your sister" (10/282); this sentence continues

$$\text{and might even in time, } \underset{\wedge}{\overset{\text{⊦———⊦ bring himself to}}{\underset{\text{⊦—————⊦}}{}}\text{ think of}}\\ \text{marrying—your sister.}$$

Dickens' many delections seem to reflect Bradley's difficulty in facing his own feelings. Here, Dickens seems to identify himself with Bradley;[8] he, like Bradley, is having trouble "bring[ing] himself to think of" a romantic connection, or at least bringing himself to express Bradley's (or his own) passion.

Headstone, in thinking of marrying Lizzie, speaks of "overcoming in his mind other inequalities of condition and other considerations" against marriage (10/282). Dickens interlines the phrase "in his mind" later, recognizing and intentionally emphasizing that Bradley cannot overcome class inequalities in any other way, and more important that he is constantly trying to overcome things "in his mind." This is his character, and it determines his fate.

Bradley next appears confronting Eugene Wrayburn in Book II, Chapter 6, "A Riddle Without An Answer." Dickens' notes for this chapter on the right side of the plan for the seventh number read

> Mortimer and Eugene living together.
> To <u>them, Young Hexam and Bradley.</u>

Evidently, Dickens had Headstone's role in this scene clearly in mind, as he does not mention him on the left side of the plans. After Bradley and Eugene exchange their first words, Dickens comments that "there was some perception between them, that set them against one another" (19/341). Modifying "perception," Dickens adds, interlinearly, "⊢———⊣ secret, ⊢———⊣ sure." It is difficult to find the right words to describe the strange kinship caused by rivalry, but Dickens makes the effort, creating a sense of that strange, secret, and sure bond. Bradley can barely restrain himself after Wrayburn's goading. Dickens writes that "He set his lips," but revises this to "He tried to set his lips" (19/341), showing that Bradley's passions are so strong that they cannot be completely controlled.

Dickens reworks violence, just as he reworks passionate gesture. He tells us that Bradley's "right-hand clutching the respectable hair-guard of the respectable watch could have strangled" Eugene (19/342). To this statement Dickens adds the concrete detail "wound it round his throat" and the phrase "on the spot," which emphasizes how close Bradley is to lashing out at Eugene; though this last phrase appears in the proofs, it is unpublished. Eugene's response to Headstone's violence is to stand "looking imperturbably at Bradley Headstone," but by interlinear additions Dickens revises this to read "looking imperturbably at the chafing Bradley Headstone with his clutching right hand" (19/342), further contrasting Eugene's easy lassitude with Bradley's barely-repressed passion.

After Charley threatens Eugene, Eugene responds by suggesting to Bradley that he take his pupil away. Dickens interlines the short paragraph that intervenes, "A pause ensued, in which the schoolmaster looked very awkward" (20/344). Bradley, though kin to Charley in selfishness, would no doubt be embarrassed by his pupil's bluster; Dickens admits this possibility through the addition of the awkward pause expressed in this paragraph.

Dickens creates or expands in scope several other gestures in this chapter. Bradley's "carefully weighed" tone of voice (20/344), his "clutching hand" (20/345), his "starting perspiration," and the "errant motion" of his hands (21/345) are all external expressions of his inner state, and all take shape through interlinear additions.

Though Dickens did not include Bradley in the eighth part number, he was still thinking of him, as his notes on the left indicate.

> Mem: Two more interviews between Bradley Headstone and Lizzie before the close of Book the Second. One in N° IX?
>
> And one in N° X?

Dickens brought about these two interviews exactly as planned, commenting on the first in his plans for the ninth number. Most interesting is his emphasis on foreshadowing: he writes on the left "Work up to scene in next N° between Lizzie, her brother, and Bradley Headstone," and on the right "Lead on to another scene between Bradley and Lizzie." In the chapter itself, he continues the same techniques of revision, interlining the adjectives "downcast and reserved," modifying Headstone's face (1/394), and the phrase "seating himself in his constrained manner" (2/395).

Dickens continues to use the dash effectively in Bradley's speech. Bradley refers, in the manuscript, to "Mr—Mr Eugene Wrayburn"; Dickens adds the phrase "I believe the name is" after the dash, and then revises the following sentence:

> He made this point of not being certain of the name, with
>   With ∧ another ~~furtive and~~ uneasy look at her,
>   that dropped
>   ~~that fell like the last that fell~~ ∧ like the last.
>
>   (4/399)

First with the dash itself, and then by creating the emphatic aside, Dickens shows us both the deceit and the attempted self-deceit of Bradley. Dickens gives the aside an extra emphasis by putting it into a paragraph by itself; though I do not reproduce it, his mark to designate a new paragraph is clearly visible in the manuscript.

Bradley's difficulty in communicating with Lizzie is manifest in his speech to her late in the chapter. Dickens writes: "'I should like to ask you,' said Bradley Headstone slowly, 'if I may without offense'" (5/401). This speech is smooth, polite, and apparently easy, but after Dickens' revisions it reads "'I should like to ask you,' said Bradley Headstone, grinding his words slowly out, as though they came from a mill, 'I should like to ask you, if I may without offense.'" Both the repetition of the phrase and the introduction of the mill metaphor make the line expressive and dramatic. Apparently, Dickens carried the metaphor further in a late set of proofs, the word "rusty," modifying "mill" in the published text, not appearing in either the manuscript or the extant proofs.

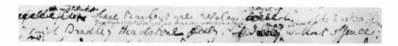

Just before he leaves Lizzie, Bradley says "I—I leave it all incomplete," "as if in a burst of irrepressible despair" (5/402). Both his statement and this last phrase are telling; both, like the "strange tremble" which passes over Bradley when Lizzie touches him (5/402), are interlinear additions, expressing Bradley's uncontrollable depth of feeling.

Though he is not mentioned in the plans, Bradley appears briefly in Chapter 14, "Strong of Purpose," telling John Rokesmith of his interest in Lizzie with "knotted" brows, "squared" jaw, and an air of "determination" (7/446). Headstone's peculiar manner is much more revealing than the content of his speech, and it is significant that all the quoted words, which help convey his manner, are interlinear additions.

Bradley's next interview with Lizzie, in Chapter 15 of Book II, is vitally important; Dickens' plans for the tenth number reflect its significance. On the left side, Dickens writes

> Declaration scene between Bradley
> and
> Lizzie
> }
> Yes

On the right, he notes the time and place, "City churchyard at dusk," the plot,

> Bradley Headstone's love
> Declared
> rejected,

a bit of dialogue,

"You could draw me to fire
                              water
                              gallows
                              what not!,"

and perhaps most important of all, a gesture:

His hand upon the
coping—
wrenching at it
while he speaks.

Dickens encloses this last set of notes by a box, something he does only rarely; clearly, he sees the gesture as particularly important.

Perhaps as a result of Dickens' careful planning, the chapter comes off brilliantly; interestingly, Bradley's gestures require less revision in this chapter than elsewhere. Still, the revisions—especially of Headstone's speech— are revealing. Bradley begins his impassioned plea to Lizzie, telling her "I have no confidence in myself," and "no government of myself"; these phrases are rewordings of "no self-respect" and "no power over myself"

(10/452). Dickens takes these issues very seriously, and struggles for precisely the right phrases, letting Bradley reveal his passion but not allowing him to step out of character. (Bradley would never admit a loss of self-respect, or of power over himself, in such a bald, explicit way.)

Dickens fleshes out the line of dialogue outlined in the number plans. In his passion, Bradley says

You could draw me to the fire, you could draw me to
the water, you could draw me to the gallows, you
                me to any death, you could draw
could draw ∧me to anything I have most avoided in life.   (11/455)

Dickens adds the interlinear phrase to the middle of the sentence in order to make it even more stiffly rhetorical. This explicit and extravagant expression of Headstone's passion was especially important to Dickens; his quoting it in the notes, intensification of it in the manuscript, and final adjustment of it in a late set of proofs (the article "the" before both "fire" and "water," and the words "in life," appear in the extant proofs, but do not appear in the published text) underscore its importance.

Headstone's most important gesture in the chapter, gripping and wrenching at the coping stone with his hand, appears four times. Significantly, these passages are almost entirely free of revisions. The gesture is a symptom of and symbol for the violence and potential for self-destruction in Bradley's repressed nature. Evidently, Dickens so carefully planned the way this symbol would work that the passages came out on paper as if rehearsed.

Though this image is unrevised, many of the most violent images in the chapter are the result of careful reworking. Bradley's "half-suffocated way" (11/455), his "bringing" his hand down upon the stone—a marvelous understatement for the act which lays his knuckles raw (11/456)—and his holding his bloody hand up as if it held "some weapon" (12/456), are all the results of interlinear additions. Similarly, Dickens revises the simple line "He smiled and said never a word" to "He bit his lip, and looked at her, and said never a word" (12/456), a line almost horrible in its realistic, underplayed violence. Dickens virtually repeats this line after Lizzie asks Headstone a second question, revising it exactly as he did the first time; the line gains power in repetition. And when Bradley is at his most violent, he exclaims of Wrayburn "I hope I may never have to kill him!" (11/456), but Dickens then deletes the words "have to." This makes his exclamation more threatening, as it implies that Headstone *may* kill Wrayburn. (However, the original reading also sheds light on Headstone—revealing him as one who may actually feel *compelled* to murder.)

Bradley's departure from the scene is particularly noteworthy. The manuscript tells us that Headstone

> uttered a ^(short) ~~strange wild~~ unearthly broken cry ^(went his way) and ~~was gone~~ (13/458)

Dickens evidently felt the original version was too extreme; his revisions, deleting "strange wild" and adding "short," make the phrase both more moderate and more realistic. He also substitutes "went his way" for "was gone," over the carelessly placed caret. The original line, in the graveyard context, seems positively ghostly: we imagine Bradley vanishing into thin air. The phrase "went his way" reinforces the fact that Bradley is human and not supernatural, emphasizing that the scene is realistic, not gothic.

Bradley does not appear in either of the next two part numbers, though Dickens mentions him briefly in the plans for N° XI. Dickens, summing up for himself the "Position of affairs at the end of the Second Book (N° X)," writes that "Lizzie has disappeared" and numbers Bradley fourth in a list of five characters related "to that part of the story." It is reasonable that Eugene should head this list; the fact that "The Doll's Dressmaker" and "Mr bad child" (Mr. Dolls) precede Bradley in the list seems to indicate simply that Dickens plans to include them earlier.

Headstone first appears in Book III in the thirteenth number. The notes make clear that Dickens means to emphasize Wrayburn; the only note on the left side for chapter ten reads

<blockquote>
Wrayburn for the last chapter?
<u>Yes</u>.
</blockquote>

On the right, Dickens writes

<blockquote>
Scene with Eugene
The schoolmaster on the watch
    "The pleasures of the chase."
</blockquote>

That Eugene is named, where Headstone is not, and that the quotation in the notes reflects Eugene's perspective and not Headstone's, underscores the fact that Dickens sees Bradley as only secondary here.

Dickens' emphasis on Eugene in the number plans is carried through in the manuscript itself; he seems to spend little creative energy on Bradley here. He revises Bradley's "torments" to "grinding torments" twice (21/606), perhaps looking back to the mill metaphor of Book II, Chapter 11; these revisions, the interlinear description of Bradley as "draggle-haired," and the note (also interlinear) that Bradley is "torturing" himself (22/608) are probably the most revealing.

Headstone plays a more important role in the next chapter, "In the Dark." Dickens' notes for Nº XIV emphasize the plot function of the chapter:

<blockquote>
Bradley Headstone and Riderhood
       / Get them together
      / Let him know where to find Riderhood
<u>Plashwater Weir Mill Lock</u>.
</blockquote>

The only other note for the chapter, enclosed in a box for emphasis, reads: "Bradley's state of mind."

Dickens manages the plot well in this chapter, and there are few significant revisions. "Bradley's state of mind" is important, and Dickens conveys it clearly and with economy. He implies that Bradley is, in fact, murderous when Riderhood tells him "And wishing that your elth may be better than your looks, which your inside must be bad indeed if it's on the footing of your out"

(2/612); this statement, which lets Bradley know that "his face revealed too much of his mind" (3/612), is crowded onto the very bottom of the manuscript folio. (When especially inspired, Dickens would often try to work his ideas onto the bottom of a page in a tiny hand, rather than interrupt his train of thought by changing slips. This is certainly one of those instances.) Bradley, meditating on Riderhood, thinks of him only in terms of plot, saying to himself "Here is an instrument. Can I use it?" (3/614). Dickens often intensively reworks dehumanization, but here the passage appears in the manuscript just as in the published text; Dickens is plotting as clearly and premeditatedly as Headstone.

In the last sentences of the chapter, Dickens describes Bradley's state of mind in strong terms: "He had been spurred and whipped and heavily sweated. If a record of the sport had usurped the places of the peaceful texts from Scripture on the wall, the most advanced of the scholars might have taken fright and run away from the master" (5/618). This, the printed version, differs in several respects from the manuscript, which is highly revised and crowded onto the bottom of a slip; in the manuscript, "the most advanced of his scholars would have been at a loss to make it read to the master's satisfaction." Through revision, Dickens transforms Bradley's state of mind from something confusing and mysterious to something horrible. Ironically, one of the most illegible interlinear phrases in the manuscript (added to modify "a record of the sport"), "though never so legibly printed," is unpublished.

Book IV opens with an important chapter for Bradley, "Setting Traps." Dickens planned it carefully, noting Bradley's role on both sides of the plan for N° XVI. The chapter is rich in significant revisions, descriptive of Bradley's appearance or tone of voice but more importantly revealing his nature. The phrases "turned away his haggard face" (2/698), "in a low voice" (3/699), and "protesting with both his tremulous hands" (6/705) are all interlinear additions, as is Bradley's look of "gloomy" fascination (4/702). In the manuscript of this chapter, Dickens first describes Bradley as a "bargeman," revising this to a "Bargeman" (1/696) and doubly under-scoring the "B" to emphasize the fact that he is, in fact, no ordinary water-man. On the next page, when Riderhood calls out to him, the manuscript reads "The bargeman stopped, and looked back" (2/697); in an interlinear addition, Dickens adds "started" before "stopped," effectively conveying Bradley's surprise and displeasure at being detected by Rogue. Unfortu-nately, this addition appears in neither the proofs nor the final text; it was probably overlooked by a compositor, and is unpublished.

Dickens carefully revises Bradley's speech in this chapter, and again not for content so much as for form. When Bradley returns to Rogue and tells him about Eugene and Lizzie's liaison, he says "I saw them walking side by side last night." Dickens revises this to read "'I saw them'—he stopped as though he were suffocating, and began again—'I saw them walking side by side last night'" (5/704). The revision effectively conveys Headstone's passion, through both the suffocation metaphor and the use of repetition.

Shortly after Bradley's "suffocation," "a great spirt of blood burst from his nose." In explaining this phenomenon to Rogue, Bradley says

> ~~It chokes me~~ I taste it, smell it, ~~it chokes~~ see it, it chokes me, and then it breaks out like this.   (5/704)

That the phrase "it chokes me" is written in and deleted before both "I taste it" and "see it" seems to indicate that both Dickens and Bradley want to defer the choking, and are painfully conscious of its impendency. Here again, Dickens may be identifying himself with Headstone. Other images of violence in the chapter are carefully reworked: in a single passage, Dickens tries and rejects "with his hand upon the dagger," "with his hand upon the dagger" again, and "with his furtive hand clutching the dagger," before arriving at "with his furtive hand laid upon the dagger" (3/701):

> with his ~~hand upon~~ furtive hand ~~clutching~~ laid upon
> ~~with his hand upon~~ ˄the dagger.

Very sensitive to the nuances of words, Dickens found "furtive" appropriately menacing, but rejected "clutching," perhaps as overly melodramatic.

Dickens adds three very important passages, too long to quote in full here, to this chapter on a separate unnumbered sheet, now bound into the manuscript immediately before Book IV (see Figure 1). These passages, all concerning Headstone, repay close attention. The first, which Dickens labels "A," is seven short paragraphs, beginning with "It ain't Locks as *you've* been a reckoning up" (697–698); it deals with Headstone's abstraction in dwelling on "spites, affronts, offences," *etc.* The second, "B," is two paragraphs, beginning with "You seem to like it" (702–703); this passage probes Headstone's morbid and suicidal tendencies, examining his "troubled soul." The last passage, "C," is six paragraphs long, beginning with "The thunder rolled heavily" (706); it traces Rogue's growing suspicion of Headstone, as the external storm crashes and lightens outside. All of these passages shed light on Bradley's character, the first revealing his re-

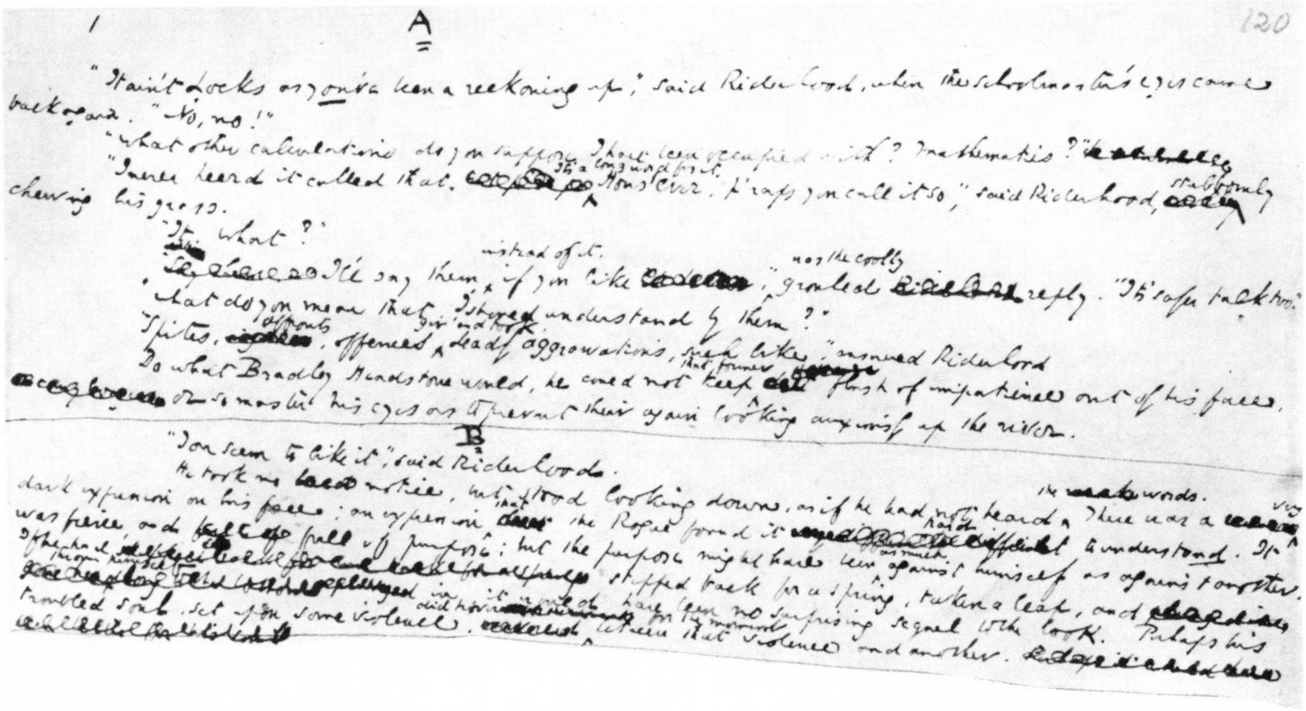

FIGURE 1. Three important additions to the manuscript of *Our Mutual Friend*, Book IV, Chapter LI (continued overleaf). By permission of the Pierpont Morgan Library, New York.

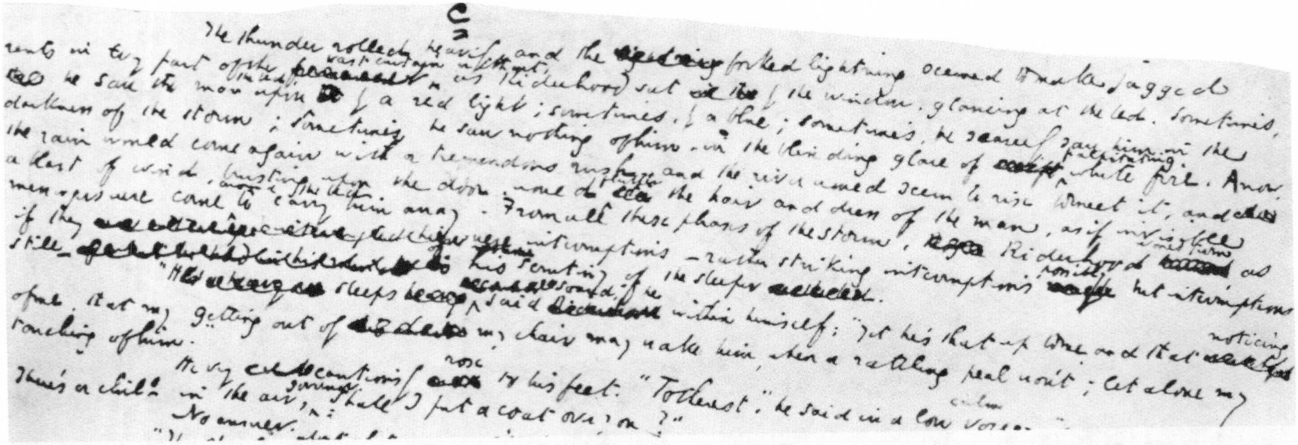

FIGURE 1 (continued).

pression, the second his violence, and the third, by extending the storm metaphor, his inner turmoil. Dickens evidently added these passages to fill out a too-short monthly number; it is significant that the first role he thinks of expanding is Bradley's.

In the notes for the seventeenth number, Dickens plans Bradley's role in Chapter 6, "A Cry for Help." It is evident that Eugene is the main focus of attention here: the left side of the notes says "The attack upon Eugene," and the right says

> Eugene alone—except for a Bargeman lying on his face.—And what is there in that?

> Scene between Eugene and Lizzie
> Attack on Eugene
> Rescue by Lizzie.

Bradley is not even named as Eugene's attacker.

In the chapter itself, there are a number of interesting revisions relevant to Headstone. When Eugene almost collides with Headstone, who is in disguise, the narrator says "The man carried something on his shoulder" (14/766). There are at least five words, three of them interlinear additions, entered and deleted from the manuscript before "something" is allowed to stand, so perhaps Dickens considered specifying Headstone's weapon here. Dickens' decision to use the vague word "something" to connote a mysterious and threatening object looks back to his repeated use of the word for George Radfoot's corpse in the first chapter of the novel.

The attack itself, the most violent act in the novel, is carefully shaped through revision (see Figure 2). The "dreadful crash" of Headstone's attack is itself an interlinear addition, and Dickens changed "there were flames in the air" to "flames shot jaggedly across the air" (15/767), a more active and disturbing image. The revisions of the attack emphasize its suddenness and brutality; the attack is the shocking culmination of Bradley's hitherto repressed passion. After its last line, " . . . a splash, and all was done," Dickens wrote in the manuscript "(Printer. A white line here)" (15/767), and then altered this to "Two white lines." The white lines appear in the extant proofs, but by chance they fall at the bottom of a page where they do not stand out as intentional. The unfortunate result is that the lines do not appear in the published text.

The chapter following the attack, "Better to be Abel than Cain," is carefully planned in Dickens' notes:

> Riderhood turns spie on Bradley
>   Indication derived therefrom, how Bradley
>   did it. All his plot shewn.
> Pursue Bradley and unrepentant state of mind.
>   Charley Hexam renounces him. The wretched
> creature affected by this selfishness.

The notes say emphatically that he plans to "pursue Bradley and unrepentant state of mind," and he certainly does this. Not only is the chapter rich in interesting revisions, but Dickens evidently wrote considerably more copy for it than would fit in the thirty-two page monthly number. There are several very interesting passages in the manuscript that do not appear either in the extant proofs or in the published text. Though some are lengthy I will give them all in full, as they provide fascinating glimpses into Bradley's character and "state of mind."

Early in the chapter, Bradley and Rogue Riderhood exchange a few lines, in a passage presumably deleted from an early set of proofs for space reasons. Headstone's unwillingness to reveal his whereabouts, and Riderhood's curiosity, are both typical. (Though there are revealing interlineations and deletions in this and in subsequent unpublished passages, I give a simplified form for the sake of clarity.)

> "T'otherest," said Riderhood in a low voice, after beckoning to him confidentially to draw nearer, "as I said to you afore, first time that ever I see you, I don't know where to find you."
> "As I said to you before," returned Bradley, "I know where to find you."
> "But you see, governor," resumed Riderhood, "I don't so much as know your name."
> "Why should you?" asked Bradley standing still.
> "Why should I?" growled Riderhood, heavily pondering an answer to the purpose: "Why should you know mine?"
> "I never asked you for it."
> "No," returned Riderhood. "Because you knowed it all along."
> "I never wanted to know it. I knew it through mere accident."
>   (18–19/[774])

Following this exchange, Bradley sets out, followed by Rogue; as Rogue fishes for Bradley's clothes, thereby sealing his fate, the narrator philosophizes on the blindness of the shedder of blood: "There are fifty doors by which discovery may enter. He double-locks and bars forty nine of them, and leaves the fiftieth standing wide open" (20/776). Dickens adds the phrase "With infinite pains and cunning" to the beginning of the second sentence, substitutes "cannot see" for "leaves," and substitutes "the nearest of the

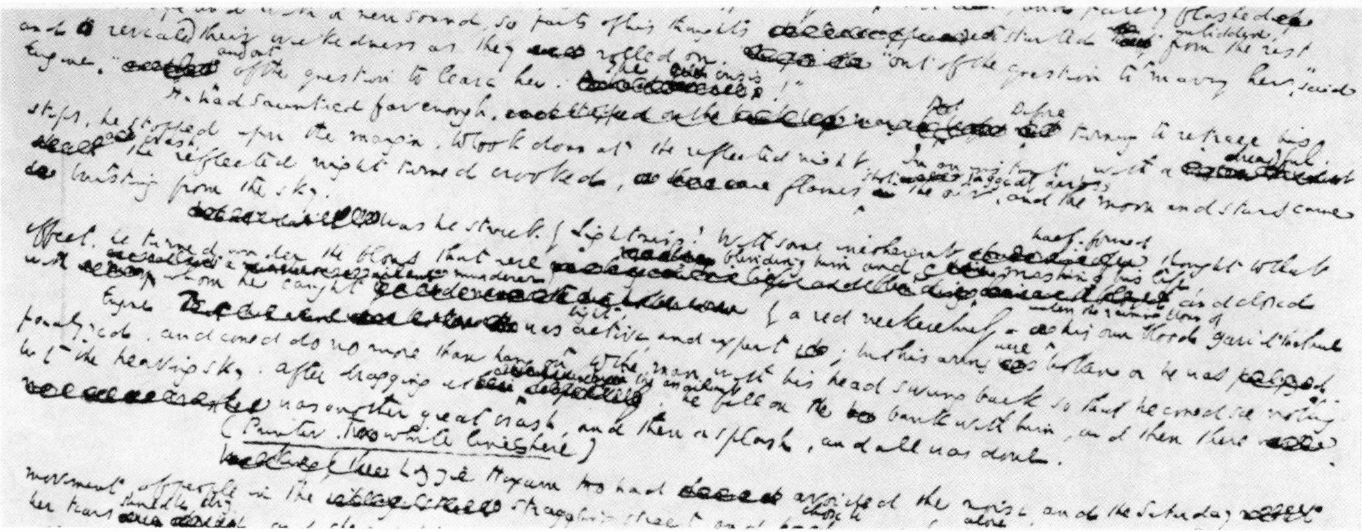

FIGURE 2. The account of Headstone's attack on Eugene (*Our Mutual Friend*, p. 767) in manuscript. By permission of the Pierpont Morgan Library, New York.

FIGURE 3. An unpublished passage from *Our Mutual Friend* (MS. pp. 22–23; Book IV, Chapter LII) further describing Bradley's state of mind. By permission of the Pierpont Morgan Library, New York.

fifty" for "the fiftieth," thereby pointing directly to Riderhood (this last reference is not in the proofs, however, and remains unpublished).

Dickens heavily revises the next paragraph, which explores "a state of mind more wearing and more wearisome than remorse" (20/776–777). Dickens writes that it "is a state that aggravates the offence by doing the deed a hundred times instead of once," and then changes "hundred" to "thousand"; Bradley's "sullen unrepentant nature," to use another phrase Dickens adds interlinearly, condemns him to commit his crime over and over. Dickens reworks Bradley's unrelievedly violent thoughts with the same care manifest earlier. Reflecting Bradley's thoughts of Eugene, Dickens writes

> Supposing he had been strangled.
> Supposing he had been shot. ∧Suppose this way, that
> way, |————| the other way. Suppose anything but getting
>   one |————| inexorably
> unchained from the ∧idea, for that was ∧impossible.
>
> (20/777)

Dickens adds the sentence "Supposing he had been strangled" as an additional violent possibility, adds the word "one" before "idea," emphasizing the prison of Bradley's monomania, and adds "inexorably," implying a sense of fatalism.

When Headstone returns to his school, he continues to dwell on the attack. This unpublished passage reveals Headstone's state of mind:

> He was neither sorry for having done it, nor pressingly afraid of being found out. His misery was that he must think of it, must take himself to task for having done it ill, must incessantly reconstruct the scheme and redo the deed. (20/[777])

On the next page, Charley Hexam confronts Headstone; Dickens writes that Bradley tried "to fix his working mouth," and then substitutes "constrain" for "fix" (21/778). The substitution is apt, as the word is more specific; Headstone is always "constraining" himself. As Headstone tries to master himself, Charley asks him where he was when the deed was done. The following unpublished passage reveals both Headstone's response, and his inner state:

> Bradley Headstone for one brief moment threw up his arms and head as if he were about to shriek. The moment passing, he sat quite still. (21/[778])

Bradley has shrieking demons within him, but he engages his powers of constraint and self-repression once more.

Young Hexam explains that he can no longer associate with Headstone, renounces him, and leaves him in a state of "unutterable misery, unrelieved

by a single tear'' (22/782). Following this, there is a long unpublished passage
further describing Bradley's state (see Figure 3). Several words are interlinear
additions in a tiny hand, very difficult to make out. (In this example, the words
in brackets are doubtful readings.)

> But he must be up and doing. He must be ever doing the deed again and again,
> better and better, with more and more of precaution, though never in a swifter
> way. His head had got to ache with the sound of the blows; in their monotonous
> repetition, they had begun to go to a horrid tune; he could vary the preliminaries
> and the attendant circumstances in doing the act again; but the act if his [mind]
> had ever been able to change, the manner of it could be changed no more. The
> same blows, without diminution of number or force, the same effects from the
> blows, the same slipping of his foot upon the grass, the same stained face fallen
> back, and turned up to the moon, the same face drifting down the stream.
> The river ran in his thoughts distractingly. Whatever he planned in correction
> of the weak defects of the scheme, that could never be [recalled], the river ran
> through all. On his way to do the murder, the river was always meeting him as
> if to keep him back. On his way from doing the murder, the river ran before him
> as if to tell the tale. Lock ho! Lock! But in recalling the cry (he in his fancy lying
> on the bed in the Lock-House) it was the river itself that seemed to call out to
> be let through to outstrip him.
> Rogue Riderhood likewise had been busy with the river that very same
> day. . . .   (22–23/[782])

Dickens took great pains with these paragraphs, compressing most of the
above lines onto the bottom of one sheet and writing the last five lines on the
top of another. Dickens was always very economical with paper, and it is
significant that he would "waste" a sheet in detailing Headstone's fantasy
about the river, which after all serves no plot function whatsoever. But
Dickens is more interested in theme and symbol than plot, and perhaps still
more in psychological truth. These details further these ends; it is ironic, and
very unfortunate, that they were left unprinted.

Headstone is not mentioned in the plans for N°. XVIII, appearing only
briefly in Chapter 11. The Milveys see him at the train station, where he seems
extremely anxious to avoid being seen by Mortimer Lightwood. Dickens
conveys Headstone's anxiety here through six interlinear additions on a single
manuscript folio (19/819–820); one example, "though always glancing
towards the door by which Lightwood had gone out" (19/819), should
sufficiently exemplify Dickens' technique here. When Milvey tells Headstone
he is going to perform the marriage service at Lizzie's wedding, Dickens
writes that Headstone's face turned "ghastly" (20/821); this appears in the
published text as "ashy." The two words convey much the same tone, both

carrying a sense of death and decay, but "ashy" emphasizes that Bradley is still human. Finally, when the attendant tells Milvey that Headstone is having a fit, he says "He was knocking about him." Dickens embellishes this, making the violence of Bradley's fit both more striking and more specific by making the line read "He was took very bad to be sure, and was biting and knocking about him" (20/281).

Bradley's final appearance is in Book IV, Chapter 15. Dickens lays the groundwork very carefully in the notes for the last part number. On the left, he writes

> Riderhood and Bradley at the Lock again.
> Riderhood turns out Bradley and shows how he (Bradley) plotted to throw the appearance of guilt on him (Riderhood). Swears he'll know all about him, and will never leave him unless well paid. Bradley seizes him on the bank of the Lock at last—"It's no use, I can't be drowned"—"We'll try!" Holds him tight, falls in with him purposely, still holds him tight. Both drowned.

On the right, he again emphasizes "Bradley's state of mind," and mentions "Riderhood in the school. And the blackboard." "The Lock House again" and "And the drowning of the two," crowded into the bottom of the section for Chapter 15, appear to be interlinear additions; again, it is Bradley's "state of mind" that seems to be of paramount importance to Dickens.

When Bradley first sees Riderhood in the school, the narrator tells us Headstone felt "he was in danger of falling" (19/864); this, the first sign of a fit, is an interlinear addition, added to intensify our sense of Bradley's peril. The phrases "in a suppressed voice" (20/865) and "and speaking in his suppressed voice" (20/866), both interlinear additions, reflect Headstone's continued tension, disclosed more dramatically when Riderhood reveals that he has found Headstone's suit of clothes. Headstone's response to this revelation is given an entire paragraph in the manuscript, which reads

> ~~The Master~~ Bradley started, and his face ~~changed dropped changed [   ]~~ ~~fell~~ changed. (21/866)

Dickens struggles for a way to describe Headstone's face, finally deciding that the simple word "changed" would force his readers to interpret the meaning of the change for themselves. He further simplifies the statement in an early set of proofs, for the paragraph in the extant proofs and in the printed text reads simply "Bradley's face changed." Dickens discloses Bradley's tension more dramatically when, in front of his pupils, Bradley "fell into the fit which had been so long impending" (21/867); this phrase, which in some sense is the culmination of Bradley's degradation, dishonoring him as it does in front of his students, is an interlinear addition to the manuscript.

After Bradley returns to the lock, he is rigid, uncommunicative, and finally ferocious. At the climax of the chapter, he clutches Rogue round the body; the sentence "He seemed to be girdled with an iron ring," which introduces the last important metaphor for Bradley, is an interlinear addition (24/874). His final speech, a response to Rogue's claim that he can't be drowned, is carefully wrought. Bradley's "desperate, clenched" voice, his chilling statement that he is "resolved to be" drowned, and his claim "I'll hold you living, and I'll hold you dead," are all realized through interlinear additions. Bradley Headstone dies a horrible death as the result of his passion, violence, and rigidity, but even that death "under the ooze and scum behind one of the rotting gates" is made to seem less horrible than his monomaniacal state of mind after his attack on Eugene.

G. K. Chesterton, writing in 1906, praised Dickens' full and serious treatment of psychology in *Our Mutual Friend*, noting that Bradley Headstone is "a fully human villain."[9] Dickens' "very particular care" in working and reworking Headstone's language, gestures, and "state of mind" shapes both Bradley's villainy and his humanity, and results in a convincing and frightening portrayal of Bradley's inner life.

NOTES

1. In citing the manuscript, now in the Pierpont Morgan Library in New York City, I first give the number assigned to the page by Dickens (who began renumbering with each new monthly part), and then the number of the page in the Penguin edition (see note 5) which corresponds to that passage. I gratefully thank the Pierpont Morgan Library for allowing me to quote unpublished passages from the manuscript and number plans. The illustrations interspersed with the text of my article appear by permission of the Pierpont Morgan Library.
2. The plans for the first ten monthly parts can be found immediately before Book I of the manuscript; the rest are before Book III. Though Dickens assigned the plans no page numbers, they are all in order; in quoting from them, I cite only the monthly part number.
3. John Butt and Kathleen Tillotson, in their *Dickens At Work* (London: Methuen, 1957), pp. 25–28, explain the function of the plans, and relate that sometimes the plans, or some part of them, seem to have been written after the number itself. For the sake of consistency, however, I always discuss the plans before the manuscript.
4. The name "Amon Headstone" appears on p. 22, and "Bradley" on p. 23, of the

working notebook Dickens entitled "Memoranda," which is now in the holdings of the Berg Collection of English and American Literature, in the New York Public Library. The book of memoranda has been published in facsimile, transcribed, and annotated by Fred Kaplan (New York: New York Public Library, 1981), who identifies the year Dickens made these entries as 1864.

5. Charles Dickens, *Our Mutual Friend*, ed. Stephen Gill (Harmondsworth, Middlesex: Penguin Books, 1971), p. 265. Subsequent references, in the form mentioned in note one above, will be given parenthetically in the body of the essay.

6. Basil Cottle, in *The Penguin Dictionary of Surnames* (Harmondsworth, Middlesex: Penguin Books, 1978), pp. 36–37, notes that "Amos" is a corruption of "Amis," which means "friend." This is clearly inappropriate for Headstone—but we must note that Dickens considered Amos for the schoolmaster's christian name, not his surname.

7. Only one set of proofs of *Our Mutual Friend* are known to have survived. They, like Dickens' book of memoranda, are in the holdings of the Berg Collection of English and American Literature, in the New York Public Library. Only certain sections of the proofs are corrected in Dickens' hand, and while these proofs—as yet unpublished, and unavailable on microform—are fascinating, they are strangely unrevealing to the scholar interested in Headstone. In the cases discussed in this paper where the manuscript and published text differ, the proofs are invariably the same as either the published text (implying the existence of an earlier set of proofs, corrected by Dickens), or the manuscript (implying the existence of a later set). The proofs *never* show Dickens actually engaged in the process of substituting a new phrase for the manuscript reading in developing Headstone's character. I gratefully thank the Henry W. and Albert A. Berg Collection, The New York Public Library, Astor, Lenox, and Tilden Foundations, for permission to cite the proofs.

8. A number of critics have identified Dickens with his creation, including John Carey, *The Violent Effigy* (London: Faber and Faber, 1973), p. 28; Mary G. Dickins, "Dickens Self-revealed," *Dickensian*, 42 (1946), 129–130; Jack Lindsay, *Charles Dickens* (London: Andrew Dakers, 1950), pp. 382–384; Hugh Kingsmill [Lunn], *The Sentimental Journey* (New York: William Morrow, 1935), p. 233; Ellen Moers, *The Dandy* (New York: Viking Press, 1960), pp. 246–249; Hesketh Pearson, *Dickens* (London: Methuen, 1949), pp. 304–305; Valerie Purton, "Dickens and 'Cheap Melodrama'," *Etudes Anglaises*, 28 (1975), 25–26; Grahame Smith, *Dickens, Money, and Society* (Berkeley: University of California Press, 1968), pp. 183–186; and Ralph Straus, *Dickens* (London: Victor Gollancz, 1928), p. 68. Many of these critics feel that Dickens' secret passion for Ellen Ternan motivates his characterization of Headstone.

9. G. K. Chesterton, *Charles Dickens* (London: Methuen, 1906), pp. 238–239.

Dickens' Fantastic Rhetoric: The Semantics of Reality and Unreality in *Our Mutual Friend*

John Kucich

Criticism has always been fascinated with the conjunction of realism and anti-realism—with what we now glibly call the fantastic—in Dickens' novels. But, as Robert Newsom points out in the introduction to his recent book, it has done little more than label that conjunction a mixture. And, Newsom argues, unless we can define the real/unreal opposition in Dickens more precisely, we remain strangely inarticulate about the most obvious source for the energy of his art.[1] One way to describe this opposition more fully, though it may appear at first to be a diversion, is to examine the relationship between purely semantic versions of realism and anti-realism in Dickens' rhetoric. In the realm of rhetoric, we can free ourselves of the epistemological conundrums that have plagued most discussions of Dickens' fantastic tendencies. We can see instead that, for Dickens, questions raised by the intersection of realism and romance, fact and fancy, description and invention, are as much questions about meaning as they are about mimesis.[2]

Dickens was, if anything, more preoccupied with the writer's relation to his own words than with his relation to the outside world, as the novels' irrepressible verbal play bears witness—more concerned, that is, with expression than with reference. And even more prominently than in the novels' explicit preoccupations with hybrid, fantastic scenes and psychology, in their semantic organization we find the strangest conjunctions of the serious and the nonsensical, the significant and the extra-significant, the meaningful and the extra-meaningful. These conjunctions have long been obvious to most readers. But to approach Dickens' real/unreal opposition through these oscillations between language's power to signify and its power to surpass significance, and outside of any concern with the actual content of that language, can help us define Dickens' predilection for fantastic oppositions in a much more fundamental way. For on the level of rhetoric, meaning and un-meaning can more easily be seen as dynamically related in Dickens, and not simply mixed.

The meaningful and the extra-meaningful are ordered by a special kind of linguistic economy in Dickens' rhetoric. It is through the complexities of this unique economy that Dickens generates many of the "inimitable" characteristics of his prose style. By the concept of "economy" in rhetoric, what I intend to suggest is a closed linguistic system, in which every aspect of rhetoric can be exchanged with a certain intended meaning or effect. Units of rhetoric and units of meaning are, to continue the metaphor, of the same kind of currency. This economy may be diverse—at any given moment, syntax might signify one thing, while metaphor signifies something else, and diction a third thing—but all aspects of such a rhetoric are doing some kind of work. That is to say, they are all dedicated to produce some kind of exchange value in terms of meaning. If there is any surplus value in such a rhetorical economy—a surplus, perhaps, in the power of literary language always to produce more than just what it literally says—that surplus will be expressible, too, as an increase in meaning, and not as an escape from it. In such an economy, then, no verbal work is wasted, or lost, in terms of its exchange value as significance. The important concept here is this closure of the system, the complete folding together of rhetoric and meaning.

But the specialness of Dickens' prose, of course, rests in its combination of two very different kinds of rhetoric: language that does do this kind of productive work and does convert itself efficiently into significance, and language that exuberantly wastes itself, flaunting its freedom from such an economical, reductive, and reasonable relation to meaning. These two rhetorics form a semantic "real" and "unreal," if you will, since "reality" is always that which can be referred to a context of significance, that which "makes sense." Nevertheless, despite the divergence in Dickens of these two kinds of rhetoric, the economic and the non-economic, the real and the unreal, both are ultimately enclosed by a second-order economy that puts them into an efficient and perfectly well-defined relationship of exchange in terms of meaning. This is the unique economical relationship we find in Dickens' rhetoric: the minting of the significant and the extra-significant within an idiosyncratic, paradoxical order of discourse that makes them a common currency and not just a clashing of sense and non-sense. Non-sense is brought into a specific relationship with sense that in this new, limited system produces its own particular kind of meaning. What this double-tiered economy shows, ultimately, is that Dickens' very attempt to synthesize the significant and the extra-significant is commented upon and reflected by the nature of the things he means to synthesize. To the extent that a dynamic synthesis does take place, its nature as a synthesis is only comprehensible through the debate about compatibility, exchange, and closure it seeks to define, and then to override. For this reason, the fantastic but nevertheless limiting economy of meaning Dickens finally achieves must be analyzed through the same distinctions between the economic and the non-economic it tries to contain.

Before going on to describe this fantastic rhetorical economy more fully, and to explain exactly how the notion of a rhetorical economy is different from the simple "mixing" of two rhetorics, I should make one point about this terminology clear. The abstract and somewhat unwieldy notion of an economy in rhetoric can help, through its very strangeness, to remove our thinking about this Dickensian dynamic from any one particular critical frame of thought—from psychology, linguistics, aesthetics, philosophy. Instead, putting the problem in these more global terms can help us see Dickens as a writer preoccupied by the need to represent human energy in general—personal, cultural, linguistic—as a force whose nature is both always contained and always uncontainable. In the novels, Dickens is concerned not so much with any particular aspect of human energy as he is with its essential nature, and its necessary relationship with limits. For this reason, it is important to see the argument about rhetoric as only one reflection—a deliberately abstract one—of a more fundamental Dickensian perception about human energy, and not as a polemic for the primacy of semantic paradox in Dickens. I will return to this point in greater depth later, to show how this rhetorical economy is reflected and enlarged by other aspects of the novels.

On the level of rhetoric first, though, Dickens establishes an impossible compatibility between two conflicting lexical systems, one efficient in relation to meaning, one inefficient. For the sake of simplicity, these two lexical systems may be termed "style" and "mode." Although these terms are as vexed as any in the linguist's repertoire, their fairly conventional differences can, I think, help convey the kind of relationship I have in mind. A few particular features of Dickens' style—syntax, metaphor, conventions of description, readability—have in common a non-economic linguistic tendency, spurning any reduction to meaning. But this "inefficient" style, I would argue, enters into a reciprocal exchange with the more efficient rhetorical category of mode. By mode I mean what Wellek and Warren call "inner form": the tone or mood of a work as derived from textual sources such as diction, point of view, or explicit statement—either by the narrator or by a character who experiences the work's mood in his own person.[3] Such "inner form" may work together with structural or generic principles, but it does not necessarily do so. Mode, in this sense, can be apprehended by immediate rhetorical cues rather than by large-scale formal imperatives like plot or genre.

To take the issue of style first: Dickens employs a set of stylistic devices or tendencies, all readily recognizable as Dickensian, that signal a deliberate escape from any economy of reference. Some of these devices include: openly transforming the figurative into the literal; interrupting narrative sequence— or what Christine Brooke-Rose would call the "conventions of readabil- ity"[4]—with a histrionic, performative prolixity; heightening the discontinui- ties of descriptive and psychological detail; estranging character and scene through external perspective; and adopting parody as a compulsive, seemingly groundless gesture. These devices—and a few others, less widely-used, such as redundancy of phrasing or elaborately extended metaphor—are all viola- tions of realistic narrative conventions. But they are more than just that. All of them are signs of a stylistic liberality unrelated to purpose, meaning, content. All of them signal the presence of a linguistic energy that exceeds efficient signification, and that returns in emphasis to the non-expressive order of the sign. All of them, no matter what local content they may carry, are the expression of a textual euphoria, the verbal trace of an energy that cannot be named in terms of what it represents.

We have often heard Dickens' language described as self-consciously artificial. But it is worth considering how this artificiality is the sign of a pointedly non-economic linguistic energy. By announcing a verbal prodigality that flaunts the efficient relation of language to meaning, Dickens' inefficient devices are the signs of a writerly energy that is unreal, in the sense that it is not directly exchangeable with referential significance.

The notion of this kind of rhetorical excess has long been acceptable to Dickens critics, but it has come under attack lately by contemporary theore- ticians. There has been considerable debate about whether such a non-signi- fying potential is strictly possible in language, given that everything in language signifies in one way or another.[5] But recent theory has, in fact, often managed simply to shift the site of this rhetorical freedom away from the personal power of the writer, and toward the impersonal power of the word.

Many structuralist and post-structuralist thinkers have found such a poten- tial for non-significance inherent in Saussure's very separation of the order of the signifier from the order of the signified, which creates a certain slippage between them, and the self-enclosure of both. Levi-Strauss, for example, in his famous discussion of "mana" in primitive mythology, posits a "surplus of the signifier'' as the source for all myth-making.[6] Similarly, Jacques Lacan's formulation of the unconscious as a representational structure hinges on an enclosure of the order of the signifier, which Lacan equates with the autonomous organization of a repressed and discontinuous psychic language.[7] Roland Barthes, too, defines his ''text of bliss'' as the creation of a gap between the signifier and the signified, a gap in which the reader ''glimpses'' non-signification.[8] What these formulations have in common is not a theory of non-signification as such, so much as a tendency to attribute to the signifier some kind of metonymic extension that can keep language circulating within the order of the signifier, in a space of excessive freedom, rather than connecting it absolutely with the signified. Indeed, one main project of post-structuralism has been to insist on the independent energy of the signifier. If all units of language must indeed signify something, such thinking goes, they may nevertheless signify only themselves—what Barthes calls ''the site of their effect''[9]—or they may refer, in a chain of metonymic displacements, to other signifiers like themselves, in an organization that resists the bridge to signification. In Dickens, this kind of enclosed circulation of the signifier is achieved through his language's continual presentation of itself as a surface, a system of purely linguistic cross-references, displacements, and self-aggrandizements. In this way Dickens' prose offers itself at least partially as a sign of its own self-enclosure, no matter what other significations it carries, and thus as a refusal of the economy of reference.

One dramatic example of how these stylistic devices refuse to exchange themselves efficiently with reference is provided by Bradley Headstone's fits of jealous passion in *Our Mutual Friend*. No matter how convincingly motivated or conceptualized, these repeatedly become an occasion for the exercise of a disruptive, self-enclosed language. In part, this language only proclaims its own prodigality, as a play of verbal extravagance across a textual surface. At one point, tortured by Eugene, Headstone is described in this way:

> Looking like the hunted and not the hunter, baffled, worn, with the exhaustion of deferred hope and consuming hate and anger in his face, white-lipped, wild-eyed, draggle-haired, seamed with jealousy and anger, and torturing himself with the conviction that he showed it all and they exulted in it, he went by them in the dark, like a haggard head suspended in the air: so completely did the force of his expression cancel his figure.[10]

In this one sentence, we have a good number of self-consciously prodigal devices. To mention just four of these: figurative self-suppression is transformed into literal self-suppression, ''transparent'' conventions of readability are interrupted with a prolix and metrically disjunctive series of modifiers, character is estranged through a bizarre externalizing of inward states, and a discontinuous physical description exaggerates the unreal fragmentation of the scene rather than establishing a coherent scenic context. In at least these ways, Dickens' style reminds us forcefully that one goal of its energies is a purely linguistic extension, a kind of verbal expense and proliferation. Despite the clear intention to evoke Headstone's rage and despair—so clear that many readers find Headstone the most deeply-felt character in the book[11]—this passage and others like it insistently designate another kind of energy, which is purely textual. Language fuels language, one rhetorical flourish preparing the way for another, as though what links them fundamentally is a narrative decision to exploit verbal extravagance. The relatively wasteful, unproductive expense of style here is not so intrusive as to negate the mimetic force of Headstone's presence in the text, but it does partially turn language into a sign for its own discontinuity from meaning and purpose, for its own stylistic self-involvement. We are at least as much aware of Dickens the rhetorician, extravagantly juggling a series of rhetorical balloons, as we are aware of Headstone's agony.

The preceding passage, taken from one of the highest pitches of Headstone's anguish, dramatically establishes the split between representation and linguistic extravagance. But elsewhere, Headstone is rendered with similar kinds of rhetorical abandon. These devices include redundancy of phrasing:

> Bradley Headstone, in his decent black coat and waistcoat, and decent white shirt, and decent formal black tie, and decent pantaloons of pepper and salt, with his decent silver watch in his pocket and its decent hair-guard round his neck, looked a thoroughly decent young man of six-and-twenty.   (II.1.266)

and absurdly extended metaphor:

> The arrangement of his wholesale warehouse, so that it might always be ready to meet the demands of retail dealers—history here, geography there, astronomy to the right, political economy to the left—natural history, the physical sciences, figures, music, the lower mathematics, and what not, all in their several places—this care had imparted to his countenance a look of care. . . . He always seemed to be uneasy lest anything should be missing from his mental warehouse, and taking stock to assure himself. . . .   (266–267)

as well as the devices mentioned above. Even at the grim climax of his story, Headstone is rendered as a rhetorical figure turned absurdly literal: "Bradley had caught him round the body. He seemed to be girded with an iron ring. . . .

When the two were found . . . he was girded still with Bradley's iron ring, and the rivets of the iron ring held tight''(IV.15.874).

In all these passages, as J. Hillis Miller might put it, Dickens' language acquires more ontological solidity as language—it becomes an "unreal" but an opaque textual object—than the reality it pretends to represent.[12] Lately, some theorists of the fantastic have turned to this non-signifying potential as the single distinctive feature of fantastic discourse. Bellemin-Noel, for example, in his critique of Tzvetan Todorov's content-oriented system, claims that, instead, "one could speak of a rhetoric of the unsayable (in fantastic literature) . . . the fantastic activity often returns to a creation of 'pure signifiers.' "[13] While we should be wary of applying such generalizations, one clear mark of the unreality of Dickens' fiction, supplied by a purely rhetorical means, is this systematic refusal of referential economy.

The stylistic liberality associated with Headstone is partly, of course, tied to the excessiveness of his character. But Headstone's emotional excesses are much more laden with meaning than are Dickens' stylistic ones. I began with Headstone deliberately, in fact, because he is such an unlikely vehicle for gratuitous linguistic play. And the same techniques used to evoke Headstone's rage are actually used in a broad spectrum of contexts in *Our Mutual Friend*, often to describe characters not nearly so extreme emotionally—in short, they transcend the contexts in which we find them.

If we turn to the novel's introduction of Noddy Boffin, for example, and compare it to the first Headstone passage, we can find a continuity of stylistic technique in a situation far removed from the earlier one in its narrative implications and its tone:

> The words referred to a broad, round-shouldered, one-sided old fellow in mourning, coming comically ambling towards the corner, dressed in a pea overcoat, and carrying a large stick. He wore thick shoes, and thick leather gaiters, and thick gloves like a hedger's. Both as to his dress and to himself, he was of an overlapping rhinoceros build, with folds in his cheeks, and his forehead, and his eyelids, and his lips, and his ears, but with bright, eager, childishly-inquiring, grey eyes, under his ragged eyebrows, and broad-brimmed hat. A very odd-looking old fellow altogether. (I.5.90)

Again, readability is interrupted by syntax, although this time of a cheerfully parallel rather than a disjunctive prolixity; character is estranged through externalization; physical discontinuities are heightened; and the figurative becomes literal. Though the object of Dickens' style has changed, the marks of that style's prodigality have not. Instead, they seem to float free of any particular context or intention. They designate an excess, but not an excess that can be tied to any particular character or narrative context, even though they clearly run parallel to these characters and contexts. The gulf between the two is crucial: represented excess becomes the occasion for an authorial excess that only loosely reflects it and remains unchanged in relation to changing narrative subjects. In this way, style generalizes Dickensian excessiveness, making its unreality seem the property of style itself rather than that of individual characters and scenes. The character of either Headstone or Boffin is distinctly separable from the language that describes them: Dickens' language remains tangential to character, stylistically, in its ostentatious self-performance.

The proof of this gulf between excesses of style and those of mimetic content is that other characters, who range far from the emotional peaks of either a Headstone or a Boffin, are presented through the exact same stylistic devices. Thus, R. Wilfer, a sympathetic but wholly reserved character, is presented in a similarly excessive style, through such means as figurative transformations into the literal, externalization of character, and discursive prolixity:

> If the conventional Cherub could ever grow up and be clothed, he might be photographed as a portrait of Wilfer. His chubby, smooth, innocent appearance was a reason for his being always treated with condescension when he was not put down. . . . So boyish was he in his curves and proportions, that his old schoolmaster meeting him in Cheapside, might have been unable to withstand the temptation of caning him on the spot. In short, he was the conventional cherub. . . .   (I.4.75)

His wife, a more expressive but still constipated character, merits the same stylistic devices:

> She was much given to tying up her head in a pocket-handkerchief, knotted under the chin. This head-gear, in conjunction with a pair of gloves worn within doors, she seemed to consider as at once a kind of armour against misfortune (invariably assuming it when in low spirits or difficulties), and as a species of full dress. It was therefore with some sinking of the spirit that her husband beheld her thus heroically attired. . . .
>
>   (77)

The point is simply that Dickens' prodigal style leaves it an open question—and an age-old critical saw—how much it is his characters and how much it is his rhetorical art that generates such extreme pitches of verbal energy.

While these techniques of Dickens' style may appear fairly commonplace after a century of stylistic analyses, the complex texture of his rhetoric remains obscured unless we can locate the non-economic impulse behind these techniques with precision.[14] For Dickens' inefficient style does not operate in a textual vacuum. Dickens is not in any way a formalist, or an unrestrainedly polysemous writer, though he has been described in this way by modern critics who privilege these stylistic attributes, or similar ones.[15] In Dickens, non-economic style is directly confronted by a number of other lexical codes or structures that are much more efficiently related to meaning. But these two different kinds of rhetoric do not simply coexist in the text, nor do they fracture it. Rather, inefficient and efficient rhetorical elements form a second-order economic relation that permits the excesses of Dickens' non-economic style to be named. Rather than being a simple companion to more conventional novelistic meaning, inefficient style is named in its very excessiveness by other lexical pressures. A direct exchange is created in rhetoric between signs of linguistic autonomy and signs that can name that autonomy in specific terms.

Because the relationships here can become very complex, it seems appropriate to explore this second-order economy through just one of these rhetorical elements, which I have earlier called mode. To begin with, one of the most striking things about mode, or "inner form," in Dickens is simply its multiplicity. We feel the shifts in Dickensian mode as a series of vivid changes in tonality, almost as if there were several different, highly theatrical narrators, each taking up an attitude appropriate to the characters and events he generates. Of course, it is a familiar idea in narrative theory that the novel owes its very existence to the convergence of numerous formal or generic categories. But no novelist exploits these differences so dramatically as Dickens. From scene to scene, or even from passage to passage, the shifts are clear-cut and decisive: the framework of formal cues is either grotesque, ironic, comic, fairy-tale-ish, satiric, melodramatic, lyric, or didactic. What we get in Dickens' novels is not so much a mixture of these modes as a distinct and precise fragmentation of them. These shifts in mode are so precise that there are never any neutral tonal moments in Dickens, as there are in writers who strive for a consistently non-intrusive or transparent prose—like early James or Forster—or in writers who adopt a limited range of modes—like Austen, Faulkner, or Joyce. And in Dickens, as we will see, constantly shifting modes imply constantly shifting and explicit authorial judgments about meaning.

The crucial point I would make here is that through this emphatic fragmentation and the extension of specific modes to all areas of the text, the contextualizing mode within which a non-economic style operates always works in readily-perceptible ways to "name" such style, to inscribe its very excessiveness within an efficient relationship of sign to meaning. Specifically, as style defines an authorial, textual distance from conventional norms of representation, mode redefines that distance as a controlling attitude of some kind. In other words, if the intrusive language describing Dickens' characters deviates from meaningful narrative norms toward writerly play, those very deviations taken as a general movement always come to express a particular kind of narrative intrusion. They indicate a particular, dominant narrative attitude, which is more immediately accessible to the reader—even if it is not in itself an exclusive index of the novel's meaning—than are the distinct psychological excesses of character that stylistic excess usually seems to parallel.

Mode, of course, can work independently of such stylistic excess—as it does in many writers. But the very prodigality of Dickens' prose defines a degree of authorial dominion that is necessary to the importunate intrusions of his abrupt modal shifts, which might seem to reflect a confusion of design without that well-defined and assertive authorial autonomy. Thus, the non-economic excessiveness of style becomes crucial, as a sign of textual distance from character, partly because that distance is more easily recuperated by mode as an excess of authorial intention. Style and mode are in this way more dynamically and more fluidly related in Dickens than they are in most novelists, fantastic or otherwise.

Dickens' prodigal style, and the autonomous, intentional attitude it comes to evoke, are named by mode much more systematically, in fact, than they can be named by the more naturalistic, psychological codes of excess that parallel stylistic excess. For these psychological codes are much more limited, and much more ambiguous, in their attempt to define the origins of rhetorical extravagance. Psychological codes may tell us, for example, that Headstone is excessively tormented, Boffin excessively avuncular, Wilfer excessively diffident, his wife excessively tyrannical. But what conditions our attitude toward these various types of psychic excess, more than anything else, is the tone of favor or disfavor, innocence or danger, seriousness or frivolity that mode establishes as a context for the stylistic freedom mounted on each character. Consider the ambiguities: Mr. Venus might well be as tormented as Headstone—his frustration is certainly analogous—and George Sampson might be as innocently diffident as Wilfer. But, in Dickens, the mode within which each character is performatively described shapes a persuasive kind of significance that is imposed on each character, a significance not the less powerful because it may actually be distinct from any we can derive by analysis and comparison of various psychological dynamics. Thus, the comic cues in the Mr. Venus passages divert us from too strong a parallel with Headstone, in ways that anticipate revelations about character and psychology that are not made, in Venus's case, for several hundred pages. In this way, mode and style, operating together, provide a powerful way of reading these characters, irrespective of our other ways of forming judgments about them. Through the interaction of style and mode, we learn not every way of reading Dickens' characters, but one persistent and controlling evaluation which we can juxtapose, if we wish, to other kinds of narrative significance.

Through clear-cut shifts in mode, then, seemingly gratuitous language, which signals authorial distance, is convertible to very different kinds of tone, as the expression of a dominant authorial attitude. Through mode, the extravagance of non-economic stylistic energies—which, through their very anti-representational qualities, express a kind of intentional autonomy—is actually put to use as the unmistakable, impassioned expression of a general authorial decision about meaning. Stylistic excess becomes the very guarantee of such meaning's depth and power. This general meaning may well be distinct from the particular object of representation in any given passage, but in Dickens mode and style together produce a kind of meaning that becomes a much more stable and comprehensive level of reference, and a more economic enclosure of non-economic rhetorical excess, than more mimetic cues.

This ability of mode to name the vagaries of style as a certain kind of authorial intention is far more complicated than I have suggested here, but a few concrete examples should help define this naming relationship as a starting point. The conversion of seemingly unbounded narrative energies to the economy of a sign/meaning relationship through mode is most clearly visible when the same vehicle for unbounded style is placed within entirely different modal registers. This variation in mode's relationship to style can also help underline the profound differences in these lexical systems, despite their interaction. To return to Bradley Headstone: through Headstone, non-economic style is most often put in the mode of melodramatic terror. But even in relation to Headstone, the significance of non-economic style can shift drastically. Such style can also become transiently comic, as it does when Headstone, informed by the Rev. Frank Milvey of Lizzie's marriage, is seized by an extravagant and unrealistic fit. In a passage too long to quote in its entirety, Headstone is presented as a comic butt, a character for whom we need feel little sympathy. And the stylistic devices used to render his fit, though similar to devices we noted earlier, retain a much more purely comic effect here. The obsessive, discontinuous details of Headstone's description—

his sidling toward shadows, or his repeatedly "plucking at his gloves" (IV.11.820), for example—are felt as explicitly comic gestures. Similarly, the arch prolixity of the narrator's introduction of Headstone to this scene works to sustain a comic reticence, a sort of mincing ridiculousness, while previously such prolixity had served melodramatic sensationalism: "There was now so evident a faltering upon him, expressive of indecision whether or no he should express his having heard himself referred to, that Mr. Milvey spoke to him." And the estrangement of Headstone through a forcefully external description of his fit makes him appear absurd, rather than threatening: "Bradley Headstone caught hold of a pillar behind him. If Mr. Milvey knew an ashy face when he saw it, he saw it then. . . . As Mr. Milvey, who had no more minutes to spare, made a suitable reply and turned back into the office, he observed the schoolmaster to lean against the pillar with his hat in his hand, and to pull at his neckcloth as if he were trying to tear it off"(821).

The cause of these tonal shifts is not that Headstone's psychological identity or the stylistic devices used to render it have changed; it is simply that prodigal stylistic energies are channeled here by the overriding comic mode of the wedding chapter. This comic mode is signaled partly just by the movement of the plot, but more importantly it is signaled by immediate cues from diction and point of view. Milvey's point of view in particular encodes the excessiveness of Headstone's fit within a comic mode when he observes casually: "There is a person outside who seems to be really ill, and to require some help, though he says he does not." More directly, Headstone's fit is rendered ridiculous by the narrator through a breezy narrative point of view that certifies coy, comic knowingness: "He seemed to be a shy man, struggling against nervousness, and spoke in a very constrained way." The passage goes on to weave the diction of comedy into the prodigal descriptions of Headstone themselves, as when an anonymous attendant describes him as "took very bad to be sure . . . biting and knocking about him . . . furiously"(821). The very choice of words like "biting" and "knocking"—which contrast with the more ominously violent modifiers of the earlier Headstone passage—or the tongue-in-cheek innocence of "took very bad to be sure" help insinuate humor into the very folds of style. By surrounding prodigal style with comic cues, mode is able to name style's histrionic excessiveness for its own purposes, and to keep it from any absolute freedom to dissipate itself in an intentional vacuum.

These comic cues take us back to earlier descriptions of Headstone as a source of fun; they treat us to the sadistic amusement of a Eugene Wrayburn but, interestingly, without qualifying our own sadistic pleasure with the ominous modal cues we find in passages bringing Wrayburn and Headstone together. In this way, mode reminds us that Headstone's significance as a character is shifted and determined as much by the demands of novelistic form as by his own personal crises. Throughout the novel, the private excesses of characters like Headstone, diverted away from the mimetic level once by Dickens' stylistic extravagance, are altered again and named by such modal cues. The complete moral transformation of Bella, for example, is defined for us partly by the confident modal register of her final chapters, more so than simply by her own declarations, which would otherwise be subject to doubt— as she herself admits—or by our own access to her interior self. Immediately after her renunciation of Boffin, an increase in stylistic excess is fused with an uncharacteristically patronizing but bouncy tone in relation to Bella:

> . . . Bella was considering . . . when whom should she see, sitting at one of the windows with the plate-glass sash raised, but R. Wilfer himself, preparing to take a slight refection!
>
> . . . Bella discerned that the refection had the appearance of a small cottage-loaf and a pennyworth of milk. Simultaneously with this discovery on her part, her father discovered her, and invoked the echoes of Mincing Lane to exclaim 'My gracious me!'

> . . . Bella hugged him and choked him to her heart's content . . .

> Sooth to say, Mr. Rokesmith not only passed the window, but came into the counting-house. And not only came into the counting-house, but, finding himself alone there with Bella and her father, rushed at Bella and caught her in his arms, with the rapturous words 'My dear, dear girl; my gallant, generous, disinterested, courageous, noble girl!' And not only that even, (which one might have thought astonishment enough for one dose), but Bella, after hanging her head for a moment, lifted it up and laid it on his breast, as if that were her head's chosen and lasting resting-place!

> (III.16.667–671)

The modal cues here, which name the narrator's sudden stylistic promontory above Bella—who, as a personality, begins to shrink proportionately in dimension—confine the meaning of Bella's transformation almost entirely within the narrative point of view. These "named" excesses of style, rather than providing any kind of unmediated presence for Bella in the text, dominate what we can say about her extravagant self-humbling, submerged as she is not simply within John Harmon's doll house but also within the reciprocal play of Dickens' rhetorical extravagance and the authority it makes available to his precise modal cues. In a similar way, Boffin's feigned miserliness, the pretext for some outrageous stylistic play, is constantly bounded as comic, which protects him from falling too far in the reader's eyes, by modal cues that could just as easily have been more bleak. The very diction of the chapter titles— "The Golden Dustman Rises a Little," "The Golden Dustman Sinks Again"—signal the essential lightness of Boffin's transformation. And throughout, Boffin is presented from a supercilious point of view, rather than from the sardonic or fearful one used for characters like Wegg, Riderhood, and Headstone. Both Bella and Mrs. Boffin, for example, consistently assert a kind of imperviousness to this change ("Don't mind him, Bella, my dear," Mrs. Boffin says [III.5.526]). The phraseology used for Mr. Boffin's enigmatic obsessions, too, repeatedly rings a comic bell ("Recollect we are not our old selves. Recollect, we must scrunch or be scrunched. Recollect, we must hold our own. Recollect, money makes money"[III.5.537]). In a novel concerned so centrally with transformation, renovation, and metamorphosis of character, it is largely the cues of mode, in conjunction with stylistic departures from representational norms, that signal what kind of authorial significance is attributed to any particular venture outside the limits of a character's prior identity.

Comparison of a single character's altered contextual treatment, like that of Headstone, defines the second order, fantastic economy of style and mode most dramatically. But at every moment in Dickens' narration the flamboyant play of prodigal style is transiently named by the shifts and demarcations of mode, and in that way subjected to an economy of meaning. Transformation of the figurative into the literal, for instance, is understood as satiric in and of itself during the Veneering's dinner party, in which Twemlow becomes the dinner-table metaphor meant to describe him. But such transformation seems an implicit gesture toward fairy-tale enchantment when it occurs during the "Arabian Nights" wedding feast of Bella and John. Thus, the old pensioner becomes a fairy-tale ogre "Old Gruff and Glum," the headwaiter becomes "the Archbishop of Greenwich," and the food is "seasoned with Bliss—an article which they are sometimes out of, at Greenwich" (IV.4). At other points, such transformation is nightmarish—for example, when Venus and Wegg together speak of his missing leg as if it were literally recalcitrant. Similarly, the kind of preposterous prolixity found in the Veneering chapters is invested with an entirely different meaning when it extends the sentimentality of the wedding chapter: "There was an innocent young waiter of a slender form and with weakish legs, as yet unversed in the wiles of waiterhood, and but too evidently of a romantic temperament, and deeply (it were not too much to add hopelessly) in love with one young female not aware of his merit.'' And prolixity is transformed yet again by the triumphant self-righteousness of the final victory over Wegg:

> A countenance of special discontent and amazement Mr. Wegg exhibited in this position, with his buttons almost as prominently on view as Sloppy's own, and with his wooden leg in a highly unaccommodating state. But, not for many seconds was his countenance visible in the room; for, Sloppy lightly trotted out with him and trotted down the staircase, Mr. Venus attending to open the street door. (IV.14.862)

To identify mode with reference is, of course, only the beginning of an analysis of the way Dickens' rhetoric signifies. There are many different ways in which mode operates to complicate or even obscure the generation of meaning. For one thing, mode can change very quickly in Dickens, not just from scene to scene but from sentence to sentence. For another, there are various ways of grouping the hierarchies of these modal shifts—ironic interludes can be controlled by an overriding comic mode, for instance, or vice versa—and it is difficult to determine which narrative attitude should be subordinate, which dominant. It goes without saying, too, that the many other, more ''naturalistic'' systems of meaning in Dickens often work together with mode, or against it, in the labeling of any particular linguistic excess. Moreover, mode itself labels more things than just style and, through it, authorial attitude: mode colors almost every aspect of Dickens' characters and scenes, whether it is mediated first by style's authorial distance or not. But the most important point here is that the clear presence of an ever-shifting series of modes, and therefore some kind of authorial intention latent in stylistic excess, invites us to make a decision about the basic significance of each narrative moment. Mode invites us to decide which attitude lies at the origin of stylistic excess, of Dickens' departure from conventional mimesis. Different readers may formulate that attitude in different ways, but all are responding to the imperative toward meaning implicit in Dickens' emphatic juxtaposition of narratively intrusive modes.

The important qualification to make here is that the relation of prodigal style to mode is not a simple economic one. As implied earlier, this naming relationship is only one moment in the conjunction of these two lexical systems. For even if mode does designate the emotional values carried by seemingly unbounded narrative energies, this naming process is not reductive. Style and mode shimmer in an uneasy harmony, neither one ever appearing finally to be dominant over the other. Mode's ability to name style makes mode fantastically compatible with stylistic energies that seem, in their own right, to overturn significance wholesale. But the very pervasiveness of prodigal stylistic devices in the novels suggests their partial independence from the economic naming function of any particular mode. In other words, what we experience during the tensions of the rhetoric is an efficient but transient compatibility between economic and non-economic linguistic energies, not an irreversible reduction. It would be an exaggeration to stress either pole as final, or transcendent. What we experience instead is a fantastic system that permits efficient and inefficient rhetorical elements to amplify each other, without a final conversion of the narrative either to a luxurious formalism or to the limitations of any particular atmospheric mood. Economic and non-economic rhetorics are interchangeable despite their essential difference.

A recognition of this second-order economy within Dickens' rhetoric is only the beginning of any serious exploration of that economy—for the tenuous compatibility of these two systems of rhetoric must always be unstable. One way to suggest some of the complexities involved is to consider for a moment longer some of the instabilities within the modal register itself. That is, the multiplication and dispersion of Dickensian modes works not only as an efficient instrument of signification; at strategic points, it also generates a kind of non-economic potential itself by radically pluralizing rhetorical attitudes. This pluralizing is most apparent at the ends of the novels, when the fragmenting quality of Dickens' formal shifts is subjected to a kind of acceleration. The carefully-paced alternation of modes throughout the work is turned into a frenzied kind of collusion. In the endings, Dickens includes all of his contextual modes in strikingly close proximity, in such a way as to dissolve their differences. This is one reason why it is so difficult to pinpoint the actual ending in a work like *Our Mutual Friend*: Dickens' plot lines seem to run together, rather than to be fully resolved in the crescendoes of a perfectly orchestrated tonal climax.

To take one example: the chapter entitled "The Feast of the Three Hobgoblins," in which Bella and John meet at her father's office to be engaged—clearly not an actual ending, but nevertheless the emotional climax of Bella and John's story—manages to include a number of Dickens' modes in rapid, almost frantic succession. The comic, of course, operates throughout this chapter, most especially in Bella and John's relation of their story to the astounded R. W.; the fairy tale association announced in the chapter title also appears throughout; and the lyric mode emerges on the walk home—during passages, for example, in which R. W. strews the path with smiles. But most important, even modes apparently incompatible with such felicity are included. In R. W.'s office, the engagement takes place within a grotesque atmosphere: we hear of "the uncongenial oddity of [the] surroundings," with "the two brass knobs of the iron safe of Chicksey, Veneering, and Stobbles staring from a corner like the eyes of some dull dragon" (III.16.673). Nevertheless, this grotesque moment does not disrupt the chapter's mood; rather, the narrator tells us that this atmospheric mood "only made it the more delightful." Or again, the chapter indulges in what might seem an irrelevant burst of satire when the three return to face Mrs. Wilfer, whose shock at Bella's return is treated in tones of the most "sublime severity" by the mocking narrator. But even satire is conscripted by the onward rush of the happy ending, as Mrs. Wilfer's satiric treatment is ultimately turned into a sign of benevolence. Without losing a bit of her ridiculous, caricatural qualities, Mrs. Wilfer's preposterous speech swings her into synch with Bella. Unable to rebuke Bella herself, Mrs. Wilfer's displaced anger at Lavinia becomes a sign of comic adjustment as it transforms Mrs. Wilfer's own perspective: " . . . if," she tells Lavinia, "making light of my warnings that the face of Mrs. Boffin alone was a face teeming with evil, you had clung to Mrs. Boffin instead of to me, and had after all come home rejected by Mrs. Boffin, trampled under foot by Mrs. Boffin, and cast out by Mrs. Boffin, do you think my feelings could have been expressed in looks?"(681). And the chapter continues in a satiric narrative blessing of "the agreeable party." In effect, the heightening of borders between all these distinct modes, and then their collective collapse in the modeless fabric of the narrative climax, becomes itself a generation of fantastic tension. The efficient signifying power of textual form is tentatively violated when various forms are splashed together in this way. The collapsing of mode as an instrument for naming style thus turns mode itself into a sign for excess, for narrative euphoria, for a namelessness of authorial attitude that enters into a fantastic tension with the clear-cut significance of individual modal cues.

This collapse of modes is only made more drastic in the penultimate chapter of the novel, "Persons and Things in General." While trying to include and resolve all lines of plot, the chapter manages to produce a prismatic shattering of tonal wholeness by accumulating the various modes associated with each plot. The chapter itself is broken into four short sections of text: a brief summary of the minor characters' fates; the satiric comedy of that "grand event" (IV.16), Mrs. Wilfer's visit; a sentimental set-piece bringing Sloppy and Jenny Wren together; and the pensive reunion of the Harmons and the Wrayburns. All four sections operate under the general rubric of the ending's providential good fortune, yet the pull of each section's individualizing tone is disorienting. The narrative attitude in these four sections is alternately cheerful, satiric, wistfully ironic, and sentimental; this problem is only further complicated by the divergence in tone of the Harmon and Wrayburn marriages themselves. What is most important here is that the differences in tone of this chapter produce a plain question on the level of the novel's meaning: what attitude does Dickens ultimately take toward the four very different marriages (two of them only promised) that are highlighted in this chapter? And if he views them all differently, then why is marriage chosen as the novel's symbolic concluding event? In short, what is the relationship between marriage as concluding event, human happiness in general, and narrative closure? The fractured tone undermines any single answer: the condescension of Lavinia and Mrs. Wilfer, the repressed ambition of George Sampson, the vulgarity of Sloppy, the sarcasm and amused resignation of Jenny—all contaminate the purity of marriage as a vehicle for narrative conclusion and narrative meaning.

Partly because of these disjunctive modes, it becomes impossible to say in any single way what Dickens means by concluding *Our Mutual Friend* in the way he does, or what he understood the structure of his story to mean. Instead, it is clear only that in some way these four stories work to undermine each other, or at least to confuse distinctions and parallels. Can we really see Jenny's relegation to Sloppy as a blessing—particularly after she recalls regretfully her fantasy of meeting a lover "from somewhere," a phrase that echoes Harmon's original sobriquet—or should we see such a marriage as an ironic comment on Lizzie's more privileged desires and fortunes? Does George's position mirror Bella's or invert it? Are there, in fact, similarities between the "beneficence" of Mrs. Wilfer and that of the Boffins? All these questions are complicated by the multiplicities of mode we encounter here, which prevent any kind of tonal resolution. We are left instead with a feeling of excessive, non-economic resolution, without that resolution being fully named because in fact it has been named so variously by these modes.

The use of mode to escape a referential economy, after it has worked so well to economize the excesses of prodigal style, suggests that the integration of the economic and the non-economic in various areas of the text is more important to Dickens as a structural principle than are the functions he assigns to any single textual system. Fantastic economies, in other words, transcend the narrative terms that produce them. At this point, it is worth suggesting how the concept of a fantastic economy reaches into other areas of Dickens' novels. For it is crucial to understand that we cannot locate this special kind of economy in Dickens' rhetoric alone. Dickens' novels are, in fact, saturated with versions of this fantastic economy. A bizarre, paradoxical economy of unlike things, a cooperation of the discordant, is absolutely central in Dickens, not just in his rhetoric but in all the important orderings of his subject matter. To locate Dickens' fantastic economy on the level of rhetoric is to discover its fundamental importance in Dickens' imagination, and to reduce it to its most primitive shape. But other areas of Dickens' texts can certainly help us fill in the implications and even the ethical significance of such a second-order economy. Very briefly, then, we should examine at least one kind of analogous thematic economy, as a way to establish some of the larger contexts and the larger implications of the argument about rhetoric.

In purely thematic terms, Dickens' fantastic economy emerges most simply, perhaps, when one considers that the novels create an urgent opposition between the economic and the non-economic properties of human desire. Economic desires, on the one hand, drive the claustrophobic and self-imprisoned phases of Dickensian psychology—a psychology of repetitive, mechanical identity, of selfishness, and of various miserly kinds of inflexible, retentive, solipsistic yearning. From the greedy self-absorption of Fagin in *Oliver Twist* to the misers and scavengers of *Our Mutual Friend*, Dickens was always deeply disturbed by personal inabilities to expend energy freely, liberally, without taking account beforehand of its profitable return. Non-economic desires, on the other hand, underlie all the dangerous, uncontrolled proclivities for violence, death, and cruelty that threaten Dickens' heroes, either internally or externally, as well as the exuberant reaches of play, generosity, and imagination the heroes eventually achieve. The ambiguity here is profound: since such non-economic exuberance is always also waste, Dickens was troubled by the latent affinities between his villains and his heroes in the willingness of both to throw themselves away—to waste themselves—on one consuming, self-regardless passion or another. For these non-economic desires always threaten in some way the wholeness and the integrity of the isolated self. If nothing else, they threaten the self's ability to control rationally its own movements and to maintain some kind of self-contained equilibrium of happiness. The waverings between individualist assertion and anti-individualist surrender of characters like Bella Wilfer, David Copperfield, and Pip in their relationships to sexual partners point up this problem. If Dickens was disgusted, then, by the monotonous economic needs of a Dombey or a Gradgrind, he was also wary of unregulated, prodigal desires, whether they take the cruel form of a Sikes or a Blandois, or the more innocent but equally dangerous form of a Dick Swiveller, a Mr. Dick, a Mrs. Harris, or a Pip. Esther Summerson, who throws away her self-regard in the most problematic way, is the cardinal instance of this ambivalence. Dickens' twin fears—of rigidly economic and solipsistic desire on the one hand, and of prodigal self-expenditure on the other—signal his need to balance or combine these two kinds of psychic energy in some higher form of psychic organization.

This opposition of two kinds of human desire, put crudely enough here, is familiar in some way to all readers of the novels.[16] Yet it is worth considering, in these terms, that on the simplest levels of plot and theme Dickens ends his novels with some kind of efficient transaction between economic and non-economic human desire.[17] The heroes' rejection of purely monetary considerations, their more general rejection of psychological self-interest, and their tentative affiliation with creative forms of violence and self-negation—all non-economic inclinations—are redeemed in the conservative economies of moral order and social stability the novels seem to cherish. *Our Mutual Friend*, which ends in an overt celebration of death within life, is the most explicit of the novels in its efforts to allow fatal expenditures of energy to circulate together with conservative recuperations of energy, in a narrative medium that contains them both despite the apparent contradiction. But Dickens' attempt to find an exchangeable value for disinterest in a world that cannot, at the same time, completely deny the premium it places on self-interest, is a concern that haunts the endings of all the novels.

There is, of course, a crucial, provocative warp in this formulation of the issue. To speak of a thematic system that puts economic and non-economic human desires into an efficient relation is in some sense to speak of a second-order economy. This second-order economy seems able to preserve the integrity of both kinds of desire while it also makes them exchangeable—convertible to each other despite their apparent irreconcilability. To put this exchange in simpler thematic terms: Dickens' heroes earn their providential good fortune only through their extreme self-negations; at the same time, they also earn the reckless emotional luxury of those self-negations through their moral circumspection (Bradley Headstone's suicidal impulses, for example, do not occupy the same moral plateau, and for that reason do not gain the same narrative approval, as Lizzie Hexam's or even Eugene Wrayburn's). Neither pole of the exchange is reduced completely to the other, yet neither is allowed to exceed the balanced system of merits and rewards. Anyone who has tried to make students tolerate what they often call the hypocrisy of Dickens' happy endings knows how subtle the workings of this second-order economy must be. In fact, a paradoxical economy of this kind is clearly a fantastic one—an imaginative projection that seems both real and unreal, possible and impossible, at the same time. The thematic economy at work here is so provisional, as an image of what human identity may actually include, that it makes sense to describe it as a wish, a waking fantasy, or perhaps the representation in art of a psychic impossibility. That is to say, the question of belief—of reality/ unreality, plausibility/implausibility—is generated by the satisfaction of the heroes' desires in relation to a thematic system that includes, fantastically, both an economic and a non-economic dimension. To describe the second-order or fantastic economy of desire in this way is to see it as the projection of a very specific split within the nature of human psychic needs, a split Freud might have described as the conflict between the psychic economy of the pleasure principle and the violation of that economy by the death instincts. But, more important to the present purpose, it is also to suggest a structural continuity between the fantastic opposition of theme and those of language in Dickens.

As I hope this discussion has suggested, the concept of a second-order economy is very complex and must be sifted out with some care. But such an impossible economy, both thematic and rhetorical, helps to explain the general, impossible compatibility of the real and the unreal, the meaningful and the non-meaningful, that most readers sense in many different phases of Dickens' novels—as opposed to the shock of the discontinuous we experience in, say, Kafka or Calvino, and universally in the Gothic. Instead, Dickens' particular economy, with its impossible reconciliations, resembles more closely that of Shakespearean comedy, or of a few Latin American novelists, like Garcia Marquez or Puig. But most important, the concept of a fantastic economy can help to make the relation between the real and the unreal in Dickens perceptible as a structural tension in his work, rather than a strictly epistemological one—a structural tension that unites a crucial and idiosyncratic rhetorical dynamic with Dickens' characteristic thematic concerns. And seeing this structural tension in Dickens can carry us beyond the reach of both psychology and linguistics, into a greater appreciation of Dickens' concern with the relationship of all human energy to limiting systems, and with the ways in which that dialectical relationship can be represented in art. Rather than insulating language, attention to rhetorical tensions can help reveal the fundamentally economic character of Dickens' novels. For in many different ways, the novels attempt to organize an exhilarating exchange between the real and the unreal, the contained and the uncontainable, that takes us beyond the limits of analytic thought toward a self-conscious expression of the (logically inconceivable) nature of human energy itself.

NOTES

1. *Dickens on the Romantic Side of Familiar Things: "Bleak House" and the Novel Tradition* (New York: Columbia University Press, 1977), pp. 1–7.

2. Recently, some theoreticians have argued that the fantastic, as a literary category, is not definable at all on the level of subject matter, but that it can only be described as a general set of structural principles, which, by inverting semantic distinctions between the real and the unreal, underlie the fundamental linguistic ambiguities of all texts. See esp. Christine Brooke-Rose, *A Rhetoric of the Unreal: Studies in Narrative and Structure, Especially of the Fantastic* (Cambridge: Cambridge University Press, 1981). See also Phillipe Harmon, "Un discours contraint," *Poetique*, 16 (1973), 411–445.

3. See Rene Wellek and Austin Warren, Chapter 16, "The Nature and Modes of Narrative Fiction," *Theory of Literature* (New York: Harcourt, Brace, 1949), pp. 219–234. An excellent discussion of "inner form" can also be found under the entry "Form" in Roger Fowler, *Linguistics and the Novel* (London: Methuen, 1977), pp. 68–71. See also Wayne C. Booth's discussion of tonal cues in Chapter 7, "The Uses of Reliable Commentary," *The Rhetoric of Fiction* (Chicago: University of Chicago Press, 1961), pp. 169–209.

4. Brooke-Rose, esp. pp. 76 and 85–86. "Conventions of readability" include: constant reference to past and future, an absence of narrator interference, plausibility, discursive predictability, a detonalized and merely assertive discourse, exhaustiveness of description (as opposed to mosaic-like description), etc.

5. Foremost in his opposition, perhaps, is Emile Benveniste, who, in *Problems in General Linguistics*, trans. Mary Elizabeth Meek (Coral Gables: University of Miami Press, 1971), argues that, at the level of the word, it is impossible to suspend relations of signification in any way. See also Andre Martinet, *Elements of General Linguistics*, trans. Elisabeth Palmer (London: Faber & Faber, 1969), or the work of Roland Barthes's middle period, particularly *Elements of Semiology*, trans. Annette Lavers and Colin Smith (London: Cape, 1967); or *S/Z*, trans. Richard Miller (New York: Hill & Wang, 1974), p. 51: "structure is not a design, a schema, a diagram: everything signifies something."

6. "Introduction a l'Oeuvre de Marcel Mauss," *Sociologie et anthropologie* (Paris: Presses universitaires de France, 1966).

7. See Jacques Lacan, "The Freudian Thing," *Ecrits*, trans. Alan Sheridan (New York: Norton, 1977). For a good discussion of Lacan's return to the Saussurean separation of signifier from signified, see Anika Lemaire, "The Lacanian Perspective in Linguistics," *Jacques Lacan*, trans. David Macey (Boston: Routledge & Kegan Paul, 1977), pp. 38–50. In general, for Lacan the existence of the unconscious at all is predicated on the ability of the psyche to detach signifiers from the signified, or unconscious discourse from conscious discourse.

8. See esp. Roland Barthes, *The Pleasure of the Text*, trans. Richard Miller (New York: Hill & Wang, 1975), pp. 4–6.

9. See *The Pleasure of the Text*, p. 6: in the text of bliss, "two edges are created: an obedient, conformist, plagiarizing edge . . . and *another edge*, mobile, blank (ready to assume any contours), which is never anything but the site of its effect: the place where the death of language is glimpsed."

10. Charles Dickens, *Our Mutual Friend*, ed. Stephen Gill (Baltimore, Maryland: Penguin, 1971), III.10.608. Further references are to volume, chapter, and page numbers in this edition.

11. See, *e.g.*, Edgar Johnson, *Charles Dickens: His Tragedy and Triumph*, 2 vols. (New York: Simon & Schuster, 1952), II. 1039–1040; or John Lucas, *The Melancholy Man: A Study of Dickens' Novels* (London: Methuen, 1970), p. 329.

12. See esp. *The Form of Victorian Fiction* (Notre Dame: University of Notre Dame Press, 1968), pp. 36–44.

13. Jean Bellemin-Noel, "Des formes fantastiques aux themes fantasmatique," *Litterature*, 2 (May, 1971), 112–113. Translated and quoted by Rosemary Jackson in *Fantasy: The Literature of Subversion* (London: Methuen, 1981), p. 38.

14. These same (or similar) stylistic devices are discussed by numerous other critics, though they are placed in very different contexts. To suggest just some of the directions taken: Garrett Stewart, in *Dickens and the Trials of Imagination* (Cambridge, Mass.: Harvard University Press, 1974), esp. pp. xiv–xviii, describes extravagant prose as Dickens' embodiment of the romantic imagination; William F. Axton, *Circle of Fire: Dickens' Vision and Style and the Popular Victorian Theater* (Lexington: University of Kentucky Press, 1966), pp. 153–155, argues that similar devices help Dickens rearrange his readers' relationship to an overly-familiar reality; James R. Kincaid, *Dickens and the Rhetoric of Laughter* (London: Oxford University Press, 1971), pp. 5–7, identifies techniques like estrangement of perspective and narrative interruption as elements in Dickens' attempt to consolidate a shared system of values; Robert Garis, *The Dickens Theatre: A Reassessment of the Novels* (London: Oxford University Press, 1965), p. 16, observes that Dickens' flamboyant style creates a theatrical, performative environment. Clearly, our awareness of Dickens' stylistic techniques lends itself to a variety of different interpretations, which do not necessarily reveal the non-economic semantic tendencies I mean to define. My own discussion of style, in *Excess and Restraint in the Novels of Charles Dickens* (Athens: University of Georgia Press, 1981), suffers from a lack of precision by subsuming similar impulses under categories like "satire" and "parody."

15. The best of these remains J. Hillis Miller, "The Fiction of Realism: *Sketches by Boz, Oliver Twist*, and Cruikshank's Illustrations," in *Dickens Centennial Essays*, ed. Ada Nisbet and Blake Nevius (Berkeley: University of California Press, 1971), pp. 1–69.

16. Modern criticism has been highly sensitive to this opposition in Dickens. See Edmund Wilson's seminal essay, "Dickens: The Two Scrooges," *The Wound and the Bow* (New York: Oxford University Press, 1941), pp. 1–104; or Humphrey House's comments in his Preface to *Oliver Twist*, collected in *All in Due Time* (London: Hart-Davis, 1955), pp. 190–200.

17. In my book, *Excess and Restraint in the Novels of Charles Dickens*, I discuss at much greater length how the novels achieve such a cooperation on the level of representation. I also argue that Dickens' ambivalence here reflects a fundamental, unresolvable psychological dilemma, which is reflected in a number of textual strategies besides those referred to in this essay.

What's in a Name: Fantasy and Calculation in Dickens

Harry Stone

Names were always magical for Dickens. We know that he collected them in his notebooks, fussed over them in his manuscripts, and discussed them endlessly with family and friends. He agonized especially over the names of his chief characters and the titles of his novels. Two of the names in *Martin Chuzzlewit* went through such intricate changes as Pick, Tick, Flick, Flicks, Fleezer, Sweezer, Sweezleden, Sweezlebach, Sweezlewag, Cottletoe, Swee-tletoe, Pottletoe, Spottletoe, Chuzzletoe, Chuzzlebog, Chubblewig, Chuzzlewig, and Chuzzlewit before they emerged in the novel as Spottletoe and Chuzzlewit. The title of *David Copperfield* went through even more changes. Dickens felt uncomfortable and inhibited, unable to proceed, until he settled on a name—the right name.[1]

That there was a right name he had no doubt. It was the name that conveyed the outward show and inward mystery of a character or a book, the name which revealed and yet concealed. Part of a name's magic lay in this latter property, this ability to be open and yet secretive. Indeed this duality was often of the essence: the blatant showing forth frequently made one overlook the inconspicuous hints glimmering within. Thus the paradox and irony: by revealing, one concealed. There is a corollary to this. Dickens' names are deceptive. They often seem clear or even simple, but this is frequently a figment of hindsight, a wisdom that comes only after we have been made privy to the grand design of a novel. We all know how much ink has been spilled over the simple title *The Mystery of Edwin Drood*, but without hindsight—and with this unfinished work there can be no full-fledged hindsight—the title retains its secret. Kate Dickens tells the story of how her aunt Georgina

191

Hogarth, shortly before Dickens' death, felt impelled to ask him, "I hope you haven't really killed poor Edwin Drood?," to which the enigmatic Master "gravely" replied, "I call my book the Mystery, not the History, of Edwin Drood"—an answer which perplexed both aunt and daughter, and a response which has been seized upon with equal avidity since then by the Homicidists and the Resurrectionists.[2]

Dickens' mode of naming is calculated and distinctive, but it is not sui generis; it has deep roots in a rich literary and dramatic tradition. His inspiration, however—or perhaps I should say his motivation—has more in common with the magic of folklore and fairy tales than with the tradition of allegory and humors, though it owes a great deal to each. Dickens' naming, in other words, is indebted to the clear, rational mode of designation that gave us Everyman, Shallow, Christian, and Allworthy—witness such generic Dickensian names (to cite *Little Dorrit* only) as Admiralty, Treasury, Horse Guards, Bar, Bishop, Bench, and so on—but his naming is even more indebted to the strange, cognate tradition that produced such curious appellatives as Cinderella, Blunderbore, Rumpelstiltskin, and Captain Murderer.

The name Captain Murderer is instructive; it exhibits some of the weird, unnerving properties that fairy-tale names often possess. Captain Murderer is the protagonist in a horrific tale that Dickens heard nightly in his childhood from the redoubtable lips of his nurse.[3] Captain Murderer had sharp pointed teeth and delighted in cannibalistic jokes. He also delighted in frequent banqueting. His mode of providing for these periodic banquets was invariable and economical. He married a succulent young girl—there was always a plentiful supply—immediately murdered her, chopped her up, had her baked in a great silver pie dish, and then feasted on her. Though his ghoulish proclivities are heralded by a host of baleful and predictive signs, he elicits no suspicion and arouses no concern. The most outrageous of the warning signs is his name: why would an endless line of eager young girls (each of whom disappears in due course) queue up to marry a terrifying killer with the telltale appellation—dare I call it a dead giveaway—of Captain Murderer? Obviously we are dealing here with a realm of fantasy, symbolism, and magic, a realm where abodes, clothing, physical attributes, and names conspire to express their true identities and yet are rarely seen for what they really are. This is the shorthand—I choose the word deliberately in view of Dickens' early career—of folklore and fairy tales. This is a way of showing us two things: that we live in a universe in which everything is meaningful and interconnected, and that few of us are able to read the plain signs that are all about us.

Dickens, however, does more than name his characters in the fairy-tale mode of Captain Murderer. He combines such names, which blend blatant showing-forth and strange, irrational lulling effects which prevent that showing-forth from being understood by the protagonists, with a less visible system of meanings, a carefully calculated and artfully articulated system that gives up its secrets only to the initiate. Such cunningly crafted names combine wild Captain Murderer fantasy and sober Daedalian calculation in equal degree.

We see this calculation everywhere in Dickens. We see it in his incidental remarks and in his meditated planning. But even if we did not have the evidence of his letters, conversations, and working notes to tell us that naming for him was a carefully weighed process, we have the irrefutable evidence of his practice: we can hardly miss the central, often critical role that names play in his writings. Oliver Twist, whose real name is Leeford, but who is named by Mr. Bumble in a manner that attests to his subjection and disinheritance by an inhuman system, must, as in the old romances, find his true name—that is, his true identity—before he can come into his fortune and his felicity. David Copperfield's name is no less crucial. When David runs away from the Murdstones' sadism, suffers the brutalities of a predatory world, and finally finds refuge with Miss Betsey, his succoring fairy godmother, she gives him a new name. That new name, Trotwood, is a protective and totemic sign that has its far-off origins in her sudden materialization, and even more sudden disappearance, at his birth. David understands the deep significance of this rechristening and the importance of his new denomination. The significance could hardly be more direct: David has been reborn. The fairy godmother who presided imperiously at his original birth presides with equal imperiousness at his rebirth. But Dickens does not let the matter rest here. A fresh beginning, he insists, demands a fresh appellation, hence the new name. As David puts it, using repetition to underline the irrefrangible union of name and identity, he is about to begin a "new life, in a new name, and with everything new about me."[4]

Other characters are vouchsafed a variety of appellations and a variety of identities, sloughing off an old name to be reborn in a new one, or giving up an old cognomen to better achieve a double or a triple identity. One thinks immediately of *Our Mutual Friend* where John Harmon appears also as Julius Handford and John Rokesmith, or of *Edwin Drood* where the true identity of Dick Datchery has spawned hundreds of articles and shelves upon shelves of books. These are special cases, but one can easily cite more ordinary examples: David Copperfield is variously known as Copperfield, Master Copperfield, Mr. Copperfield, Copperfull, Brooks of Sheffield, Young Innocent, Trotwood, Trot, David, Davy, Mas'r Davy, Doady, and Daisy—and all these names have special significances; in *Bleak House* Esther Summerson—women also partake of the potent magic of names—is called, among other sobriquets, Old Woman, Little Old Woman, Cobweb, Mrs. Shipton, Mother Hubbard, and Dame Durden (names which accentuate the connection between Dickens' naming and fairy tales and folklore).

We know that names are important, then, because of the meaningful roles they play in the novels. But names are not simply emanations of the plot. For Dickens, names often had a shamanistic significance: the name not only stood for the thing named but took on the very life and attributes of the thing named. The name was part of the thing itself: change the name and you change the thing, change the thing and you must change the name. Hence, in *Martin Chuzzlewit*, shabby sharper Montague Tigg metamorphoses into prosperous swindler Tigg Montague (Tigg's names exactly mirror his topsy-turvy transformation, which is a transformation—to make Dickens' pun explicit—in name only), or in *Bleak House*, romantic rakish Captain Hawdon dwindles into the blank nullity of self-denominated Nemo (another fairy-tale name). With Dickens certainly (to paraphrase Shakespeare), the name's the thing.

All this can be observed from the outside. But in this essay I would like to examine Dickens in the very process of formulating his names; I would like to follow the working of his mind over several novels and during many years as he fashioned names that would incorporate the potent fusion of fantasy and calculation, concealment and revelation, that I have been tracing. For this purpose I have selected four related names about which we have special knowledge. The first name is the most familiar and seemingly the most straightforward.

As Dickens contemplated the first number (that is, the first three chapters) of *David Copperfield*, he also contemplated the name of the character who was finally to bear the very Captain Murderer-like epithet of Mr. Murdstone. Dickens' first notion when he sought to name this character was to emphasize the hardness of the man and his hardening effect on others, and he jotted down in the first number plan the name "Mr. Harden." But then he began to play with the idea of murder or murderous—Mr. Murdstone is, of course, a metaphorical murderer of impressionable young widows and helpless young children—and he wrote below "Harden" two additional names, "Murdle" and "Murden," the first focusing on the concept of murder, the second combining murder with the last four letters of his original idea, "Harden." But apparently the reverberations of "hard" were too muffled in "Murden," and Dickens, writing now to the right of the first three names, turned to a new conception, "Murdstone," which combined the ideas of murder and hardness with equal emphasis and openness.

Murdstone was clearly better for Dickens' purposes than the other three names, not only because it more exactly delineated the two chief components of Murdstone's character but because the "stone" of Murdstone connects that flinty child-queller with another, much more concealed and much more magical, constellation of crucial images in *Copperfield*, the intricate images that help give meaning to one strong motif in the first number and in the novel. For Mr. Murdstone, the hard, implacable risen father, whose very name is a form of "stone," is through that name associated with the chief emblem of the dead father, the ever-present stone, always visible from David's bedroom window, that marks his father's grave. It is that stone, the cold, lonely gravestone, not the father (the father himself would be too threatening and guilt-engendering) that David feels—so he tells us—he has cruelly barred from the cozy fireside where he blissfully sits with his playful mother (1.2). Hence David's extraordinary reaction, one Sunday evening, when his mother reads him the story of how Lazarus was raised from the dead. He is terror-stricken. He cannot be quieted. Finally, later that night, Peggotty and his mother are obliged to take him out of bed and show him through his bedroom window that the dead are all lying at rest in their silent graves. What David sees—it is the one really crucial perception for him—is that his father is lying at rest. Hence his willingness, at last, to be consoled. He has finally been reassured that his banished father sleeping peacefully under the nearby gravestone will not rise again, will not, that is, reclaim his rightful place at the domestic hearth and punish his supplanter. Hence David's special horror much later when he comes home from a holiday cunningly arranged to get him out of the way and finds an interloper—a stern, inimical father—in possession of his household and his mother (2.11; 3.32).

This is to state explicitly what is only delicately insinuated by Dickens' art. Dickens' art is indirect and dramatic. By names, images, symbols, and hints, by elemental scenes and emblematic actions, he conveys his sense of the profound fears and hopes that shape us. By the time David returns from his enforced holiday we have begun to understand the forces that shape him, and we have begun to understand the signs and premonitions that hedge him all about. Now we can feel the full significance of his reaction when Peggotty informs him "You have got a Pa!" "Something," David writes, "—I don't know what, or how—connected with the grave in the churchyard, and the raising of the dead, seemed to strike me like an unwholesome wind" (3.32).

David reacts but does not comprehend. Yet his reaction and the images in which it is couched allow us to fathom the "what" and "how" of that unnamed "something." Furthermore, we know why that unnamed "something," risen from the grave, envelops David like an "unwholesome wind." He has sinned—so he feels—against his dead father. Now he must pay for that grievous sin. His worst nightmare fears, slumbering uneasily with the slumbering dead, have suddenly risen up, become living flesh and blood. His banished father, dark and vengeful, murderous and stonelike, has emerged wrathfully from beneath his quiet gravestone to punish and torment him. All this and more Dickens has prepared us to see and understand. Significantly, in view of David's complicated feelings concerning his buried real father, his real father's gravestone, his stonelike surrogate father, and his consanguinity with each (and as further evidence of Dickens' consciousness of these intricate relationships and their centrality to his theme), the earliest working notes for *Copperfield* show that Dickens considered many combinations of names with "bury" or "stone" in them, including "Stonebury" and "Copperstone," as possible surnames for David.

The rich elaboration of ideas and meanings that enmesh David, his mother, his dead and risen fathers, and others—the names in *Copperfield* are only part of that elaboration—are intricately suggested throughout the first number. That this elaboration is not the fanciful projection of overwrought criticism is further demonstrated by the working notes, this time by some of Dickens' entries on the right-hand side of the opening number plan. Dickens' very first entry is: "Father dead—Gravestone outside the house," thus suggesting the importance of the dead father and his constant presence as personified in the accusatory gravestone. The penultimate entry on the right-hand side compounds this meaning; it reads: "comes home 'father.'" The meaning, reduced in the notes to the barest shorthand, is clear. Coming home from his banishment to Yarmouth and the Peggottys he finds his dark "father" ("Black whiskers and black dog," as the number plan has it) risen now and murderously threatening, no longer safe in the "quiet churchyard," no longer slumbering with the peaceful dead, "all lying in their graves at rest, below the solemn moon" (2.11). The notes, therefore, not only show Dickens carefully fashioning the name "Murdstone," but shaping the name and controlling the attendant imagery (and the motifs that the name and the imagery embody) so that each enriches and illuminates the other.

By such carefully wrought means, and by other means, by combining, for example, the arcane foreshadowings of signs and portents with the realistic presentation of causes and effects (each demonstration supplementing the

others, and all reinforcing the central meaning), Dickens conveys his transcendental vision of life. We see this process at work with the name
Murdstone. We see how Dickens makes David's fearful fantasies consort with
real objects, reverberating associations, and thematic parallels to give the
name its ultimate import. This import, in turn, is reciprocal and reflexive: the
name confers additional meaning on the very elements that help (so symbiotic
is the relationship) to give additional meaning to the name. The process does
not stop here. A name such as Murdstone is shaped by the past, but in due
course it helps shape the future. The generative impulse in the name—the
initial combining of "murder" and "stone"—was rooted for Dickens in
powerful pre-*Copperfield* associations that went back to his most resentful
childhood feelings toward his parents, feelings of having been neglected,
abandoned, and betrayed, of having been left to spiritual and perhaps even to
physical death. David's childhood fathers act out Dickens' childhood nightmare. David's natural father abandons him, is replaced by a stone; his
surrogate father attempts to murder his very soul. The name Murdstone, at its
most elemental level, is for Dickens a personal conflation of horror, revulsion,
coldness, and mortality. These old associations, freshly called forth and
conjoined by the act of conceiving and then naming Murdstone, were mod-
ified by that act, but the new commingling that then emerged soon underwent
further transformations. As Dickens worked on the novel, the old associations
and the new conjunction, both now at the core of the name, became intertwined with the slowly emerging network of consonant associations in the
evolving book. When *Copperfield* was complete, the name Murdstone and its
rich freight of emotionally linked images and meanings did not vanish from
Dickens' consciousness. What remained—a reanimated and reconstituted
fusion of words, ideas, and deeply charged associations—strongly influenced
(though not rigidly or limitingly) the cognate naming yet to come.

It is easy to see this process of recapitulation and elaboration at work in
Dickens' subsequent naming, for chords from the Murdstone christening
resound beyond the boundaries of *Copperfield*. One reflex of that germinal
naming occurs more than six years later in *Little Dorrit*. In that novel, a name
Dickens had earlier rejected for Mr. Murdstone—"Murdle"—reappears like
an insistent ghost as the name of the swindler-financier, Mr. Merdle. Mr.
Merdle, like Mr. Murdstone, is a surrogate father who exploits and betrays his
trusting progeny—in this case the childlike investors who clamor to give him
money. The changed spelling of his name (changed from "Murdle" to
"Merdle"), while leaving the original pronunciation untouched, delicately
distances Merdle's connection with murder and accentuates his kinship with

the French word "merde," both as a noun and as an expletive. (Dickens knew French well.) The character Merdle is still associated with Murder: his ruin causes the deaths—literally the murders—of dozens of innocent victims, and his downfall culminates with his own self-murder. But Mr. Merdle lacks the outward hardness of Mr. Murdstone—his name seems to echo "muddle" as well as "merde" and "murder"—and Dickens' disgust at his high-society criminality and the mass misery and victimization it causes is rendered not through associations with stoniness, but through images of murder, muddle, and offal, images that culminate when Merdle's naked body, in its hot, wet, steamy receptacle, becomes merely "certain carrion at the bottom of a bath"—all of which, of course, is consonant with his name (II.25.537).

Mr. Merdle and Mr. Murdstone are kin, but they are also remarkably different, and their kinship and their differences are evident in their names.[5] That this is so, that these related names diverge in ways that embody the divergent identities they are meant to shadow forth, gives us further insights into Dickens' art. It tells us, for instance, that at the very outset of his post-*Chuzzlewit* designs, Dickens knows, in all fundamental respects, who his characters are, what they must do, and how they will end. Another afterglow of the naming of Murdstone ("Murdstone" in these linked namings is the ur-name) will again illustrate this point, and again demonstrate how Dickens incorporates concealment and revelation, recapitulation and elaboration, into many of his names.

In *Our Mutual Friend*, some fifteen years after formulating the name Murdstone for *Copperfield* and nine years after fashioning the name Merdle for *Little Dorrit*, Dickens once more played in his number plans with the name of a murderer. Like Mr. Murdstone, this murderer would have the outward appearance of middle-class sobriety and decorum, would profess a puritanical code of conduct, and would have a smug satisfaction in his own superiority and rectitude. But unlike Edward Murdstone, whose cold exterior mirrors the exploitive iciness within, Bradley Headstone's stony surface, conventional and self-deluding, disguises a barely suppressed, yet totally hidden—from himself as much as from anyone else—anarchic and destructive (because unacknowledged and unnurtured) passionateness. The association of Headstone with gravestone does not indicate, as the association of Murdstone with gravestone did in *Copperfield*, a dark, murderous, risen father, but a grave, murderous incarnation of death itself. Headstone, the respectable schoolmaster, carries death buried in his inmost self; the passion which in a different society and with a different upbringing might have ignited him into life here consumes him utterly and preordains his murderous onslaughts and his death.

Hence the deceptive and contrary connotations of his name. On the one hand, most ironically, and in keeping with his occupation as a prop and guide to the young (in this role the schoolmaster is another surrogate father), his name suggests—is indeed a version of—cornerstone (that is, headstone). On the other hand, most truly, his name also suggests deadness (stone) and gravestone or deathstone (again headstone)—the names Murdstone (murderous stone) and Headstone (death stone) are, we see, cognate. At the same time Headstone's name also hints at the tragic flaw of his socially engendered character: the glorification of control and rationality at the expense of freedom and emotion (Head-stone rather than Heart-stone). That death and deadness were powerful in Dickens' initial conception of Bradley Headstone may be seen with great clarity in the working notes, for in the plan for Number VI he twice contemplates and then rejects the name "Deadstone." "Headstone," of course, includes ironies and complexities beyond the reach of "Deadstone," and Deadstone, perhaps, was too obvious as well as too narrow a name. Interestingly, Dickens also twice rejected the given name Amos, and thus rejected a cluster of consonant and predictive associations. For Headstone, like the prophet Amos, was stern and unbending and full of terrifying visions, and though he did not, like Amos, preach of sin, punishment, and the final judgment, these subjects had a special relevance for him. Perhaps Dickens' decision here owed more to euphony than to associations.

One last example of naming, an odd name that Dickens conceived in 1869—twenty years after he named Murdstone, fourteen years after he named Merdle, and five years after he named Headstone—will again affirm this continuity of germinal idea, number-plan cogitation, and old-new association and elaboration. In the first number plan for *Edwin Drood*, Dickens twice wrote the surname "Durdles." (In his Book of Memoranda, probably in 1864, he had jotted down the name "Duddle"—possibly a way station on the road from Merdle and Muddle, through Duddle, to Durdles.)[6] "Durdles," of course, echoes the name "Merdle." But soon Dickens added a sobriquet to the unadorned Durdles. In the last entry on the right-hand side of Number Plan I—the last entry in the plan—he transmuted Durdles into a more complex appellation: "Stoney Durdles." Stoney Durdles combined in one name the "stone" and "murder" associations of Murdstone and Headstone with the "merde," "muddle," and "murder" associations of Merdle. "Stoney Durdles" was changed slightly to "Stony Durdles" in the printed text of the novel, but in both versions of the name the root signifiers, "stone" and "merdle" (the latter transformed to "durdles"), called up the old constellation of associations and connotations—or perhaps the root ideas of murder, stoniness, and death called up the old congeries of names. In any case, as all the Durdles entries in Number Plan I suggest, Stony Durdles is to be an incarnation of the dusty tomb.

Stony Durdles is a drunken stonemason. He is at once ordinary and extraordinary. We quickly grasp his special significance. We are informed at the outset (in passages that elaborate the notes in Number Plan I) that he is "chiefly in the gravestone, tomb, and monument way, and wholly of their color from head to foot" (4.25). A moment later we are told that "with the Cathedral crypt he is better acquainted than any living authority" or "any dead one." Dickens refers to Durdles's "stony calling" and then goes on to tell us that he lives in a stone house, dines while sitting on tombstones, and suffers from a form of rheumatism that he insists upon calling "Tombatism" (4.25–26). His very helpers and attendants are embodiments of his office. He employs two journeyman stonecutters who are "emblematical of Time and Death" (4.26). These stony and sepulchral associations are compounded and enlarged by all that follows. It does not surprise us to discover in Chapter V that Stony Durdles is associated with Deputy, an aggressive imp or devil ("Baby-Devil," Jasper calls him) whom Durdles has employed, so muddled and wayward is the stonemason once he has begun his incessant evening drinking, to stone him home each night to his stony house (5.28). This bizarre compact is symbolic: it whispers dark truths about relationships and values in the quiet cathedral city of Cloisterham (another name that reveals and conceals). In the peaceful precincts of that cloistered refuge all is corrupt; human concern (as between Deputy and Durdles, for example) has dwindled into a mere accommodation of drunkenness on the one hand and violence on the other. The most basic laws of nature are inoperative or askew. That which should be high is low; that which should be low is high. Disease and disorder abound. Anarchy is everywhere. The natural roles of adult and child (always crucial touchstones for Dickens) are parodied and reversed. In this topsy-turvy society, the savage, untutored child becomes the demonic guardian of the uncouth, irresponsible man.

Names reinforce these ironies and disparities. Deputy has been deputized: he is both the warder and the surrogate of death-environed Durdles. But Deputy is also a baby devil, an infant deputy of the devil himself. Who—or what—then is Durdles? A grown-up devil? A grown-up deputy of the devil? Surely the stonemason in his stony stupor is no less destructive, no less a devil (he becomes an accessory to murder) than his savage deputy. Yet poor, benighted Stony Durdles and ragged, neglected Deputy are also victims. Their names, like their identities, arraign the social order—or rather disorder—they represent, and both names and identities help enforce Dickens' monitory message. Dickens epitomizes the pathological engagement of these two stony night creatures in Number Plan II: "Deputy engaged to stone Durdles nightly."

Stones, stoniness, disorder, and death are ubiquitous in *Edwin Drood*; the novel is redolent of crypts, murders, graveyards, tombstones, stone dust, and the sharp flinty hail of flying rocks. Durdles, Dickens tells us, playing on names and words, is "the Stony (and stoned) One"; Deputy, chilling bundle of destructiveness, monstrous manifestation of Durdles's besotted befuddlement and society's callous neglect, occupies his nighttime leisure, when no human target is at hand, in a fitting occupation: "in the unholy office of stoning the dead, through the railings of the churchyard" (5.28; 23.187).

In one of the many night scenes in *Edwin Drood*—it is the scene which opens Chapter V, the scene in which we first see Durdles and Deputy together—Dickens conjures up a portentous graveyard picture fraught with the special burial-ground symbolism of *Drood* but conjugate also with the "quiet churchyard" and the moonlit graves of *Copperfield*. The two scenes are similar, but the *Drood* scene whispers more overtly of unseemliness and threat. We can hardly miss that unseemliness or that threat. In the serene precincts of the old cathedral, hard by its peaceful cloister arches, on the verge of the tranquil graves themselves, we witness a profane "spectacle": "Stony Durdles, dinner-bundle and all, leaning his back against the iron railing of the burial-ground . . . and a hideous small boy in rags flinging stones at him . . . in the moonlight" (5.28). The violence that starts up from these quiet graves, though still oblique, is menacing and palpable; it vibrates with sinister dissonances and with unmistakable suggestions of graveyard violence to come. As in *Copperfield*, we know—but much more directly now—that something dark and violent, something stony and murderous, will rise out of the seemingly tranquil moonlit graves.

Such scenes and many more give mythic significance to the sodden stonemason, his granitic attributes, and his carefully crafted name. Surly and stolid, drunken and muddled, sleeping heavily in tomb and crypt, grey with the dust of tombstones and of corpses, Stony Durdles like Bradley Headstone before him is, as we gradually come to understand, the stony embodiment of ignoble Death. He is also, but now unlike Headstone, the somnolent guardian of the nether regions, the negligent keeper of the keys (he always carries crypt keys on his person), the stony but befuddled warder of cold crypt, dank sepulcher, and moldering tomb. As his encounters with Jasper make clear, and as his name subliminally suggests (a name with far from subliminal associations for Dickens), Stony Durdles will be directly and fittingly, though not volitionally, implicated in—indeed he will preside over—murder and entombment. Dead drunk in the echoing crypt, Durdles sleeps his stony sleep, while Jasper, purloiner of the keys, rehearses his murderous deed. As Dickens puts it in Number Plan III, in his notes for Chapter XII, a chapter cunningly titled, "A Night with Durdles": "Lay the ground for the manner of the Murder; to / come out at last."

Stony Durdles seems to be the most autonomous of the four names surveyed here. The surname "Durdles," taken by itself, is certainly the most remote from connotations of "murder" and of "stone." But the apparent autonomy of the name will not bear scrutiny. It vanishes as soon as we delve beneath the surface of the name—the entire name—and examine the intricate echoes and recapitulations that bind it to Murdstone, Merdle, and Headstone. Such an examination demonstrates that all four names, despite striking differences, are counterparts, distinct branches of a single tree. Their individuality and their commonality instruct us in a variety of ways. The Murdstone-Merdle-Headstone-Durdles collocation shows us the continuity over many years in Dickens' imaginative associations. But this is not all. We perceive as well a coequal impulse: continuity is modulated by innovation. Dickens lends a special nicety and particularity, a carefully calculated originality, to each fresh calling forth of the old constellation of long-linked images and ideas. Each new summoning up is unique, yet each is a permutation of old associations.

Dickens' naming helps us appreciate these truths. His naming also helps us appreciate the richness of his art. We get glimpses of that complex richness when we ask ourselves a simple question: "What's in a name?" With Dickens, our answer must surely be, "Much more than at first meets the eye." We see that this is so in the names just surveyed. Murder and death pervade the essence and the destinies of Murdstone, Merdle, Headstone, and Durdles, so stony and implacable in their very different ways. Their divergent yet related names, so direct and obvious at first, or conversely so puzzling or odd, reveal at last the fullness of their hidden signalling; they proclaim with intricate subtlety the divergent yet related identities of the persons named and their divergent yet related roles: Murdstone, hard and murderous, who kills through his cold, ruthless dominion over others; Merdle, treacherous swindler, purveyor of offal, offal and carrion himself, who muddles and murders gullible multitudes with the promise of easy wealth; Headstone, stolid citizen, cold headmaster, monument of probity, who is betrayed by a passion he hardly dreamed existed, and who turns love into savage assault, calculated murder, and ferocious self-destruction; and Stony Durdles, flinty stonemason, dweller in crypts, haunter of tombs, keeper of the infernal keys, who becomes the rough unconscious tutelary spirit of foul murder and ghastly entombment.

Each character enacts his name. Each name, in turn, signals the truth within; each name is a token of being and of destiny. Each name, to use a formula from the catechism that Dickens loved to echo and to parody, is an outward and visible sign of an inward and spiritual grace—or, in these four instances, gracelessness. Yet personifications of gracelessness, even when linked by origins and nomenclature, take many forms. Of these memorable characters, diverse tributaries of a single fount, only Headstone engages our pity and fear. He is the sole tragic figure of the four. Namesake of the grave, entombed in his own flesh, he is indeed, as his end makes clear and his name predicts, the foundation, author, and memorial of his own death and of death itself.

What then can we conclude from the process I have just been tracing? Simply this: that Dickens' names are quintessential embodiments of what one sees everywhere in his art, a fusion of the wild, the portentous, and the fantastic with the rational and the everyday. His names, like his whispering houses, terrifying streets, primordial storms, and spell-casting witches are at once wildly expressionistic and improbable and profoundly real and ordinary. Dickens conveys with the same stroke the surface of things and the hidden springs of meaning. His world is discrete, tangible, and familiar, but also interconnected, fantastic, and mysterious. Like his great middle and late novels, whose clarity of image and identity conceals mysteries and consanguinities which only emerge as the novel slowly unfolds, so his names, which seem so obvious at first—Miss Barbary, Dick Swiveller, Miss Flite, Esther Summerson, Abel Magwitch—reveal hidden depths of complex meanings as the names and the novels express their ripened import. Dickens' notes make clear that he planned it that way, that he fused the unambiguous surface with the treacherous, ambiguous depths. Dickens distorts, intensifies, and transcends reality in order to be profoundly true to reality. Through that double vision he conveys his sense of the quiddity and wonder of life. The names Murdstone, Merdle, Headstone, and Durdles testify in their varying degrees to this richly ramifying vision, so simple and so complex, that one finds everywhere in Dickens.

NOTES

1. The information about trial names and trial titles in this paragraph, and all subsequent information concerning Dickens' notes and number plans, is taken from Harry Stone, *Dickens' Working Notes for His Novels*, to be published in 1985 by the University of Chicago Press.

2. Kate [Dickens] Perugini, " 'Edwin Drood' and the Last Days of Charles Dickens," *Pall Mall Magazine*, XXXVII (June 1906), 654.

3. See "Nurse's Stories," *All the Year Round*, III (8 September 1860), 517–521. This piece was subsequently collected in *The Uncommercial Traveller*, First Series (1861).

4. *David Copperfield* (London: Bradbury & Evans, 1850), 14.153. All references to Dickens' novels are taken from first editions and are cited hereafter in the text by book, chapter, and page number as relevant. The chapter designations allow the reader to locate references in any edition of Dickens' writings.

5. Their kinship and their differences are also evident in the notes that helped shape their names. In his Book of Memoranda, in a half-page list of names written in 1855 when he was planning *Little Dorrit* and conceiving Mr. Merdle, Dickens wrote one beneath the other the names "Harden," "Merdle," and "Murden," and later in the list "Stonebury." As we have already seen, he had formulated all these names six years earlier when planning *Copperfield*, the first three while searching for a name for Mr. Murdstone, the last while hunting for a surname for David and a title for the novel. In the *Copperfield* notes he had written the names Harden, Murdle, and Murden (spelled thus in the *Copperfield* version), one beneath the other (that is, with no intervening names) and in that order. He had written "Murdstone" to the right of these names. The *Copperfield* entry is thus the prototype for the Book of Memoranda listing, not only in substance but in format and order as well. There is no evidence to suggest that Dickens copied Harden, Merdle, Murden, and Stonebury from the *Copperfield* working notes into the Book of Memoranda list. On the contrary, as far as we know—and there is much corroboratory evidence here—once he had completed a novel, he never returned to the manuscript for any purpose whatsoever. He must therefore (as his changed spelling of Merdle also suggests) have conjured up the four names afresh when, mulling over some of the elements destined for *Little Dorrit*, he again searched for a surname with some of the old Murdstone attributes. The remarkable reemergence of the same names, in the same format, called up by a similar need, destined for a similar end—all this after a dormancy of six long years— demonstrates the extraordinary tenacity of Dickens' associations and illustrates once more how intimately intertwined, yet also carefully differentiated, are the names and meanings I have been discussing in this essay. For the Book of Memoranda list of names, see *Charles Dickens' Book of Memoranda*, ed. Fred Kaplan (New York: The New York Public Library, 1981), entry 14.

6. Kaplan, entry 109. In the list of names containing "Duddle," Dickens also jotted down "Amon Headstone," and in a continuation of the list on the following page, "Bradley"—juxtapositions that provide some additional linkages between Bradley Headstone and the Merdle-Duddle-Durdles conjunction.

Household Words Anthologies
for American Readers

Anne Lohrli

Dickens' *Household Words* (1850–1859) won high praise from the American press. The New York *Tribune* (8 November 1852) pronounced the periodical "one of the most valuable" of the day, "an indispensable work for the family library." The New York *Times* found *Household Words* "a captivating magazine." And the *Home Journal* proclaimed:

> We have so often and so highly recommended "Household Words" to our readers, that the vocabulary of praise is exhausted. Its presence in a home adds to the pleasure and the knowledge of all who are within it. It is always pure, genial, and humane; and a family to which it ministers has an additional safeguard to the virtue and intelligence of its younger members. We commend it heartily to all the world.[1]

Despite the extravagant laudation of American reviewers, *Household Words* did not, apparently, have a wide circulation in the United States. Various reasons were cited for the limited sale: that the journal was not adequately promoted and publicized, that its "true character" was not understood by the general public, that its price was too high, that it contained no pictures, and that, as an English periodical, it dealt with much local and temporary material that was not of interest to American readers.[2]

The topical nature of much that was published in *Household Words* was cited by American publishers as a main reason for their bringing out anthologies of the periodical for American readers. A second reason was the ephemeral nature of periodical publication: many of the admirable stories and articles that appeared in Dickens' journal, stated the publishers, deserved the permanency of book publication.

There were two series of *Household Words* anthologies—the G. P. Putnam series, 1852 (continued by Bunce, 1854): *Home and Social Philosophy, The*

World Here and There, and *Home Narratives*; and the Beardsley series, 1854: *Choice Stories from Dickens' Household Words* (also titled *Pearl-Fishing*). In addition there was the one-volume Peck & Bliss anthology, 1854: *Sunshine on Daily Paths*.[3] The anthologies contained 137 prose items (not counting duplications, twelve in number) selected from the first eight volumes of *Household Words*.

The *Household Words* anthologies are of interest both for the prefatory publishers' comments on the journal and on Dickens, and for the selections contained in each (see tables of contents, below). Since items published in *Household Words* appeared without authors' names,[4] the selection of articles and stories to be included in the anthologies had to be made solely on the basis of the interest that the items were thought to have for American readers. Had authors' names been attached to items, it is probable that the anthologies would have contained more items by Dickens than the two that they did.

Of the 137 items included in the anthologies, approximately one hundred were articles of information and instruction or stories that served as the vehicle for information and instruction; about thirty were stories written for story interest.

Of the informational and instructional items about half were accounts of travel, life, and work on the Continent, in the British colonies, and elsewhere. Some of these were of interest; others were decidedly not. The reading public of the mid-century, as George Haven Putnam remarked in the memoir of his father, "was prepared to interest itself in travel narratives" that later generations would find "neither exciting nor informing."[5] The remaining items provided readers with information and instruction on any number of subjects—the physical universe, the human constitution, elementary science, manufactures—with some of the information and instruction presented in story form. It is difficult, today, to understand the appeal of this form of presentation to mid-century readers.

Of the some thirty stories selected for the anthologies a few were worth the reprinting; most were not. The critical judgment of the publishers, one notes, was not always in accord with that of Dickens. Included in one of the anthologies was the story by Anna Mary Howitt that Dickens had damned as "just passable"; not included in any of the anthologies was "Our Society at Cranford," a story with which Dickens had been so delighted that (as he wrote to the author) he "put it first in the number."

Indeed, few *Household Words* items that had appeared "first in the number" were selected by the American publishers for inclusion in their anthologies. In the eight *Household Words* volumes here under consideration, most of the lead items were articles rather than stories, and the articles, well adapted in content and spirit to the periodical's English readers, did not for the most part provide the sober instruction and information that American publishers apparently wanted for their American readers. Only eighteen lead items were reprinted in the anthologies.

The anthologies were meant for casual reading by a non-critical public. The stories that they contained, as the reviewer of one collection suggested, might well serve to "alleviate the tedium of a long journey, or to amuse a vacant or a sick hour at home,"[6] and the informative and instructional selections, perhaps read aloud to the family circle, would serve to edify young and old in homes where the name of Dickens was "as 'familiar as household words.'"

For this non-scholarly public, publishers felt no obligation to handle the *Household Words* text with exactitude. They arbitrarily made changes in punctuation and capitalization. They retained on one page the English spelling of a word, changed it on another page to American. They corrected some typographical errors that had appeared in *Household Words*, let others stand, and introduced some of their own. To detach the selections from the ephemerality of periodical publication, the publishers did not record with them the dates on which they had appeared in *Household Words*. These omissions led at times to confusion: in an article in Putnam's travel anthology, for instance, the statement that "our heroes . . . set out from Shanghae, on the 15th of last November" left the reader ignorant of the year of the heroes' journey. Confusion likewise resulted from the retention in the anthologies of cross-references as they had appeared in *Household Words*, as for instance in the reference to what had been explained "in our first Volume, pp. 466–67."[7] Of the four publishers, it was Peck & Bliss that handled the material most arbitrarily. Some articles they retitled; from some they omitted words, sentences, whole paragraphs, without indication of omission. In some they changed phraseology, at times to adapt the material to its American printing ("in England" for "in this country"), at times for no apparent reason ("We were three in number" for "There were three of us").[8]

The anthologies represented the writing of some sixty *Household Words* contributors, those most largely represented being Henry Morley, John Capper, Richard H. Horne, and Harriet Martineau. Morley—"the dullest" of all of Dickens' writers, remarked Sir Robertson Nicoll[9]—was the anthologists' favorite. From his *Household Words* articles and stories they chose thirteen, two of which appeared in two of the collections. From the writings of Capper, as also from those of Horne, the compilers selected nine items, two of

Capper's and one of Horne's being included in two of the collections. Martineau was represented by eight items.

Capper and Martineau were the writers who included in their own collections the largest number of their items that had been selected for inclusion in the anthologies; each reprinted six. Among the other writers one reprinted five, one reprinted four, and fourteen each reprinted one or two, making a total of forty-three items. That is, fewer than a third of the items contained in the anthologies were considered by their authors worth collecting and reprinting.

The important fact about *Household Words* was that it was "conducted by Charles Dickens," as announced on the masthead of every number. Publishers of anthologies naturally made as intimate as possible the association of Dickens with their volumes of selections. The prefatory notice to the First Series of the Beardsley anthologies, for instance, suggested that "the hand of the master" might be "readily discerned" in the selections. The three Bunce anthologies, on spine and cover, read *Home and Social Philosophy by Charles Dickens*, *The World Here and There by Charles Dickens*, and *Home Narratives by Charles Dickens*, and certain advertisements announced them as books "by Chas. Dickens" or as "Dickens's Household Books" from *Household Words* (New York *Tribune*, 20 April 1854, 16 March 1855).

Actually, however, the anthologies were practically *Household Words sans* Dickens. As stated above, only two of the 137 items included were his writing.

The publishers' policy of excluding from their anthologies material of temporary and local concern, material that scarcely touched "the popular mind of American readers," meant the exclusion of most of Dickens' articles—his tirades against Government, his disparagement of officialdom, his denunciation of social wrong, his ridicule of what seemed to him folly. The policy was a sensible one. Such articles as "Lively Turtle," for instance, or "A Narrative of Extraordinary Suffering" would have been inappropriate for the readers for whom the anthologies were intended—and unintelligible to them. American magazine publishers who did reprint such articles felt obliged, at all events, to provide a clue to their meaning.[10]

Nevertheless, it seems a somewhat perverse judgment on the part of the publishers to omit from their compilations the amusing "Bill-Sticking" or the pleasant "Gone Astray." Obviously they had little taste for Dickens' characteristic humor—or they considered their American readers to have little taste for it.

The anonymous Dickens was not the favorite *Household Words* author of

American readers. Their admiration of Dickens was reserved for writings that bore his name.

THE *HOUSEHOLD WORDS* ANTHOLOGIES

The Putnam Anthologies, 1852

George P. Putnam, the first publisher of *Household Words* anthologies for American readers, had been the first to bring out Dickens' journal in the United States.[11] His brief role as *Household Words* publisher and anthologist, however, was apparently of minor importance to Putnam in his busy life; no mention of it occurs in the memoir of him written by his son.

Putnam's plan, in 1852, to make *Household Words* selections available to American readers was well thought out—and ambitious. Putnam explained it in the preface to the first of his anthologies, *Home and Social Philosophy: or, Chapters on Every-day Topics. From "Household Words," Edited by Charles Dickens*:

> This volume is the first of a classified reprint of Dickens's "Household Words." Under the title of *"Home and Social Philosophy"* it is proposed thus to preserve, in a portable and permanent shape, all those valuable, pithy and entertaining essays which relate to domestic and social economy, familiar illustrations of natural philosophy, and kindred topics. *"The World Here and There"* will be the title of a series of travellers' narratives and geographical notes. *"Home Narratives,"* including the best of the stories and imaginative sketches, will form the third series. It is thus intended to make a complete reprint of Dickens's admirable work from the commencement, and to continue the series, omitting the articles which are of temporary or local interest.

Home and Social Philosophy, First Series,[12] contained eighteen items, selected from Volumes 2 and 3 of *Household Words*:[13]

Dreams (2:566–572. 8 March 1851) by Thomas Stone
Ice (3:481–484. 16 August 1851: lead item) by Henry Morley and William Henry Wills
Some Account of Chloroform (3:151–155. 10 May 1851) by Percival Leigh
"Births. Mrs. Meek, of a Son" (2:505–507. 22 February 1851: lead item) by Charles Dickens [rpt.]
Atlantic Waves (2:22–24. 28 September 1850) by William Blanchard Jerrold [rpt.]
German Advertisements (2:33–35. 5 October 1850) by William Henry Wills, Grenville Murray, and Walker (prob. Thomas Walker)

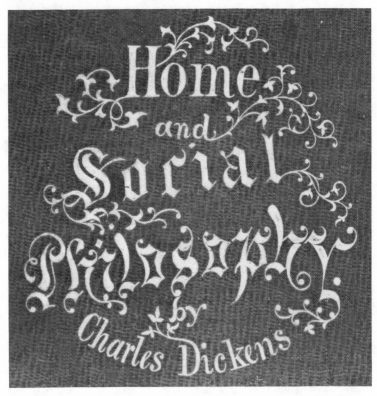

Cover design of *Home and Social Philosophy*, Bunce & Brother, 1854.
Courtesy of the Department of Special Collections, Research Library,
University of California, Los Angeles.

The Methusaleh Pill (2:36–38. 5 October 1850) by William Blanchard Jerrold [rpt.]

Mr. Van Ploos on Penmanship (2:38–42. 5 October 1850) by Richard H. Horne

The Mysteries of a Tea-kettle (2:176–181. 16 November 1850) by Percival Leigh

The Magic Crystal (2:284–288. 14 December 1850) by T. H. Wilson, Dudley Costello, and William Henry Wills

The Private History of the Palace of Glass (2:385–391. 18 January 1851: lead item) by William Henry Wills [rpt.]

Physiology of Intemperance (2:413–417. 25 January 1851) by Thomas Stone

Sleep (2:470–475. 8 February 1851) by Thomas Stone

The Chemistry of a Pint of Beer (2:498–502. 15 February 1851) by Percival Leigh

The Rational Doctor (3:13–18. 29 March 1851) by Percival Leigh

Somnambulism (3:132–138. 3 May 1851) by Thomas Stone

The World of Water (3:204–209. 24 May 1851) by Henry Morley

The Wind and the Rain (3:217–222. 31 May 1851: lead item) by Charles Dickens and Henry Morley

Home and Social Philosophy provided readers with instruction, advice, and information on a variety of topics. The eight selections concerned with "domestic and social economy" dealt with health, medicine, and related matters. Among these articles were four by Dr. Thomas Stone—"Sleep," "Dreams," "Somnambulism," and "Physiology of Intemperance"; two were by Percival Leigh— "Some Account of Chloroform" and "The Rational Doctor." The last-named, presented in story form, depicted a sensible young doctor instructing Mr. Bagges on the nature and treatment of disease. Also presented in story form were Dickens' "'Births. Mrs. Meek of a Son'" and William Blanchard Jerrold's "The Methusaleh Pill." Dickens' selection voiced Mr. Meek's protest against the tight swaddling and the physicking of new-born infants; Jerrold's concerned the vast profits made by the sale of quack remedies to the gullible public.

The "familiar illustrations of natural philosophy" promised in the preface to the anthology included six articles. "The World of Water" and "The Wind and the Rain," by Henry Morley—later a member of the *Household Words* staff—explained ocean currents, tides, wind zones, and other natural phenomena. "Atlantic Waves," by Jerrold, pictured William Scoresby, F. R. S., on board the *Hibernia*, measuring the height and breadth of storm waves. Morley's "Ice," practical rather than theoretical, included directions for the construction of an ice-stack to preserve ice for summer use. "The Mysteries of a Tea-kettle" and "The Chemistry of a Pint of Beer," by Leigh, were science for the layman. In the first, a forward young lad explained to his long-suffering uncle certain principles of physics that he had learned by attending Professor Faraday's lectures; in the second, an amateur chemist delivered to the members of a mechanics' institute a lengthy discourse on brewing.

The remaining articles dealt with miscellaneous matters. "German Advertisements," by Grenville Murray and Walker (probably Thomas Walker), cited examples of "personals" from German and Austrian newspapers. "Mr. Van Ploos on Penmanship," after a dull narrative beginning, turned into a "gossip" on handwriting; the author was Richard H. Horne of the *Household Words* staff. "The Magic Crystal," by T. H. Wilson and Dudley Costello, denounced the belief in divination and deplored the pernicious influence of *Zadkiel's Almanac*. In "The Private History of the Palace of Glass," William Henry Wills—Dickens' subeditor on *Household Words*—discussed the design of the Crystal Palace, explaining the origin of the design in Joseph Paxton's vast conservatory built for housing the *Victoria regia*.

Of the eighteen items contained in the anthology, four, as indicated in the listing above, had appeared in *Household Words* in lead position—the position allotted to the most important item in a number; and four, as also indicated above, were reprinted by their authors in collections of their periodical writings.

*   *   *

In the same year in which he brought out the First Series of *Home and Social Philosophy*, Putnam published the Second Series. This contained seventeen items, selected from the first four volumes of *Household Words*:

The Work of the World (3:589–592. 13 September 1851) by Henry Morley
The Chemistry of a Candle (1:439–444. 3 August 1850) by Percival Leigh
A Paris Newspaper (1:164–167. 11 May 1850) by Joseph Archer Crowe
Ballooning (4:97–105. 25 October 1851: lead item) by Richard H. Horne
Fate Days (1:596–598. 14 September 1850) by William Blanchard Jerrold [rpt.]
Tea (*H.W.* title: Illustrations of Cheapness. Tea. 1:253–256. 8 June 1850) by Charles Knight [rpt.]
Winged Telegraphs (1:454–456. 3 August 1850) by William Henry Wills and Thomasina Ross
Three "Detective" Anecdotes (1:577–580. 14 September 1850: lead item) by Charles Dickens [rpt.]
The Way I Made My Fortune (4:105–107. 25 October 1851) by Cramer
Disappearances (3:246–250. 7 June 1851) by Elizabeth Gaskell [rpt.]
The Nineveh Bull (2:468–469. 8 February 1851) by W. H. Stone

A Witch in the Nursery (3:601–609. 20 September 1851: lead item) by Richard
  H. Horne
Liberty, Equality, Fraternity, and Musketry (4:313–318. 27 December 1851:
  lead item) by George Augustus Sala [rpt.]
My Uncle (4:241–246. 6 December 1851: lead item) by William Henry Wills
  and Charles Dickens [rpt. by Wills]
English Songs (4:173–178. 15 November 1851) by James Hannay
The First Time, and the Last Way, of Asking (4:164–166. 8 November 1851)
  by Henry Morley
The Wonders of Nails and Screws (4:138–142. 1 November 1851) by Harriet
  Martineau [rpt.]

The Second Series of *Home and Social Philosophy* was more diversified in
content than the First, some of the selections hardly concerning "Every-day
Topics." Like other publishers of *Household Words* anthologies, Putnam
observed rather loosely the limits set by the titles of his volumes.

Three of the articles included in the book would have appeared more
appropriately in Putnam's travel anthology, *The World Here and There*:
"Liberty, Equality, Fraternity, and Musketry," by George Augustus Sala,
was that writer's account of Paris immediately after the coup d'état of 2
December 1851; "A Paris Newspaper," by Joseph Archer Crowe, described
Crowe's visit to the office of *Le Constitutionnel*; and "Winged Telegraphs,"
by Thomasina Ross, related the training methods used by the Society of
Antwerp Pigeon Fanciers—the information being translated from Johann
Georg Kohl's *Reisen in den Niederlanden*, 1850.

Only one article in the anthology dealt with laboratory science—Leigh's
"The Chemistry of a Candle"; but Morley's "The Work of the World"
considered the far-reaching results of scientific discoveries. Inventions, business, and manufacturing were the subjects of other articles: Horne's "Ballooning" discussed man's attempts to master the air by means of wings, air
ships, balloons, and parachutes, and gave an account of the writer's balloon
trip; Charles Knight's "Tea" was part of a *Household Words* series titled
"Illustrations of Cheapness"; Cramer's "The Way I Made My Fortune" (a
story rather than an article) illustrated the axiom that "the next best thing to
capital is credit." "My Uncle" by Wills—with "masterly touches" by
Dickens' hand[14]—detailed the daily transactions of a pawnbroker's shop.
"The Wonders of Nails and Screws," by Harriet Martineau, conducted the
reader through a Birmingham steel mill.

Three articles in the anthology dealt with cultural rather than practical
matters. "The Nineveh Bull," by W. H. Stone, was the soliloquy of the
famed Assyrian statue excavated by Austen Henry Layard and sent to England

in 1850. "English Songs," by James Hannay, was a brief history of English
lyric poetry from Taillefer to Tennyson. "A Witch in the Nursery" was
Horne's denunciation of nursery tales and rhymes for their depiction of
violence and horror.

Among miscellaneous articles was Jerrold's "Fate Days," which, like
"The Magic Crystal" in the First Series of the anthology, ridiculed supersti-
tions. "Three 'Detective' Anecdotes," by Dickens, related exploits of the
London Detective Police; and "Disappearances," by Mrs. Gaskell, recounted
various instances of missing persons—persons whose whereabouts would
have been speedily ascertained, she was certain, had the Detective Police been
in charge of investigations. Finally, there was Morley's "The First Time, and
the Last Way, of Asking"—one of the few pieces that must have been
included in the Putnam anthologies merely for amusement. It was the com-
plaint of a young butcher-shop helper that his application to the Matrimonial
Alliance Association had not yet resulted in his getting a rich, beautiful lady
for wife.

Of the items contained in the Second Series of *Home and Social Philosophy*, five had appeared in *Household Words* in lead position. Seven were
reprinted by their authors in collections of their periodical writings.

                    *   *   *

The second of Putnam's *Household Words* anthologies was a volume of
"travellers' narratives and geographical notes," titled *The World Here and
There: or, Notes of Travellers. From "Household Words," Edited by Charles
Dickens*. The book contained sixteen articles, selected from Volumes 1, 3,
and 4 of the periodical:

> Short Cuts across the Globe (1:65–68. 13 April 1850) by William Weir and
>   William Henry Wills
> The Isthmus of Suez (*H.W.* title: Short Cuts across the Globe. The Isthmus of
>   Suez. 1:167–168. 11 May 1850) by William Weir and William Henry Wills
> The Golden City (1:313–317. 29 June 1850: lead item) by William Henry Wills
>   [rpt.]
> Our Phantom Ship among the Ice (3:66–72. 12 April 1851) by Henry Morley
> My Pearl-Fishing Expedition (3:75–80. 19 April 1851) by John Capper [rpt.]
> Our Phantom Ship. Japan (3:160–167. 10 May 1851) by Henry Morley
> Short Trip into Bosnia (3:182–187. 17 May 1851) by Otto von Wenckstern
> A Peep at the "Peraharra" (3:252–256. 7 June 1851) by John Capper [rpt.]

THE WORLD

HERE AND THERE:

OR,

Notes of Travellers.

FROM "HOUSEHOLD WORDS," EDITED BY CHARLES DICKENS.

NEW-YORK:

G. P. PUTNAM, 155 BROADWAY.

1852.

Student Life in Paris (3:286–288. 14 June 1851) by Sidney Laman Blanchard
[rpt.]

Tahiti (3:301–305. 21 June 1851) by Thomasina Ross

Old Cairo and Its Mosque (3:332–334. 28 June 1851) by Bayle St. John or
James Augustus St. John

The "Mouth" of China (3:348–353. 5 July 1851) by Thomasina Ross

Lost in London (3:372–378. 12 July 1851) by Otto von Wenckstern

South American Scraps (3:425–430. 26 July 1851) by Dr. Von Corning, Keys,
and William Henry Wills

The Jews in China (3:452–456. 2 August 1851) by Soutar, Keys, and Henry
Morley

The Art of Catching Elephants (4:305–310. 20 December 1851) by John Capper
[rpt.]

The first two articles in the anthology, by the journalist William
Weir, were sensible, well-informed discussions of the need for a canal
through the Isthmus of Panama and one through the Isthmus of Suez. The
two "Phantom Ship" articles by Morley provided information on the Arctic
regions and on Japan by the childish device of having the reader (clad in his
"phantom" cloak) travel with the narrator on an imaginary ship (Dickens
was apparently the propounder of the idea). Three of the articles in the anthology were based on popular books of the day: Thomasina Ross's "Tahiti" and "The 'Mouth' of China" consisted of passages translated from
Ida Pfeiffer's *Eine Frauenfahrt um die Welt*, 1850; and Wills's "The
Golden City," an account of San Francisco, was taken in large part from
Bayard Taylor's *Eldorado*, 1850. Soutar's "The Jews in China," motivated
by the great public interest at the time in the Jewish colony of K'ai-feng Fu,
related the early history of the colony and summarized the information
newly received in England concerning it; almost half of the article consisted
of quotation from a letter written by the Jesuit missionary Jean-Paul Gozani,
in 1704.

The remaining articles, however, were not derivative. They were actual
"travellers' narratives," based on the writers' own observations and experiences.

Some of the articles made their content clear by their titles: "Student Life
in Paris," by the young journalist Sidney Laman Blanchard; "Old Cairo and
Its Mosque," by Bayle St. John or by his father—both well-known travellers;
and "Short Trip into Bosnia," by Otto von Wenckstern. "Lost in London,"
a second article by Wenckstern, told of the poverty and misery that that writer
endured during his first weeks in the country to which he had fled for political
freedom. The three interesting articles on Ceylon were by the journalist John

Capper, long a resident of that island: "My Pearl-Fishing Expedition," "A Peep at the 'Peraharra'" (an account of a Buddhist festival), and "The Art of Catching Elephants."

The selection of Von Corning's "South American Scraps" for inclusion in an anthology would have appalled Dickens. The slovenliness of the article, he wrote to his subeditor after seeing the article in print, was disgraceful to *Household Words*. In its violations of grammar, its faults of composition, its unintelligibility, the article was "utterly detestable." Wills should not have let "such a bestial piece of bewilderment" find admission to the periodical.[15] No other *Household Words* article provoked Dickens to quite the pitch of indignation that "South American Scraps" did. The writer, obviously, was not a native speaker of English, and the revision of his article had failed to make it entirely idiomatic or grammatically acceptable.

Of the articles included in *The World Here and There*, only one had appeared as lead item in *Household Words*. Five were reprinted by their authors in collections of their periodical writings.

The New York *Tribune* (11 March 1852) praised *The World Here and There* as an "instructive and fascinating volume," containing *Household Words* sketches "by several of the most spirited travelers in various parts of the world, including Bayard Taylor, Ida Pfeiffer, and others." Neither Bayard Taylor nor Ida Pfeiffer, of course, wrote for *Household Words*. The *Home Journal* described the anthology as "made up of the cream of those felicitous travelling sketches" that had appeared in *Household Words*, and the Albany *Argus* praised the book as "written in Dickens's own peculiar style."[16]

*   *   *

The third of the Putnam anthologies—*Home Narratives: or, Stories from "Household Words." Edited by Charles Dickens*—was described by the publisher as a collection of "the best of the stories and imaginative sketches" from Dickens' journal. The book contained fifteen items, selected from the first three volumes of *Household Words*:

The Serf of Pobereze (1:342–350. 6 July 1850) by Mme. Szczepanowska and
    William Henry Wills
Loaded Dice (1:77–82. 20 April 1850) by Catherine Crowe
The Ghost of the Late Mr. James Barber. A Yarn Ashore (1:87–90. 20 April
    1850) by William Henry Wills [rpt.]

The Young Jew of Tunis (1:118–120. 27 April 1850) by Geraldine Endsor Jewsbury

An Excellent Opportunity (1:421–426. 27 July 1850) by Julia Kavanagh and William Henry Wills [rpt. by Kavanagh]

The Gentleman Beggar. An Attorney's Story (1:510–514. 24 August 1850) by Samuel Sidney [rpt.]

The Other Garret (2:364–369. 11 January 1851) by William Moy Thomas [rpt.]

The Ghost That Appeared to Mrs. Wharton (2:139–143. 2 November 1850) by Harriet Martineau

"Judge Not" (2:431–432. 25 January 1851) by Mary Anne Hoare

The Right One (3:473–477. 9 August 1851) by Anna Mary Howitt

A Gallop for Life (3:577–581. 13 September 1851: lead item) by Samuel Sidney [rpt.]

A Specimen of Russian Justice (2:598–600. 15 March 1851) by Ignacy Jackowski and William Henry Wills

The Modern Haroun-al-Raschid (2:617–620. 22 March 1851) by Mary Anne Hoare

Dust, or Ugliness Redeemed (1:379–384. 13 July 1850) by Richard H. Horne

A Penitent Confession (3:436–445. 2 August 1851) by Richard H. Horne

The stories contained in the volume were, for the most part, mildly entertaining, but in no way distinctive. Anna Mary Howitt's "The Right One," indeed, had been admitted to *Household Words* only on sufferance, Dickens having found it "poor—but I think just passable" (to Wills, 27 July 1851).[17] Its message was that a man's choice of a wife should rest on her beauty of soul, and that happy marriage was based on the husband's and wife's living by the words of the marriage rite. Wills's story of the ghost of James Barber, intended to be humorous, was also a moral tale, the ghost motivating a sailor's turning from drunkenness and dissipation to sober industry. Catherine Crowe's "Loaded Dice," a curiously matter-of-fact story, told of a young man whose cheating at dice and cards brings about the suicide of his sister's fiancé. Dickens thought the story "horribly dismal" (to Wills, 28 February 1850). Julia Kavanagh's "An Excellent Opportunity," laid in France, as were many of that writer's stories, dealt with two unscrupulous mercers, each duping the other. Also laid in France was "The Other Garret," by William Moy Thomas, a simple love story, quietly and pleasantly told. It was the best of the stories contained in the volume.

Horne's "A Penitent Confession," which had appeared in *Household Words* during the time of the Great Exhibition, recounted the dream of Mr. Simon Sparks that he had been successful in stealing the Koh-i-noor from its display case in the Crystal Palace. The same writer's "Dust, or Ugliness Redeemed" centered about a London dust-heap. It was a story that readers of

Our Mutual Friend, in 1865, remembered having read years before in *Household Words*.[18] Both of Horne's stories were overlong and tedious.

Of the two stories by Samuel Sidney, one was pronounced by Dickens to be "surprisingly good."[19] This was "A Gallop for Life," an account of a man's fording a dangerous river channel on horseback (Sidney was an authority on horses), leading to a rather effective scene at the close. "The Gentleman Beggar" was the story of the illegitimate son of an English nobleman "by a Spanish lady of rank"; rescued from beggary, the man falls dead while proposing a toast at an elegant dinner.

Not all of the selections, however, were fiction. The "ghost" that appeared to Mrs. Wharton in Harriet Martineau's story was explained to be not a ghost at all, and the story itself to be "perfectly and literally true." The account of the young Jew of Tunis who attempted to rid himself of one of his two wives was likewise factual, stated Geraldine Jewsbury, it having been communicated to her by a friend "who had it from the French Consul himself." Mrs. Hoare's "The Modern Haroun-al-Raschid" was the account of a contemporary Algerian sheik, translated (without acknowledgment of source) from Alexandre Dumas's *Le Véloce*; and her "Judge Not" was the relation of certain events in the life of the Polish writer and statesman Stanislaw Staszic. "The Serf of Pobereze," written by a Polish refugee living in England, may also have been in part factual. The opening sentence stated that the writer had "last year" travelled in the district of Poland in which the misfortunes of the peasant heroine began. The story was factual, at least, in showing the Poles' hatred of Russian domination. Ignacy Jackowski's "A Specimen of Russian Justice" recounted the sad fate of a young French girl at the hands of corrupt government officials—a "melancholy tale, which the censorship of the press in Russia prevented from ever before being publicly related."

Of the selections contained in *Home Narratives*, only one had appeared in lead position in *Household Words*. Five were reprinted by their authors in collections of their periodical writings.

*   *   *

In the prefatory remarks to the first of his *Household Words* anthologies, Putnam had stated his intention of continuing the volumes so as to make (with appropriate omissions) "a complete reprint of Dickens's admirable work from the commencement." The only one of his anthologies that Putnam continued was *Home and Social Philosophy*, of which—as stated above—he brought out a Second Series in the same year as the First.

Although he abandoned his ambitious project, Putnam made extensive use of the anthologies that he had published. Issued as volumes in Putnam's Semi-Monthly Library, they formed part, at various times, of such collections as Putnam's Library for Travellers and the Fireside, Putnam's Library for Travellers and the Home Circle, and Putnam's Library for the People.[20]

The Putnam Anthologies Continued by Bunce, 1854

In 1854, the New York publishers Bunce & Brother took over the Putnam anthologies. In mid-April of that year they announced the following as among their books "in press—and nearly ready for publication": *Home and Social Philosophy*, and, in "Enlarged edition," both *The World Here and There* and *Home Narratives* (New York *Tribune*, 20 April). The only contribution of Bunce & Brother to the compiling and publishing of *Household Words* anthologies was the addition of selections to *The World Here and There* and to *Home Narratives*. The four volumes of the Putnam anthologies they merely printed from the Putnam plates, as is evident from the typography and the arrangement of text on the pages.

Of *Home and Social Philosophy* Putnam had published a First and a Second Series, with a preface to the First Series. The Bunce issuance of this anthology omitted the Putnam preface and also the table of contents; the first page of the text, however, appeared as page 9 (unnumbered), as in the Putnam volume. Bunce bound in one volume the two series of *Home and Social Philosophy*, each series separately paged, but not designated First Series, Second Series.

Of his second *Household Words* anthology, *The World Here and There*, Putnam had brought out only one series, consisting of sixteen selections. To these sixteen, Bunce & Brother added eleven selections, to make their "Enlarged edition." They placed the added selections after the original sixteen, and paged the whole continuously.

The Putnam anthology had contained fifteen articles taken from the first and third volumes of *Household Words* and one taken from Volume 4. Bunce & Brother, instead of continuing the selection of items from Volume 4 and perhaps from the following two volumes (1852–1853), arbitrarily made their selections from Volumes 7 and 8 (1853–1854). The selections were as follows:

The Stop the Way Company (8:449–454. 7 January 1854) by John Capper

Regular Trappers (8:471–476. 14 January 1854) by John Capper
By Dawk to Delhi (8:365–370. 17 December 1853) by Clark
Varna (8:373–377. 17 December 1853) by Bayle St. John and William Henry
    Wills
Only an Earthquake (8:235–238. 5 November 1853) by W. L. Reynolds and
    Henry Morley
Summer in Rome (7:257–261. 14 May 1853) [author not recorded]
A French Audience (7:349–352. 11 June 1853) by John Oxenford
Dunkerque Tower (7:357–360. 11 June 1853) by Edmund Saul Dixon
Canvass Town (7:361–367. 18 June 1853: lead item) by Richard H. Horne
Cats' Mount (7:385–390. 25 June 1853: lead item) by Edmund Saul Dixon
Leaves from Lima (7:202–205. 30 April 1853) by Clements Robert Markham

The first two selections in the anthology—John Capper's condemnation of
the policy and practices of the Hudson's Bay Company—were based on
official documents, published journals, and other materials. The remaining
articles, however, recorded the writers' own experiences and observations. In
"By Dawk to Delhi" an "old Indian" told of his nine hundred miles' travel
on the Grand Trunk Road. In "Varna" Bayle St. John wrote of the Bulgarian
port that—with the approach of the Crimean War—was fast becoming a point
of interest to readers. "Only an Earthquake" told of a clerk's short holiday
trip in Albania; and "Summer in Rome" was an Englishwoman's mild
account of her summer's residence abroad. Three articles had France as their
background: "A French Audience," by John Oxenford, the well-known
dramatist and critic, was an analysis of French theatre-goers; "Dunkerque
Tower," by Edmund Saul Dixon, was an account of Dunkerque and its
environs; and "Cats' Mount," by the same writer, told of his visit to a
Trappist monastery. Of the two remaining items, one dealt with Australia, the
other with Peru. In "Canvass Town" Horne described living conditions in and
near Melbourne during Gold Rush days; and in "Leaves from Lima"
Clements Robert Markham—not yet famous as a geographer—wrote of his
excursions in the vicinity of Lima.

Of the eleven articles selected by Bunce & Brother for inclusion in their
enlarged edition of this anthology, only two had appeared in lead position in
Household Words. None were reprinted by their authors.

*   *   *

Home Narratives, the third *Household Words* anthology published by
Putnam, contained fifteen items. To these fifteen, Bunce & Brother added

nine, placing them after the Putnam selections and paging the whole continuously. Like their selections for *The World Here and There*, the Bunce
selections for *Home Narratives* were taken from Volumes 7 and 8 of *Household Words*:

> Amy the Child (8:431–432. 31 December 1853) by Townsend
> The Sack of Chestnuts (8:460–466. 14 January 1854) by Louisa Stuart Costello
> Pharisees and Sinners (8:486–491. 21 January 1854) by Eliza Lynn
> The Cradle and the Grave (8:317–325. 3 December 1853) by William Hogarth
>   or James Hogarth, and Henry Morley
> Two Cousins (8:246–252. 12 November 1853) by Eliza Lynn [rpt.]
> Little Children (8:289–293. 26 November 1853: lead item) by George Augustus
>   Sala [rpt.]
> A Shepherd's Autobiography (7:309–312. 28 May 1853) by Lewis Hough [rpt.]
> The Sensitive Mother (7:414–419. 2 July 1853) by Eliza Lynn
> The Borrowed Book (7:317–324. 4 June 1853) by William Moy Thomas [rpt.]

"Amy the Child," the opening story in the Bunce anthology, was an
unfortunate selection—a sentimental tale translated from "an old German
pocket-book." The best of the selections was "The Sack of Chestnuts,"
Louisa Stuart Costello's story of a haunted chamber—a story made memorable by its evidence of the author's intimate acquaintance with France, with
French ways and French people.

Of the three stories by Eliza Lynn (later Mrs. Lynn Linton), the first,
"Pharisees and Sinners," depicted a grand, cold family of pious Christians
who disown the love-child of their erring brother, but at length come to accept
and love her; the second, "Two Cousins," told of an indolent young
gentleman, content to be engaged to a mild, conventional young lady, until he
comes to know her vivacious cousin; and the third, "The Sensitive Mother,"
pictured a possessive mother who ruins her daughter's life. In contrast to Eliza
Lynn's society stories was Lewis Hough's story of humble life: a shepherd's
recital of the cruel injustices and the harsh misfortunes that bring him and his
wife to the workhouse. In Thomas's "The Borrowed Book," the interest lay
in plot and atmosphere: the murder of a watchman on a lonely stretch of
Suffolk coast.

Two of the selections were, actually, not stories. "The Cradle and the
Grave," by either William Hogarth or James Hogarth, was the account—
apparently factual—of the writer's going to the Turon gold diggings in
company with a partner who he becomes convinced is a murderer from
California. "Little Children," by Sala, was a lengthy disquisition on the
innocence and goodness of little children, echoing some of Dickens' ideas on
childhood.

Of the nine selections, Sala's article was the only one that had appeared in lead position in *Household Words*. That article and three of the stories in the anthology were reprinted by their authors.

For about a year after bringing out the three anthologies, Bunce & Brother advertised them, quoting laudatory opinions of the press and themselves praising the books. "A more delightful series than these volumes," they declared, "can scarcely be found" (New York *Tribune*, 28 October 1854). They did not continue the series.

The Beardsley Anthologies, 1854

The Beardsley anthologies, 1854, consisted of a First Series and a Second Series.

The First Series appeared under two titles: the simple, explanatory title *Choice Stories from Dickens' Household Words*; and a double title, in which the explanatory title was preceded by a fanciful one: *Pearl-Fishing. Choice Stories, from Dickens' Household Words.*

The designation "First Series" did not appear on the title page of *Choice Stories from Dickens' Household Words*; it did appear on the title page of *Pearl-Fishing*. The publisher recorded on the title page of *Choice Stories* was John E. Beardsley of Auburn and Buffalo; the joint publishers recorded on the title page of *Pearl-Fishing* were Alden, Beardsley & Co. of Auburn, and Wanzer, Beardsley & Co. of Rochester. The copyright notice was identical in the book under both titles, recording copyright by Alden, Beardsley & Co., 1854.

The "Publishers' Notice" prefaced to the book, under its two titles, was dated February 1854. Concerning Dickens' "admirable publication" *Household Words*, it stated:

> That work has had a smaller circulation in this country than its merits entitle it to, in consequence of its being issued in such form as to make it troublesome to preserve the numbers, and have them bound. Many of its papers, too, are of local and somewhat temporary interest, which scarcely touches the popular mind of American readers. It is believed, therefore, that judicious selections from its pages, embracing some of its best stories, in which the hand of the master is readily discerned, will be welcomed with delight in many a home in which the name of DICKENS has become as "familiar as household words."
>
> This volume is intended to be the first in a series gathered from the same publication. It is enriched with an admirable likeness of DICKENS, engraved for this work.[21] The Publishers commend the volume as pure in sentiment, whole-

CHOICE STORIES

FROM

Dickens' Household Words

———

AUBURN & BUFFALO:
JOHN E. BEARDSLEY.

Title page of *Choice Stories from Dickens' Household
Words*, First Series, John E. Beardsley (c. 1854). Cour-
tesy of the Rare Book Room, Buffalo and Erie County
Public Library, Buffalo, New York.

PEARL-FISHING.

CHOICE STORIES,

FROM

Dickens' Household Words.

FIRST SERIES

AUBURN:
ALDEN, BEARDSLEY & CO.
ROCHESTER:
WANZER, BEARDSLEY & CO.
1854.

Title page of *Pearl-Fishing.*, First Series, Alden, Beardsley & Co., 1854. Courtesy of the Department of Special Collections, Research Library, University of California, Los Angeles.

some in morals, and abounding in such incident and interest as cannot fail to secure a friendly reception and a wide circulation among American readers.

The ten selections that constituted the First Series of the anthology were taken from the first volume of *Household Words*:

Loaded Dice (1:77–82. 20 April 1850) by Catherine Crowe

The Serf of Pobereze (1:342–350. 6 July 1850) by Mme. Szczepanowska and William Henry Wills

My Wonderful Adventures in Skitzland (1:225–229. 1 June 1850) by Henry Morley [rpt.]

Lizzie Leigh (1:2–6. 30 March 1850, and the two following numbers) by Elizabeth Gaskell [rpt.]

The Old Churchyard Tree. A Prose Poem (1:377–378. 13 July 1850) by [author not recorded] and Richard H. Horne

The Modern "Officer's" Progress (1:304–307. 22 June 1850, and the two following numbers) by Dudley Costello

Father and Son (1:213–216. 25 May 1850) by Mary Anne Hoare [rpt.]

The Miner's Daughter.—A Tale of the Peak (1:125–130. 4 May 1850, and the two following numbers) by William Howitt

The Ghost of the Late Mr. James Barber. A Yarn Ashore (1:87–90. 20 April 1850) by William Henry Wills [rpt.]

A Tale of the Good Old Times (1:103–106. 27 April 1850) by Percival Leigh

Of the ten selections, three—"Loaded Dice," "The Serf of Pobereze," and "The Ghost of the Late Mr. James Barber"—had been included in the Putnam anthology *Home Narratives*; they are briefly discussed above. Of the selections that had not before been included in an anthology, three were stories of humble life. Mrs. Gaskell's "Lizzie Leigh" was the account of a mother's search for her fallen daughter. The story had become familiar to American readers by being reprinted at least four times in the United States as the writing of Dickens. William Howitt's "The Miner's Daughters" (mistitled in the anthology "The Miner's Daughter") told of a father's harsh treatment of his two daughters, of their hard work and their devotion to each other, which is rewarded by good fortune. "The Old Churchyard Tree" (author not recorded) was a "prose poem" depicting scenes in the life of a husband and wife, and in the life of their son, whose debauchery brings them in sorrow to the grave.

Mrs. Hoare's "Father and Son" was a historical tale. Laid in the "dark time in Ireland's annals," it told of the rising of peasants against landowners and of the circumstances that saved one landowner's life. "The Modern

'Officer's' Progress,'' by Dudley Costello (a retired army man), was an exposé of the idleness, ignorance, and incompetence of young officers who hold their commissions by purchase.

Morley's ''My Wonderful Adventures in Skitzland'' was a dream-fantasy on the theme of a person's losing all parts of the body of which he does not make use. Intended to be amusing and satirical, it was unpleasant reading anatomically. Also presented in the form of fantasy was Leigh's ''A Tale of the Good Old Times,'' in which a conservative alderman comes to understand that the true ''good old times'' are not in the past, but in the present and the future. Dickens had, of course, been delighted with the story.

None of the selections contained in the volume had appeared as lead item in *Household Words*. Four were reprinted by their authors in collections of their periodical writings; Morley, indeed, thought so well of his ''Skitzland'' that he included it in three of his collections.

*   *   *

The Second Series of the Beardsley anthology appeared under the title *Pearl-Fishing. Choice Stories, from Dickens' Household Words*,[22] the publishers being recorded on the title page as Alden, Beardsley & Co. of Auburn; and Wanzer, Beardsley & Co. of Rochester. The publication of the Second Series, stated the publishers, was motivated by the popularity that the First Series had enjoyed. The prefatory notice, dated June 1854, read:

> The large demand for the *First Series* of this publication, has confirmed the publishers in their opinion of its worth and its adaptability to meet the wants and tastes of the reading public, and induced them to issue, in rapid succession, the present volume, which will be found not less interesting and worthy of attention.
> The publishers also announce their intention of continuing this series, which has been received with so much public favor.

Again, the selections were taken from the first volume of *Household Words*:

The Young Advocate (1:292–297. 22 June 1850) by Catherine Crowe [rpt.]
The Last of a Long Line (1:433–439. 3 August 1850, and the following number. Chap. i, lead item) by William Howitt
The Gentleman Beggar. An Attorney's Story (1:510–514. 24 August 1850) by Samuel Sidney [rpt.]
''Evil Is Wrought by Want of Thought'' (1:580–587. 14 September 1850) by Coventry Patmore
Bed (1:333–336. 29 June 1850) by Robert Hogarth Patterson

The Home of Woodruffe the Gardener (1:518–524. 24 August 1850, and the two
    following numbers) by Harriet Martineau
The Water-Drops. A Fairy Tale (1:482–489. 17 August 1850) by Henry Morley
An Excellent Opportunity (1:421–426. 27 July 1850) by Julia Kavanagh and
    William Henry Wills [rpt. by Kavanagh]

Of the eight items, "The Gentleman Beggar" and "An Excellent Opportunity" had been included in the Putnam anthology *Home Narratives*; they are
mentioned above.

The six items here appearing in an anthology for the first time were diverse
in content and purpose. Mrs. Crowe's "The Young Advocate" was a tale of
nemesis: the young advocate dies of terror on seeing what he believes to be
the ghost of the innocent man whom he has been instrumental in convicting
of murder. "The Last of a Long Line" was Howitt's account of the dying out
of an inbred, aristocratic family, and the rise to wealth—and a baronetcy—of
a man of pauper blood. Coventry Patmore's childish story, titled by a line
from Thomas Hood, contrasted foolish, impulsive generosity with sensible,
reasoned action. "The Home of Woodruffe the Gardener" was one of Harriet
Martineau's instructive tales for the humbler classes: here given was advice on
draining water-logged land and foul-smelling, disease-carrying ditches. Likewise concerned with sanitation was Morley's "The Water-Drops," a documented account of the filthy drinking water and the putrid drains of London.
In an unfortunate attempt at sprightliness, Morley presented his material by
means of the activities and conversation of fairy water-drops—Nubis, Neph-
elo, and their fellows. "Bed," by Robert Hogarth Patterson, was not a story,
but rather a familiar essay, being that writer's pleasant reflections on sleep,
dreams, and kindred matters.

In *Household Words*, the first chapter of "The Last of a Long Line" had
appeared in lead position. Howitt did not reprint the story, but three of the
other stories included in the anthology were reprinted by their authors.

Their selecting anthology items entirely from the first volume of *Household
Words*, while eight volumes of the periodical were available, indicated that the
Beardsleys did actually intend, as they stated, to continue the series. They did
not do so. But the two series of their anthology—separately or jointly—were
several times reissued by other publishers. These included J. C. Derby, New
York; Arundel Print, New York; Burnett & Bostick, New Orleans; and
Belford, Clarke & Co., Chicago. The last-named publisher titled the First
Series of the anthology *The Dickens Story Teller* (1884, also 1886), and the
Second Series *Dickens' Shorter Tales* (1884). Each of the two titles bore the
subtitle *Choice Stories from Dickens' Household Words*.

DICKENS' SHORTER TALES.

CHOICE STORIES

FROM

DICKENS' HOUSEHOLD WORDS.

————

CHICAGO AND NEW YORK:
BELFORD, CLARKE & CO.
1884.

Title page of *Dickens' Shorter Tales.*, Belford, Clarke & Co., 1884, a reissue of the Second Series of the Beardsley anthology. Courtesy of the University Libraries, the University of Iowa, Iowa City.

The Peck & Bliss Anthology, 1854

In the same year in which the two series of the Beardsley anthology were first brought out for American readers appeared an anthology published by the Philadelphia firm H. C. Peck & Theo. Bliss: *Sunshine on Daily Paths; or the Revelation of Beauty and Wonder in Common Things. From Household Words, by Charles Dickens*. The book contained forty-five selections, more than any other *Household Words* anthology. Its two-page publishers' preface was longer than the preface of the other anthologies, and more extravagantly laudatory of Dickens and of *Household Words*.

No journal, stated the preface, had "ever met with a more immediate and wide-spread acceptance" than had *Household Words*—a publication that found a welcome at "thousands of happy firesides." American readers were familiar with *Household Words* not only from their reading of the journal itself, but from seeing selections from its pages reprinted in "numberless newspapers and similar ephemeral publications." But *Household Words* articles deserved more permanency than this:

> . . . their value is too great, and their beauty too rare, for them to be allowed to perish with the local gossip of to-day, or to pass into oblivion with the Congressional flare-up of yesterday. Their merits demand a more permanent form, and this we have given in the present volume, wherein will be found a selection—and, we believe, a judicious one—of the most striking and interesting pieces that have hitherto appeared.

The basis on which the judicious selection was made was stated in the subtitle: *Sunshine on Daily Paths* was to consist of articles that revealed the "beauty and wonder in common things." The subtitle echoed a thought from Dickens' "Preliminary Word" to *Household Words*: one of the objects of the journal was to show "that in all familiar things, even in those which are repellant on the surface, there is Romance enough, if we will find it out."

The preface to *Sunshine on Daily Paths* pointed out to the reader a distinction that existed between the writing of an earlier day and the writing of the day, as exemplified in Dickens and his journal: the literature of "our ancestors," explained the preface, made a sharp distinction between "fact and fiction" and the manner in which each was treated. Fiction "was considered equivalent to falsehood, and to it were offered up fancy, imagination, the graces of rhetoric, and the gifts of poetry." Fact (scientific treatises, history, biography, accounts of travel, "personal narratives of real events") was "magnified in importance, but could be clothed only in the drab monotony of threadbare narrative, or dry-as-dust didactics." If a writer "became enter-

Sunshine on Daily Paths;

OR THE

REVELATION OF BEAUTY AND WONDER IN COMMON THINGS.

From Household Words,

BY CHARLES DICKENS.

WITH EIGHT ORIGINAL ILLUSTRATIONS.

PHILADELPHIA:
H. C. PECK & THEO. BLISS.
1854.

taining, he was checked with the suspicion of 'romance.'" But this state of things no longer prevailed:

> . . . a change has recently come over our literature in regard to this matter; and it is to Charles Dickens, more than any other, that we are indebted for the recognition of the important fact that falsehood is no more an essential attribute of works addressed to the sentiments of beauty, of wonder, of reverence, or of human sympathy, than stupidity is a necessary element of the truth. The pen of the ready writer may now exert its utmost powers to throw the charms of its art over details, to whose inherent interest we have been hitherto blinded only by familiarity.

The preface then turned directly to Dickens:

> It is said of one of old, *nihil tetigit quod non ornavit*, and the same may be said of our author. Over every subject he treats, he casts the warm sunshine of his own genial and cheery nature, dispelling the fog and the smoke-cloud from above the dwellings of the humble, gilding cottage and factory and sooty furnace with the glory of the dawn, and flashing back from the dew-drop on the wayside weed a many-coloured iris as bright as was ever refracted from the Kohinoor. Nothing can conceal from him "the soul of good in things evil," or obscure the beauty and interest that are inseparable from this so curious human life of ours, and the wondrous world in which we dwell.

The glowing words again reflected the sentiment voiced in Dickens' "Preliminary Word": there is "good in everything," and it is man's privilege to live in "this summer-dawn of time."

Fortunately, according to the preface, this romantic world-view was held not by Dickens alone; it was shared by the writers who contributed to his journal:

> The same spirit he [Dickens] imparts to his collaborators; and so they go on, month after month, singing their song, or telling their tale, while thousands of old and young listen in rapt attention. We also have listened, and find the interest too great to be suffered to expire with the echoes of the hour. Therefore have we endeavoured to give to these sketches that more permanent form, which we trust will be found acceptable by many readers.

Their selection of forty-five articles too fine to be allowed "to expire with the echoes of the hour" the publishers took from the first seven volumes of *Household Words*:

My Pearl-Fishing Expedition (3:75–80. 19 April 1851) by John Capper [rpt.]
A Visit to a Gunpowder Mill (*H.W.* title: Gunpowder. 4:457–465. 7 February
    1852: lead item) by Richard H. Horne
Down in a Silver Mine (5:593–596. 4 September 1852) by William Duthie [rpt.]

A Voyage in the Air (*H. W.* title: Ballooning. 4:97–105. 25 October 1851: lead item) by Richard H. Horne

Gold, and Gold-Seeking (*H.W.* title: Gold. 4:77–82. 18 October 1851) by Henry Morley

Papier-Mache (*H.W.* title: Flower Shows in a Birmingham Hot-house. 4:82–85. 18 October 1851) by Harriet Martineau [rpt.]

The True Story of a Coal Fire (1:26–31. 6 April 1850, and the two following numbers) by Richard H. Horne

The Art of Catching Elephants (4:305–310. 20 December 1851) by John Capper [rpt.]

Needles (4:540–546. 28 February 1852) by Harriet Martineau [rpt.]

The City of Sudden Death (5:171–176. 8 May 1852) by John Delaware Lewis

A Dash among the Whales (*H.W.* title: Black-Skin A-head! 6:399–404. 8 January 1853) by Samuel Rinder

Redhot Bubble-Blowing (7:175–179. 23 April 1853) by Edmund Saul Dixon

Time and the Hour (4:555–559. 6 March 1852) by Harriet Martineau [rpt.]

The Guano Diggings (6:42–46. 25 September 1852) by Samuel Rinder

How We Went Hunting in Canada (1:364–368. 13 July 1850) by Alexander Mackay

Light-Houses and Light-Boats (2:373–379. 11 January 1851) by Richard H. Horne

The Coral Fishery in the Mediterranean (2:379–383. 11 January 1851) by Henry G. Wreford

Pottery and Porcelain (4:32–37. 4 October 1851) by Henry Morley

A Day at Waterloo (3:539–544. 30 August 1851) by William Howitt

Ice, and Its Uses (*H.W.* title: Ice. 3:481–484. 16 August 1851: lead item) by Henry Morley and William Henry Wills

Coffee-Planting in Ceylon (3:109–114. 26 April 1851) by John Capper [rpt.]

Fishing for Tunny (7:499–503. 23 July 1853) by Edward Henry Michelsen and Henry Morley

The Crusade of the Needle (6:306–309. 11 December 1852) by John Capper

A Walk through a Mountain (7:9–13. 5 March 1853) by William Duthie and Henry Morley [rpt. by Duthie]

Hermit Island (7:88–94. 26 March 1853) by Edmund Saul Dixon

Shawls (5:552–556. 28 August 1852) by Harriet Martineau [rpt.]

Quails (7:448–450. 9 July 1853) by Henry G. Wreford and Henry Morley

The River of Yesterday (7:450–454. 9 July 1853) by Henry Morley

The Cocoa-Nut Palm (2:585–589. 15 March 1851) by John Capper [rpt.]

Plate-Glass (2:433–437. 1 February 1851: lead item) by Charles Dickens and William Henry Wills [rpt. by Wills]

How We Went Fishing in Canada (1:243–245. 8 June 1850) by Alexander Mackay

Christmas in the Frozen Regions (2:306–309. 21 December 1850) by Robert McCormick and Charles Dickens

A New Phase of Bee-Life (2:353–355. 4 January 1851) by Thomas Satchell

Hunting the Boar (*H.W.* title: The Roving Englishman. After the Boars. 7:118–120. 2 April 1853) by Grenville Murray

Among the Moors (5:276–279. 5 June 1852) by Mrs. Grenville Murray

Guns and Pistols (4:580–585. 13 March 1852) by Harriet Martineau [rpt.]

Pipe-Clay and Clay Pipes (4:526–528. 21 February 1852) by William Blanchard Jerrold [rpt.]

Our Phantom Ship among the Ice (3:66–72. 12 April 1851) by Henry Morley

Zoological Stories (4:564–567. 6 March 1852) by Henry Morley

An Ascent of Adam's Peak (4:420–424. 24 January 1852) by William Knighton

An Indian Wedding (4:505–510. 21 February 1852: lead item) by John Capper [rpt.]

Three Guns in Albania (5:16–19. 20 March 1852) by Hale

A Visit to Vesuvius (*H.W.* title: Up Vesuvius. 5:235–236. 22 May 1852) by Dulton

The "Mouth" of China (3:348–353. 5 July 1851) by Thomasina Ross

Leaves from Lima (7:202–205. 30 April 1853) by Clements Robert Markham

Reading the forty-five selections in *Sunshine on Daily Paths*, one finds it difficult to connect them with the title of the book and with the assertions of the preface. The selections do not cast "sunshine on daily paths" in the sense of disseminating cheer or optimism, and the travel articles (more numerous than other articles in the anthology) concern not "common things" but exotic. Actually, the only articles that the publishers can have had in mind as illustrating the presentation of factual material in novel and entertaining form were "The True Story of a Coal Fire" and the articles describing the manufacture of various common products—glass, gunpowder, tobacco-pipes, shawls.

Such "process" articles customarily introduced their subject by explaining the narrator's presence at the mill or factory or relating his journey there, by telling something of the history of the product manufactured or discussing the scientific discoveries that had made its invention possible. The narrator then led the reader from one factory workroom or storeroom or laboratory to another, describing the pieces of equipment and machinery, and explaining the tasks of the workers.

Of the ten such articles included in the anthology, five were—appropriately—by Harriet Martineau, a manufacturer's daughter. Martineau's articles explained the manufacture of needles, watches, guns and pistols, papier-mâché, and shawls. Dixon, in "Redhot Bubble-Blowing," described the manufacture of bottle-glass in a French glass mill; and an article by Wills (again, with "masterly touches" by Dickens' hand) described the smelting, casting, cooling, and polishing operations that took place in the works of the Thames Plate Glass Company. (From this article the anthology omitted the introductory paragraphs telling of the narrator's railway journey to the glass works.) Horne conducted the reader through a vast gunpowder plant, and Jerrold led him into the dingy warehouse where clay tobacco-pipes were made. Capper's "The Crusade of the Needle" differed somewhat from the other process articles. Though it described the activities of a "sewed muslin establishment," its basic purpose was to show that Irish peasants, if they could be induced to give up their "old time-worn habits of idle wretchedness," could earn money by cottage industry.

More numerous than the accounts of manufactures in the Peck & Bliss anthology were the accounts of travel, life, work, and adventure in foreign parts. These ranged from Alexander Mackay's "How We Went Fishing in Canada," "How We Went Hunting in Canada"—articles as dull as their titles—to Capper's well-written, informative articles on Ceylon.

Articles that recorded their author's days on the Continent included two by the journeyman-goldsmith William Duthie, who told of his visit to a silver mine in Freiberg and to a salt mine in Hallein. They included "A Day at Waterloo," in which Howitt described his tour of the battlefield and set down some of his reflections on the famous site of victory and defeat. Murray's article on boar-hunting in France and Hale's "Three Guns in Albania" were sportsmen's sketches; "Among the Moors," by Murray's wife, told of a visit to Tangier, which had its origin in Cadiz. Among articles with Italy as a setting were Dulton's account of climbing Vesuvius and John Delaware Lewis's account of his visit to Pompeii. E. H. Michelsen's "Fishing for Tunny" described the work of Ligurian fishermen; and Henry Wreford's "Quails" told of quail-netting and quail-gunning by the *cantadini* of Capri. A second article by Wreford, "The Coral Fishery in the Mediterranean," recounted the work of coral fishermen and told of the cruel hardships under which they labored.

Three articles had South America as their setting: Thomas Satchell's "A New Phase of Bee-Life" recorded a naturalist's findings in British Guiana, and Markham's "Leaves from Lima" (mentioned above, as included in the Bunce anthology, *The World Here and There*) told of trips in the vicinity of Lima. Samuel Rinder's "The Guano Diggings," the most interesting of the three articles, was a sailor's account of taking on cargo at the Chincha Islands off the coast of Peru.

"A Dash among the Whales" ("Black-Skin A-head!" in *Household Words*) was the same writer's account of his first cruise on a South Seas whaler. "Christmas in the Frozen Regions," by Robert McCormick, described the Christmas 1841 and New Year's 1842 festivities of the crews of the *Erebus* and the *Terror*, on Captain Ross's Antarctic expedition. McCormick, appointed to the *Erebus*, had served as surgeon to the expedition.

Six articles in the anthology dealt with Ceylon. One of these, "An Ascent of Adam's Peak," was by William Knighton; the others were by Capper. Capper's "An Indian Wedding" (actually, a Cingalese wedding) pictured the squalid native quarter of Colombo and gave a ludicrous picture of the Cingalese attempting to imitate European customs. The other four Capper articles (two of which had been included in Putnam's *The World Here and There*) dealt with the agricultural and other activities of the island—coffee planting, cocoanut-palm cultivation, pearl fishing, and elephant catching and taming. They were the best of the articles on life abroad included in the Peck & Bliss anthology.

In addition to the articles in which writers recorded what they themselves had seen, heard, or experienced in foreign lands, were the articles that provided readers with geographical or travel material from published sources. Two of these derivative articles—Thomasina Ross's "The 'Mouth' of China" and Morley's "Our Phantom Ship among the Ice"—had been included in the Putnam anthology *The World Here and There* and are mentioned above. A second derivative article by Morley was "The River of Yesterday," taken (without acknowledgment of source) from John Gilmary Shea's *Discovery and Exploration of the Mississippi Valley*, 1852. Dixon's "Hermit Island," the account of a visit to an island off the north coast of Tunisia, was also derivative material unacknowledged to its source. Dickens, in a letter to Wills (10 March 1853) damned the article as "a wretched translation from a wretched original."

Seven miscellaneous articles completed the Peck & Bliss anthology; four were by Morley, three by Horne. Morley's "Zoological Stories," "Gold, and Gold-Seeking," "Ice, and Its Uses," and "Pottery and Porcelain" indicated their content in their titles, the last named being based on Joseph Marryat's *Collections towards a History of Pottery and Porcelain*, 1850. Morley's article on ice, as also Horne's on ballooning (here titled "A Voyage in the Air") had been included in Putnam's *Home and Social Philosophy*, one in the First Series, the other in the Second (see above). Horne's "Light-Houses and Light-Boats" was based in large part on Alan Stevenson's *A Rudimentary Treatise on the History, Construction, and Illumination of Lighthouses*, 1850, though Horne attempted to give a personal interest to the article by picturing "our visitor" as being admitted to the North Foreland Lighthouse and being shown the interior by the light-keeper. Finally, Horne's "The True Story of a Coal Fire" related the origin, mining, and transportation of coal, through the medium of a dream or vision that comes upon Flashley Dalton—a ''dashing young fellow 'from town''—as he dozes before a dying coal fire in his uncle's home in the ''remote coal country.''

Like some of the accounts of manufactures, ''The True Story of a Coal Fire'' represented the new manner of writing discussed in the preface to *Sunshine on Daily Paths*—the writing that clothed ''fact'' not in the ''drab monotony of threadbare narrative, or dry-as-dust didactics,'' but presented it in a novel, fanciful manner. Horne exemplified the writer whose pen exerted ''its utmost powers to throw the charms of its art over details, to whose inherent interest we have been hitherto blinded only by familiarity.''

Actually, though ''The True Story of a Coal Fire'' contained interesting information on coal mining, the presentation of the information through the person of ''poor Flashley'' was unfortunate, as was the presentation of material in other *Household Words* pieces written in the spirit of Dickens' editorial injunction ''KEEP HOUSEHOLD WORDS IMAGINATIVE!''[23]—pieces that resorted to all manner of literary contrivances and devices to take the place of straightforward exposition.

Much of the information conveyed in the Peck & Bliss selections was of interest, and some of the articles were well written. Of none, however, can it be said that their value was ''too great, and their beauty too rare'' for them to be allowed to pass into oblivion.

Of the forty-five selections contained in the anthology, five had appeared in lead position in *Household Words*. Fourteen were reprinted by their authors in collections of their periodical writings.

A reviewer in the New York *National Magazine* (August, 1854) found *Sunshine on Daily Paths* a ''very interesting compilation,'' though—unlike the Beardsley editors—he did not discern ''the hand of the master'' in the selections that the anthology contained:[24]

> Charles Dickens, perhaps, wrote not one of these pages; but as he is the responsible editor of the *Household Words*, we have his endorsement of them, and the reader will pronounce them fully worthy of his pen.

A Projected Anthology, 1854

In his tentative plans for the journal that was to become *Household Words*, Dickens had thought of the numbers as ''always having, if possible, a little good poetry.''[25] It was the *Household Words* prose, not the verse, that attracted the four anthology publishers, but a verse anthology was also planned, though apparently not published. This was *Household Poems*, "a collection of the choicest gems of poetry, from Dickens's Household Words," announced in 1854 by McElrath & Barker as "in press" and soon to be published (New York *Tribune*, 11 March). I have not found the title listed in any catalogue or bibliography. McElrath & Barker did not look with favor on the publication of volumes of prose selections from *Household Words*; it seems clear that they decided against the publication of *Household Poems*.

Dickens wrote no verse for his periodical. *Household Poems* would have been *Household Words* entirely *sans* Dickens.

*   *   *

The anthologies published by the Beardsleys were reissued by other publishers as late as the 1880s, as stated above, but the actual compiling and publishing of *Household Words* anthologies came to an end in 1854. Publishers who had stated their intention of continuing their series did not do so. The demand for the books was apparently less enthusiastic than they had expected it to be. "[I]t is thought," suggested an 1854 advertisement of McElrath & Barker (then publishers of *Household Words* in the United States), "that readers, generally, would prefer the entire publication rather than any disjointed or mutilated selections (New York *Tribune*, 29 March). This may well have been so. Reprinted in nondescript anthologies, the *Household Words* articles and stories lost much of the interest that their appearance under Dickens' famous masthead had temporarily lent them.

NOTES

1. The comment of the *Times* and that of the *Home Journal* are cited from an advertisement for *Household Words* that appeared in *Putnam's Monthly Magazine*, May 1854 (advertising pages in back of number).
2. William E. Buckler, "'Household Words' in America," *Papers of the Bibliographical Society of America*, 45 (1951) 160–166, quotes letters of 1853 and 1854 from persons connected with American publishing firms, commenting on the limited sale of *Household Words* and suggesting plans to increase the sale. American advertisements for *Household Words*, however, naturally stressed the large sale of the journal.
3. Not included in this discussion are the booklets, each containing from one to four *Household Words* items, brought out by the two New York firms DeWitt & Davenport and Stringer & Townsend, to take advantage of the popular interest in

Dickens' periodical on its first appearance. The booklets were not anthologies in the sense of being collections of selected items. They consisted simply of one or more items rushed into print—as Stringer & Townsend explained—"as fast as the London copy can be procured" (statement on advertising page, facing first page of text, in *Stories from Household Words*, 1850).

4. For an account of the few exceptions to the *Household Words* policy of anonymous publication, see my *Household Words . . . List of Contributors and Their Contributions* (University of Toronto Press, 1973), pp. 12–13 and note. None of the items collected in the anthologies here discussed appeared in *Household Words* with the author's name.

5. *George Palmer Putnam, a Memoir* (New York: G. P. Putnam's Sons, 1912), p. 217.

6. Boston *Traveller*, quoted on advertising page facing title page in *Home and Social Philosophy*, Bunce edition.

7. "The Jews in China," *The World Here and There*, Putnam edition, p. 211; "My Pearl-Fishing Expedition," *The World Here and There*, Putnam edition, p. 64n.

8. "Plate-Glass," *Sunshine on Daily Paths*, p. 317; "How We Went Fishing in Canada," *Sunshine on Daily Paths*, p. 325.

9. *Dickens's Own Story. Side-lights on His Life and Personality* (London: Chapman and Hall, 1923), p. 190.

10. Reprinting "Lively Turtle," *Harper's New Monthly Magazine* (December, 1850) made clear the point of the article by expanding the title: "Lively Turtle. A Sketch of a Conservative." The *Albion* (9 August 1851) prefaced its reprinting of "A Narrative of Extraordinary Suffering" by identifying Bradshaw's Railway Guides, and the *Literary World* (27 April 1850), reprinting the first of the "Raven in the Happy Family" articles, explained that London shopmen's "caged exhibitions of the smaller hostile animals" were "facetiously designated 'Happy Families'."

11. Nos. 1–72 (30 March 1850–9 August 1851, inclusive).

12. Putnam used the word "Series" in two distinct senses. In the preface here quoted, he used the word to refer to each of the three anthologies that he planned. He used the word also to designate the first and the second volumes of *Home and Social Philosophy*.

13. In the following listing (as also in subsequent listings), the items appear in the order in which they appeared in the anthology. The title of an item is given as the title appeared in the anthology; if that title differed markedly from the title under which the item had appeared in *Household Words*, the *Household Words* title is also stated. Following the title is given the location of the item in *Household Words*. Lead items are so marked. Names of authors are recorded from my *Household Words*. For a discussion of the dual or triple authorship assignment of certain items, see my *Household Words*, pp. 40–42. In general, Dickens' name attached to an item jointly with that of another writer indicates that Dickens revised the item or added material to it, not that he collaborated in the writing of it. (For suggestion as to what may have been Dickens' part in the four anthology items assigned jointly to him and to another writer, see Harry Stone, ed., *Charles Dickens' Uncollected Writings from "Household Words"*, Indiana University

Press, 1968.) William Henry Wills's name attached to an item jointly with the name of another writer (except Dickens)—or jointly with the names of other writers—indicates that Wills revised the item, not that he collaborated in the writing of it. Henry Morley's name attached to an item jointly with the name of another writer or writers (except Dickens or Wills) indicates that Morley revised the item, not that he collaborated in the writing of it. Richard H. Horne revised the item to which his name is jointly attached with that of an unnamed *Household Words* contributor. Wills, Morley, and Horne were on the *Household Words* staff. Keys, whose name appears in connection with two items ("South American Scraps," "The Jews in China"), seems to have been engaged very briefly as a reviser of *Household Words* articles.

Items reprinted by authors in collections of their periodical writings are marked "rpt." For information on the reprinting, see my *Household Words*.

14. The words appear in Wills's dedication to Dickens of *Old Leaves: Gathered from Household Words* (London: Chapman and Hall, 1860), in which collection Wills reprinted the article.

15. Dickens to Wills, 23 July 1851. MS: The Henry E. Huntington Library. Quoted by permission.

16. The comment of the *Home Journal* and that of the *Argus* are cited from an advertisement for *The World Here and There* that appeared in *Putnam's Monthly Magazine*, March 1853 (advertising pages in back of number).

17. Unless otherwise stated, quotations from Dickens' letters are from *The Letters of Charles Dickens*, ed. Walter Dexter, Bloomsbury: Nonesuch Press, 1938.

18. "Mr. Dickens's Romance of a Dust-heap," *Eclectic and Congregational Review*, November 1865: " . . . Mr. Dickens has now, to our knowledge, for sixteen years been haunted by a great Dust-heap. In the *Household Words* for 1850 first appeared the account of that amazing mound" (cited in Philip Collins, ed., *Dickens: The Critical Heritage* [New York: Barnes & Noble, 1971], p. 458).

19. Dickens to Wills, 31 August 1851. MS: The Henry E. Huntington Library. Quoted by permission.

20. So advertised, during 1852, in the New York *Tribune*, *Spirit of the Times*, *Literary World*, and other periodicals.

21. An engraving of the 1839 portrait of Dickens by Daniel Maclise. It does not appear in all copies of the anthology.

22. Roorbach, *Bibliotheca Americana*, Supplement 1855 (p. 38), lists the Second Series under the title *Choice Stories from Dickens' Household Words*. I have not seen a copy of the Second Series so titled.

23. Dickens to Wills, 17 November 1853.

24. An earlier number of the *National Magazine* (February 1854) had explained that Dickens had placed *Household Words* "entirely in the hands of an assistant editor" and had "nothing to do with it beyond furnishing a weekly article" ("Editorial Notes and Gleanings").

25. Dickens to John Forster, 7 October 1849.

Surrealization and the Redoubled Self: Fantasy in *David Copperfield* and *Pendennis*

Carol Hanbery MacKay

When Charles Dickens and William Makepeace Thackeray fictionalize their lives, fantasy emerges as a central element: Dickens' world resembles a dream, a phantasmagoria of suppressed emotions which are "surrealized," while Thackeray's world is one of displacement and redoubled versions of himself—a world in which fantasy is analyzed and appears as theme, rather than dream. *David Copperfield*'s first-person account lets us see what a fantasist sees and presents us with characters whose "surreality" suggests that they are shaped in large part by the narrator's subconscious: what emerges from the effort to bury or suppress emotions is indeed surreal. *Pendennis*, on the other hand, shows us how fantasists look and act, and then its discursive omniscient narrator comments on the relative success and failure of fantasy in his characters' lives. So Dickens places us inside David's fantasies, where we are caught up and even trapped by them, whereas Thackeray looks down on Pen's world, inviting us to share his larger insights and perspective. Thus, point of view can encourage yet limit fantasy, or it can open it up for scrutiny and analysis. Between *David Copperfield* and *Pendennis*, we see how auto-biographical fiction can both penetrate and dissect fantasy to personal and artistic ends.

In the intimate relationship of such apparent opposites as fantasy and reality, we can begin to discover how paradox informs this study—how autobiographical fiction reveals and conceals, how doubles reflect and invert, how fantasy communicates and isolates—finally raising fundamental questions about creativity and suppression. To fictionalize one's autobiography is, in the first place, to utilize fantasy in an especially personal, even paradoxical way—to create an imaginative realm, however much it may or may not be based on one's own construct of "reality." Secondly, because Dickens and Thackeray are fictionalizing their lives, some suppression would almost inevitably occur as they transform elements of their personal experience into their newly created fictions. As a result, *David Copperfield* and *Pendennis* can be profitably studied *as if* they express hidden emotions of their authors—even if we could claim no special insight into their lives and minds. We may recall that some of the important autobiographical implications of *David Copperfield* were not realized until John Forster published his biography in 1872–74. In contrast, many of Thackeray's readers were too quick to assume an easy correspondence between his life and that of his titular character; in fact, his son-in-law Leslie Stephen later felt impelled to warn them against reading *Pendennis* as straight autobiography.[1] We will need to consider these auto-biographical provocations and transformations, but I am postponing an explicit discussion of them to a later section of this essay. In the meantime, we can immediately perceive that both Dickens and Thackeray recognize the value of working with fantasy to portray and understand character—Dickens through David's surreal haze, Thackeray through displacement of his "hero" into two characters, who serve to elucidate the underlying theme of appearance versus reality.

Even before isolating the common elements of fantasy and autobiographical fiction, we could build a case for comparing and contrasting these two novels to promising critical effect. Serialized contemporaneously (*David Copperfield* from May 1849 to November 1850; *Pendennis* from November 1848 to December 1850—with a three-month hiatus at the end of 1849 due to Thackeray's illness), the two novels virtually invited comparison.[2] Their authors' popularity guaranteed a considerable readership, and whether partisan or not, immediate and subsequent generations of readers have noted basic similarities. Both novels could be called examples of the *Bildungsroman*, specifically the subtype of the *Kunstlerroman*. They both detail the growth into maturity of young men who become writers, although both protagonists remain somewhat passive—drifting into their profession rather than actively choosing it. The mothers of the two only-sons (David's half-brother lives only a short time, after all) influence their offspring long after they die, and an aunt or uncle sponsors each young man's social rite of passage. Furthermore, both David and Pen "develop" through a series of romantic interests, and each finally gets a second chance at marital happiness with a sister-figure.

On the other hand, close study of these two novels also brings to the fore their differences, which seem largely to stem from their different narrative points of view. David Masson, who jointly reviewed *David Copperfield* and *Pendennis* in 1851, emphasized the differences more generally as an opposition between the two authors, acknowledging at the same time the critical value of juxtaposing them:

> There can be no doubt that the writers bring out and throw into relief each other's peculiarities—that they are, in some respects, the opposites of each other; and that each is most accurately studied when his differences from the other are noted and scrutinized.[3]

Thus, although many of the differences can ostensibly be attributed to point of view, we do well to look beyond it to understand the choice of viewpoint and its implications for style and theme. After all, Dickens elsewhere employs an omniscient stance, and Thackeray's subsequent semi-autobiographical novels—*The Newcomes* and *Philip*—show him using first-person character-narrators. Most critics and readers concur that Dickens in general welcomes the free play of fanciful imagery, enhanced here by a subjective viewpoint that can unleash nightmarish threats to self-esteem. In contrast, Thackeray's distanced outlook emphasizes his brand of social realism, with its satiric edge that can invoke fantasy partly to cut through its façade. Their emphases and perspectives differ, yet both authors draw on a kind of fantastic realism to write fiction: Dickens' surrealism creates a gritty fantasy, while Thackeray's redoubling produces a multi-dimensional reality.

I

Fantasy can both help and hinder personal growth: it can isolate the individual as well as nurture the seeds for eventual communication. As Bruno Bettelheim has amply demonstrated, fairy tales provide children with an important outlet for coming to terms with reality. And Viktor Frankl reports that imaginative escapes into the past seemed to increase the survival rate among concentration camp prisoners.[4] But both these hypotheses are predicated on the assumption that the individual overcomes isolation and adopts a future-orientation. In *David Copperfield*, fantasy elements protect and invade David's worldview as a child, and they continue to inform his mode of assessment as he looks back over his life and tries to comprehend its meaning. To a certain extent, the adult David is conscious of the role of fantasy in shaping the man he has become. As he resurrects and relives specific memories, he playfully indulges in self-conscious fairy-tale ascriptions and openly invokes the "enchantments" that captivated him. David's first visit to

Yarmouth is only one of many such memories. Note how he describes Mr. Peggotty's home:

> If it had been Aladdin's palace, roc's egg and all, I suppose I could not have been more charmed with the romantic idea of living in it. There was a delightful door cut in the side, and it was roofed in, and there were little windows in it; but the wonderful charm of it was, that it was a real boat which had no doubt been upon the water hundreds of times, and which had never been intended to be lived in, on dry land. That was the captivation of it to me. If it had ever been meant to be lived in, I might have thought it small, or inconvenient, or lonely; but never having been designed for any such use, it became a perfect abode.[5]

The fantasy is all the more appealing because it inverts reality. This is part of the process that charms us, that makes us believe that we are indeed witnessing the child's mind at work. At the same time, however, the narrator may get caught up in his own imagery and once again seek solace in the innocence it can imply. This propensity to revert to childhood's protective fantasies helps to explain why David never confronts his own nightmares—or perceives that they are borne out by shadow selves—and why he continues to cloak Agnes in unreal robes of sainthood.

Telling stories—essentially relating fantasies—generally has a positive effect on David's life. It is a communicative, creative endeavor, one that forces him to reexamine past experiences as he recasts them in relation to his present, ongoing sense of self. This is true even of his retelling the plots of novels to his fellow students at Salem House, despite the negative cast he later pretends to put on it: "Whatever I had within me that was romantic and dreamy, was encouraged by so much story-telling in the dark; and in that respect the pursuit may not have been very profitable to me" (DC 7.146). In the process of committing "ravages" on his favorite authors, David reinterprets them in a more positive, public context—compared with his isolated, compensatory first act of reading them at Blunderstone. Furthermore, retelling these stories helps David to sharpen his memory and to hone his "simple, earnest manner of narrating" (145)—skills which later serve him in his literary profession and in the retelling of his own life-story. In fact, this overall act of recounting his past, even if "he never meant [it] to be published on any account," makes him more conscious of how that past has determined his present and can give meaning to his future.[6]

Although the power of storytelling can counter fantasy's isolating propensity, it can also encourage isolation and retreat from the world. We recognize this tendency in David's very imagery. As he enters the "caverns of Memory," he imparts new layers of fantasy upon the events that he first saw through the eyes of fantasy—creating a softening effect, a veritable cocoon of language surrounding and covering over what the narrator is still unable and unwilling to see with clear eyes. This language emerges in particular when David is dealing with the early stages of his relationship to Dora Spenlow, before he acknowledges the reality of her impracticality and his own unsuccessful attempts to deal with it. Full of himself, ego-isolated, David exaggerates and amplifies what has contributed to his fantasy. He builds his cocoon, into which he encases Dora and Julia Mills, assuming a perfect state of mutual understanding: "we all seemed, to my thinking, to go straight up to the seventh heaven" (33.546). It is almost as if David knows that his later insights about Dora—incomplete as they still are with regard to his own feelings—might invade and destroy the innocent bliss associated with his courtship days, and so he invites and encourages these protective layers of imagery, allowing only a modicum of self-mockery.

David may be increasingly surrounded in fact by many loving friends and relatives and in narrative by his own cocoons of imagery, but he continues to have nightmares and a darker vision of life. This darker vision manifests itself in his shadow selves—"surrealized" versions of his own projections— namely, James Steerforth and Uriah Heep.[7] Apparent opposites, Steerforth and Heep have in common their attractions to Emily and Agnes, the two "other women" in David's life. And both Steerforth and Heep actively pursue these women, while David passively sits by, experiencing merely restless nights and strange forebodings. This "doubling" of suppressed emotions in *David Copperfield* is not just a matter of imaginative projections of David's psyche, of course. Steerforth and Heep exist in the world that surrounds David: Steerforth is indeed cruelly indifferent to the feelings of others, and Heep is truly a grotesque, disturbing figure. Although their very names point to them as fantastical creations, these names also assert their meaning in the novel—giving it more reality: Steerforth steers forth into the lives of others, and Uriah Heep twists "God is light" into the scum of the earth. But as competitors for Emily and Agnes, they also bring into relief David's repressed sexual longings—as did Uriah's wife Bathsheba in the Bible—extending and inverting them until, as symbolic shades of the self, they look ahead to the unreliable narrator's protection from self-understanding.

Fantasy elements thus pervade the very infrastructure of *David Copperfield*, infiltrating imagery and character, in short, the novel's world view. Through a fantasist's eyes, perfect communication can be assumed and asserted, as we see in the idyllic scenes at Yarmouth or during David's courtship of Dora. We need to read these assertions against David's propensity to fantasize, however, to recognize when the fantasy elements represent conscious, superficial ascriptions—ones he has already come to terms with—and when they continue to obscure or transform deep-seated fears and self-doubts. As unresolved protective mechanisms, these fantasy elements perpetuate isolation, even within the apparent community of home and family.

In contrast, *Pendennis* presents us with a world view that generally exposes fantasy and deals directly with the theme of isolation and façades. Early in the novel, the narrator reminds us that "a distinct universe walks about under your hat and under mine—all things in nature are different to each . . . you and I are but a pair of infinite isolations, with some fellow-islands a little more or less near to us."[8] Along with constant images of sight and eyes, and references to façades, faces, and individuals' perceptions, we recognize a related concern with how something is written or said, biased stories and accounts, withheld thoughts. The novel takes up the theme of blocked communication and separations between characters, and fantasy contributes to that theme by distorting characters' perceptions of themselves and one another. At the same time, however, Thackeray is not oblivious to the attractions of fantasy to accomplish his own ends. In the guise of narrator, he invokes society in multifarious, organic imagery that makes it come to life: society constitutes the fantastic for Thackeray, and he grants his narrator a rhetorical indulgence that would betray a weakness in a character with a less distanced perspective.[9]

By establishing contrasts between reality and appearance, Thackeray lets his narrator and characters occasionally treat fantasy as appropriate or desirable, but the novel more often demonstrates that the reality principle should either hold sway or that it would be the preferable choice. For example, Arthur Pendennis—dubbed Pen by his friends and family—indulges in daydreams and soliloquies, which are expressed through an emotive, melodramatic rhetoric that reveals him as conceited and dilettantish. With only the slightest encouragement, he is quick to predict his success as a writer. Nonetheless, Pen catches himself and halts his "Alnaschar dreams"—his propensity to count his chickens before they are hatched:[10]

> Dearest old mother, what a pride will you have, if I can do anything worthy of our name! and you, Laura, you won't scorn me as the worthless idler and spendthrift, when you see that I—when I have achieved a—psha! what an Alnaschar I am because I have made five pounds by my poems, and am engaged to write half a dozen articles for a newspaper.   (PEN 1.32.365)

Although Pen skirts rationalization and the dangers of self-delusion, his melodramatic gestures reflect a creative handling of life: they point him toward the future, which prevents him from feeling the isolating constraints of fate. At the same time, entertaining his fantasies provokes Pen to self-insight, however short-lived it may be. This is the positive side of fantasizing, nurtured in Pen since the days of his permissive childhood, when he was happily allowed "a world of his own" (1.3.32).

Elsewhere, however, Pen almost plays out a fantasy role with Fanny Bolton and runs the risk of falling into a marriage of incompatibility—not to mention a serious breach of family communications. Here Pen comes much closer than David to acting the part of seducer: he is so gratified by Fanny's evident adoration that he is tempted to indulge both their fantasies.[11] As for Fanny, she is a victim of the circulating library's vision of the romantic hero: "The Prince had appeared and subjugated the poor handmaid" (2.9.105). Thackeray underscores this theme with his decorative-initial illustrations; that of the previous chapter, entitled "Monseigneur s'amuse," depicts a chin-chucking chevalier and a little maid (2.8.87; see Figure 4, page 250). But reality intrudes in the convenient form of Pen's fever—a sort of visitation of fantasy—alerting the "avenging angels" of his mother and Laura, who dismiss the diligent Fanny. No one emerges from this episode unscathed in the reader's eyes: Pen dallies, Fanny flirts, and Helen and Laura reveal their snobbery, suspicious natures, and jealousy.

The novel's realist would seem to be George Warrington. After all, he stops many of Pen's flights of fancy, and his own experience testifies to the lesson learned from an incompatible marriage. But even Warrington is subject to the enticements of wishful thinking and his own fantasies, and when he returns to reality he overreacts, succumbing too readily to the limitations of fate—itself a fantasy, something he constructs to ease his pain and justify his passivity toward life. Note how he releases his suppressed feelings for Laura, only to settle for resignation:

> "Even if I could, she would not have me," George thought. "What has an ugly, rough old fellow like me, to make any woman like him? I'm getting old, and I've made no mark in life. I've neither good looks, nor youth, nor money, nor reputation. A man must be able to do something besides stare at her and offer on his knees his uncouth devotion, to make a woman like him. What can I do? Lots of young fellows have passed me in the race—what they call the prizes of life didn't seem to me worth the trouble of the struggle. But for *her*. If she had been mine and liked a diamond—ah! shouldn't she have worn it! Psha, what a fool I am to brag of what I would have done! We are the slaves of destiny. Our lots are shaped for us, and mine is ordained long ago." (2.15.170)

Like Pen, Warrington breaks off his fantasy with self-castigation, but his rationalizing propensity limits his insight. Essentially spinning out a version of "what might have been" to counter the reality of his entrapped marriage, Warrington is still directed by the past. Thackeray makes it clear that society poses considerable obstacles to a man in Warrington's position, but ultimately it is Warrington's decision to accept his fate—to be a realist for everyone except himself.

As if to emphasize the paradoxical nature of fantasy with respect to isolation and the stripping away of façades, Thackeray reserves the novel's main arena of self-expression for moments of isolation—soliloquy or the privacy of one's own thoughts. Thus, even when a character arrives at a measure of self-understanding, the test of its fulfillment in relation to others remains ahead. Narrative layers further obscure and distance such awareness, until fantasy and reality commingle, and what emerges is the implication that it is difficult for any of us to sort them out, to know whether or not we are fooling ourselves about what governs our lives. Thackeray's irony involves the intersection of fantasies. Laura Bell's thoughts make a good case in point. When she is speculating about Warrington's past, her fantasy that "he must have been the victim of some unhappy attachment" (2.15.161) is ironically close to the reality that still remains hidden from her. Later, when her allegiance shifts back to Pen, we learn about this shift through the narrator's speculation about her thoughts—in which she apparently denies the reality of her previous attraction to Warrington and insists on her current obsessional fantasies about Pen (2.36.396–397).

Toward the end of the novel, when we are not certain about how much growth we have witnessed in pampered Pen, who has never experienced any serious privations, Thackeray grants him one speech in which he would seem to understand the limitations of fantasy and appearance. Laura interrupts him on the word "but" and then asks, "But what? What is that wicked but? and why are you always calling it up?" (2.33.370). Pen's reply puts him on equal footing with the narrator, perhaps setting him up for that role in the future novels of *The Newcomes* and *Philip*:

> "But will come in spite of us. But is reflection. But is the sceptic's familiar, with whom he has made a compact; and if he forgets it, and indulges in happy day-dreams, or building of air-castles, or listens to sweet music let us say, or the bells ringing to church, But taps at the door, and says, Master, I am here. You are my master; but I am yours. Go where you will you can't travel without me. I will whisper to you when you are on your knees at church. I will be at your

marriage pillow. I will sit down at your table with your children. I will be behind
your death-bed curtain. That is what But is,'' Pen said.   (2.33.370)

That ''but,'' that reminder of reality, could well be a disturbing fantasy, an
emergent suppression. ''But's'' reality gains meaning in juxtaposition with its
opposite—the will to fantasy.

By opposing reality to fantasy, Dickens and Thackeray share a common
interest in their implied paradox and alternating movement. Thackeray implicitly and explicitly announces his theme of reality versus appearance from
the outset, through both Major Pendennis's vain façade of youth and Pen's
fascination with an actress, and his decorative-initial illustrations provide a
fantastic commentary on the realistic full-page ones that follow.[12] Dickens
also raises these elements from the outset and alerts us to his alternating
patterns. Note, for example, how David's viewpoint on the raffling of his own
birth caul makes the whole proceeding seem fantastic, despite the apparently
offhand, realistic description (DC 1.50). On the level of individual character
and speech, Micawber, too, demonstrates the tension between fantasy and
reality, for he often builds his extravagant rhetorical flourishes to an ''in
short,'' which introduces a straightforward, realistic summary of what has
preceded it.[13] The principle of alternating oppositions generally governs the
number plans, whether we are talking about comedy and tragedy, the conscious and the unconscious, or fantasy and reality. And when Dickens
prepared his reading from *Daivd Copperfield*, his favorite presentation, he
employed this same alternating principle—emphasizing the contrast between humor and pathos, which highlights the opposition of fantasy and
reality.[14]

Nonetheless, these two authors' handling of this opposition reminds us
again of their own essential opposition—the basic difference between a
subjective and an analytical approach to their subject. The difference is once
more brought to the fore in their prefaces to the two novels. Whereas Dickens
seems emotionally involved with his work, calling it his ''favorite child'' in
the 1867 Preface (DC 47), Thackeray seems intellectually impassioned,
challenging himself and the reader with questions of truth and honesty (PEN
ix). Each pretends to risk boredom, but for different reasons, which typify
their two approaches. Dickens worries that ''personal confidences'' and
''private emotions'' might weary the reader (DC 45), while Thackeray acknowledges that ''confidential talk between writer and reader . . . must often
be dull'' (PEN x).[15] Thackeray even takes the issue of judging by appearances
and extends it to the author-reader relationship, applying the theme of reality
and illusion to art in general and this novel in particular:

FIGURES 1–6. Some examples of Thackeray's decorative-initial illustrations for *Pendennis* (see note 12).

If truth is not always pleasant; at any rate truth is best, from whatever chair—
from those whence graver writers or thinkers argue, as from that at which the
story-teller sits as he concludes his labor, and bids his kind reader farewell.

(PEN xii)

Having just dramatized and reiterated their relationship to their art, both
Dickens and Thackeray reify themselves at the end of their prefaces as they
bid their readers farewell—doubly encouraging us to look to their personal
histories for further insight into their autobiographical fictions.

II

Turning to Dickens' biography for additional insight into *David Copperfield*, we can build upon the general analysis of the blacking warehouse
experience and concentrate instead upon some of the personal provocations
that seemed to demand suppression through surrealized characterization.[16] In
doing so, we uncover the process of hidden doubling that lies behind many of
the transformations from reality to fantasy. It is the women in Dickens' life
who kept him in emotional turmoil and fueled his artistic mill, where they split
primarily into fantastic eccentrics or innocuous shells. The doubling of David
into Steerforth and Uriah reflects some of Dickens' general attitudes toward
women, but what happens when Dickens tries to deal with his resentment
toward his mother, who was ''warm'' for his return to the ignominy of
Warren's Blacking House? As Michael Slater suggests in his recent study of
Dickens and women, we can see the author's ambivalent feelings for his
mother dramatized in light and dark doubles—namely, Mrs. Micawber and
Miss Murdstone. And because the ignominy of Warren's haunted Dickens'
social aspirations, and his mother's apparently hard heart complicated his
expectations of women, Dickens felt even more keenly the cruel flirtation of
Maria Beadnell—who undergoes her own series of light and dark doubling in
this novel, into both Dora and Steerforth.[17]

Society initiates and perpetuates stereotypes about women—''accepted''
fantasies, if you will. In the case of Dickens—and many of his fellow
Victorians, including Thackeray—stereotypes and personal experience clash
and confirm, creating problematic relationships. In *David Copperfield*, we
may see how women have become a problem for Dickens through his repeated
use of a romantic-maternal syndrome and his resolution with a ''sisterly''
heroine. Clara Copperfield, David's child-mother, is ineffectual yet attractive—a solution to the problem of an overbearing mother and perhaps equally

desirable in a romantic interest. Although Clara's resurrection in Dora reflects David's choice, Dora also tells us something about Dickens—at least as a young suitor. Agnes Wickfield is another matter, however, especially given her prominence at the end of the novel. Whereas the fantasy surrounding Dora gives way to reality for both her and David (and hence Dickens), we get no double view or distanced irony on Agnes. Agnes is too close to the faultless Mary Hogarth, Dickens' sister-in-law who died at the young age of seventeen and remained changeless in his eyes and in his angelic heroines.[18]

Perhaps yet another doubling process is at work in *David Copperfield*, one in which the female characters represent more than stages for David and suggest fantasized counterparts to him—and to Dickens as well. In Dora, we discover childhood innocence; in Emily, goodness temporarily succumbing to temptation; and in Agnes, frozen idealization. None of these women as they are portrayed simply suggests the timeless feminine component of the self that David (or Dickens) might need to come to terms with in order to integrate himself.[19] Instead, they represent the typical Victorian view of women as arrested in their development. In this respect, they may unconsciously reflect the limited, time-bound perspectives of both their erstwhile suitor and their creator, both of whom remain trapped by their fantasies.

Whereas Dickens transforms actual people from his life into pairs of characters, likewise giving David a pair of antithetical doubles, Thackeray provides us with doubles of himself in the complementary characters of Pen and Warrington. Pen is the youthful Thackeray, frivolous much of the time, trying to decide on his vocation, while Warrington reflects the worldly-wise author, trapped by the reality of a marriage in name only. Between them, they fill out the concept of "hero" for the novel—Pen providing the conventional paradigm, Warrington eliciting our respect and admiration. Despite their primarily complementary roles, they also share the double's propensity to reflect and oppose his "other" half.[20] When Warrington confesses about his past to save Pen from further attacking his mother for her treatment of Fanny, he admits that he was drawn to the younger man by their shared "great unreasonable attachment for a woman" (PEN 2.19.211). On the other hand, Warrington alternately opposes Pen's innocence with his wisdom, his skepticism with certainty, his fantasies with reality.

Thackeray could hardly be unconscious of Warrington's predicament as paralleling his own. His own marriage to Isabella Shawe, whose hopeless insanity required that she receive constant care in an isolated, protected environment, left Thackeray in a state of "perpetual bachelorhood."[21] This is not unlike Warrington's situation, the result of allowing himself to be trapped in a loveless marriage to a lower-class woman, who let her family effect the terms of exchange. From the beginning of his writing career, Thackeray dealt openly with feelings of ambivalence and self-doubt, addressing his reading public in his own voice or those of thinly-disguised narrators. Charles Batchelor, in *Lovel the Widower*, shows just how far he was willing to go to expose this side of himself.[22] Yet—unlike Dickens—Thackeray never even attempted his own autobiography, and he left strict proscriptions to his daughters against writing his biography. And he was not above a little wishful thinking in *Pendennis*, projecting fantasies that might not always stem from fully conscious thoughts.[23] By displacing himself into both Pen and Warrington, he retains Warrington's sense of integrity while getting the girl in the end.

The debates between Pen and Warrington thus assume a unique status in the novel. In a sense, they are like the self-debates of a soliloquist—namely Thackeray—with Warrington acting the part of Pen's conscience or the voice of reason.[24] They show Pen, with a grandiloquence that sometimes rivals Micawber's, falsely posturing and then being led, in almost Socratic fashion, to see the errors of his ways.[25] One debate in particular hits especially close to the mark. On this occasion, Pen and Warrington are discussing Pen's autobiographical novel, "Leaves from the Lifebook of Walter Lorraine." Warrington could indeed be speaking for Thackeray when he says,

> That's the way of poets. . . . They fall in love, jilt, or are jilted; they suffer and they cry out that they suffer more than any other mortals: and when they have experienced feelings enough they note them down in a book, and take the book to market. All poets are humbugs, all literary men are humbugs; directly a man begins to sell his feelings for money he's a humbug. If a poet gets a pain in his side from too good a dinner, he bellows Ai, Ai, louder than Prometheus.
>
> (PEN 2.3.26)[26]

This, then, is one voice of Thackeray, eschewing the autobiographical mode that *Pendennis* itself represents. Stimulated by this issue, he is still willing to bring it forward in analytical debate, ultimately losing the argument through the reality of his own fantasy. Warrington maintains his own terms for the author, however. When Pen, after first ensuring that the embers are dead, performs the melodramatic gesture of tossing his novel onto the fire, Warrington chides him for his pretentiousness—while gently rescuing the manuscript with the firetongs so it can be sent off to a publisher (2.3.29; see Figure 7).

Whether we are talking about character or author, we can gauge degree of suppression by relation to the shadow. A character learns from interacting with his double—or he testifies to his continued self-delusion by standing aloof and failing to confront that part of himself in another. The debates

FIGURE 7. Warrington rescuing Pen's manuscript from the dead
fire—by Thackeray for *Pendennis* (2.3.29).

between Pen and Warrington show Pen benefiting from their synthesis by confronting his hypocrisy. On the other hand, David shrinks from dealing with Heep—who nonetheless fascinates him. Although he finally does strike Heep and call him "villain"—afterwards he lies "tormented half the night" (DC 42.686–687)—David abandons Agnes and Mr. Wickfield to Heep's criminal devices, and he participates in the overthrow of Heep only at Micawber's behest. And neither name-calling nor conquest constitutes the kind of confrontation that permits learning to occur. Seeing Heep as the model prisoner raises the possibility of David's recognizing the criminal and the hypocrite in himself, but the scene dissipates in superficial satire.[27] David's relation to Steerforth, however, falls somewhere in between. Because David can eventually see both the good and evil in Steerforth, he comes closer to accepting himself and realizing his own inner conflicts. In terms of the authors, Thackeray is thus less removed than is Dickens from his shadow figures, since Thackeray's doubles represent versions of himself that have already been resolved in complementary figures. In contrast, Dickens is dealing with doubles of a created, albeit autobiographical, character. Twice removed from their author, these shadows increase the potential for exposing unguarded elements of the psyche, but they may also erect additional layers of protection between the self and self-knowledge.

III

"Whether I shall turn out to be the hero of my own life, or whether that station will be held by anybody else, these pages must show" (DC 1.49). So begins *David Copperfield*, its paradoxical question prefiguring the tension between David and his larger-than-life shades. It raises the question of heroism only to undermine it by suggesting that the self's centrality in its own life could be supplanted by someone else. *Pendennis* implicitly poses the same problem for its ostensible protagonist—first by diverting our attention to another Pendennis, namely the Major, then by splitting our interest between Pen and Warrington. Furthermore, echoes of *Vanity Fair*'s subtitle—*A Novel Without a Hero*—abound in *Pendennis*. Thackeray reminds us on several occasions that Pen is no hero or model (PEN 1.19.204 and 2.15.164), although the point that eventually emerges is more general, based on how reality bursts the bubble of any fantasy: "A duke is no more a hero to his *valet-de-chambre* than you or I" (1.36.399). Finally, the narrator insists, "our endeavor is merely to follow out, in its progress, the development of the mind of a worldly and selfish, but not ungenerous or unkind or truth-avoiding man'' (2.23.269). Given his final equation between Agnes and truth, is this not what David would call a realistic assessment of his own attempt at telling his life story?

Deflating false assumptions about heroism cannot make either David or Pen command our interest, however. In many respects, the subplots in *David Copperfield* hold more interest than David's own story, and Pen's self-complacency risks losing our (and the narrator's) allegiance. But as the realist Warrington interacts with Pen to make his story more compelling, so David's narrative interaction with the entourage of fantasticos who inhabit the fringes of his existence gives his story meaning. As recorders and catalysts, David and Pen do interact with others and thus grow in self-awareness. Yet the implied thesis here, on the part of both Dickens and Thackeray, is that none of us is whole. Doubling characters and displacing oneself would seem to confirm this observation. People are unhappy with their lives, so they have to compensate for a reality that does not fit their desires or illusions by creating more fantasies. Recall Thackeray's comment that we are all separate universes: we can approach one another but never really touch. It is only the author, with the creative power of presenting complementary figures and building a whole novel out of many parts, of addressing and reaching an absent audience, who bridges those gaps—ironically enough, by expressing them.

In this light, we can also see how negativity and emptiness characterize both David and Pen. David's incident with ''the friendly waiter'' is an emblem for his emptiness. Ashamed to eat because everyone assumes he has consumed the food that the waiter appropriated, David does not assert himself. He is literally empty—and his fellow travellers ''create'' a David to amuse themselves. Because David holds his emotions inside, suppressing them, his only response to this situation is to stay empty (DC 5.116–121). Pen, too, is like a shell: he represents one-half of the author, but Warrington has the greater content, eclipsing the shallow Pen. As a half-shadow of his author, Pen is truly penumbral.

The fictions of these shadow-heroes constitute a vacuity at the center of the novels that contain them. Supposed artists, David and Pen hardly seem like protagonists in *Kuntslerromane*, for we learn very little about their work or what impels them to write; their authors are more interested in them for their emotional development than for their professional aspirations or activities. David is especially circumspect about his writing. Only by treating the account we are reading as indeed his own— that is, only by accepting the reality of Dickens' fantasy—can we find evidence of David's artistry, and even so, we must provide our own analysis of it.[28] Pen, on the other hand, gets histrionic about his poetry and autobiographical novel, but these very histrionics betray a hollow core. His melodramatic gesture of tossing his manuscript onto the dead fire underscores his superficiality. True, we do learn more about his novel when Blanche Amory, herself the author of "Mes Larmes," talks about how it moved her to tears (PEN 2.2.21), but the most important information that we acquire is that Pen's autobiographical novel has two heroes—reflecting the split-interest between Pen and Warrington, whose work as a journalist merits Thackeray's more realistic discussion and exposure. In fact, at the end of *Pendennis*, the narrator reveals that is Warrington who is the "abler" writer: Pen's works may have "procured him more reputation," but "the best men do not draw the great prizes in life" (2.37.423).[29]

Dickens and Thackeray are so dispersed among their two protagonists and their doubles that David and Pen seem watered down, not fully dimensional, passive. But even though the protagonists are apparently lax creatures, we sense a tension in the novels. This tension exists between David and his paradoxically more real shades, and between Pen and Warrington. Ultimately, it is a tension that reflects upon the authors themselves as they produce these suppressed *Kuntslerromane*.[30] The ostensible structure of these two autobiographical novels would seem to dictate an artistic component that is mysteriously absent—or notably suppressed. The very hapless, goal-less quality of *David Copperfield* and *Pendennis* points to suppression and an unwillingness to examine closely questions of talent and creativity. To examine such questions too closely is to risk discovering weakness or limitations. On the other hand, to explore them through doubling and redoubling, through displacement and surrealization, is to allow creativity to occur contemporaneously with its own brand of self-analysis. Once again, we recognize that the real interest in these novels emerges from the psychological interplay of suppression and fantasy—whether or not that fantasy is subjected to abstract analysis.

At the end of *David Copperfield* and *Pendennis*, attention is deflected away from the heroes and focuses on the two heroines, Agnes and Laura. This deflection signals yet another form of suppression and return to fantasy, for the Victorian perception of women constitutes an accepted fantasy that neither Dickens nor Thackeray is willing to give up. Agnes and Laura are indeed comparable: they both seem associated with love and truth, and they provide their mates with a second chance at happiness—David through remarriage, Pen through marriage to someone realistic enough to have turned him down when his first proposal was insincere. Now we witness an odd displacement, wherein everything gets shifted onto the women—attention, meaning, hope, idealism, the future. Such displacement reflects not only the idealization of women but the weight placed on marriage—as both the means to happiness and the end-point in life's journey, itself a "death" and therefore all the more fitting an end to narrative. Yet as abstractions, Agnes and Laura also reflect the vacuity already noted in David and Pen, and their unions hint at an incestuous matching that disturbs more than it resolves.[31]

By hanging onto the angelic attributes of Agnes at the end of his narrative, David tries to transcend the realities of this world, to wrap himself anew in a cocoon of fantasy and enter a realm where suppression is no longer necessary:

> O Agnes, O my soul, so may thy face be by me when I close my life indeed; so may I, when realities are melting from me, like the shadows which I now dismiss, still find thee near me, pointing upward!   (DC 64.950)

It is almost as if David's previous initiation into reality by outgrowing the fantasy of his first marriage comes to naught, for we have no indication that he can fully dismiss his shadow selves, now or in the future. Moreover, as Alexander Welsh points out, Agnes is also an "angel of death."[32] She announces Dora's death to David, and despite their growing family, David's idealization of her suggests an asexuality, an end to life. Death in this guise does not break through fantasy—it perpetuates it. Idealization and its enforced lifelessness are David's projections, however. Since we see Agnes only through his eyes, any attacks on her as one-dimensional or death-instilling must take this limited vision into account.

In his attempt to disparage Agnes as the most disagreeable of Dickens' heroines—"the real legless angel of Victorian romance"—George Orwell can resort to no worse a charge than to call her "almost as bad as Thackeray's Laura."[33] But which Laura is Orwell maligning? After all, she exists in several stages as she reappears in *The Newcomes* and *Philip*. In one respect, her conventionality in *Pendennis* may deserve reproach, but as Ina Ferris argues, Laura also falls away from "a sure sense of self," becoming "a strident, dogmatic bully" by Thackeray's last completed novel.[34] True, the Laura of *Pendennis* suffers in our eyes because of her angelic attributions, but like Agnes, she acquires some of these attributes from her "brotherly" lover. When Pen writes to Blanche about their projected marriage, he says of Laura, "she must be our Sister, Blanche, our Saint, our good Angel" (PEN 34.376). Within the world of the novel, Laura's role is also compromised because she acts as Helen Pendennis's surrogate: Helen raises the orphaned daughter of her first love to marry her only son. The incestuous layering redoubles as this sister-figure fulfills their mother's most fervent fantasy, and neither Pen nor

FIGURE 8. By Hablôt Knight Browne for David Copperfield (43.698)—an example of
how Browne's illustrations could recreate the cocoon effect of Dickens' imagery.

Laura can think fondly of their approaching marriage without evoking Helen, their possessive guardian angel, in prayer (2.36.395 and 397).[35]

But Laura is also more humanized than Agnes because the narrator of *Pendennis* enters her mind, reporting her unspoken thoughts and fantasies. For example, despite Pen's idealization of Laura, we discover her smug cattiness regarding Fanny when she says to herself, "well, now really! is *this* the creature about whom we were all so frightened? What *could* he see in her?" (398). Furthermore, we learn more about Laura through the love triangle that exists only in fantasies: Warrington reveals his love for Laura in soliloquy, and she changes toward him, moving toward Pen, in her unspoken soliloquies. Ironically, characters become more real to us as readers when we see them in their most isolated moments—indulging in their fantasies—either because the fantasy is narrated directly, as with David, or because it is reported through omniscient eyes, as in *Pendennis*. Thus, there is a distinction between how fantasy operates in the "real" world of the novel—mostly as self-protection that risks setting up constrictive barriers of self-deception and secrecy—and its mode of operation in the writing of the novel, where fantasy is largely creative and relief-giving (unless it, too, is suppressed).

Both Dickens and Thackeray distance themselves from their suppressed emotions—Dickens through layered cocoons of fantasy and doubling, Thackeray through trivialization and displacement. Both authors erect layers but their perspectives differ: Dickens moves inward, embedding himself in his own encasements, while Thackeray moves outward, rising above the levels of reality he has created. Note, too, the greater ironic distance of Thackeray from his released suppressions: we view the silliness of Pen throwing his manuscript onto the fire, whereas Dickens makes us join him in responding to Heep as a true grotesque—perhaps partly because he never truly confronts him. We stand outside Pen, evaluating his gesture even before Warrington or the narrator can do so for us, while we are pulled into David's horror at Heep's writhing.[36] Dickens is, at the same time, both distant and intimate with his fantasies: he produces shades of a created character, not another side of himself, but he also gets drawn into the subjectivity of David's nightmare world. Thackeray, on the other hand, shows us how fantasy implies an intellectual rejection, creating a tension that we see in satire, ambivalence, and puppet characters. Thus, the fantasy and reality that merge in Dickens remain separate but occasionally cross over in Thackeray. After all, one man's fantasy may be another man's reality, and the goals of fantasy in *David Copperfield* may indeed be the reality valued in *Pendennis*. When Pen is still infatuated with the actress known as the Fotheringay, he sees her in a performance of *The Stranger*, the play that leaves David "so dreadfully cut up" just before he succumbs to Dora's charms (DC 26.446). But even in the "balderdash" of this dramatic fantasy, Thackeray's narrator reminds us that "there runs that reality of love, children and forgiveness of wrong, which will be listened to wherever it is preached, and sets all the world sympathizing" (PEN 1.4.41).

NOTES

1. Leslie Stephen, "The Writings of W. M. Thackeray," in *The Writings of W. M. Thackeray*, 24 (London: Smith, Elder, 1879), 319. In time, Forster had to give a similar warning.

2. See, for example, [David Masson], "*Pendennis* and *Copperfield*: Thackeray and Dickens," *North British Review*, 15 (May 1851), 57–89; Samuel Phillips, "David Copperfield and Arthur Pendennis," *The Times*, 11 June 1851, 8; and "*David Copperfield* and *Pendennis*," *Prospective Review*, 7 (July 1851), 157–191—as well as Thackeray's letter to Masson, 6(?) May 1851, *The Letters and Private Papers of William Makepeace Thackeray*, ed. Gordon N. Ray (Cambridge, Mass.: Harvard University Press, 1952), II, 771–773. Masson later revised his review and developed it into a general comparison, in which he acknowledges the inevitable pressure to evaluate each author in terms of the other: "But whether simultaneously visible or alternate, the two are now so closely associated in the public mind, that whenever the one is mentioned the other is thought of. . . . Nay not content with associating them people have got in the habit of contrasting them and naming them in opposition to each other. . . . [T]here is no debate more common, wherever literary talk goes on, than the debate as to the respective merits of Dickens and Thackeray." See *British Novelists and Their Styles: Being a Critical Sketch of the History of British Prose Style* (Cambridge: Macmillan, 1859), p. 240.

3. Masson, *British Novelists*, p. 243.

4. See Bruno Bettelheim, *The Uses of Enchantment: The Meaning and Importance of Fairy Tales* (New York: Alfred A. Knopf, 1976), and Viktor Frankl, *Man's Search for Meaning: An Introduction to Logotherapy*, trans. Ilse Lasch (New York: Pocket Books, 1963). Bettelheim in fact begins by discussing how Dickens acknowledged that fairy tales had a "deep formative impact . . . on him and his creative genius" (p. 23). See also Thackeray's views on being sure his daughter Anny received an "extensive and instructive learning" in fairy tales (*Letters*, I, 394–395). For an overview of Dickens' use of fantasy, see Harry Stone, *Dickens and the Invisible World: Fairy Tales, Fantasy, and Novel-Making* (Bloomington: Indiana University Press, 1979).

5. Charles Dickens, *The Personal History of David Copperfield*, ed. Trevor Blount (Harmondsworth: Penguin Books, 1966), ch. 3, p. 79. Further citations of this edition will appear in parentheses in the text.

6. Sylvia Manning also demonstrates how narrative helps David to conquer his past. See her article, "David Copperfield and Scheherazada: The Necessity of Narrative," *Studies in the Novel*, 14 (1982), 327–336.

7. For an intriguing discussion of how *déja vu* works through Heep to reveal David's repressed sexual attraction to Agnes, see Stanley Friedman, "Dickens' Mid-Victorian Theodicy: *David Copperfield*," *Dickens Studies Annual*, ed. Robert B. Partlow, 7 (1978), 137–139 especially.

8. William Makepeace Thackeray, *The History of Pendennis: His Fortunes and Misfortunes, His Friends and His Greatest Enemy*, 1 (London: Smith, Elder, 1878), ch. 16, pp. 160–161. Subsequent references to this and other novels by Thackeray will be to this edition of *The Works* (1878–79) and will appear in parentheses in the text. For a visual rendition of this essential separation, see the decorative-initial illustration that opens *Lovel the Widower*: it depicts people walking around with muffs over their heads and faces (p. 3).

9. See 1.22.225 and 2.11.116–117 for examples of how fantasy comes alive in metaphors about society, past and present. In the second half of the novel, Pen's perspective begins to merge with the narrator's, and he too weaves fantasies about society, "in his own satirical way," when he tells Blanche Amory about the Chevalier's imprisonment and Altamont's "gallant rescue" (2.26.300).

10. Alnaschar appears in "The Barber's Fifth Night" of *The Arabian Nights*. He invests all his money in glassware in order to impress the Vizier's daughter, but during a dream about his future bride he becomes angry and upsets the merchandise, breaking it to pieces. See also the chapter entitled "In Which Pendennis Counts His Eggs," with its decorative-initial illustration depicting a young woman balancing a basket full of eggs on her head (2.31.350).

11. Thackeray deals with the question of propriety in fiction and the priggishness of the Victorian Age in his preface, where he notes, "since the author of Tom Jones was buried, no writer of fiction among us has been permitted to depict to his utmost power a MAN" (p. xi). So, despite Pen's temptation, he does not try to seduce Fanny, and Thackeray later covers his tracks somewhat by making Fanny more conniving than when she first appears. The issue of seduction has an interesting symbolic importance vis-à-vis fantasy: it may reflect sexual suppression, and its act of sexual initiation marks a loss of either fantasy or reality—depending on one's point of view.

12. Since Thackeray illustrated most of his own novels, his illustrations constitute an integral part of his presentation. See Figures 1–6, page 250, for some examples of his decorative-initial fantasies, including a mermaid with a cup (PEN 1.18.184), a dragonslayer (1.28.306), a courtier waving farewell to a woman at a window (2.10.109), the previously discussed chin-chucking chevalier and maid (2.8.87), a fairy with a magic wand (2.22.241), and Eve with her serpent (2.26.293). In contrast, his story-line illustrations fall within the tradition of domestic realism (see Figure 7, page 254, showing Warrington rescuing Pen's manuscript from the dead fire [2.3.29]). For an example of how Hablôt K. Browne's illustrations could recreate the cocoon effect of Dickens' imagery, see especially the illustration entitled, "I Am Married" (DC 43.698), depicted in Figure 8, page 259.

13. James R. Kincaid discusses Micawber's two styles and the author's contrasting

movements in "Dickens's Subversive Humor: *David Copperfield*," *Nineteenth-Century Fiction*, 22 (1968), 313–329, while he analyzes the novel's symbolic patterning of the conflict between illusion and reality in "Symbol and Subversion in *David Copperfield*," *Studies in the Novel*, 1 (1969), 196–206.

14. For the authoritative text of this reading, see *Charles Dickens: The Public Readings*, ed. Philip Collins (Oxford: Clarendon Press, 1975), pp. 213–248. Collins observes that Dickens delivered the reading some seventy times.

15. Although this kind of self-consciousness sometimes blends into subjectivity with Thackeray, it still involves a degree of role-playing. For further discussion of this issue, see Winslow Rogers, "Thackeray's Self-Consciousness," in *The Worlds of Victorian Fiction*, ed. Jerome H. Buckley (Cambridge, Mass.: Harvard University Press, 1975), pp. 149–164.

16. For a study of some of the more positive aspects of Dickens' childhood employment, see Albert D. Hutter, "Reconstructive Autobiography: The Experience at Warren's Blacking," *Dickens Studies Annual*, ed. Robert B. Partlow, 6 (1977), 1–14. C. D. Cox conjectures that Dickens' fantasticos reflect as much about his "characteristic adult vision of life" as they do his childhood experience—which in most cases informs the adult's outlook. See "Realism and Fantasy in *David Copperfield*," *Bulletin of the John Rylands Library*, 52 (1970), 267–283.

17. Michael Slater, *Dickens and Women* (Stanford, Calif.: Stanford University Press, 1983), chs. 1 and 4 especially. Maria later reappears in the single devastating portrait of Flora Finching in *Little Dorrit*. In his full-length novels, Dickens does not create the tension of doubling within a single character until John Jasper in *The Mystery of Edwin Drood*—and that remains unfinished. This tension is prefigured and fantasticated, however, in his last Christmas story, *The Haunted Man* (1848)—which immediately precedes *David Copperfield*.

18. Writing to Thomas Beard about Mary [17 May 1827], Dickens observes, "she had not a fault." See *The Letters of Charles Dickens*, ed. Madeline House and Graham Storey, I (Oxford: Clarendon Press, 1965), 259.

19. This reading draws on the Jungian concepts of animus and anima. (This kind of reading is even more strongly suggested by Vladimir Nabokov's strangely autobiographical novel, *Ada*.)

20. Claire Rosenfield notes how complementary doubles usually comment on the struggling personality of the protagonist, as in Dostoyevsky's *Crime and Punishment* and Melville's *Pierre*. See "The Shadow Within: The Conscious and Unconscious Use of the Double," *Daedalus*, 92 (1963), 326–344. Masson speaks directly to Pen's and Warrington's opposition in his review-essay: "[I]n this antimony between Pen and Warrington, we may, without any injustice, discern the main features of the author's own philosophy of life." This doubling of the author looks ahead to the later pairings of Pen with Clive and Philip—when Pen assumes the role that Warrington has been playing.

21. In her self-protective, childlike state of fantasy, Isabella outlived her husband by thirty years, her daughter Anne Thackeray Ritchie eventually feeling like a mother to her own mother. See "The Psychiatric Case History of Isabella Shawe Thackeray," written by Dr. Stanley Cobb from evidence in the letters (*Letters*, I, 518–520).

22. In contrast to my reading, Ina Ferris concludes that the character-narrator's convoluted interiorization reflects Thackeray's own disintegration. See "The Breakdown of Thackeray's Narrator: *Lovel the Widower,*" *Nineteenth-Century Fiction,* 32 (1977), 36–53.

23. Although he has Pen leave "Oxbridge" just as he left Cambridge, Thackeray also lets Pen return (with Laura's money) to earn the degree he himself never received.

24. Juliet McMaster also notes Warrington's role as "the voice of Pen's conscience" in *Thackeray: The Major Novels* (Toronto: University of Toronto Press, 1971), p. 80.

25. Pen is not the only young writer who responds in extravagant verbal posturings to his artistic calling, of course. Note Stephen Dedalus's grandiloquence at the end of James Joyce's *Kuntslerroman:* "Welcome, O life! I go to encounter for the millionth time the reality of experience and to forge in the smithy of my soul the uncreated conscience of my race." See *Portrait of the Artist as a Young Man* (New York: The Viking Press, 1964), pp. 252–253.

26. This speech caused Thackeray to be attacked by numerous critics, who concluded that he was being false to his own profession. For Thackeray's reply to them, see his letter to the editor, "The Dignity of Literature," *The Morning Chronicle,* 12 January 1850. Within *Pendennis* already lies at least one answer. See Warrington's earlier tribute to that "great engine"—the Press—that "never sleeps" (1.30.340).

27. For an opposing reading, one that views David as beginning to discover his own incomplete repentance in this scene, see Carl Bandelin, "David Copperfield: A Third Interesting Penitent," *Studies in English Literature,* 16 (1976), 601–611.

28. For an interpretation that emphasizes this reading and the importance of memory to the narrative, see Carl Dawson, *Victorian Noon: English Literature in 1850* (Baltimore, Maryland: Johns Hopkins University Press, 1979), pp. 127–143. Time and narrative memory also grant meaning to *Pendennis,* of course. For a thorough examination of this issue in Thackeray, see Jean Sudrann, "The Philosopher's Property: Thackeray and the Use of Time," *Victorian Studies,* 10 (1976), 359–388.

29. Note, too, that Warrington gets Pen his first writing assignment and substitutes for him when he is sick. The narrator's voice at the end also echoes Warrington's earlier rationalization about fate, thereby lending some support to his resignation.

30. For further discussion of *Pendennis* as a *Kuntslerroman,* see McMaster, pp. 77–85.

31. Blanche's name also points to her emptiness. In fact, Pen and Blanche conjoin in hypocrisy to reveal their emptiness to Laura (1.24.260–261). As for the incestuous undertones, Warrington's perfect submission to "the part of Godpapa" further compounds them (2.37.423).

32. Alexander Welsh, *The City of Dickens* (Oxford: Clarendon Press, 1971), pp. 180–183. For a reading that works with Welsh's insights but then goes on to see Agnes as transcending "the paradigm of the immobilized angel," see Nina Auerbach, *Woman and the Demon: The Life of a Victorian Myth* (Cambridge, Mass.: Harvard University Press, 1982), pp. 84–88 especially.

33. George Orwell, "Charles Dickens," in *A Collection of Essays* (New York: Harcourt, Brace, 1946), p. 102.

34. Ina Ferris, "The Demystification of Laura Pendennis," *Studies in the Novel*, 13 (1981), 122–132.

35. Both Helen and Laura were received enthusiastically by Thackeray's reading public, while modern critical attention emphasizes their hypocrisy and idealization. Thackeray leaves no doubt that Helen experiences sexual jealousy in the Fanny Bolton affair, but his explicit angelic attributions would seem to counter that interpretation or suggest that he later puts his blinders on. Instead, we do well to read this division as an indication of his ambivalence toward his own mother, the acknowledged model. Let me also add John Forster's reminder that Thackeray cheerfully admitted some of the resemblances between his mother and Mrs. Steerforth. See *The Life of Charles Dickens*, ed. A. J. Hoppé, rev. ed. (London: Dent, 1969), II, 108. For an argument that Helen is the most important character in the novel, see Robert Bledsoe, "*Pendennis* and the Power of Sentimentality: A Study of Motherly Love," *PMLA*, 91 (1976), 871–873.

36. Some of Virginia Woolf's comments are pertinent here. She notes that "while we are under their spell these great geniuses make us see the world in any shape they choose. We remodel our psychological geography when we read Dickens." She also places *David Copperfield* among the "stories communicated by word of mouth in those tender years when fact and fiction merge." Ironically, from her vantage point, she assumes that Dickens is "of all great writers . . . the least personally present in his books." See "David Copperfield," *Nation and Athenaeum*, 22 August 1925; rpt. *The Moment and Other Essays* (New York: Harcourt, Brace, 1948), pp. 75–80.

Magic Casements and Victorian Transparencies: Post-Romantic Modes of Perception

Michael Greenstein

> "The Understanding is indeed thy window,
> too clear thou canst not make it."
> *Sartor Resartus*

If one were to extend M. H. Abrams's line of inquiry in *The Mirror and the Lamp* through the nineteenth century, the "window" would emerge as a central image rivalling the aesthetic roles of neo-classical mirrors and Romantic lamps.[1] Just as a glass window may function physically as a reflector or a source of light, so metaphorically it may be aligned with the mimetic or expressive theories of art which post-Romantic aesthetics inherited from its eighteenth- and early-nineteenth-century precursors. In their attempts to accommodate these critical traditions, Victorian poets, painters, and novelists resort increasingly to window imagery, which allowed them to focus on scenes of mimetic Realism or expressive Romanticism, an opposition characterized by Jakobson's structural distinction between metonymy and metaphor. Thus, while Victorian windows demonstrate predominantly metonymic modes of perception, characteristic of a Realism concerned with social and moral issues, occasionally Romantic impulses continue through a dialectical interplay between these two modes. When the pre-Romantics hold a window up to nature, they copy it; the Romantics stain it, as Shelley's "dome of many-coloured glass, / Stains the white radiance of Eternity"; post-Romantic windows mediate between reflection and projection as they frame and "contain" nature and perceiver.

When the Lady of Shalott abandons her mirror in favor of a more direct view of the external world, she seems to be moving in a direction paradigmatic of a Victorian shift to fenestrated modes of perception—modes involving a conflict between domestic security or imprisonment on one side of the threshold and a Romantic longing for adventure or freedom beyond. Her mirror symbolically cracks as a result of her defiant move: "The new terror of the mirror, on occasion also the smashing of the glass in order to break free from the pursuing double and thus, if possible, return to the great whole . . . was an important motif in the works both of Storm and Stress and Romanticism."[2] "Half sick of shadows" from their domestic interiors, Victorians seek to restore "the great whole" outdoors with views of society that "double" the position of the viewer, or views of nature from which the skeptical viewer is protected by the glass pane. Where Romantic projection is accompanied by iconoclastic activity (as in the smashing of glass in "The Lady of Shalott" or shattered window-panes in *Wuthering Heights*),[3] Victorians construct a glass barrier to contemplate a metonymic perspective situated in a middle distance between the extremes of self-absorbing foregrounds or remote backgrounds, between vantage point and vanishing point.

Though one finds many casements through which glimpses of the landscape transform the mind in the poetry of Coleridge and Wordsworth, the Romantics on the whole prefer to bypass the window in unmediated vision and direct contact with nature. At his sister's deathbed, De Quincey's epiphany of the "blue depths [which] seemed to express types of infinity"[4] outside a large window reveals a vertical, metaphoric mode of perception: instead of a contiguous foreground the eye is presented with an unspecified emptiness to be filled by an imaginative metaphoric leap. The same process occurs in Keats's "magic casements, opening on the foam / Of perilous seas, in faery lands forlorn": once again vision becomes cancelled when nothing but an abyss or absence meets the eye, which must fill the void through expressive projection.

I

Blake concludes "A Vision of the Last Judgment" by rejecting the empirical window which is responsible for division rather than vision: "I question not my Corporeal or Vegetative Eye any more than I would question a Window concerning a Sight. I look thro' it & not with it."[5] Where the Romantics look *through* the casement upon a vast, vertical universe beyond space and time, the skeptical Victorians in their prose, poetry, and painting tend increasingly to question *with* the window a more specific, horizontal reality foregrounded in space and time. Where Romantic vision goes to extremes of either direct contact with nature outdoors or isolated self-absorption indoors, Victorian vision compromises by retreating from both and seeking refuge behind the window, where the self can securely interact with nature or society.

If the correspondent breeze is a dominant Romantic metaphor uniting man and nature, then the correspondent window becomes an equally important post-Romantic trope, simultaneously linking and separating man and his environment. In denouncing "the despotism of the eye" and invoking their "viewless winds," Blake, Wordsworth, Coleridge, and Shelley were reacting against the dualism and mechanism of the Enlightenment. Skeptical Victorians, in turn, developed strategies in response to this Romantic revolt: post-Romantic iconology displaced the aural wind-harp with the visual wind-eye (the original meaning of window), where insight rather than inspiration predominates. But this reappearance of the seen differs from earlier empiricism in its degree of particularization: Victorian vistas are channeled into the window, where they are confined, filtered, and restrained by an individualized point of view. The boundlessness of Promethean vision and action at the beginning of the century contrasts with the eclipse of the Victorian hero, bound to his window, searching in vain for vertical transcendence and settling instead for the limitations of horizontal correspondence.

During the course of the nineteenth century, vision narrows in focus from Keats's magic casements and De Quincey's large window to F. H. Bradley's "limited transparencies": "Contact with reality is through a limited aperture. For [we] cannot get at it directly except through . . . one small opening."[6] To establish contact with reality through these limited apertures, Victorians developed an aesthetic of metonymic particularity: "By the Victorian period, the sense of the particularity of experience and the disintegration of belief in the reality of universals had increased to such an extent that poets were forced to develop new aesthetics to deal with this particularity and its relationship to universality."[7] Not only in their poetry, but also in their painting, fiction, and social history, the Victorians focused on windows as a medium for exploring the interrelationships between particularity and universality, solitude and society, interior privacy and the external public spectacle. Reacting against the egotistical sublime, post-Romantic aesthetics limited itself to more circumscribed views of reality. By "containing" both external threat and internal projection, Bradley's "one small opening" was admirably suited to the Victorian temper. Limited apertures limit both view and viewer: the selected and framed view restricts the viewer's horizon so that he no longer immerses himself in "faery lands forlorn," "blue depths of infinity," or many-colored domes of Eternity.

II

While it may be impossible to establish any direct causal connection between the history of glass and the prevalence of window imagery in the nineteenth century, nevertheless certain architectural, mechanical, and optical developments exemplify individual perception of material gain and human deprivation in the public scene. The window tax, for example, which had been in effect since the seventeenth century, was relaxed just before Queen Victoria ascended the throne:

> In the ordinary home, decent lighting was not to be found until late in the century. In the period 1808–23 the window tax, a relic dating from 1696, reached its highest level. Houses with six windows or less were taxed 6s.6d. to 8s. annually; seven-window houses, a pound; nine-window houses, two guineas, and so on up. Even an aperture only a foot square was considered a window. Although in 1823 the tax was halved, and in 1825 houses with less than eight windows were exempted, builders still were discouraged from putting any more openings in a house than were absolutely necessary, with the result that only one-seventh of all the houses in Britain fell under the tax.[8]

Whereas the poorer classes were deprived of light, the middle classes who could afford windows ironically limited these apertures with heavy, defensive curtains.[9]

In his *Rural Rides* William Cobbett noted that laborers were liable to punishment for looking out of their factory window, and in *Nicholas Nickleby* the windows of Dotheboys Hall are stuffed with rags.[10] In 1850 Dickens, replying to Charles Knight concerning the duty on paper, shifted from the opaque medium of print to the transparent window of vision which occupied so many of his characters around the middle of the century: "I quite agree with you in all you say so well of the injustice and impolicy of this excessive taxation. But when I think of the condition of the great masses of the people, I fear that I could hardly find the heart to press for justice in this respect, before the window-duty is removed. They cannot read without light. They cannot have an average chance of life and health without it."[11] Houses with bricked-up windows testify to the injustices of this tax: a moral, social, and architectural blight upon England, the window tax was finally removed in 1851 as part of the spirit of reform, and glass began to be used increasingly in construction in the second half of the century. The *Illustrated London News* celebrated "the abolition of the tax; the triple fenestration no longer imposes triple penalty, and Palladian forms of window emancipated from the tax seem to rejoice as they gaily reflect the broad light from their ample surfaces."[12] Obviously any increase in the size and number of windows should result in an increase in daylight reading and a propensity for gazing at external vistas—the causal and contiguous relationship between light and reading. The history of the window tax reflects the Victorians' social and artistic sensitivity to this architectural opening: on the one hand, public celebration of the material benefits of industrial progress; on the other, a private shrinking from its demonic aspect and social inequalities.

An *annus mirabilis*, 1851 also saw the completion of Paxton's Crystal Palace, another architectural eye-opener, dubbed by Thackeray "The Palace made o' windows!" *The Eclectic Review* summarized Victorian progress and optimism as reflected in the Great Exhibition: "the year 1851, when compared with the year 1801, is as the palace of glass when compared with the houses built under the regime of the window duty."[13] It goes on to praise the "architectural veracity" of glass: "Quite in keeping is the building, too, with the age. It is the aesthetic blossom of its practical character, and of the practical tendency of the English nation. . . . [It] expresses its realities, as far as they go: material rather than spiritual."[14] *Punch* echoes this essentially pragmatic opinion by emphasizing the relationship between container and contained: "Beautiful as were the contents of the glass, the glass itself was the prime glory."[15] Indeed, the mixing of classes, the ordering of scientific exhibits, the relationship between the glass container and its contents, and the proximity between the large elm trees within the glass structure and the others in Hyde Park all reinforced metonymic modes of perception. Tennyson depicted the pacific restraints of this limiting microcosm:

> She brought a vast design to pass
> When Europe and the scattered ends
> Of our fierce world did meet as friends
> And brethren in her halls of glass.

Reviewing the architectural achievements of the middle of the nineteenth century, Sir John Summerson concludes that "Many Victorians saw in the Crystal Palace the first glimpse of the new style which was to characterise the new age. The whole force of a most attractive analogy came into operation. We were to have crystal cathedrals and crystal homes."[16] This attractive analogy made its way into Victorian consciousness as the various classes awakened to the new architectural potential of glass in public and private dwellings.

If the Crystal Palace display captured reality in glass, so too did photography with its glass lenses, plates, and windowed studios along Glasshouse Street near Regent Street in London. The Great Exhibition "encouraged photography by establishing display *salons*, and, with wider effect, by advancing the universalist idea to Western peoples of a new global perspective: the world under one roof. The camera, the youngest child of science and technology, was the inevitable instrument for achieving this perspective by bringing the variety of the nations under a common gaze."[17] Fox Talbot, who had taken the world's first negative (a view of his latticed window at Lacock Abbey), wrote to *The Times* (August 13, 1852): "Ever since the Great Exhibition I have felt a new era has commenced for photography."

Photography represents reality metonymically as the camera and finished photograph select and frame a particular slice of life. (Hence Realists and Naturalists frequently resort to photographic analogies in their theories of art.) Photographic albums displayed family histories in their visual narratives, while *cartes-de-visite* encouraged a vicarious mixing of classes since photographs of the rich and famous could be inserted into private family albums. Also by mid-century, window screens displayed photographic imagery of landscapes as well as portraits, thereby focusing on continuity between individual interior and public exterior. Books began to be illustrated with photographs, the visual contiguity of word and picture furthering a metonymic effect. Carl Dawson has argued that "the autobiographical impulse and autobiographical forms of mid-century literature are related to new theories of perception (including the mechanical eye of photography), new theories of history, new literary idols, and new permutations of Romantic literary styles."[18] Indeed, as domesticated Victorians documented the world through limited apertures of glass, theories of perception inevitably changed from earlier Romantic styles. Instead of losing the organic self through egotistical immersion or escape into nature, post-Romanticism tried to find itself, through a distancing removal behind the mechanical confines of glass to gain perspective and security in its outlook on realistic detail.

Henry Peach Robinson's photographs "Fading Away" (1858) and "Sleep" (1867) illustrate the natural alliance between photography and the window. Remarkably similar to scenes in *Dombey and Son*, "Fading Away" depicts a family's concern for its moribund daughter, the title suggesting not only her condition but also the sentimental quality of light shed upon her emotional and physical debility. At this photograph's center the window emphasizes a black-and-white contrast between dark, vertical parental figures at the left and lighter, angular, younger figures to the right, between external light and a heavily-curtained Victorian chamber within. The girl's father turns away from the poignant domestic interior toward the light outside. The window serves as a structural, narrative, and imagistic frame counterpointing the photograph's external borders, while the empty sky and outdoor fountain imply release from the internal mood. "Sleep" recalls Henry Wallis's *The Death of Chatterton* (1856) in its positioning of horizontal figures beneath a centrally located lattice window, which acts as a mediator between the dreamlike Romantic sea and the dreams of two sleeping girls. By "containing" the sea without, the window protects the dormant girls while at the same time providing an opening for their Romantic dreams. Both of Robinson's photographs exhibit the Victorian dilemma between the window's combinative axis of metonymic Realism and the selective axis of metaphoric Romance (a dilemma shared by the Pre-Raphaelites in their use of photographic detail on both sides of their casements).

Expansion of railways in the nineteenth century coincides with the development of photography, and is aligned to metonymic habits of perception and an awareness of class distinctions. As opposed to the stationary window at home, the train's window afforded an opportunity to view the landscape kinetically, with the visual emphasis on horizontal perspective and contrast between inside and outside. Furthermore, railway travel encouraged reading inside the carriage alternating with views outside the source of light. Visiting England in 1847, Ralph Waldo Emerson describes his experience of railway travelling: "Cushioned and comforted in every manner, the traveller rides as on a cannon-ball, high and low, over rivers and towns, through mountains in tunnels of three or four miles, at near twice the speed of our trains; and reads quietly the 'Times' newspaper."[19] Emerson's comments depict the domestic comfort of the interior, the point-to-point succession of the landscape, and the connection between travel and reading. The following year W. H. Smith established his first bookstall at London's Euston Station, and by mid-century passengers were able to purchase books to take along on their journeys. On August 9, 1851 Samuel Phillips's article "Literature of the Rail" appeared in the *Times*, showing the connection between train travel and reading.

Dickens exploits this kinetic window in the train rides in *Dombey and Son*. Just before the villainous Carker throws himself in front of an onrushing train, he asks a waiter at his inn what day of the week it is. Sensing that Carker's temporal bewilderment stems from his train journey, the waiter comments, "Very confusing, Sir. Not much in the habit of travelling by rail myself, Sir, but gentlemen frequently say so."[20] Another gentleman who would "say so" is Carker's pursuing alter ego, Dombey, who earlier in the novel also undertakes a train ride associated with death. Dickens' syntactical parallelisms imitate the rhythm of the wheels, the vanishing perspective of the rails, and the kaleidoscopic change of scenery outdoors. At the train station and during his trip Dombey wishes to exclude those undesirable characters, particularly the lower-class father and son, Toodle and Grinder, who constantly intrude on his mourning for his own dead son: "To think that this lost child, who was to have divided with him his riches, and his projects, and his power, and allied with whom he was to have shut out all the world as with a double door of gold, should have let in such a herd to insult him with their knowledge of his defeated hopes, and their boasts of claiming community of feeling with himself, so far removed: if not of having crept into the place wherein he would have lorded it, alone!" (p. 275).

Dickens repeats "to think" in parallel to establish Dombey's "train of thought," divided from nature and humanity on the other side of the glass partition. In place of transparency, Dombey prefers an opaque loneliness or solipsistic protection that excludes any reminder by lower classes of his own situation. "Tortured by these thoughts he carried monotony with him, through the rushing landscape, and hurried headlong, not through a rich and varied country, but a wilderness of blighted plans and gnawing jealousies" (p. 275). The rejected mixing of classes within the train and train station finds its counterpart in the view of rich and poor dwellings succeeding each other during the journey. "As Mr. Dombey looks out of his carriage window, it is never in his thoughts that the monster who has brought him there has let the light of day in on these things: not made or caused them" (p. 277). Dombey tries to remain blind to the view from his carriage window (a scene whose social implications Dickens emphatically denounces) for the landscape reveals severe injustices. The locomotive allows Dickens to witness social problems, to convey psychological disturbances within his characters, and to display a verbal virtuosity that imitates the kaleidoscopic sense of time and space experienced by Victorians.

Domestic windows, train windows, the Crystal Palace, and photography metonymically let the light of day in on social realities of the Two Nations, underlining the need for reform. While none of these limited transparencies caused "the condition of England question," they did emphasize the perceptual means whereby Victorians mediated between their domestic serenity and external public challenge to it. The Romantic escapism of Pre-Raphaelitism and Art for Art's Sake was still possible but, as Ruskin and Morris demonstrated, increasingly difficult in an age when social reform became imperative and transmuted magic casements.

III

According to Graham Reynolds, the domestication of Victorian painting parallels literary developments as domestic scenes peaked around the middle of the century: "This upsurge of domesticity coincides with the height of influence of the Victorian novel, as well as with the researches of Mayhew into the life of the London Poor; with journalism and photography it makes the mid-century an accessible one for explanation and understanding."[21] While there are significant precursors from the Renaissance and from the Dutch genre painters of the seventeenth century, nineteenth-century painters "place the open window in the center, while in Dutch genres it is seen obliquely, in strong foreshortening, as a source of light but not an opening into space."[22] As in literature, Romanticism ushers in the major shift in the window's emphasis: "It is in the work of the genre painters after 1810, on the threshold between classicism and romanticism, that the *figure at the window* first appears as a favorite motif. The typical picture of this kind shows an interior of fairly ordinary character, with a figure quietly at work or absorbed in meditation near a window."[23] The viewer of the painting repeats the contemplation of the figure at the window—which may be viewed phenomenologically if emphasis is placed on the visual process of interaction between the observer's emotions and the view, or structurally with the frame isolating and containing objects on the outside juxtaposed with those indoors.

> The pure window-view is a romantic innovation—neither landscape, nor interior, but a curious combination of both. It brings the confinement of an interior into the most immediate contrast with an immensity of space outside, outdoors, a space which need not be a landscape, but can be a view of houses or of the empty sky. It often places the beholder so close to the window that little more than an enclosing frame of darkness remains of the interior, but this is sufficient to maintain the suggestion of a separation between him and the world outside.[24]

The Victorians narrow and limit this Romantic immensity of outside space and illuminate the interior by focusing on particular details on both sides of the window.

In the 1850s Mrs. Sophie Anderson's sentimental *No Walk To-day* magnifies a window, thereby dwarfing a young girl disappointed by the rain that prevents her from walking outdoors. The large glass panes serve as a medium for pathetic fallacy, as individual raindrops clinging to them reflect tears of disappointment. Her delicate fingers resting on the wooden frame suggest gentle confinement behind the thin glass, which separates and joins the floral pattern on the curtains with the vegetation immediately in front of a scene entirely devoted to detailed foreground. Protected by glass and by layers of clothing, she must forego action and settle for contemplation; framed by a static window of domestic imprisonment and security, the Victorian female as the century progresses seeks active emancipation where earlier she had to be satisfied with visual and oneiric escape.

In Augustus Egg's *The Travelling Companions* (1862) the carriage window provides the canvas with a symmetry not only between the calm repose of domestic interior and distanced exterior, but also between the "twin" women identically dressed, one sleeping while the other reads. Like an inset painting the central window panel, flanked by two smaller ones, frames a landscape unobserved by either of the two heavily-robed Victorian women, whose ample dresses seem in shape and color to parallel the mountains in the distance. Beside each traveller lies a reminder of the external world brought indoors for her pleasure—a bouquet of flowers for the reader and a food basket next to the sleeper. In contrast to the luxury and harmony at Egg's window, Charles Rossiter in *To Brighton and Back for 3/6d* (1859) portrays the crowded, uncomfortable conditions of third-class travel, where the carriage has no windows to protect the poor. Similarly, Abraham Solomon compares class comforts in *First Class—The Meeting* and *Second Class—The Parting*.

Just as Egg uses a triptych effect with the windows of *The Travelling Companions*, so he employs a triple framing device in his moralistic narrative series *Past and Present* (1858). Part I reveals a crowded Victorian interior with the "fallen" mother on the floor, surrounded by her husband, children, and domestic luxury. At the room's center, a mirror reflects the woman's guilt for having upset the claustral domestic order. In Part II, a decade later, the grown daughters bemoan their mother's adultery: in place of the earlier mirror, a window is now situated at the center. This pivotal window opens on a bleak cityscape reflecting their mother's guilt and preparing for the depiction of her fate in the third panel. The view opens and becomes more explicit in Part III as the woman, thrust outdoors, descends further into the underworld of lower-class prostitutes and derelicts: an arch now divides the city from her present situation under a bridge.

This metonymic series displays a causal progression from past acts to present consequences. In the same manner, William Frith's series *The Road to Ruin* uses windows in its first and last sections to relate the consequences of a debauched private life to the world at large, with a descent from elaborately furnished decor to an impoverished garret. The first part, "College," demonstrates how the young gamblers remain oblivious to the natural order of time (suggested by dawn breaking outside the window) and academic training (suggested by college spires); the window of "The End" relates the protagonist's suicide in his garret to an indifferent urban wasteland beyond.

Window vision in Pre-Raphaelite painting becomes far more complex and detailed than in these sentimental portraits: ambiguities arise from the tensions between Victorian constraints and individual license, between precise Realism and voluptuous Romance. From Millais's *Mariana* (1851) to Holman Hunt's *The Awakening Conscience* (1852) and *The Lady of Shalott*, windows help to organize a repetitive pattern between interior and exterior details. These repeated patterns contribute to a *mise en abîme* effect, just as the multiple repetitions in Tennyson's poem place Mariana on the brink of a visual abyss where she succumbs to vertigo: details "did all confound / Her sense." Millais's windows reproduce Mariana's state of mind as well as her physical dilemma; accumulation of particular details of composition and iconography result in a post-Romantic blend of metonymic and metaphoric modes of perception. Similarly, various types of lighting and multiple framing devices in *The Awakening Conscience* create a pentimento which may be seen as spatial superimposition of a metonymic mirror and window in such a way as to create its metaphoric effect. The complex *trompe l'oeil* reflects the woman's and the viewer's moral confusion, each one trying to escape the confinement of Victorian frames.

Doubtful about vague Romantic distances and equally fearful of Victorian realities outside, post-Romantic painters sought domestic protection, but in their retreat they could not abandon views of the external world. Consequently, to mitigate claustrophobia, their vision repeatedly alighted upon fenestrated perception, which allowed them to select combinations of realistic or fantastic details in perpetual struggle.

IV

Pictures of imprisoned characters yearning for freedom at their windows recur throughout nineteenth-century fiction: in the Brontës' juvenile Glass Town or Verreopolis and any of their mature novels; in Dickens' *The Old Curiosity Shop, Martin Chuzzlewit, Dombey and Son,* and *Bleak House*; in George Eliot's *Adam Bede, Felix Holt,* and *Middlemarch*; and in many of

Henry James's houses of fiction with their "million windows."[25] Of all of these, perhaps the most elaborate pattern of window imagery appears in *Dombey and Son*.

Dickens' sensitivity to the window may be seen not only from his remarks about the window tax, but from windows that altered both his mode of perception and emotional outlook. He recalls his childhood visits to coffee-shops:

> In the door there was an oval glass plate, with COFFEE-ROOM painted on it, addressed towards the street. If I ever find myself in a very different kind of coffee-room now, but where there is such an inscription on glass, and read it backward on the wrong side MOOЯ-ƎƎꟻꟻOƆ (as I often used to do then, in a dismal reverie), a shock goes through my blood.[26]

The window in the door acts as a kind of mirror (the converse of Alice's looking-glass) that transforms a mode of perception; the glass interface between inner and outer worlds transforms public and private points of view, and the door-window-mirror displays the internal presence of an observer, who internalizes the world beyond the glass. But the "shock" of the coffee-room window was probably not as traumatic as the humiliation Dickens felt at being on display at the blacking warehouse: "We worked for the light's sake, near the second window as you came from Bedford-street; and we were so brisk at it, that the people used to stop and look in. Sometimes there would be quite a little crowd there. I saw my father coming in at the door one day when we were very busy, and I wondered how he could bear it."[27] Similarly, in *Dombey and Son* Dickens displays his major characters at windows which reveal their imprisonment and excessive contemplation.

From the open windows in the first chapter of *Dombey and Son*, when twilight gathers at Mrs. Dombey's death, to the open window at the very end of the novel where a reformed Dombey, Florence, and Walter sit listening to the roar of the waves, the window forms an integral part of the novel's structure, relating characters to each other and to nature, linking plots and subplots, and combining houses of fiction in Portland-place, Leadenhall Street, Princess' Place, Brig Place, Brighton, Leamington, and Dijon. One of Dombey's flaws, his inability to distinguish between home and work, may be represented by the similarity of views presented at the windows of his house and his office. From his corner house, frowned upon by barred windows and leered at by crooked-eyed doors leading to dust-bins, Dombey, frozen and immobile, may look out upon a gravelled yard or at the dirty house opposite which "addressed a dismal eloquence to Mr. Dombey's windows" (p. 24)—

the oxymoron epitomizing the split in his life between house and home, public and private, appearance and reality. For a solipsistic Dombey who attempts to project his will, the views from his windows merely reflect a passive, static reality.

The windows at his office repeat the kind of vision confronting Dombey at home: they mirror his ego, foreshorten the distance between an isolated self and the other, and freeze action, time, and temperature. "Such vapid and flat daylight as filtered through the ground-glass windows and skylights, leaving a black sediment upon the panes, showed the books and papers, and the figures bending over them, enveloped in a studious gloom, and as much abstracted in appearance, from the world without, as if they were assembled at the bottom of the sea" (p. 170). Through the window the reader witnesses an accumulation of realistic detail mixed with similes that add a Dickensian blend of fantasy and fairy tale. Dombey is "stared at, through a dome-shaped window in the leads, by ugly chimney pots and backs of houses, and especially by the bold window of a hair-cutting saloon on a first floor, where a waxen effigy, bald as a Mussulman in the morning, and covered, after eleven o'clock in the day, with luxuriant hair and whiskers in the latest Christian fashion, showed the wrong side of its head for ever" (p. 171). Dombey becomes what he beholds: the ugly, animated domiciles stare at him daily at work just as at home the personified windows frown upon his objectified existence. Perceiver and perceived are both framed by the window behind which he, the Caliph Haroun Alraschid, confronts the Mussulman, a kind of ironic Doppelgänger; the wrong side of the effigy corresponds with Dombey's perverse pride in not recognizing the truth in the humanity of father and child (just as the "wrong side" of COFFEE-ROOM recalled the distance between child and adult for Dickens). The ironic conversion of Mussulman into Christian every morning represents the shallowness of mere public appearance in Dombey and Son as opposed to the unrealized truth of family feelings.[28]

Other limited apertures in the novel equate character and vista, the one doubling the other. Yet the external view, in mirroring the internal private situation, points to the optical illusion of doubling: while Dombey's pride blinds him to the unlikelihood of duplicating himself through Son, other characters may see the truth of their correspondent selves, but the vision offers no resolution to their predicament since it denies action. After Paul's death Florence assumes her brother's post at the window, watching motherless children across the street. When she witnesses the daily reunion between a neighboring father and daughter, she "would hide behind the curtain as if she were frightened, or would hurry from the window. Yet she could not help returning'' (p. 243). The centripetal visual force of the window compels Florence to see the life that she wishes could belong to herself and her father. When the neighbors go out of their window onto the balcony Florence retreats from her window and hides herself, because the ideal must not approach the real too closely, and her loneliness must not be discovered by the happy faces across the way. Where her father remains immobile at his windows, Florence actively seeks visual and emotional release from a confining interior—but to little avail, for the external world throws back in her face a reflexive situation that makes her life all the more painful. Once again the window mediates between an internal projector and an external reflector.

Florence's dog, Diogenes, soon acquires the human habit of window-gazing.

> He would lay his head upon the window-ledge, and placidly open and shut his eyes upon the street, all through a summer morning; sometimes pricking up his head to look with great significance after some noisy dog in a cart, who was barking his way along, and sometimes, with an exasperated and unaccountable recollection of his supposed enemy in the neighbourhood, rushing to the door, whence, after a deafening disturbance, he would come jogging back with a ridiculous complacency that belonged to him, and lay his jaw upon the window-ledge again, with the air of a dog who had done a public service.
>
> (p. 313)

Like Florence, Diogenes finds his counterpart outside the window, where he oscillates between active, public confirmation and lethargic, private contemplation. Repeatedly Dickens' private vision and "public service" interact at a fictional window.

Yet no character participates in window viewing as extensively as Lucretia Tox. Miss Tox and Major Bagstock exchange views at Princess' Place that reiterate the Doppelgänger motif as well as differences between public and private, revelation and concealment, motion and stasis, separation and reunion, metonymic reality and metaphoric fantasy. Her bedroom commands a vista of Mews, where she carries on a Platonic dalliance with Bagstock: "Miss Tox had been wont, once upon a time, to look out at one of her dark little windows by accident, and blushingly to return the Major's greeting" (p. 88). From this limited aperture her vision ranges from a realistic foreground to a Romantic distance: "At about this same period too, she was seized with a passion for looking at . . . the moon, of which she would take long observations from her chamber window. But whatever she looked at; sun, moon, stars, or bracelets; she looked no more at the Major" (p. 89). Her Romantic vision projects from telescopic astronomy to microscopic jewelry, but the absence of human content in the middle distance prepares for her own reversal of fortune at the hands of Bagstock, who informs Dombey of her matrimonial ambitions.

Once Bagstock gains his victory over his neighbor by displacing her with Edith, the windows at Princess' Place no longer communicate; instead they focus on the pathos in Miss Tox's loneliness as she engages in a flight of reverie on the window-seat. The narrator relates her domestic habits, which pass "by a natural association of ideas" from the Bird Waltz on the harpsichord to her canary and on to her plants. Following her customary activities, the narrator pauses with his character at the window to retard the narrative pace, to enter her mind, and to describe in detail the summer morning in Princess' Place where the pot-boy trickling water parallels Miss Tox's watering indoors—yet another instance of the Dickensian use of the public external scene doubling and confirming private internal activity.

The natural association of ideas at this phenomenologically active yet structurally static window turns Miss Tox's thoughts to the country, as the fresh outdoor scents exhilarate her beyond metonymic particularism to a metaphoric window, where flights of reverie transform smoky urban sparrows (the external counterpart of her canary) into "glorified sparrows, unconnected with chimneys." The narrative camera then reverts to the metonymic middle-ground window of Princess' Arms, which displays "legends in praise of Ginger Beer, with pictorial representations of thirsty customers submerged in the effervescence, or stunned by flying corks." The opposite illustrations, like so many pub and COFFEE-ROOM signs in Dickens' imagination, reveal gregariousness—in contrast to Miss Tox's loneliness, which finds its escape in a little scoopful of tea that creates "a flight of fancy" like the flying corks or sparrows hopping across the courtyard, a sentimental abyss not unlike the void of Dombey's imprisonment and Florence's lonely windows.

The narrator re-enters Miss Tox's mind to uncover thoughts of family relationships and passing time.

> Miss Tox sat down upon the window-seat, and thought of her good Papa deceased—Mr. Tox, of the Customs Department of the public service; and of her childhood, passed at a seaport, among a considerable quantity of cold tar, and some rusticity. She fell into a softened remembrance of meadows, in old time, gleaming with buttercups, like so many inverted firmaments of golden stars; and how she had made chains of dandelion-stalks for youthful vowers of eternal constancy, dressed chiefly in nankeen; and how soon those fetters had withered and broken.
> Sitting on the window-seat, and looking out upon the sparrows and the blink

of sun, Miss Tox thought likewise of her good Mama deceased—sister to the owner of the powdered head and pigtail—of her virtues and her rheumatism. And when a man with bulgy legs, and a rough voice, and a heavy basket on his head that crushed his hat into a mere black muffin, came crying flowers down Princess's Place, making his timid little roots of daisies shudder in the vibration of every yell he gave, as though he had been an ogre, hawking little children, summer recollections were so strong upon Miss Tox, that she shook her head, and murmured she would be comparatively old before she knew it—which seemed likely.

In her pensive mood, Miss Tox's thoughts went wandering on Mr. Dombey's track; probably because the Major had returned home to his lodgings opposite, and had just bowed to her from his window. What other reason could Miss Tox have for connecting Mr. Dombey with her summer days and dandelion fetters?

(pp. 395–396)

The answer to this rhetorical question may be the window itself: Dickens carefully structures her mental peregrinations there, the window serving as a framing fetter which simultaneously isolates her from and connects her with Dombey. The secrets of her private life are hidden from human sight, like her pair of ancient gloves that Dickens likens to "dead leaves," a reminder of those autumnal leaves blighted by Dombey. Similarly, her father's position in the public service recalls Diogenes's "public service" at his window, as well as Dickens' own childhood, as the narration shrinks the distance between private autobiography and public fiction. The parallel structures of the first two paragraphs lead dialectically from memories of her parents' past to the present and future of the third paragraph. There Miss Tox wonders if Dombey will marry again, while the transitory summer days and dandelion fetters turn to the eternity of solitude and the sterility of old age, the flashback retarding the narrative pace in line with her slowness in coming to the plants.

In contrast to her own stasis, the man with the bulgy legs and rough voice represents the sexual drive addressing the void in the spinster, which like the roots of the daisies shudders in the vibration of his yell. Her summer recollections stress the frustrations of her repressed existence: "A flush—it was warm weather—overspread Miss Tox's face." This woman confronts the painful reality of past, present, and future at her window, where she can gain self-awareness through psychological interaction with the world beyond; at her window the process of self-examination through internal monologue should help her answer her own rhetorical question, "What sort of person now!" Her metaphoric, associative process (assisted by the narrator's similes) unravels at the contiguous window filled with synecdochic sights and particularized detail. The converse of the Lady of Shalott, the Lady of Princess' Place, herself a sadly ironic princess, moves from casement to mirror: "she turned her head, and was surprised by the reflection of her thoughtful image in the chimney-glass.'' Her examined life proceeds from a window that freezes time, frames and localizes the private self; its startling confirmation is revealed at the mirror, which merely reflects the metamorphosis achieved at the window. Her limited aperture provides her with the illusion of escape from domestic confinement, but any form of Romantic projection is defeated by a mimetic Victorian reality. Lucretia Tox's casement, like other fenestrated epiphanies in *Dombey and Son*, deconstructs the central theme of doubling or repetition surrounding Dombey's attempt to duplicate himself through Son. For its views and vision reveal double absences or the failures of repetition in public and private, in reality and the dreamer's stance.

Ruskin's remark that ''the painter of interiors feels like a caged bird, unless he can throw a window open,''[29] applies to Miss Tox, Mariana, the Lady of Shalott, Florence Dombey, Jane Eyre, Lucy Snowe, Little Nell, Esther Summerson, or Dorothea Brooke, for all of these Victorians attempt to escape domestic confinement through limited transparencies. ''The Window is charged with contradiction and ambiguity. There is the many-faceted contrast between outside and inside worlds. There is also the singular uncertainty whether the window serves as a bridge or as a barrier to the world beyond, because it actually functions in both ways: for the eye it is a bridge, for the body it is a barrier.''[30] Hence the figure at the window becomes an archetypal image during an age of paradox, when mimesis and expressiveness compete in Victorian aesthetics.

Ruskin offers two methods for perceiving such a work of art:

> Look at the bars of your window-frame, so as to get a clear image of their lines and form, and you cannot, while your eye is fixed on them, perceive anything but the most indistinct and shadowy images of whatever objects may be visible beyond. But fix your eyes on those objects, so as to see them clearly, and though they are just beyond and apparently beside the window-frame, that frame will only be felt or seen as a vague, flitting, obscure interruption to whatever is perceived beyond it.[31]

Transparencies often blind us because we take their presence for granted, but once we arrest our focus on the pane we see the centrality of window vision in the lives of the Victorians. Isolated in domestic interiors, Victorians sought communion at their windows, but with society and nature increasingly red in tooth and claw, they could not escape as readily as their Romantic predecessors through magic casements toward transcendental realms. Instead, they remained fixed at their more limited apertures to examine particularistic details in metonymic modes of perception grounded in skepticism and anxiety.

Spontaneous overflow of emotion was held in check by glass "containers": in an epistemological reorientation, projection and expression were counterbalanced by protection and repression—the mirror turned lamp turned window.

NOTES

1. See especially: Edward Engelberg, *The Symbolist Poem* (New York: Dutton, 1967), pp. 31–33; Gerhard Joseph, "Victorian Frames: The Windows and Mirrors of Browning, Arnold, and Tennyson," *Victorian Poetry*, 16 (1978), 70–87; and W. David Shaw, "The Optical Metaphor: Victorian Poetics and the Theory of Knowledge," *Victorian Studies*, 23 (1980), 293–324. While my remarks are restricted to the British scene, examples may also be found in America, France, and Germany: Poe's "The Man of the Crowd," Melville's "Bartleby," Hawthorne's *The House of the Seven Gables*, and Henry James's houses of fiction with their "million windows"; *Madame Bovary*, Mallarmé's "Les Fenêtres," the novels of Zola and Proust; E. T. A. Hoffmann's "The Cousin's Corner Window" and the paintings of Friedrich, Schwind, and Spitzweg. See Jean Rousset's discussion of *Madame Bovary* in *Forme et Signification* (Paris, 1962), pp. 109–133; Naomi Schor, "Zola: From Window to Window," *Yale French Studies* 42 (1969), 38–51; and John Lapp, "Proust's Windows to Reality," *The Romanic Review*, 67 (1976), 38–49.
2. Peter Ure, "The Looking-Glass of *Richard II*," *Philological Quarterly*, 34 (1955), 224.
3. See Dorothy Van Ghent's discussion in *The English Novel: Form and Function* (New York: Harper, 1961), pp. 161–166.
4. Thomas De Quincey, *Autobiography from 1785 to 1803*, in *Collected Writings*, ed. David Masson (London: A. & C. Black, 1896), I, 38.
5. *The Poetry and Prose of William Blake*, ed. David Erdman (Garden City, N.Y.: Doubleday, 1965), p. 555.
6. F. H. Bradley, *Appearance and Reality: A Metaphysical Essay* (Oxford: Clarendon Press, 1930), p. 229.
7. Carol Christ, *The Finer Optic: The Aesthetics of Particularity in Victorian Poetry* (New Haven, Conn.: Yale University Press, 1975), p. 6.
8. Richard Altick, *The English Common Reader* (Chicago, Ill.: University of Chicago Press, 1957), p. 92.
9. See Mario Praz, "The Victorian Mood: A Reappraisal," in *Backgrounds to Victorian Literature*, ed. Richard Levine (San Francisco, Calif.: Chandler, 1967), p. 66.
10. William Cobbett, *Rural Rides*, ed. George Woodcock (Harmondsworth: Penguin, 1967), p. 127.
11. *The Letters of Charles Dickens*, eds. Sister-in-Law and Eldest Daughter (London: Macmillan, 1893), p. 214.

12. Quoted in Henry-Russell Hitchcock, *Early Victorian Architecture in Britain* (New Haven, Conn.: Yale University Press, 1954), I, 406.

13. Quoted in Asa Briggs, *1851* (London: The Historical Association, 1951), p. 5.

14. *The Eclectic Review*, June, 1851, 752.

15. See Anthony Bird, *Paxton's Palace* (London: Cassell, 1976), p. 162; and Christopher Hobhouse, *1851 and the Crystal Palace Exhibition* (London: John Murray, 1937), p. 174.

16. Sir John Summerson, ''1851—a New Age, a New Style,'' in *Ideas and Beliefs of the Victorians* (no author) (London: BBC, 1949), p. 65.

17. Alan Thomas, *Time in a Frame: Photography and the Nineteenth-Century Mind* (New York: Schocken, 1977), p. 11.

18. Carl Dawson, *Victorian Noon: English Literature in 1850* (Baltimore, Md.: Johns Hopkins University Press, 1979), p. 9.

19. Ralph Waldo Emerson, *English Traits* (Boston, Mass.: Houghton Mifflin, 1856), p. 38.

20. Charles Dickens, *Dombey and Son*, ed. Alan Horsman (Oxford: Clarendon Press, 1974), p. 740. All future references are to this edition.

21. Graham Reynolds, *Victorian Painting* (London: Studio Vista, 1966), pp. 95–96.

22. Lorenz Eitner, ''The Open Window and the Storm-Tossed Boat: An Essay in the Iconography of Romanticism,'' *The Art Bulletin*, 37 (1955), 285.

23. *Ibid.*, 284.

24. *Ibid.*, 285–286.

25. Kathleen Tillotson mentions the image in *Jane Eyre* in *Novels of the Eighteen-Forties* (London: Oxford University Press, 1962), p. 300. On George Eliot's windows see Reva Stump, *Movement and Vision in George Eliot's Novels* (Seattle: University of Washington Press, 1959), p. 171, and Barbara Hardy, *The Novels of George Eliot* (New York: Oxford University Press, 1967), p. 199. On James's windows see Maurice Beebe, *Ivory Towers and Sacred Founts* (New York: New York University Press, 1964), pp. 204–205 and Philip Weinstein, *Henry James and the Requirements of the Imagination* (Cambridge, Mass.: Harvard University Press, 1971), p. 6.

26. John Forster, *The Life of Charles Dickens* (London: Chapman and Hall, 1904), p. 29.

27. *Ibid.*, p. 37.

28. On Dombey's frozen nature, see Susan Horton, *Interpreting, Interpreting* (Baltimore, Md.: Johns Hopkins University Press, 1979) and Julian Moynahan, ''Dealings with the Firm of Dombey and Son: *Firmness* versus *Wetness*,'' in *Dickens and the Twentieth Century*, ed. John Gross and Gabriel Pearson (Toronto: University of Toronto Press, 1962), pp. 121–131. For a discussion of the houses in the novel see Henri Talon, ''Dombey and Son: A Closer Look at the Text,'' *Dickens Studies Annual*, 1, Robert L. Partlow, Jr., ed. (Carbondale: Southern Illinois University Press, 1970), pp. 148–151.

29. John Ruskin, *Modern Painters*, Vol. 2, p. 82; as quoted in Landow, p. 84.

30. Carla Gottlieb, ''The Role of the Window in the Art of Matisse,'' *Journal of Aesthetics and Art Criticism*, 22 (1964), 420. Michael Riffaterre makes a similar comment in *Semiotics of Poetry* (Bloomington: Indiana University Press, 1978),

p. 43: "'Literary' windows serve as settings for contemplation, as symbols of contact between the inner life and the world of sensation. Their glass panes permit visual communication but prevent direct touch, and so they may also be a metaphor for absence, separation, longing, memory."

31. John Ruskin, *Modern Painters*, ed. Cook and Wedderburn (London: George Allen, 1903), I, 320. Ruskin anticipates Ortega y Gasset in *The Dehumanization of Art and Other Essays*, trans. Willard Trask (Princeton, N.J.: Princeton University Press, 1958), p. 10; and Roland Barthes in *Mythologies*, trans. Annette Lavers (New York: Hill and Wang, 1979), pp. 123–124.

Autobiographical Fantasies of a Female Anti-Feminist: Eliza Lynn Linton as Christopher Kirkland and Theodora Desanges

Nancy F. Anderson

The novelist Eliza Lynn Linton was the most prominent and vociferous female opponent of women's emancipation in Victorian England. She established her reputation as a critic of women in her scathing *Saturday Review* articles in the 1860s, most notably with her sensational "Girl of the Period" piece. For the next thirty years, she would in her many novels and journal essays attack with increasing ferocity the "Shrieking Sisters," the "Wild Women," and the "New Hussies," who sought the right to participate in the political, educational, and occupational life theretofore reserved exclusively for men.

Many Victorian women opposed women's rights, as evidenced by the thousands of signatures to the women's "Appeal Against Female Suffrage" of 1889.[1] What makes Eliza Lynn Linton of particular interest, and what confused her contemporaries and infuriated her opponents, was that she herself was an Advanced Woman, emancipated from the constraints of conventional ladyhood. Born in 1822 in the Lake District town of Keswick into the comfortably endowed clerical Lynn family, she was the youngest of twelve children, whose mother died when she was five months old. As a young girl in her teens, she rebelled against her father, a conservative Anglican vicar, and became a freethinker and political radical. Intensely ambitious, restless and disharmonious in the family vicarage, she went alone to London at age twenty-three to support herself as a writer.

The young Eliza Lynn achieved early success. Considering herself to be "in the vanguard of the independent women,"[2] she was the first English woman to draw a fixed salary as a journalist. Her first novel, published in 1846, received modest but laudatory critical attention. She became part of the avant-garde London society of the 1840s, and frequented most of the important literary and radical gatherings. She was for example a regular guest at John Chapman's, whence reports of her literary achievements reached the envious Marian Evans, who was then still confined in Coventry nursing her dying father and known only as the translator of Strauss's *Leben Jesu*.[3] Though George Eliot's later success made Linton painfully jealous, in these early days it was Eliza Lynn who was the celebrity.

Linton's youthful writings were characterized by fiery iconoclastic attacks on Victorian respectability. She championed republicanism, socialism, and free love. Her 1851 novel *Realities* was so bold that John Chapman backed out of his commitment to publish it because he felt it was "addressed [to] and excited the sensual nature and [was] therefore injurious."[4] She wrote more socially acceptable essays and stories for Dickens' *Household Words*, but Dickens warned his subeditor W. H. Wills that Miss Lynn "gets so near the sexual side of things as to be a little dangerous to us at times."[5]

On the nascent Woman Question, Linton was in her youth theoretically in favor of women's emancipation. Even then, however, despite her own independent life style, she was ambivalent about women's proper role, an ambivalence she most clearly revealed in two contrasting essays she wrote in 1854. For the radical *English Republic*, she wrote a stirring piece praising Mary Wollstonecraft for "asserting by her own life the truth of her equality with man, and boldly claiming as her right an equal share in the privileges hitherto reserved for himself alone." Linton concluded the essay with a passionate plea for Englishwomen to follow Mary's example by throwing off their "stigma of cowardice and the slave's degradation."[6] In the same year Linton wrote an essay for *Household Words* with quite a different message on the "Rights and Wrongs of Women." In this polemic she urged women to stay in their womanly domestic sphere. "The shadow of man darkens the path of woman, and while walking by his side, she yet walks not in the same light with him. Her home is in the shade."[7] The inconsistency between these two essays shows not only Linton's chameleonlike ability to match the editorial tone of diverse journals, but also her conflicted feelings about the role of women and her own life choices.

In 1858, at age thirty-six, Eliza Lynn temporarily gave up her independent life style to marry a widower, the Chartist engraver William James Linton, and to take care of his many children. She now styled herself "E. Lynn Linton," keeping her maiden name in equal prominence with her husband's name in order to maintain her "cherished individualism."[8] The marriage was a failure almost from the beginning. She publicly if unintentionally revealed her dissatisfaction when, only two months after her wedding, she published a story in *National Magazine* entitled "Crooked Sticks," a tale of a maid sent into the woods to choose a stick. Finding none that was just right, the maid, when leaving the woods, finally picked up an old crooked one. Linton compared this to a girl who kept rejecting suitors, and ended up with an unsuitable one. She concluded the story with a warning for young people to take her advice "and remember that I speak from experience; do not be too fastidious; and remember the story of the pretty maid who went through the wood, and came out with a crooked stick at the end of it."[9]

After several years of painful and probably unconsummated union, Eliza and William James Linton separated, and she returned to her active unfettered life in the London literary world she so loved. She maintained her self-image as a social and political rebel but became in fact increasingly conservative. A vigilant guardian of respectability, she soon was one of Mrs. Grundy's most loyal lieutenants. She resolved her ambivalence about woman's place in society (and tried to eliminate competition) by enjoying freedom herself in the man's world, while emphatically insisting that other women remain in their prescribed sphere. She ostensibly idealized the sheltered womanly woman, but her arguments against women's emancipation revealed strong misogynist feelings, which she admitted in a personal letter when she confessed that "I hate women as a race. I think we are demons. Individually we are all right, but as a race we are monkeyish, cruel, irresponsible, superficial."[10]

Hostility to women permeated her writings. In her 1894 novel *The One Too Many*, for example, she ridiculed and condemned three independent Girton girls, and yet ended the story with the sweet, self-sacrificing, submissive heroine, with no means of livelihood, drowning herself, sinking "as a dead thing might, without a struggle to her doom." (Many readers commented on the peculiar message of the book, and, as the *Athenaeum* suggested, "the plain person can hardly fail to rise from a perusal of the story without an impression that it is the view of the writer that it is wiser to revolt rather than to submit.")[11]

Though Eliza Lynn Linton was an enigma to her contemporaries because of the contradiction between her independent professional life style and her anti-feminist, misogynist opinions, she did provide the key to the puzzle of her personality in her self-portrayal in *The Autobiography of Christopher Kirkland*. Written in 1885 when she was sixty-three, this is her autobiography, signed with her own name, in the persona of a man. Despite the sex reversal, the book was, she said, "my own history, travestied in the sense of sex and certain experiences." She explained that she could not publish her autobiography "without some such veil as this of changed sex and personation"—it was, she said, "a screen which takes off the sting of boldness and self-exposure."[12] Like many fictional autobiographies in the Bildungsroman tradition, *Christopher Kirkland* interestingly crosses and recrosses the narrow boundary between fiction and autobiography.

The sex reversal was in fact not a screen, but a mirror which reflected Linton's deep unconscious sense of male identity. The disguise was an inadvertent vehicle for expressing her true feelings about herself. Although the male identification was unconscious, she once remarked that when she was born, a boy was expected, "and only the top coating miscarried."[13] Having always seen herself as big and robust, the transformation into the tall strong Christopher Kirkland was both reversal and self-realization. This masculine self-image helps explain how Linton could escape her own devaluation of women, and why she could so easily insist that women remain dependent and submissive in the home while at the same time priding herself on her own independence.

The inner conflicts this role and gender reversal inevitably aroused in Linton she handled, in her long obsessional struggle against women's emancipation, by projecting and condemning in women's-rights women those characteristics most distinctive in her own personality. "There is in them a curious inversion of sex, which does not necessarily appear in the body, but is evident enough in the mind." Frantically warning against a blurring of distinctions between the sexes, she pleaded that "men be men, and women women, sharply, unmistakably defined . . . not an ambiguous sex which is neither one nor the other"[14]—ironic words from a woman who wrote her life story as a man. She had been the breadwinner and dominant force in her brief marriage, and in *Christopher Kirkland* had easily transmuted her husband into a woman, described with psychological congruence as Christopher's wife. At the same time in her anti-feminist polemics she insisted that wives remain submissive and obedient to their husbands: "when two people ride on one horse one must ride behind."[15] She damned as emasculating the emancipated women who she claimed wanted to seize the reins of authority from their natural male masters.

In *Christopher Kirkland*, Linton provided abundant material that explains the development of her male-identified personality and her misogyny. She described with heartrending pathos, as the crucial aspect of her childhood, the devastating emotional consequences of her mother's death after her own birth. With no mothering figure, not even a maiden aunt, to nurture her, her childhood was, she lamented, one of loneliness and pain. She blamed her father, who was in her opinion weak and ineffectual, for not exercising supervision over his twelve children. Their house was "like nothing so much as a farmyard full of cockerels and pullets forever spurring and pecking at one another" (I.47). She claimed that as the youngest she suffered the most, either by being ignored and neglected or abused by her family. This treatment made her recalcitrant and rebellious, which increased all the more her sense of loneliness. "I was so isolated in the family, so out of harmony with them all, and by my own faults of temperament such a little Ishmaelite and outcast, that as much despair as can exist with childhood overwhelmed and possessed me" (I.60).

Linton felt that if only her mother had lived, everything would have been different. Her later invectives against women's emancipation contain the child's voice of rage against the mother who deserted her by dying. When she would repeatedly insist that a woman's place was by the cradle, she was in part expressing her own feelings of maternal deprivation. The personality characteristics she developed in that unhappy chaotic childhood—her wish to escape, to become famous and therefore noticed and loved, her need actively to struggle and compete—these characteristics were considered masculine in her adult patriarchal society, with its rigid polarization of sexual personality.

In contrast to her own tough, tomboyish personality, Linton presents her one-year-older, angelic sister Lucy, to whom she had a strong but ambivalent attachment. In *Christopher Kirkland*, Linton also reversed Lucy's sex, but wrote of her in unmistakably feminine terms:

> He [i.e., Lucy] was like one of Sir Joshua's cherubs. His head was covered with bright golden curls, his skin was like a pale monthly rose, and he had big soft blue eyes which no one could resist. Everyone loved and petted him. Our father, who saw in him the reproduction of our dead mother, had even a more tender feeling for him than any of his other favourites.   (I.58)

Linton's jealousy of Lucy was intense. "I had sometimes broken my young heart over the difference made between us" (I.184). She recounted, surely with distorted memory but with emotional authenticity, that once, when her father kissed Lucy, she asked him to kiss her too. "I longed to receive the same love that was given to others, to be included, to be taken out of the solitude and banishment in which I lived." She claimed he refused because, he said, he did not respect her (I.146).

Linton dealt with her jealousy by not competing with this quintessentially feminine sister, and by shaping her own self-identity as a purposeful opposition to her sister. Ostensibly idealizing Lucy, she assumed the male role of devoted protector. Underneath the idealization were strong feelings of hostility, revealed in extravagant poems she wrote in her adolescence to Lucy, repeatedly expressing the fear, surely a disguised wish, that Lucy would die:

> Oh sweet! thy cheek is pale . . .
> Lucy! my soul's best love
> Soft death will come from this world of folly
> To bear thee to Heaven above![16]

In other poems she uses the image of Lucy as a fair dove in a cage whom she will carefully guard. This relationship was the prototype for her later fervent efforts to keep the idealized angelic womanly woman encaged in the house.

The rage Linton felt against her mother and sister was for the most part repressed, and reappeared in her virulent attacks on women. Her conscious rage was against her unloving father. In her adolescence she expressed her anger at her father with her opposition to what she saw as his cold-hearted, selfish Toryism, and with an impassioned defense of democracy and socialism. On a more fundamental level she challenged Vicar Lynn by rejecting his religion. In her original draft of *Christopher Kirkland* she indicates that she first began to doubt Christianity when she was seventeen: the pregnancy of their unmarried servant girl made her question the truth of the Virgin Birth. "It was the persistent denial of this girl, and her repeated assurance that it was and must have been a 'bogle' which set me thinking." Her publisher George Bentley, repelled by such blasphemy, insisted this part be changed. Linton reluctantly agreed to bowdlerize it, writing instead that she began to question the truth of Christianity while reading Ovid's *Metamorphoses*, when she noted the similarities between Greek myths and Biblical stories, including virgin births.[17] She dramatically detailed the shock of considering the possibility that Mary may have lied:

> A terrible faintness took hold of me. The perspiration streamed over my face like rain, and I trembled like a frightened horse. . . . The light grew dim; the earth was vapoury and unstable; and, overpowered by an awful dread, I fell back among the long grass where I was sitting as if I had been struck down by an unseen hand. (I.36)

Such doubts eventually led Linton to agnosticism. Her loss of faith engendered great emotional turmoil in her, for as she asked, "who that has known the hour when the Father is not, and Law has taken the Place of Love, can ever forget it?" (II.151). Her religious struggles were of such central importance to her autobiographical narrative that she considered titling her book "Confessions of an Agnostic."[18] Linton's loss of faith alienated her even more from her family, especially her father, and confirmed her childhood feeling, repeatedly recreated and reexperienced in adulthood, that she was an outcast, an Ishmaelite. Her insistence that she was banished from love by Christ and the Church (III.256) explains the significance of her pseudonym Christopher Kirkland, although ironically in this pseudonym she identified with her perceived oppressors. Linton's rejection of Christianity strengthened her sense of maleness, for she considered agnosticism to be masculine, whereas

> the religious sentiment, shifting, personal, emotional, subject to the pressure of affection and the relief of compassion . . . is feminine. The fundamental doctrines of Christianity . . . are essentially feminine. . . . Does not the whole world lie between these two limits? Surely!—the whole world of masculine self-control and feminine obedience; masculine reason and feminine emotion.
>
> (III.159–160)

She apparently never felt any inconsistency in priding herself on her manly agnosticism, while urging women to remain within the Church, to receive the restraint and support their weak dependent natures required.

Another aspect of Linton's personality inadvertently revealed through her male persona in *Christopher Kirkland* was her strong sexual attraction to women. Writing her autobiography as a man, she was able safely to describe her homoerotic feelings (which coexisted with her misogynist opinions). Her intense relationships with women, which were probably only unconsciously sexual, became in *Christopher Kirkland* passionate love affairs, portrayed as heterosexual romances. The reader for Bentley, although recommending *Christopher Kirkland* for publication, complained that Christopher's "love affairs are somewhat numerous," and that "we should be content to hear less about the exact shape of ladies' limbs, and the quality of their complexions" (a frequent criticism reviewers made of Linton's novels).[19] Linton, as Christopher, explained why she liked to have women around:

> I like to hear the frou-frou of a woman's dress about me, I like to hear the softer tones of her voice, and to look at her shining hair and the smooth outlines of her flower-like face . . . the sense of her softness, sweetness, and dainty smallness

compared to my own sinewy bulk, and the feeling that I can protect her if need be, soothe what I suppose is my masculine vanity.   (III.207)

As an example of her romantic attachments to women, Linton describes in great detail in *Christopher Kirkland* an adolescent crush on an older married woman, a Mrs. Dalrymple, a character Linton later explained was "partly true, partly evolved."[20] The young Christopher adores Mrs. Dalrymple, who is "the most exquisite creature under heaven . . . a woman more like . . . a spirit half-transparently incarnate, than a living solid flesh and blood reality" (I.173). When Mrs. Dalrymple tries to teach Christopher to dance, he is too awkward and clumsy, as well as too intoxicated by the beautiful woman's nearness, to learn. "My head swam when Adeline Dalrymple laid her long white hand on my shoulder, and I put my arm around her supple stayless waist; and I was faint and giddy before I had made a couple of turns round the room" (I.181).

The climax—literally—of this semi-fantasized relationship comes when Christopher goes one moonlit night to her garden. Mrs. Dalrymple comes down to join him, and they sit hand in hand in the summer house until dawn. She then kisses him on the forehead and eyes. "Overpowered by an emotion so powerful as to be physical pain, I knelt on the ground at her feet; and I think that for a moment I died" (I.208–209). Christopher, his passion so intense, soon thereafter is stricken with brain fever, and when he recovers he learns that the Dalrymples have moved away.

Just as Linton did not consciously recognize her sense of male identity, and defensively condemned mannish women, so she did not acknowledge her lesbian feelings, and warned others of the dangers of sexual relationships among emancipated women. In her 1880 novel *The Rebel in the Family*, for example, Linton created the character of Bell, a mannish man-hating women's righter, who frightens the innocent young heroine Perdita "by taking her in her arms and kissing her with strange warmth." On another occasion Bell kisses Perdita fondly, and calls her "my darling" under her breath. When Bell urges Perdita to leave home, to become self-supporting and to enjoy friendships with those of her own sex, Perdita replies that she cannot live without love. Bell, tenderly putting her arm around Connie, the woman she lives with and calls her "little wife," tells Perdita that if she wants love, "you have it here—the best and truest that the world can give—the love between women without the degrading and disturbing interference of man." Such a prospect, however, does not appeal to Perdita, who feels "revolted by something too vague to name yet too real to ignore."[21]

Eliza Lynn Linton's fictionalized autobiography clearly dramatizes her own hard-fought and paradoxical struggle against women's emancipation. Though she insisted that women should not be mere chattel, but should have certain rights such as control over their own property and children, there she drew the line:

> I could not accept the doctrine that no such thing as natural limitation of sphere is included in the fact of sex, and that individual women may, if they have the will and the power, do all those things which have hitherto been exclusively assigned to men. Nor can I deny the value of inherent modesty; nor despise domestic duties; nor look on maternity as a curse and degradation—'making a woman no better than a cow,' as one of these ladies, herself a mother, once said to me indignantly; nor do I join in the hostility to men which comes in as the correlative of all that has gone before.   (III.4)

She was especially opposed to women becoming doctors and artists, because without separate female educational facilities it required them to attend mixed medical schools and mixed drawing classes from the nude. "These two things seemed to me to be repugnant to every sentiment of morality or decency in either sex" (III.7). In addition to what she considered her rational arguments against female emancipation, as Christopher she confessed that much of her early opposition to the woman's movement was because she thought advanced women ugly and unfeminine, fulfilling the epigram that "Women's Rights Are Men's Lefts." She claimed however that she was "always ashamed of my own childishness of judgement" (III.5). As one would expect, in Linton's autobiography the subject of the appropriate role for women appears in almost every situation. For instance, when Christopher is visiting a beloved friend on his deathbed, the friend, with almost his last breath, "broke off abruptly into the woman question, on the main points of which we were thoroughly agreed." After a long exposition of the sins of the movement, they agree that a mother does more for humanity "than does the sister who prefers individuality and a paying profession to the self-continuance, self-sacrifice, and devotion of maternity." With that off his chest, the friend expires shortly thereafter (III.271–272).

   Linton, reflecting on her career as a critic of women, complained that her writings brought her "more obloquy than praise . . . those at whom I struck were naturally indignant, and gave me back blow for blow, sometimes hitting below the belt, with even a few odd scratchings thrown in" (III.95). She concluded the autobiography, therefore, with a reiteration of her lament for the "intrinsic isolation of my life." She had "made, or attracted to myself, as the dominant circumstances of my life—Loneliness and Loss" (III.313, 308). Commenting in later years on *Christopher Kirkland*, Linton said that it was "an outpour no one hears me make by word of mouth, a confession of sorrow, suffering, trial, and determination not to be beaten, which few suspect as the underlying truth of my life."[22]

Appropriately, the pain and frustration which Linton said were central to her life were extended to the publication of her autobiography. The publisher had demanded so many changes and had so delayed publication that Linton was frantic. She repeatedly implored Bentley to publish it immediately:

> Do you think this throbbing heart is *quite* dead! . . . I have put my very Soul, my Life into those pages, and I feel as if I am being slowly killed through them. . . . I all the while eating out my heart for the anguish of disappointment, humiliation, and illusion. It cannot go on . . . I am nearly heartbroken and only my strength of will keeps me from brain fever.[23]

When finally published, *The Autobiography of Christopher Kirkland* was a literary and financial failure. Linton's friend and biographer George Somes Layard attributed the bad reviews to the confusion created by the sex reversals. "To those who could read between the lines, the effect was somewhat bizarre, while to those not in the secret the story was in parts incomprehensible." Bentley spent more than was usual on advertising, but it did not sell well, and he lost money on the publication. The irrepressible Linton nevertheless repeatedly begged him to issue a second edition. "My beloved Christopher! I want him to shine again." She later urged a cheap edition, so that Christopher "would reach so many who now do not hear of him."[24] It was however not reissued until 1976, as part of the Garland *Novels of Faith and Doubt* reprint series.

Eliza Lynn Linton's sense of male identification, as revealed in *The Autobiography of Christopher Kirkland*, allowed her to achieve success in her patriarchal society. Though she delighted in her achievements and independence, she was at the same time painfully envious of her antitype, the beautiful womanly woman, who like her sister Lucy received the love Linton herself had so yearned for as a child. She once confessed that she "would renounce any intellectual gifts to which she might lay claim, for the compelling power of great physical beauty."[25] This wish she gratified in another autobiographical fantasy, *The Second Youth of Theodora Desanges*, written just before she died in 1898. *Theodora Desanges* is dissimilar but complementary to *Christopher Kirkland*, and together they illuminate in full dimension the conflicts and complexities in Linton's personality.

In *The Second Youth of Theodora Desanges*, Linton fantasized that she, in the character of the elderly Theodora, was miraculously transformed into a young woman, "younger-looking, more beautiful, more attractive than the pretty women I had admired thirty years before . . . not merely the rival but the superior of those who had been so far above me." She describes the transformed Theodora as looking and feeling like a goddess, a "divinely appointed priestess, whose will was law and whose mind was as the mind of God" (hence the significance of the name Theodora, gift of God). Men flock around her, and fall madly in love. A woman friend warns her not to become too free. "You have been so long our old mentor and faultfinder, our putter-to-rights and moral policeman, it would never do for you to go over the border and set a bad example to us poor, silly little butterflies." Theodora is, however, like an iceberg, and unmoved by men's passions. She enjoys rather the sense of power and control over the men, feeling like a puppeteer pulling strings. "I swayed them as I would. I bent them to my will."[26]

Linton, as the beautiful Theodora, encounters many people from her past. One of her admirers is a man closely modeled on George Lewes, whom Linton had known in her early London years. She changed him into an artist, but describes the character with exactly the same words as she did George Lewes in a non-fictional reminiscence written at the same time.[27] This artist wants to paint Theodora as Boadicea, with "diaphanous drapery, showing the fine contour of the limbs beneath, the leopard-skin over half the naked breast" (p. 68). Theodora is shocked, even as Linton claimed she as a young woman had been shocked by Lewes's familiarities, which had, however, apparently not been directed at her. The fantasized version allowed Linton to enjoy attracting and then cutting down a man whom she despised. The fantasy of this adoration also gave her a feeling of superiority over her most envied professional rival, George Eliot.

In the novel, the women friends of the elderly Theodora become bitterly jealous and hostile to the transformed beautiful woman, an indication of the strength of Linton's own projected feelings of jealousy. Even the fictional representation of the woman who had lived with Linton for many years as her adopted daughter, Beatrice Hartley, called Esther in *Theodora* (curiously the same pseudonym given to William James Linton in *Christopher Kirkland*), is consumed with jealousy. Esther's husband, however, is able to exercise enough self-control to resist his infatuation for Theodora, but her son, conflicted and confused because of his desire for the woman he had always called Granny, commits suicide.

The youthful Theodora remains, as she had been before her metamorphosis, "an uncompromising opponent of the New Woman in all her hateful phases"

(p. 134). She uses the power of her beauty and wisdom to fight women's suffrage, as well as other emasculating threats to the British Empire, such as Little Englandism, vegetarianism, and antivivisection. To effect her purpose, she gains complete influence over an important Member of Parliament, Lord Keswick, the future Duke of Crosthwaite (Linton's birth town and parish). Lord Keswick is weak and spineless, similar to Linton's view of her father and husband. Skirting around the incongruity of a woman gaining control over a man in order to maintain male dominance, Theodora says that she is willing to manipulate him because she had "the more practicable manly view of things" (p. 207). (Her male identification persisted even as she fantasized herself a voluptuous female.)

To control Lord Keswick, Theodora has to come between him and his wife, a saintly woman who is a deluded advocate of women's rights and other so-called visionary fads. "For all his loyal love for his wife I quite knew that Lord Keswick could not withstand my influence when I choose to exert it" (p. 219). Lady Keswick dies of heartbreak, and Theodora is blamed for murdering her "by mental desire—by the criminal concentration of thought and will" (p. 230). Lord Keswick remarries a malicious evil woman. Theodora is the unwitting cause of his death, and then also of the second Lady Keswick, as well as various others. Theodora, accused of being in league with the devil, is called "a fiend-woman," "a vampire who lives on human blood" (pp. 255, 301).

The oedipal nature of Theodora's triangular relationship with Lord Keswick and each of his wives (the mother-image split into a good and bad representation) indicates the conflicts embedded in the mind of a daughter whose mother died in her childbirth. Linton repeatedly insisted that Theodora is a sinless Cain, blameless for the deaths she has caused, as if she herself were seeking absolution for the primal guilt of matricide, as well as for the murderous feelings, also rooted in oedipal jealousy, that she experienced towards her sister Lucy. Her rage moreover at her weak rejecting father caused her to have Theodora kill, however unintentionally, the father image Lord Keswick. ("Desanges" suggests blood in the sense of death and family ties.)

The disasters Linton imagined would have happened if indeed her secret wish to be a seductively beautiful woman had been fulfilled helps explain why in reality she had sought safety by developing an antithetical, male-identified personality. Gratified wishes were too dangerous, and so she has Theodora conclude that "my strange experience has taught me that things are better ordered for us than we could order them for ourselves" (p. 334). Linton ends her novelistic fantasy with Theodora longing only for death, "that sweet faced genius who is our releaser from pain and perplexity" (p. 334). Ironically, Linton herself died even before she finished her final revision of the book. Published posthumously in 1900, two years after her death, the book was an "unexpected voice from the grave,"[28] and received scant attention.

A reviewer of *Theodora Desanges* commented that the melancholy tone of the book must be "the net result of the preaching of obstructive and destructive doctrines, the net result of a too exclusive contemplation of the blots and blemishes in feminine nature, the net result of a thirty-years' occupancy of the seat of self-appointed censor."[29] Certainly Linton's increasingly single-minded and hysterical campaign to keep women encaged within the home diminished her popularity. Through most of her professional life, she had been a respected writer, the author of popular novels and a contributor to the leading periodicals. She had been a valuable ally to the male opposition to women's emancipation. By the 1890s, however, she became an object of ridicule, mocked for what a critic called her "wearisome iteration concerning blatant noisy unsexed and wild women, few of whom are more blatant, noisy, unsexed and wild than Mrs. Lynn Linton." Her later novels were not popular because, as a reviewer commented, "the veins of purpose were too often black and swollen with anger to the detriment of their artistic value."[30]

Eliza Lynn Linton's obsessive anti-feminism and misogyny were the psychic cost of the self-alienation that characterized her fictionalized autobiographical fantasies. Not conforming to the constricting norm of Victorian womanhood in that age of extreme sexual polarization, she developed a sense of maleness so strong that she could only write her autobiography in the persona of a man. She reaped the benefits in the form of personal freedom and success. She was, however, painfully jealous of the womanly woman, a feeling clearly revealed in *Theodora Desanges*, which fueled her relentless war on women. In addition, her social incongruence fostered in her a vicious self-hatred, which she turned outward in the form of anti-feminist diatribes. She was once described, because of her polemics, as a "lady flagellant,"[31] but her attacks were to a large extent self-flagellation. Neither as the male Christopher Kirkland nor as the voluptuous Theodora Desanges could she present her life as other than one of pain and estrangement.

NOTES

1. *Nineteenth Century*, June, 1889, 781–788, and August, 1889, 357–384.
2. E. Lynn Linton, *The Autobiography of Christopher Kirkland* (London: Richard Bentley and Son, 1885), I, 253.

3. *George Eliot Letters*, Gordon S. Haight, ed. (New Haven, Conn.: Yale University Press, 1954), I. 225.

4. John Chapman's Diary, 12 January, 1851, published in Gordon Haight, *George Eliot and John Chapman, With Chapman's Diaries* (New Haven, Conn.: Yale University Press, 1940), p. 131.

5. Quoted in Anne Lohrli, *Household Words: A Weekly Journal 1850–1859 Conducted by Charles Dickens* (Toronto: University of Toronto Press, 1973), p. 344. In addition to the professional relationship between Linton and Dickens, they had a personal connection in that Gadshill, Dickens' house in Kent, had originally belonged to Linton's father, and she had lived there for five years in her childhood. In 1856, after Vicar Lynn's death, she as executor sold the house to Dickens.

6. Eliza Lynn, "Mary Wollstonecraft," *English Republic* IV (1854), 418–424.

7. [Eliza Lynn], "Rights and Wrongs of Women," *Household Words*, April 1, 1854, 158–161.

8. E. Lynn Linton, *Lizzie Lorton of Greyrigg* (New York: Harper and Brothers, 1866), p. 137.

9. E. L. L[inton], "Crooked Sticks," *National Magazine*, June, 1858, 98–100.

10. Quoted in George Somes Layard, *Mrs. Lynn Linton: Her Life, Letters and Opinions* (London: Methuen and Co., 1901), p. 249.

11. E. Lynn Linton, *The One Too Many* (London: Chatto and Windus, 1894), p. 358; *Athenaeum*, March 17, 1894, 342.

12. Layard, p. 249; E. Lynn Linton to [George] Bentley, February 21, 1885, in the Bentley Collection, University of Illinois Library, Urbana, Illinois.

13. Layard, p. 21.

14. E. Lynn Linton, "The Wild Women as Politicians," *Nineteenth Century*, July 1891, 79; [Linton], "Epicene Sex," *Saturday Review*, August 24, 1872, 243.

15. E. Lynn Linton, "The Judicial Shock to Marriage," *Nineteenth Century*, May 1891, 697.

16. "To Lucy," September 21, [1844], Notebook, E. Lynn Linton MSS, Keswick Museum, Keswick, England.

17. Linton to Bentley, December 21, 1884, and March 12, 1885, Bentley Collection.

18. Linton to Bentley, December 13, 1884, Bentley Collection.

19. Unsigned reader's report on *The Autobiography of Christopher Kirkland*, Bentley Collection.

20. E. Lynn Linton to Rhoda Broughton, September 30, 1885, quoted in Layard, p. 247.

21. E. Lynn Linton, *The Rebel of the Family* (3 vols., 1880; A New Edition, 3 vols. in 1, London: Chatto and Windus, 1886), pp. 32, 159–160, 35, 151.

22. Layard, p. vii.

23. Linton to Bentley, April 24, 1885, and May 11, 1885, Bentley Collection.

24. Layard, p. vii; Royal A. Gettman, *A Victorian Publisher: A Study of the Bentley Papers* (Cambridge: Cambridge University Press, 1960), pp. 126–127; Linton to Bentley, November 28, 1885, and March 13, 1887, Bentley Collection.

25. Layard, p. 100.

26. E. Lynn Linton, *The Second Youth of Theodora Desanges* (London: Hutchinson and Co., 1900), pp. 8–9, 247, 120, 242.

27. E. Lynn Linton, *My Literary Life* (London: Hodder and Stoughton, 1899), pp. 19–21.

28. *Graphic*, July 6, 1901, 20.

29. George Paston [Emily Symonds], "A Censor of Modern Womanhood," *Fortnightly Review*, September 1, 1901, 518.

30. *Review of Reviews*, September 1893, 312; Paston, *Fortnightly Review*, 512.

31. *Illustrated London News*, September 4, 1869, 242.

The Modern Family
and the Ancient Image
in *Romola*

Karen Chase

One of George Eliot's finest ethical maxims appears in the thirty-ninth chapter of *Romola*, when the narrator looks on Tito's inexorable descent into egoism and sternly comments that "our lives make a moral tradition for our individual selves, as the life of mankind at large makes a moral tradition for the race; and to have once acted nobly seems a reason why we should always be noble" (ch. 39).[1] This perfectly characteristic sentiment aligns two pairs of terms that drift ceaselessly through the fiction of George Eliot. On the one hand, moral value lies embedded within tradition; on the other, the life of the individual stands in studious parallel to the life of the race. *Felix Holt, the Radical*, *Middlemarch*, and *Daniel Deronda* concern themselves with various forms of these oppositions, but clearly they acquire a special importance within the genre of the historical novel. The strain that nearly everyone finds in *Romola* is only partly due to the weight of its scholarship. More significantly it reflects the complex historical intention that seeks to bring such large and forbidding concepts as morality, tradition, individual, and race into coherent imaginative relation. The chief instrument in this effort is the family, but the family submitted to so many exacting demands that it ceases to be the domestic unit so prominent in Victorian fiction and becomes instead the bearer of that moral tradition on which the individual and the race depend.

By setting her fiction in Renaissance Florence, at a time when a resurgence of Christian piety accompanied a revival of classical learning, George Eliot unsettles the relations between past and present, and no sooner raises the question of history than she raises the related one of modernity. In the opening phase of the novel the historical emphasis falls upon those Florentine human-

303

ists who, in the words of Bardo, follow "the clear lights of reason and philosophy" and who regard Christian faith as a "dim mysticism" (ch. 12) inappropriate to a modern age. On the other hand, when Savonarola enters the novel he insists precisely on the modernity of Christianity, and assails those contemporary pagans who emulate the ancients, "deaf to the work of God that has been since their time" (ch. 40). The distinctive situation of fifteenth-century Florence allowed George Eliot to present Bardo and Savonarola, classical reason and Christian faith, as contemporary rivals each with a strong claim to the modern mind.

In *Romola*, however, the dilemma of historical consciousness fully emerges only for a subsequent generation, the generation of Romola and Tito, which possesses neither Christian piety nor classical fervor. Romola has been taught to ignore "any claims the Church could have to regulate the belief and action of beings with a cultivated reason" (ch. 15). Yet she has "never used" and "never needed" the contemporary alternative to Christianity, the "grand severity of the stoical philosophy" (ch. 36). As for Tito, he regards himself as a "man of clear intellect," as distant from the "simpleton who swallowed whole one of the old systems of philosophy" as from those "fanatics who believed in the coming Scourge and Renovation" (ch. 57). Tito and Romola thus mark the position of modernity in this historical novel, the condition of those who live after an age of belief and who must decide how to stand towards a history which is, and is not, theirs. Characteristically, George Eliot expresses this difficulty in its most imposing form. *Romola* asks nothing less than how a post-Classical, post-Christian consciousness can recover the past.

I

It is useful to begin by tracing the sinuous course of a metaphor. At an important moment in the novel Tito Melema begins to regret his failure to perform "what his fellow-men called obligations" (ch. 16), and the narrator offers the following image for his moral predicament.

> [O]ur deeds are like children that are born to us; they live and act apart from our own will. Nay, children may be strangled, but deeds never: they have an indestructible life both in and out of our consciousness; and that dreadful vitality of deeds was pressing hard on Tito for the first time.   (ch. 16)

Soon thereafter, Tito's impulsive public denial of his adoptive father, Baldassarre Calvo, is compared to a "sudden birth that had been begotten and nourished in the darkness'' (ch. 23). Deeds are children; that is the first metaphoric identity, but the conceit goes further. When he becomes implicated in complex political intrigue, we learn that ''all the motives which might have made Tito shrink from the triple deceit that came before him . . . had been slowly strangled in him by the successive falsities of his life'' (ch. 39). Deeds cannot be strangled, but evidently they can strangle. They not only persist in their ''indestructible life'' as an index of character; they narrow the possibilities for future action. Tito experiences ''that inexorable law of human souls, that we prepare ourselves for sudden deeds by the reiterated choice of good or evil which gradually determines character'' (ch. 27). Here is the daunting circularity of the moral life in George Eliot: we prepare ourselves for deeds that are themselves preparations; the choices that we make determine the character who will choose; freely we invent our constraints. In terms of the conceit, we create our parents in creating our children. Thus, elsewhere, ''inward shame'' is said to ''rush to the deed of fidelity and pity as inevitably as the brute mother shields her young from the attack of the hereditary enemy'' (ch. 9)—a startling image that confirms the general pattern. We give birth to acts which then beget the possibilities for future action: the self spawns its ancestry; the individual moral psyche is its own family.

But that is only the first movement of the metaphor, for the family itself is reinterpreted in metaphoric terms. By far the most important instance is the image that stands out conspicuously at the center of the novel: the Father as the Past. Bardo and Baldassarre embody the past—a point George Eliot emphasizes by making them zealous classical scholars. More significantly, they register the *claim* of the past upon the present. Bardo's demands upon Romola, including the demands that persist after his death, possess the authority that historical events have for a contemporary generation: they constitute the unalterable given which demands a response. Baldassarre's desperate appeal to Tito represents a moment ''when the Past had grasped him [Tito] with living quivering hands, and he had disowned it'' (ch. 34). The problem of tradition is posed vividly and ineluctably within the family, which is not for George Eliot what it is for so many of her contemporaries, a ''walled garden,'' a refuge from history.[2] On the contrary, history establishes the structure of the family, and Romola's movement through the novel is a family progress conceived in rigorously historical terms. The three generations are the three categories of time; the obligation to obey the parent and to teach the child manifests itself as an obligation to history.

Yet, if we press still further and ask how George Eliot imagines history, we find that she conceives history in terms of the *individual*. As the narrator concisely puts it, "the eager theorising of ages is compressed, as in a seed, in the momentary want of a single mind" (ch. 17). *Romola* begins by conjuring the "spirit of a Florentine citizen," "a man of the fifteenth century" who is less man than century, existing merely as the condensation of cultural traits; it continues by identifying major historical periods with individual exemplars.[3] Bacchus and Antigone come to signify the dichotomous temperament of the classical age, much as the Holy Mother comes to stand for all Christendom. Of Savonarola we are told that the moral emotions of his time "had found a very remarkable utterance in the voice of a single man" (ch. 21). And Romola, it is clear, exemplifies the possibilities for moral consciousness in the modern age. History is "compressed" within representative individuals who summarize the experience of vast epochs and in this way serve as convenient tokens of an intricate cultural inheritance.

With this braid of overlapping metaphors, George Eliot weaves her way around a circle. What is the individual? The individual is a family of dispositions, choices, and deeds. What is the family? The family is a living history, a transaction between past and future. What is history? History is the succession of individuals who epitomize the possibilities of their age. Through this series of metaphoric displacements, the novel creates an imaginative solidarity among three regions of experience: the relation of a self to its past resembles the relation of a child to its parent, which in turn resembles the relation of a community to its traditions. When Romola leaves her home, she feels "orphaned in those wide spaces of sea and sky" (ch. 61); when Lorenzo de' Medici dies, he leaves "Florence orphaned" (ch. 4). The family metaphor links individual and community, and allows George Eliot to establish continuity between the most intimate emotions and the broadest historical movements. "Our sentiments," she once wrote, "may be called organised traditions."[4] And her Theophrastus Such calls it "blasphemy" to wish that one had been born in another age; it is like wishing that one "had had other parents"—a remark that vividly conjoins personal identity, family origin and historical epoch.[5] These metaphors may be seen as marking the place where a realist allows herself to wish. They establish an imaginative identity which determines the goal towards which the novel moves—moving, it is true, only haltingly because moral realism must tread over rough ground that the imagination need not touch.

II

In attempting to defend *Romola* against an ever-lengthening litany of complaints, a number of critics have argued that readers have sought the wrong satisfactions in the novel because they have incorrectly identified its genre. Felicia Bonaparte, for instance, calls *Romola* "the first distinctly modern epic," "in its entirety, a poem" and insists that it cannot be evaluated according to the standard norms of Victorian fiction.[6] George Levine, on the other hand, has suggested that the relevant generic rubric is the fable.[7] These proposals have been salutary, reminding us that *Romola* has certain distinctive ambitions that need to be respected, but before we permit ourselves a relieved sigh—oh, *of course*, it's not a failure, it's an epic—we must surely recall the homely truth that whatever else *Romola* is, it is first of all a novel, and however great its ambitions it relies on conventions of realism in order to approach them. Specifically, it offers a psychological analysis of individuals and a social analysis of institutions, and it locates both within a precisely rendered historical milieu. In the realist narrative that is the scaffolding of the novel, the family occupies a central place, as it does so often in Victorian realism: the dramatic action turns on problems of love and marriage, domestic crises and domestic resolutions. Through the circle of metaphors that we have been tracing George Eliot allows herself to imagine a certain unity of experience, in which the family is embedded in conceptions of the individual on one side and history on the other. But on the realist plane of the novel the figural unity dissolves into literal conflict.

In the relationship between parent and child George Eliot finds a primitive moral relationship in which, to use her distinction, love rather than duty establishes the bond. Natural expressions of sentiment create a circuit of affections that depends on neither ethical maxims nor social insitutions. Romola's devotion to her father needs no justification and can withstand his weakness; it has the stability of an absolute claim, absolutely acknowledged. Moreover, in a strong sense it constitutes her identity. Her early years with her father will be described as a "young filial life" (ch. 54), and all through the opening of the novel Romola is deeply and essentially filial. This is not an incidental virtue but a defining characteristic, and Piero di Cosimo aptly chooses Bardo and Romola as models for his painting of Oedipus and Antigone. George Eliot puts the precedent of Antigone to many uses in this novel, but chief among them is the representation of a perfect daughterly devotion, which receives its consummate expression in the attitude of mourning. Indeed mourning is a fundamental disposition in George Eliot's heroines, for whom it is a sign of moral character. Even before her father's death Romola assumes the bearing of a mourner who lives with an irrevocable sense of loss. Romola, we are told, "had inherited nothing but memories— memories of a dead mother, of a lost brother, of a blind father's happier time—memories of far-off light, love and beauty, that lay embedded in dark mines of books" (ch. 6). As the good daughter her moral orientation is retrospective, and mourning is only the final expression of this unqualified fidelity to the parent.[8]

But the inevitable movement of family history unsettles the simplicity of this relationship. When Tito first enters the Bardo household, he seems a providential addition to the family configuration, destined to fill the place left by Bardo's son Dino, who has deserted classical philosophy for Christian mysticism. Indeed Tito's approach to Romola is by way of the parent; he will become her husband by being son to her father. Thus Romola tells old Bardo that "I wish to marry [Tito], that we may both be your children and never part" (ch. 12). This is what the novel calls "the dream of a triple life" (ch. 27), a terse expression of the novel's persistent hope for family continuity.

George Eliot interrupted her work on *Romola* in order to write *Silas Marner*, which concludes by posing just this problem of fathers and husbands. When Eppie tells Silas that she would prefer not to marry, that she would "sooner things didn't change," Silas points out that "things *will* change, whether we like it or no" and encourages her to accept Aaron's offer of marriage. On the day of her wedding Eppie echoes Romola's sentiment, telling Marner that "you won't be giving me away . . . you'll only be taking Aaron to be a son to you," and as the novel ends it gives us no reason to doubt the smooth continuity of generational change.[9]

If *Silas Marner* offers an ideal picture of the domestic tradition, in which inevitable change need not bring discord, *Romola* asks what happens when the ideal fails to obtain. For it quickly becomes evident that Tito, unlike Aaron, grants no priority to the claim of the father and sees marriage as a transaction in the present, not a negotiation with the past. In this as in all else, Tito exemplifies modernity in its most skeptical and anti-traditional guise. Possessing no "traditional attachments" himself (ch. 57), he regards the "sentiment of society" as "a mere tangle of anomalous traditions and opinions" (ch. 11) and asks that Romola "never look backward" (ch. 20), encouraging her to enjoy "the soft waters of forgetfulness" (ch. 32). The capacity to mourn, I have suggested, is a test of moral character in George Eliot. Tito cannot mourn; he seeks instead to "strip himself of the past, as of rehearsal clothing, and [to] throw away the old bundle'' (ch. 57). The marriage, in short, represents not only a familiar clash between egoism and altruism; it is a collision between rival principles of history.

Only with Bardo's death does the extent of this conflict become evident. Romola's first thought in the midst of her sorrow is that her "life with Tito will be more perfect now" (ch. 27), but she will quickly learn that the ties of the living depend on what the novel evocatively calls "the common interest in the dead" (ch. 31). The decisive event, of course, is Tito's refusal to heed Bardo's "longest, dearest wish" (ch 31), that his great collection of books and antiquities be permanently assembled in a library under his name. Having secretly sold the collection to French and Milanese bidders, Tito tries to persuade Romola that no "substantial good" (ch. 32) would have come of the library: "Any rational person looking at the case from a due distance will see that I have taken the wisest course" (ch. 32). But the appeal to reason and distance has no meaning for Romola, whose "religion" is "tenderness and fellow-feeling for the near and the loved" (ch. 36). To be a faithful daughter is to *inherit* feelings; this is the sense in which George Eliot can speak of sentiments as traditions. "It was a yearning of *his* heart," she tells Tito, "and therefore it is a yearning of mine" (ch. 32).

Tito's egoism itself provides a sufficient explanation for the failure of the "triple life," but it is worth pointing out that there is another form of egoism which contributes to that failure, namely the marriage tie itself. In all of George Eliot's work there persists a lingering suspicion of marriage as too emotionally narrow and too morally exclusive; the insistent demands of private life jeopardize wider commitments and turn the life of the emotions dangerously inward. Marriage, she writes in *Romola*, "must be a relation either of sympathy or of conquest" (ch. 48). Sympathy she characteristically reserves for those—such as Will and Dorothea or Deronda and Mirah—who have engaged in long and painful moral struggle and who marry almost as an afterthought. Those who rush to marriage in the headlong pursuit of private happiness—Lydgate and Rosamond, Gwendolen and Grandcourt—typically come to suffer within the confinements of their intimacy. When Tito abruptly breaks off discussion with Romola by asserting that "the event is irrevocable, the library is sold, and you are my wife" (ch. 32), he gives curt expression to the peremptory character of the marital bond, which jealously guards its prerogatives against any outer claims. Even in her unhappiness, Romola refuses to divulge her growing disappointment with Tito—a reticence which wins the somewhat sanctimonious approval of the narrator: "She who willingly lifts up the veil of her married life has profaned it from a sanctuary into a vulgar place'' (ch. 31). Such a remark conforms to a dominant Victorian ideal, but in the wider domain of *Romola* it raises a difficulty. The very intimacy of married life is a mark of that life's emotional restrictions and moral exclusions.

Romola's decision to leave Tito is a rejection of the egoism of marriage, but that rejection carries its own narrowness. In reasserting the claim of the father, Romola substitutes one form of moral limitation for another—a point well emphasized in her first dialogue with Savonarola. When Romola declares her irrevocable commitment to Bardo, Savonarola pointedly inquires, ''and do you own no tie but that of a child to her father in the flesh?'' (ch. 40), a question that shakes the foundations of the family ethic which has hitherto dominated the novel.

In persuading Romola to return to her husband, Savonarola appeals not to a domestic ideal but to a moral imperative founded upon duty rather than affection: ''can man or woman choose duties? No more than they can choose their birthplace or their father and mother'' (ch. 40). The immediate effect of Savonarola's influence is to send Romola back to Tito, but the marriage tie is sustained only at the cost of its ethical priority. The province of duty is far wider than that of affection, and once Romola acknowledges its claim she relinquishes the self-sufficiency of family values. Savonarola challenges her isolation from the ''common life,'' demanding that she recognize obligations to the community into which she was born: ''Live for Florence—for your own people, whom God is preparing to bless the earth'' (ch. 40).

Romola thus becomes ''a daughter of Florence'' (ch. 41) who exchanges her old filial devotion for this broader one: ''All that ardour of her nature which could no longer spend itself in the woman's tenderness for father and husband, had transformed itself into an enthusiasm of sympathy with the general life'' (ch. 44). It must be emphasized that this is not only a broadening of the moral goal; it is a change in the moral emotion. Romola's motives now exist ''apart from personal enjoyment and personal affection'' (ch. 44), much as Savonarola had shown her the possibility of care ''apart from any personal feeling'' (ch. 40). The movement from family to community and personal sentiment to impersonal fellowship brings Romola towards the Comtean religion of humanity, whose importance for the novel has been well established.[10] But it is worth noting that in order to express this advance to a wider moral sphere, George Eliot must rely on metaphors drawn from the narrower ambit. Romola is a ''child of Florence'' (ch. 40); ''[t]he idea of home had come to be identified for her less with the house in the Via de' Bardi, where she sat in frequent loneliness, than with the towered circuit of Florence'' (ch. 43). Here is another form of that metaphoric unity which we have considered: the historical life of a community pictured as a home and the emotions of public service conceived in terms of family feelings. And yet this smooth transfer of metaphor must not conceal the tension on the literal plane. Romola's embrace of social responsibility requires an overcoming of the family ethic—as Tito bitterly observes, ''a husband's influence is powerless against the Frate's'' (ch. 45).

The family is threatened from two sides: from the standpoint of a skeptical individualism, which asks ''what motive could any man really have, except his own interest?'', and from the standpoint of a communal ideal, which seeks to assimilate family duties within a broader ethical conception. Thus Tito casually anticipates a future without his wife, while Romola, for her part, is willing to denounce her husband in order to ''guard the Republic from further treachery'' (ch. 46). Correctly believing Tito to be plotting against Savonarola, she asks in a moment of withering contempt, ''what if I am your wife?'' (ch. 46). In one of its most serious purposes *Romola* attempts to offer an historical analysis of social insititutions, and within this context it dramatizes the pressures which make the family such a fragile configuration.

At the same time, however, the novel provides a psychological analysis of moral emotions, and in this context the family proves to be durable and resilient. It remains a powerful source of sentiments that plague the egoist much as they haunt the altruist. Baldassarre's obsessive pursuit of Tito into death itself is not only an image of unappeasable Nemesis; it marks a final resurgence of the family tie, which withstands any attempt to break it. A similar resurgence occurs in Romola's relation to Savonarola, although here it is not imposed from without but wells up from within, reappearing in the clamorous intrusions of personal affection into the domain of impersonal obligation.

This second conflict reaches its highest dramatic pitch in the late scene between Romola and Savonarola, when she begs him to intercede for her godfather who has been sentenced to death, and he refuses. Romola pleads for ''the old man I love best in the world,'' while Savonarola defends the ''common good,'' insisting that ''affections must give way to the needs of the Republic'' (ch. 59). The conflict here, as others have noted, follows the Sophoclean treatment of the struggle between Creon and Antigone; like Hegel, George Eliot saw the tragedy of that struggle as ''an antagonism between valid claims'': ''two principles, both having their validity, are at war with each [other].''[11] In *Romola* the moment of tragic balance reflects a moral stasis, where a strict historical realism can offer no more than the competing and irreconcilable pressures of two moral goods. It is easy for the novel to dismiss Tito's egoism, but it is a more difficult task to avoid "a collision between two kinds of faithfulness" (ch. 60).

For the novel to advance its argument beyond this point it must find an imaginative mode that will permit it to reconcile these rival claims. In her metaphors, as we have seen, George Eliot envisions continuity between disparate realms of experience, but her commitment to fact was too great to allow her to find a solution that was merely metaphoric. What she sought was a way to locate metaphor within history, to establish the practical aspect of figural truth. How this is possible is far from obvious, and in order to make an approach to this question it will be necessary to make an oblique turn towards some issues whose pertinence will only gradually become evident.

III

Romola is George Eliot's most pictorial novel, and its argument, even at its most abstract, is cast in visual terms. In the attempt to render the daily texture of a distant period, a task which she undertook with great solemnity, George Eliot relied on painterly detail as her most valuable resource. Florence appears primarily in the aspect of social pageantry and public spectacle. Procession, carnival, trial, sermon, execution, and riot—these are the characteristic urban events of the novel, each described in minute detail, a twentieth of which, according to Henry James, would have been enough.[12] Lavish description is of course a stock device of historical fiction, but in *Romola* it offers far more than a strong dose of period flavor, though it certainly offers that. The emphasis on visual experience extends to the most intimate personal relationships, and to an extraordinary degree (especially for George Eliot) the plot of the novel relies on dreams, images and visions, reading and painting, the exchange of glances and the recognition of resemblance, foresight, and imagination and blindness.

In trying to account for this persistent attention to seeing and sight, we should recall the description of Savonarola's preaching: it "never insisted on gifts to the invisible powers, but only on help to visible need" (ch. 43). George Eliot might well have said with Arnold that conduct is the object of religion, and certainly the great appeal of Savonarola to the author of *Romola* is the moral content of his teaching.[13] The novel takes great pains to separate his unwarranted "supernatural claims" from his "*clear-sighted* demand for the subjection of selfish interests to the general good'' (ch. 25, my emphasis). It is insofar as Savonarola brings piety into public life that he serves as an exemplary figure, and once the ''invisible'' and ''supernatural'' elements have been set aside, then Savonarola reveals himself to be ''labouring for the very highest end—the moral welfare of men'' (ch. 71). It should not be surprising that a religious leader embodies George Eliot's humanist ideal, for her humanism might be best described as visible religion.

One might come at this question from the opposite direction, from the direction of individual psychology. *Romola* contains some of George Eliot's most astute psychological analysis, but unlike her later work it does not attempt to construct a complex inner world as the arena of emotional conflict. On the contrary, it repeatedly gives public expression to private sentiment. The most pointed manifestation of this tendency is the marked attention which the novel bestows upon human faces. From the opening scene Tito's ''bright face'' becomes almost an independent character. It launches a thousand schemes, and carefully tended by the barber Nello it makes a rapid ascent in Florentine society. After years of separation Baldassarre longed to see his adopted son ''face to face'' (ch. 30), while Tito, who wants nothing of the sort, prepares himself ''to see [Baldassarre's] face rise up continually like the intermittent blotch that comes in diseased vision'' (ch. 29). Tessa ''could read nothing else, but she had learned to read a good deal in her husband's face'' (ch. 50), and Tito's final living moment is spent staring at Baldassarre, who presents him ''with the face of the hideous past'' (ch. 67). These are but a few of the countless cases in which the novel locates emotion in the features of the countenance. An early description of Romola is particularly noteworthy.

> At that moment the doubtful attractiveness of Romola's face, in which pride and passion seemed to be quivering in the balance with native refinement and intelligence, was transfigured to the most lovable womanliness by mingled pity and affection: it was evident that the deepest fount of feeling within her had not yet wrought its way to the less changeful features, and only found its outlet through her eyes.   (ch. 5)

The notion of feeling in search of an ''outlet'' is fundamental to the method of *Romola*, which continually places ''pride and passion,'' ''pity and affection'' not in the mind but on the face. Much as religion is cast in terms of visible need, so is emotion conceived in terms of its visual expression. Late in the novel, when Romola learns that an appeal may be granted to her godfather, the narrator observes that the ''colour had risen to her face like a visible thought'' (ch. 58), and when Tito recognizes a crisis in their marriage we learn that "the husband's determination to mastery, which lay deep below all blandness and beseechingness, had risen permanently to the surface now, and seemed to alter his face, as a face is altered by a hidden muscular tension, with which a man is secretly throttling or stamping out the life from something feeble, yet dangerous" (ch. 48). Thought and emotion ascend to the surface of the skin, and the intimacies of personal experience are gradually but ineluctably displayed to view, much as Tito's armor becomes a "garment of fear," transforming his private terror into a heavy carapace, and as Romola in a very different emphasis becomes the "Visible Madonna." Virtue and vice cannot be concealed; they find a way to expose themselves to view.

The education of the senses is thus an ethical activity, and learning to see, in particular learning to read faces, is a way of learning how to assay value. When Romola first meets Tito, she assumes that because he looks "bright and gentle," he "must feel, as she did": "A girl of eighteen imagines the feelings behind the face that has moved her with its symbolic youth, as easily as primitive people imagined the humours of the gods in fair weather: what is she to believe in, if not in this vision woven from within?" (ch. 6). And when Bernardo del Nero cautions her against falling in love with "the first pair of bright eyes," she responds that "beauty is part of the finished language by which goodness speaks" (ch. 19). This had been Nello's opinion: "I shall never look at such an outside as [Tito's] without taking it as a sign of a lovable nature" (ch. 4). Romola's development to moral maturity depends on abandoning this identification of aesthetic and ethical values. She will come to recoil from Tito's "loathsome beauty" (ch. 32), while she learns to admire Savonarola's face which is "strong-featured" but "not beautiful" (ch. 40). The task of moral seeing is to distinguish goodness from beauty or, more exactly, to recognize the beauty appropriate to goodness. "I think all lines of the human face have something either touching or grand," says a wiser Romola, "unless they seem to come from low passions" (ch. 51).

One form of seeing, however, frustrates sound interpretation and accordingly poses special problems for a community which seeks an ethical consensus. *Romola* contains many characters who style themselves as visionaries and grant an unquestioned authority to their private spectres. The chief example, of course, is Savonarola, who had possessed this "mode of seeing" from his youth (ch. 21) and whose "enigmatic visions" and "false certitude about the Divine intentions" (ch. 25) are said to be more responsible for his wide appeal than his piety. From Romola's standpoint, and no doubt from the standpoint of George Eliot, Savonarola's vision-mongering is offset by his persistent attention to "visible need," but the visionaries who surround him are not similarly redeemed. Romola chides her brother for placing "visions before natural duties" (ch. 15), and she shrinks from her confessor Fra Salvestro's "peculiar liability to visions, dependent apparently on a constitution given to somnambulism" (ch. 41). The most wicked seer is Camilla Rucellai, "whose faculties seemed all wrought up into fantasies, leaving nothing for emotion and thought," and who claims to have been visited by Romola's angel descending to accuse Bernardo del Nero. Angry and distraught, Romola wonders why Savonarola did not denounce such "pretended revelations" and then realizes the answer: "he was fettered inwardly by the consciousness that such revelations were not, in their basis, distinctly separable from his own visions" (ch. 52). Savonarola, that is, has no criterion for disputing rival seers, who can defend their premonitions quite as vehemently as he can. Visions are inescapably private: as Machiavelli puts it (in Nello's paraphrase), "there is as wonderful a power of stretching in the meaning of visions as in Dido's bull's hide. It seems to me a dream may mean whatever comes after it" (ch. 29). Because no public norms can regulate the interpretation of visions, they undermine the attempt to build a community based on ethical observation. In this respect, visions resemble Tito's bland beauty, which welcomes any emotion the observer happens to feel, leading the narrator to query, "was it that Tito's face attracted or repelled according to the mental attitude of the observer? Was it a cypher with more than one key?" (ch. 10).

That question brings us to the concept which dominates George Eliot's account of visual experience in *Romola*, and which will let us see the bearing of that account on the main issues of our argument. The concept is the "image," which appears with startling frequency and serves to characterize the greatest variety of representations. The term is not used systematically, and its prominence seems more a reflex of the imagination than the result of a conscious decision. But for just this reason, its movements provide a way to follow George Eliot's own attempt to establish close bonds between private and public experience.

On the one hand, the image points to a psychological realm in opposition to the external world, a distinction firmly emphasized in the description of the blind Bardo perpetually seeking assurance "that the outward fact continued to correspond with the image which lived to the minutest detail in his mind" (ch. 5). In the same vein we learn that as Baldassarre plots revenge against the faithless Tito, his mind "narrow[s] to one image" (ch. 34). On the other hand, the novel abounds with external representations: the lofty personages of Florentine history are immortalized in "votive waxen images" (ch. 14), and the churches are full of the "images of sacred things" (ch. 8). Nello sees Tito as a "pretty image of self-forgetful sadness" (ch. 16), while Tito regards Romola as "an image of that loving, pitying devotedness" from which he himself shrinks (ch. 12).

George Eliot thus relies on an ambiguity in the term which lets it suggest both a mental picture and a public representation. Moreover—unlike visions, which are inescapably private—mental images (for George Eliot as for the tradition of empiricism behind her) have their source in the external world, and they can reappear there. A controlling movement in the novel, I have suggested, is the passage from an invisible to a visible realm; the transition from private to public images is the leading example of this movement, and its chief agent is the painter Piero di Cosimo, whose role in the novel is precisely to make visible what is concealed. He depicts Tito "with an expression of such intense fear" that the latter feels "a cold stream through his veins, as if he were being thrown into sympathy with his *imaged self*"(ch. 18, my emphasis). After her father's death, Romola anxiously awaits Piero's portrait of him, "lest his image should grow dim in her mind" (ch. 28), and when it arrives she observes that it is "less like him now than the image I have in my mind, but then that might fade with the years" (ch. 31).

This last remark expresses the problem of vision in a way that quickly returns us to the issue of history and tradition. Romola's memory possesses emotional immediacy, but Piero's painting guarantees continuity; it is through "outward symbols" that "our active life is knit together so as to make an inexorable external identity for us, not to be shaken by our wavering consciousness" (ch. 36). Lambent subjectivity finds a stability in physical representations that it can never secure for itself. It is worth noting, if only in passing, that George Eliot seems to have thought of her own fiction in such terms, as a personal creation that took on the solidity and impersonality of an objective artifact. In a letter to Sara Sophia Hennell she acknowledges that Romola may be too "ideal": "I feel it acutely in the reproof my own soul is constantly getting *from the image it has made*. My own books scourge me."[14]

There is a second aspect to this question. When Bernardo del Nero comes to look at the portrait, Romola asks her godfather whether he wants his spectacles—so anxious is she that "he should see just what she saw." Then after the two exchange impressions, she discerns "a feeling that accorded with her own" (ch. 31). Through seeing what she sees, Bernardo feels in accordance with her feeling. The importance of the motif should now be clear. The visible image not only gives the individual a way to sustain continuity, it encourages common perceptions that can arouse common emotions. To the

threat of impermanence it offers the persistence of a material form. To the
threat of egoism it offers sociality. In *Romola* seeing constitutes a community;
it establishes a shared space within which moral relations can be established.
The demand that religion answer to "visible need," and the construal of inner
states in terms of outer expression, reflect George Eliot's resolute desire to
establish a public arena, a moral amphitheatre where questions of moment can
be safely disposed. Moreover—and here we can begin to collect the strands
of our argument—the image bears closely on two other major concerns, the
problem of modernity and the problem of the family.

In the Proem to *Romola* George Eliot offers her well-known argument for
"the broad sameness of the human lot," insisting that "we still resemble the
men of the past more than we differ from them" and that there persists a
"likeness" that is "broader and deeper than all possible change." The
narrator imagines the return of a shade, dead since the fifteenth century, "the
spirit of a Florentine citizen" risen to gaze again upon his home, for whom
"the sense of familiarity is so much stronger than the perception of change."
But when, having surveyed the outlines of the city and having recalled old
struggles and divisions, the spirit agrees that the "changes have not been so
great" and announces his desire to enter the city, then the narrator reverses the
opening proposition and enjoins, "go not down, good Spirit! for the changes
are great and the speech of Florentines would sound as a riddle in your ears."
This reversal would be unintelligible, if the narrator did not immediately offer
a qualification that sets up a distinction fundamental to the workings of this
historical novel. If you go, instructs the narrator, "mingle with no politicians," "ask no questions about trade," "confuse yourself with no inquiries
into scholarship."

> Only look at the sunlight and shadows on the grand walls that were built solidly,
> and have endured in their grandeur; look at the faces of the little children,
> making another sunlight amid the shadows of age; look, if you will, into the
> churches, and hear the same chants, see the same images of old . . .

One might well have thought that images would belong with politics, scholarship, and trade as a fugitive historical manifestation—especially in light of
George Eliot's rejection of Christianity and her uncompromising commitment
to a scientifically inspired humanism. In her elusive but rigorous conception,
however, images can retain a moral force even when the beliefs they reflect
have been discarded. This is so because images express the yearnings that
underlie and *outlive* beliefs, the moral emotions of which specific beliefs are
only the outer husk.

When Savonarola first achieves influence over Romola, he points to a crucifix and says "conform your life to that image" (ch. 40). Indeed she does—not insofar as she adopts Christian faith but insofar as she assumes a moral mien consistent with "images of willing anguish for a great end, of beneficent love and ascending glory" (Proem). She scarcely pauses to consider the truths of religion, but she gives herself freely to religious emotion. In the reversal of perspective that Feuerbach taught her, George Eliot pays reverence not to a Supreme Being but to the human imagination which can envision such a being. As she put it in another context, "the mere fact that mankind has a conception of what is pure and lovely, might be fairly taken as a ground of faith in the human nature out of which the conception was born."[15] Here, again, George Eliot is close to Arnold, the Arnold who wrote that "our religion has materialized itself in the fact, in the supposed fact; it has attached its emotion to the fact, and now the fact is failing it. But for poetry the idea is everything; the rest is a world of illusion, of divine illusion. Poetry attaches its emotion to the idea; the idea *is* the fact."[16] Replace "idea" with "image," and one has a clear statement of George Eliot's position. The image is the fact.

Indeed it is more than just the fact; it is the historical fact. As I have already suggested, it is what remains when faith has waned, and it is the fate of modern consciousness, as George Eliot presents it, to exist among these visible reminders of bygone convictions. One form of modern response, Tito's response, is to regard them as mere idols which are an affront to the rational intellect and which can exert no influence upon an enlightened temperament. But in the person of Romola, the novel suggests another attitude for modernity, according to which one accepts from the past not its beliefs—towards which George Eliot can be as stern as any skeptic—but its *representations* and through those representations its emotions. When a religion, a culture, a morality disappear, they leave their images behind, not as mere relics for the archeologist but as links in a moral tradition. Images, in that generous sense on which the novel relies, are the physical bearers of moral sentiment and therefore central to the hope for historical continuity.

IV

Here it will be useful to recall the terms of conflict that brought the argument of the novel to an impasse. The clash between Romola and Savonarola is a struggle between "family affections" and "the common good'' (ch. 59), between ''inner moral facts'' and ''outward law'' (ch. 56), between a perspective that sees ''with the eyes of personal tenderness,'' and one that sees ''with the eyes of theoretic conviction'' (ch. 61). These rival demands reflect a division in George Eliot's moral psychology, which requires, on the one hand, that ideas be taken ''in a solvent of feeling'' (ch. 52) and, on the other, that ''the transcendent moral life'' (ch. 55) overcome the narrowness of affection. Because George Eliot regards these as competing ethical goods, she can offer no resolution of the conflict within the terms of her realism.

The chapter called ''Drifting Away'' marks a rupture with the very terms of that conflict. Romola longs to ''be freed from the burden of choice,'' she wishes ''that she might be gliding into death'' (ch. 61), and she wakes to a ''new baptism'' (ch. 69) when she finds herself in a plague-ridden village where the pressing needs of others revive her exhausted altruism. In the context of such moral urgency Romola reestablishes ''the simpler relations of the human being to his fellow men'' (ch. 69). And this is possible because she is no longer beset by those institutional relations that had brought her to moral paralysis; she acts without ''all the special ties of marriage, the State and religious discipleship'' and discovers that the ''reasons for living, enduring, labouring, never took the form of argument'' (ch. 69). Here, it would seem, Romola completes her development. The conflicts between individual and community, family and state, inner sentiments and outer law, yield before the claims of morality in its ineliminable aspect, and Romola herself, free from the constraints of her historical position, seems to embody ethical consciousness in its purest form. No personal demands or theoretical obligations interfere with the exercise of the moral will. A healthy agent confronts human suffering and responds without reflection. Romola acts on the basis of mere fellowship, which contains its own warrant, independent of family affection or religious doctrine.

Before we embrace this conclusion, however, an essential element of the dramatic sequence must be considered. For in removing Romola from all the usual conditions of real ethical experience, in placing her, as it were, in a moral laboratory, George Eliot also loosens the realist bonds that have secured the identity of her heroine. When one of the village boys first sees her, he believes that he has seen ''the Holy Mother, come to take care of the people who have the pestilence'' (ch. 68), and the frightened village priest, ''unable to banish the image the boy had raised of the Mother with the glory about her tending the sick'' (ch. 68), surrenders to Romola's authority and returns to the duties he had neglected. Furthermore, one of the first tasks that Romola assumes is to bury the unburied dead who lie in the village—a responsibility that once again links her firmly to Antigone. Romola, in short, does not appear as one moral actor among others but precisely as that heir to two traditions whom Piero di Cosimo calls "Madonna Antigone" (ch. 28).

Early in this essay it is argued that in her metaphors George Eliot allows herself to imagine reconciliations that she disallows elsewhere in her fiction. "Madonna Antigone" is another and central metaphor, suggesting, as is clear, a convergence of classical and Christian values, in particular a union of personal loyalty and universal charity.[17] This resolution must remain metaphoric, but as the discussion of the image was intended to show, this does not mean that metaphor belongs to some self-subsistent imaginative sphere distinct from human concerns. It participates in the realm of practical consequence, the metaphor as *fact*, as itself an "organised tradition" which embodies the wisdom of history and encourages us to act in its light. Romola may be free of the ties of family, religion, and state, but she is no pure moral consciousness; she is entangled in the figures which history has drawn. These figures offer her a way to act, and offer others a way to respond. What rouses the village priest to responsibility is not a person but a living image, who guides him by invoking a tradition of guidance. Within this conception metaphors and images are not merely incidental to the workings of morality; to a substantial degree they govern the moral sense, shaping our notion of virtue and inciting us to its pursuit.

"Madonna Antigone" carries a further implication that we must follow, for apart from suggesting a union of classical and Christian virtues, it brings together the two family roles that dominate the novel's representation of the moral self. All through the opening of the novel, as we have seen, virtue is measured in terms of filial sentiment; devotion to the father provides a decisive test of character. But through the course of the narrative Romola, though childless, appears increasingly in the guise of a mother whose "ready maternal instinct" (ch. 56) finds many willing objects. A concern for the future overlays a devotion to the past, and while Romola never abandons her attachment to tradition, its values are placed in the service of posterity—a point perhaps too well emphasized in her guardianship of the orphaned Hebrew baby and her position as "Mamma Romola" in the novel's epilogue.

The movement from daughter to mother, simple though it may appear, raises some noteworthy issues concerning the centrality of the family in George Eliot's historical vision. The first point involves the question we have been considering, the relation of characters towards time. In the Victorian novel generally and the novels of George Eliot in particular, history often enters the fiction not by way of notable public events but through the immediate concerns of individual characters, and the problem of time manifests itself in such personal activities as memory and expectation, regret and hope, "the tumultuous waves of retrospect and anticipation" (ch. 54). Through these psychological categories *Romola* dramatizes the threat to a satisfactory historical perspective. Tito, of course, represents the novel's clearest instance of what one might call temporal pathology. He suppresses the past and considers the future only insofar as it will satisfy present desires. But the difficulty extends beyond Tito. Bardo concedes that even before his blindness, "it was with the great dead that I lived; while the living often seemed to me mere spectres" (ch. 5)—with the result that Romola "had been brought up in learned seclusion from the interests of actual life, and had been accustomed to think of heroic deeds and great principles as something antithetic to the vulgar present" (ch. 27). The visionaries in the novel treat the future as Bardo treats the past, placing it at a remove from the concerns of living history. Thus Dino's "prevision" of Romola's marriage prevents "the revelation [about Tito] that might have come from the simple questions of filial and brotherly affection" (ch. 15). Part of Romola's role as an historical agent is to secure temporal continuity and thus to restore the possibility of a genuine moral tradition. She does this by conceiving historical commitment in family terms. The past no longer appears as a sterile antiquarianism but as the felt claim of the parent. The future no longer exists only through insubstantial presentiments but through the immediate needs of children. In the guise of Madonna Antigone, Romola is able to domesticate time and thus to recover effective historical agency.

The second point returns us to the issue of marriage. It is striking, after all, that within the symbolic configuration that suggests a form for moral engagement no place is granted to the marital tie. In *Romola* the image of Madonna Antigone expresses a reverence for children and parents, but neither the symbolism nor the narrative points to an equivalent concern for the husband or wife. Romola's development is envisioned as a progress from daughter to mother, but marriage is not seen as a natural stage in an harmonious course, rather as an obstacle that must be surmounted. Love for the parent and love for the child provide the basis for moral sentiments, but love for the husband proves to be a moral danger; Romola's pursuit of virtue consistently depends on overcoming the limitations of her marriage. The novel imagines a growth from daughterly faith to maternal devotion that does not depend on wifely affection. Thus does a humanist render the Virgin Birth.[18]

In the particular terms of the novel's plot, Tito's immorality accounts for

Romola's revulsion from her marriage, but as I have suggested, his villainy overlays a deeper suspicion towards marriage, and in the context of our recent concerns it should be possible to enlarge this point. When Savonarola deprecates Romola's single-minded attachment to "her father in the flesh" (ch. 40), his remark allows two emphases. In the original conversation the stress seems to fall on *father*, in line with Savonarola's demand that Romola overcome the privacy of her affections and learn to feel "the glow of a common life" (ch. 40). In the further course of the novel, however, it becomes clear that the important issue concerns not the father but *the flesh*. Savonarola, of course, means to turn Romola's glance towards her Heavenly Father. But from the standpoint of George Eliot's humanism the opposite of the flesh is not the spirit, it is the image—in the sense in which we have approached it here: the metaphoric manifestation of a real yearning. In these terms Romola indeed heeds Savonarola's plea. Bernardo del Nero becomes her "second father" (ch. 37), and Savonarola becomes a third. When the latter stops her outside Florence and enjoins her to return to duty, "the title which she had never given him before came to her lips without forethought: 'My father'" (ch. 40). And certainly for Romola this is more than a formal title; it is another outlet for filial reverence. So too, as we have seen, is Florence itself, whose "daughter" Romola becomes.

The two emphases in Savonarola's remark confirm one another. By not confining her devotion to the fleshly father, Romola can discover the paternal image outside the family. Learning to see metaphorically is the way to combine personal affection with public responsibility. This, indeed, is the secret of Romola's maternity. When she finds the Hebrew baby orphaned by the plague, her first thought is to "find some woman in the village whose mother's heart will not let her refuse to tend this helpless child" (ch. 68). She will soon learn that she is that woman. The childlessness which prevents her from being a mother "in the flesh" only makes her a more vivid *image* of the mother, one who need not restrict her beneficence to the narrow confines of the family but can extend it through a widening community. As we have seen, this is the moral force of the image in *Romola*: it allows one to move from the intimacies of private feeling to the shared emotions of a common life.

The problem with marriage is that it frustrates this movement. It is the one family tie that cannot be the source of a moral image: its claim is too exclusive. What concerns George Eliot, not just in *Romola* but throughout her work, is that the marital bond cannot be extended, that it cannot offer an archetype for other relations. One cannot (at least George Eliot cannot) scold a wife for attention to her "husband in the flesh," as if there could be a figural marriage beyond the literal. It is precisely Tito's baseness to ignore the restrictions of marriage; far from a welcome enlargement of affections, his "marriage" to Tessa appears as only a sordid adultery. Romola, on the other hand, can have several "fathers" without jeopardizing her fidelity to any one of them. The asymmetry here goes some distance towards clarifying George Eliot's exacting notion of family responsibility. Tito invites great opprobrium for having "two wives," while Romola can be promiscuously filial and wantonly maternal without attracting censure. Husbands and wives are not fungible; they justly lay claim to singularity, but in so doing they threaten an expansive moral vision. Parent and child, on the other hand, permit a graceful recasting in metaphoric terms, and thus allow family affections to extend to the world beyond the family.

When Romola returns to Florence she assembles an improbable domestic circle—comprising her husband's secret wife, the children of that marriage, and her own aging cousin—which seems almost an affront to the conventions of family life. Surely that is its point. A great risk in the Victorian moral imagination was that in celebrating the values which the family engendered it would isolate those values in the attempt to protect them. Certainly this is a tendency in Dickens and in more complicated ways in Thackeray, but all of *Romola* is set in opposition to that tendency. The ambition of the novel, and its burden, is to show how family affections can exist as social sentiments. This is not a question of some tender-minded vision of society as a large family; George Eliot retains too keen a feeling for the dissonance between private and public life to entertain that hope. Rather, it is an effort to envision a society in which public roles would be based on personal images—where an image, it must be emphasized again, is not something insubstantial or impractical, but on the contrary the very basis of practical morality. Bernardo del Nero notes at one point that he will always consider Piero de' Medici a "lad," just as "I have always been 'little father' to him" (ch. 6). The quotation marks indicate not an insufficiency but an opportunity. George Eliot, as it were, pries open the family and distributes its contents through the community; she frees characters from their literal relationships ("in the flesh"), so that they can have many "children" and many "parents" (but not many "husbands" and "wives"), and in this way ensures that personal sentiments will also be social ligatures. In place of the citizen and mother *Romola* offers the maternal citizen.

No conclusion could bear the weight of a work such as *Romola*, but the epilogue in its modest way indicates the massive ambition of the novel. It records a simple event, a conversation in which Lillo, the son of Tessa and

Tito, asks Romola what he ought to become. He insists that he wants to do something that will make him great without keeping him ''from having a great deal of pleasure.'' Romola gently reproves him and suggests other goals by telling him the stories of her father who ''had the greatness that belongs to integrity,'' of Savonarola who ''had the greatness which belongs to a life spent in struggling against powerful wrong,'' and then of Tito, whom she does not name but describes as a negative instance, a seeker of pleasure whom ''calamity overtook.'' Romola, that is, summons these figures from her personal past and converts them into moral examples who might guide domestic life. In this respect the epilogue recapitulates that broad movement we have traced: the transformation of history into image within the context of a family tradition. Indeed Savonarola, as the epilogue reveals, has become a household god enshrined in a candle-lit altar and a ''small full-length portrait.'' Then, lest we think that Romola has succumbed to narrow idolatry, the novel ends with the arrival of Nello and Piero di Cosimo, unrepentant humanists who nevertheless bring flowers to decorate the altar.

It is a strained final picture but it testifies again to the extraordinary *viscosity* of George Eliot's conception, and it presents her most exacting and most hopeful view of the family, that of a cluster of highly diverse ties that nevertheless constitute a close network of emotions. When Romola decides to leave the valley of the plague and return to Florence, she reasons that ''in strictness there is no replacing of relations'' and then wonders, ''could anything utterly cease for her that had once mingled itself with the current of her life's blood?'' (ch. 69). This is how the family grows: through an accumulation of relationships, none of which can ever dissolve, so that the household becomes a living record of the past. It is composed of almost willfully heterogeneous materials—natural ties, moral relations, bonds of friendship, love, and reverence—and it includes within it the vivid memories of those who have ceased to live but have not ceased to represent.

The question of past and present and the question of individual and community receive at the last a common solution. George Eliot offers a category of experience, the image, and a configuration of relationships, the family, that together will allow diverse values to achieve not unity but continuity. It is an attempt—resolute, uncompromising, solemn, Victorian— to avoid both domestic narrowness and abstract sociality, and to overcome a competition between history and modernity. Far from isolating the family, George Eliot hurls it violently into history and contemplates with equanimity the dislocations it endures. For they allow her to entertain her imperious vision of a family that is itself a community, a present that is compounded of past and future, and a reality that is dense with images.

NOTES

1. All quotations from George Eliot's novels are from *The Works of George Eliot*, Cabinet edition (Edinburgh: William Blackwood & Sons, n. d.). References are cited by chapter, and those to *Romola* are included parenthetically within the text.
2. Walter E. Houghton, *The Victorian Frame of Mind: 1830:1870* (New Haven, Conn.: Yale University Press, 1957), p. 343.
3. See Thomas Deegan, "George Eliot's Novels of the Historical Imagination," *CLIO*, 1 (June, 1972), p. 27. William Myers writes astutely of the "translatability" of ideas in *Romola*, although he wants to insist, as I do not, that George Eliot fails "to grasp human events in other than personal terms." William Myers, "George Eliot: Politics and Personality," in *Literature and Politics in the Nineteenth Century*, ed. John Lucas (London: Metheun, 1971), pp. 114 and 123.
4. George Eliot, "The Influence of Rationalism," in *Essays of George Eliot*, ed. Thomas Pinney (New York: Columbia University Press, 1963), p. 409.
5. George Eliot, *Impressions of Theophrastus Such*, in *The Works of George Eliot*, vol. 11, 29.
6. Felicia Bonaparte, *The Triptych and the Cross: The Central Myths of George Eliot's Poetic Imagination* (New York: New York University Press, 1979), pp. 27 and 10. Bonaparte, it must be said, has provided by far the most careful general reading of the novel. Her meticulous attention to its background, especially the religious and mythological sources, and to its symbolic apparatus, should make it possible again for *Romola* to be taken with the seriousness it deserves.
7. Levine goes on to argue that the mode of the novel remains mixed, that it moves between norms of romance and norms of realism. George Levine, "'Romola' as Fable," in *Critical Essays on George Eliot*, ed. Barbara Hardy (New York: Barnes & Noble, 1970), pp. 78–98.
8. Thomas Pinney has written on the importance of retrospection in George Eliot, arguing that her characters "seek self-knowledge through memory in order to determine their duties no less than their privileges." Thomas Pinney, "The Authority of the Past in George Eliot's Novels," *Nineteenth-Century Fiction*, 21 (September, 1966), 140.
9. George Eliot, *Silas Marner*, ch. 15 and conclusion.
10. For the bearing of Comtean philosophy on *Romola*, see J. B. Bullen, "George Eliot's *Romola* as a Positivist Allegory," *Review of English Studies*, n. s. 26 (November, 1975), 425–435; U. C. Knoepflmacher, *Religious Humanism and the Victorian Novel* (Princeton, N. J.: Princeton University Press, 1965), pp. 40–41n; and Bonaparte, pp. 117 and 194–207.
11. George Eliot, "The Antigone and Its Moral," *The Leader*, 29 March 1856, 306. For discussions of George Eliot and Sophocles, see David Moldstad, "*The Mill on the Floss* and *Antigone*," *PMLA*, 96 (January, 1981), 22–35; and Vernon

Rendall, "George Eliot and the Classics," *Notes & Queries*, 192 (December 13 and December 27, 1947), 544–545 and 564–65.

12. Henry James, "George Eliot's Life," *Atlantic Monthly*, LV (May, 1885), 675.

13. "And so, when we are asked, what is the object of religion?—let us reply: *Conduct*. And when we are asked further, what is conduct?—let us answer: *Three-fourths of life.*" For George Eliot, the proportion would be, if anything, still higher. Matthew Arnold, *Literature and Dogma*, vol. VI of *The Complete Prose Works of Matthew Arnold*, ed. R. H. Super (Ann Arbor: University of Michigan Press, 1968), 175.

14. Letter to Sara Sophia Hennell, 23 August 1863, in *The George Eliot Letters*, ed. Gordon S. Haight, IV (New Haven, Conn.: Yale University Press, 1955), pp. 103–104, my emphasis.

15. George Eliot, quoted in K. K. Collins, "Questions of Method: Some Unpublished Late Essays," *Nineteenth-Century Fiction*, 35 (December, 1980), 392.

16. Matthew Arnold, "The Study of Poetry," vol. IX of *The Complete Prose Works*, (1973), 161. The quotation first appeared in slightly altered form in Arnold's Preface to *The Hundred Greatest Men*, rpt. as "On Poetry" in *The Complete Prose Works*, vol. IX, 63.

17. Bonaparte, p. 203.

18. Tito attempts to promulgate a rival symbolism, that of Bacchus and Ariadne as the type of the blissfully married pair. This image, however, reveals itself as a groundless fantasy that fails to correspond to emotional truth—a fact bluntly emphasized in the title of Chapter 36: "Ariadne Discrowns Herself."

Toward a Poetics of Hardy's Novels: *The Woodlanders*

William E. Buckler

My topic is large, uncharted, and exploratory, and I shall be able here to carry it forward but a little way. I believe we need a poetics of Hardy's novels for this reason: the novels are "organic, animated, expressive"; the criticism is, for the most part, "conventional, derivative, inexpressive."[1]

What do I mean by "a poetics"? What shape should one take? What purpose would one serve?

I am not using the term *poetics* as some structuralists or propagandists for structuralism might use it—as a specialized trope in "a systematic theory of literature."[2] I am using it to designate the results of an orderly, empirical, critical effort to identify specifically what it means to speak of the poetry of Hardy's novels, to say that Hardy's novels are poetic. I mean nothing scientific or impressionistic; I mean something organic, verifiable, critical.

The three statements of poetics that Hardy knew and studied thoroughly and sympathetically were Aristotle's *Poetics*, Wordsworth's preface to the second edition of *Lyrical Ballads*, and Arnold's preface to the first edition of *Poems* (1853). When Hardy spoke of poetry in relation to his novels, he used those three statements as touchstones.

Hardy's discontent with the popular novel and his enforced complicity in it were deep and painful. That is clear: it is written all over the face of Hardy's record of himself.[3] The fact that he expressed dissatisfaction with his involvement in novel-writing so strongly and recurrently makes it the major point of stress in his creative life for the twenty-five years in which he pursued it. Being a good hand at a serial was a dreary, mechanical, tasking business that had nothing to do with art, and so he "cared little about it as art" (179). It was "'gradually losing artistic form, with a beginning, middle, and end, and becoming a spasmodic inventory of items'" (291).

The "it" here is the popular novel form—that conventional, inorganic, misshapen, romantically exaggerated, philosophically vacuous product of the popular press. The "he" is a poet-in-exile, a man who later described himself in language strongly reminiscent of John Henry Newman's recollection of the painful distress of spirit that characterized his own pilgrimage: "'A sense of the truth of poetry, of its supreme place in literature, had awakened itself in me. At the risk of ruining all my worldly prospects I dabbled in it . . . was forced out of it. . . . It came back upon me. . . . All was of the nature of being led by a mood, without foresight, or regard to whither it led'" (385). The "action" is that *this man* was caught in *that trap*, and the subject of my critical exploration here is how the poet imprisoned in that spiritual darkness found a way to transform the sow's ear of the popular novel into the silk purse of the most organically poetic novel canon in English.

Hardy tells us, in the understated way he tells us everthing, how he did it: by "keeping his narratives close to natural life and as near to poetry in their subject as the conditions would allow," often regretting that "those conditions would not let him keep them nearer still" (291). That is really enough to go on and is essentially what I will go on, but I want to reinforce and condition it with two or three other statements of Hardy's about his "art" or poetics. "My art," he said, "is to intensify the expression of things . . . so that the heart and inner meaning is made vividly visible" (177). The "principles that make for permanence" in art are "organic form and symmetry, the force of reserve, and the emphasis of understatement" (363). The idealism he strove for in his art was "'an idealism of Fancy,'" not of dogma—that is, "'an idealism in which fancy is no longer tricked out and made to masquerade as belief, but is frankly and honestly accepted as an imaginative solace in the lack of any substantial solace to be found in life'" (310). Finally, the role of the reader in this art of the unapparent, this art that thrives on the art of concealing art, is to be ready and able to "look through the insistent, and often grotesque, substance at the thing signified."[4]

In the background of each of the operative terms in Hardy's statement of how he dealt creatively with the distress of the popular novel, one recognizes the image of Wordsworth—in "close to natural life," in "near to poetry in their subject," and in the resistant, crippling "conditions." Though Hardy was not, like Wordsworth, trying to do anything so grand as save poetry, he was trying to do something more modest and more complex—to save the poet in himself by channeling it into a form of literature both alien and inimical to it. Hardy used Wordsworth throughout this period as a sort of critical correspondent, testing his own way of looking at creative problems with

Wordsworth's way. For example: "*'January* 1881. Consider the Words-worthian dictum (the more perfectly the natural object is reproduced, the more truly poetic the picture). This reproduction is achieved by seeing into the *heart of a thing* (as rain, wind, for instance), and is realism, in fact, though through being pursued by means of the imagination it is confounded with invention, which is pursued by the same means. It is, in short, reached by what M[atthew] Arnold calls "the imaginative reason"'" (147).

By "natural life," Hardy meant, like Wordsworth, the opposite to the unnatural life dominated by the factitious and tangential accoutrements of a so-called apex of civilization, the unnatural life of fashionable literature, smart, brittle, inflated, and false, the equivalent to what Wordsworth had bundled together as "frantic novels, sickly and stupid German tragedies, and deluges of idle and extravagant stories in verse."[5] This rather fully and exactly characterizes the unnatural life of the popular novel, to which Hardy was opposing the "natural life" that he tried to keep close to in his own novels. Like Wordsworth's, Hardy's motive was poetic—fundamentally literary and artistic. Like Wordsworth, the particular metaphors upon which Hardy drew—all the dense fabric of details included in the mythic kingdom of Wessex—were those in the storehouse of memory, the particular mother of *his* muse, upon which he drew and, through drawing upon it, constantly replenished. Thus Hardy's is a *created*, not a copied world—just as *created and natural* as the mythic worlds of Apuleius and Ovid, where he perpetually found his analogues. Like Wordsworth and like Apuleius and Ovid, Hardy kept his narratives "close to natural life" because he knew that only thus could he keep his subject imaginatively pure and his delineations poetically clear and strong. *The Woodlanders* is, in part, a testing of natural life against unnatural life—of literary organicism against literary convention—and the testing inheres in the language, action or myth, and architecture of the novel.

Hardy's phrase "near to poetry in their subject" also links his thought intimately with the thought of Aristotle, Wordsworth, and Arnold, of course, but it was probably most immediately prompted by Arnold's assertion that, in poetry, "the subject is everything": "'All depends upon the subject; choose a fitting action, penetrate yourself with the feeling of its situations; this done, everything else will follow.'"[6] That is the advice that Hardy took, as Wordsworth, drawing upon Arnold's sources, had taken it before him. Hence, while I can agree with A. Alvarez that the "feelings" of Hardy's novels "are those which were later given perfect form in Hardy's best poetry," I cannot agree that their unity is "emotional" rather than Aristotelian; and I think that Alvarez's assertion that their "power" is "less fictional than poetic" is not

only a gross non sequitur but also a surprising critical confusion.[7] Hardy was
a poet, not a rhetorician, and he held as steady as did Aristotle, Wordsworth,
and Arnold in the poetic recognition that "the feeling therein developed [be
it ever so "spontaneous" and "overflowing"] gives importance to the action
and situation, and not the action and situation to the feeling."[8]

To think of the poetry (and hence of the poetics) of Hardy's novels is to
think specifically in these terms—not necessarily to these conclusions, but in
these terms.

In discussions of the topic before us, poetics, there is current a variety of
terms that may strike some as confusing: Aristotle speaks of "plot" as Arnold
speaks of "subject," "action," and "myth," and as Hardy speaks of
"subject" and "story." To what Wordsworth calls "the organic mind" of the
poet,[9] they are all one and the same thing: in poetry, beauty is truth, truth
beauty. But our "meditative world," said Hardy, is "older, more invidious,
more nervous, more quizzical, than it once was, and being unhappily perplexed by—

Riddles of Death Thebes never knew,

may be less ready and less able" than the ancient Greeks and the Elizabethans
were to see them as organically or poetically one.[10] Still, they are one in
Hardy's novels, as in his poems, and any sign in them that we think we see
to the contrary has to be scrutinized with a good deal of skeptical care to
determine whether it is not rather a delusion of the reader's or a strategy of the
poet's.

The narrator is a primary example. The narrator is a part of the myth or
action of a Hardy novel or poem, partaking of that faithful realism and/or
imaginative invention that Hardy calls "the imaginative reason." He is the
recorder of the action and, like the Celestial Spirits in *The Dynasts*, he is given
powers of penetration beyond the physical. As the human way is, he often
converts what he sees into general interpretive comments. But he is given no
special authority over the ultimate significance of what he sees and, like many
people, sometimes abstracts what he knows sententiously and discordantly.
Examples in *The Woodlanders* are the narrator's reference in the first chapter
to "dramas of a grandeur and unity truly Sophoclean," his comparison in the
middle of Mrs. Charmond's sight of the wounded Fitzpiers with the Sudarium
of St. Veronica, and his characterization at the end of Marty South's apparent
indifference to the "attribute of sex" as an example of "the loftier quality of
abstract humanism." The narrator has his story-telling function, but it is not
to convert poetic fancy into belief or high-mindedness; it is to enable the poet

to efface himself entirely and to concentrate his imaginative energy on enabling his action to subsist as it did in nature.

The primary value Hardy sets on "organic form and symmetry" is crucial here. Symmetry is the more obvious part of it, being the element of design most readily visible to the naked eye. And if it were merely mechanical, as some critics have rather peremptorily suggested, then it would have an interesting but limited value in the poetry of a major artist. But it is not mechanical; it is the outward sign of the inward action, the oblique, emphatically understated clue to the "rational content" that the architectural structure carries "inside [its] artistic form" (301). In *The Woodlanders*, Marty South is this clue. She is both the proof of the book's symmetry and the chief indication of its true subject. Moreover, the scale of her role in the novel shows that by "the emphasis of understatement" Hardy meant an organic rather than a superficial element in a work of art.

"Organic form," being "*the heart of [the] thing*," is more central if not more absolutely important. The term suggests that the form is both organic in itself—grows naturally from its own seed—and organic *with* something—is a natural and commensurate outgrowth of an idea of which it is a metaphor. Thus we are led back to the "organic mind" of the poet from which both—the form and the idea—grew and in which they are one. Connecting this with what has been said of the function of symmetry or design, and specifically in *The Woodlanders* with the structural role of Marty South, we conclude that her role is the clue to the "rational content" or "imaginative reason" carried "inside [the] artistic form" of *The Woodlanders*. And this is Hardy's severely poetic way both of enabling us to talk about the *subject* of the novel as its *action* or *myth* without the need to separate the two, and of "enabling a noble action to subsist as it did in nature."[11]

In a world of unromantic romanticism—a world of aggression and flight, of exploitation, self-deception, adaptation, and compromise, of human struggle and human survival or extinction in a relentless process of natural/human selection—only Marty South, the unfavored, hermaphroditic, astute, realistic, honest, and stoically self-contained daughter of the earth in this Vale of Tempe, touches true "sublimity." By the sentimental standards that fuel the romantic hopes and dreams even of the world of *The Woodlanders*, Marty has little, but that little is enough. She knows who she is, where she is, and the conditions of her life there. The tender *Magnificat* she chants over her dead god's grave renders him as much immortality as the earth offers. He has now suffered the second death of being forgotten by her for whom he died. To her for whom he realized no selfish, ego-satisfying, romantic dreams, but for whom he was the model of man fulfilling the law of his own being, he will live in memory so long as she knows who she is—in this world *or* the next. Marty is a native growth of that austere classical wisdom, Hebraic as well as Hellenic, that Goethe had learned from Spinoza and wise men learn from life—creative stoicism. Her epiphany may be muted to a whisper, but it has the beauty of being true, and if that is all she ever knows in life, it is all she ever really needs to know—as Goethe and Wordsworth knew earlier and at a profounder level than did Keats, and as the Gospel writers and the Greek dramatists knew earlier and better still.[12]

Counterpointing the action as it is embodied in the story of Marty, and giving the novel body, tension, and an enlarged critical content, are many varieties of romanticism. The most obvious, of course, are those rooted in Kant, Schleiermacher, and the German Romantic Idealists embodied parodically in Fitzpiers; and in Sterne, Méry, Alexandre Dumas, and the French Romanticists mirrored with ironic pathos in the Emma Bovary-like Felice Charmond. More shadowy and in some ways more ominous are the dismantled Faust metaphor that repeatedly surfaces and the Byronic gentleman from South Carolina who punctuates the story at various points like Nemesis. These examples have a pop art quality that is interesting in itself, but their function, as in a painting, is to direct the attention of the inquisitive reader toward the more native, quotidian, organic role of romanticism in a story substantially fueled by the weaving of romantic plots and the resulting dislocation, sometimes the fatal dislocation, of human lives.

Mr. Melbury, of course, is the chief engine of this. He bustles and deceives himself in the most romantically exaggerated, sentimentally pathetic way over such matters as success and failure and the pleasures, anxieties, and power of money; he has the most naive, unrealistic notions about the talismanic powers of education; and he uses the deceptive but affective ruse of conscientious high-mindedness to free himself of an obligation romantically induced in order to become a romantic fabricator of other people's lives. It is an activity for which his ineptness is matched only by his relentlessness, and after destroying one of the two people he presumably cares most for in life and leaving the other astray forever, he walks home in the darkness with his paid chorus of local supporters without the least understanding of who he really is and what he has done to the world of which he is the center. All the other characters are, in varying degrees, drawn into this net, and each has a distinctive role to play under its provisoes.

But certain other romantic motifs get implicit critical exposure in the way the fiction as a whole works—e.g., the romantic temptation to view nature in her most benign and sensuously beautiful aspect as the whole truth without regard to her endless, often fatal, inner struggles; the correlative and equally romantic temptation to see people living away from the harsh urban roar as enjoying Arcadian peace, idyllic tranquillity, and unblemished moral integrity; the romantic temptation to see the brutalities of the cash nexus and the moody, haunted disease of modern *Weltschmerz* as a wholly foreign, imported infection of the soul having no perennial, home-grown varieties.

The novel is not, however, trapped in its own critique of romanticism. Savages are not noble, nature's plan is not holy, and though nature may never have betrayed the heart that loved her she is quite ready to leave high and dry people who confuse ethics with physics, human nature with apple blossoms, and who expect nature to do for them what they must do for themselves. Arcadia has its savage prototype in Plato's *Republic*, as well as its pastoral prototype in the *Idylls* of Theocritus and the seventh and tenth *Eclogues* of Virgil. The Arcadia of King Lycaon, the wolfman whose "actions so disillusioned Zeus that he decided to destroy the entire race by a deluge,"[13] is just as real as the Arcadia of love, song, and rustic simplicity, and both are included, with art's proper force of reserve, in the poet-novelist's vision.

Painterliness itself, as in the poetry of Tennyson, is a fully organic metaphor of the novel's art. *The Woodlanders* is one continuous wall-tapestry reminiscent of the Flemish school, homeliness set off at various points by alien images and scenes that make the homeliness at once solid, ingratiating, and quizzical. At points along the way, the narrator-guide touches scenes into life, and we have a motion-painting. The canonical eye is that of the narrator, but we are repeatedly reminded of the critical significance of different ways of seeing by the narrator's views of others seeing.[14] Mr. Percomb's view of Marty South at the beginning is the paradigm. The scene is framed by the window, with us looking from the dark outside into the fire-lit room, and the narrator creates so detailed and complete a visual composition that from it anyone with a canvas, paints, and facility with the brush could create a faithful painting of "The Girlish Spar-maker." But to Mr. Percomb, self-absorbed in his mission, the scene "composed itself into an impression-picture of the extremest type, wherein the girl's hair alone, as the focus of observation, was depicted with intensity and distinctness, while her face, shoulders, hands, and figure in general was a blurred mass of unimportant detail lost in haze and obscurity." There are many variations on this double perspective, and it becomes the poet-novelist's method of metamorphosis, transforming the focus from the way things are to the way things appear to be to each of the characters, the subtle discrepancy between them being the point at which the critical content is concentrated and the natural magic by which artistic form and rational content manifest themselves as one and the same thing.

The two most lurid examples of this relentless inwardness of outward vision are John South's diabolical tree and Tim Tangs's diabolical man-trap. South's morbid self-consciousness has transformed his relationship to nature into an apocalyptic vision of himself as the victim of man's most egotistical and romantic doctrine of all, that of Final Causes, or the doctrine that man is the end and purpose toward which all creation moves. In South's scenario, thus extrapolated, nature is poised to take a terrible revenge upon her alienated conqueror, whose equally grotesque romantic lamentation is that he did not "exterminate the brute" when he still could. Tim Tangs is also poised for revenge, and seen from his perspective, the man-trap is perfectly apt. He is a wolfman in Arcadia, and when a self-indulgent, supercilious, alien popinjay comes between the wolf and his female, the wolf attacks with vicious teeth. The monstrous trap gets only a mouthful of silk, like the lioness in Ovid's tale of Pyramus and Thisbe, but, as in the myth, it is enough to bring about a series of metaphoric transformations. The iron trap of old barbarous times becomes the silken trap of new, civilized, modern times; the stagey bargaining that has been going on between Grace and Fitzpiers gets an irresistible sexual impetus that cuts through all the bargaining and leads to immediate sexual gratification; and a remembered past, momentarily forgotten, gets a promised future mirrored in Ovid's next tale of the inconstant and meretricious love between Aphrodite and Ares. Young Tim Tangs is trapped in himself and in his marriage, and he has yet to learn that a romantic journey to the antipodes is no antidote for his wife's gipsy lust or for his own rough soul. But Grace is trapped too, and one wonders if, even after all she thinks she has been through, she will be any wiser or more successful in dealing with her promised future than Tim will be with his.

As organic as painterliness, then, is the allusive-metaphoric texture of the poet-novelist's art, which gives it a power that is largely evocative and suggestive rather than discursive. For example, Giles Winterborne suddenly finds his life "being frayed away" by a confluence beyond his power to cope. The imminent loss of his worldly possessions combines with the imminent collapse of his romantic dreams to "discompose" him: "The sense that the paths he was pacing, the cabbage-plots, the apple-trees, his dwelling, cider-cellar, wring-house, stables, weather-cock, were all slipping away over his head and beneath his feet as if they were painted on a magic-lantern slide, was curious" (XIII). His "shrouding" of John South's demonic tree is a double entendre, and as he climbs upward he lops away his "perches" one by one and cuts "himself off more and more from all intercourse with the sublunary world," becoming only "a dark grey spot on the light grey zenith." When Grace breaks with him from below, he remains aloft, completely enclosed in "the fog and the night," "motionless and silent in that gloomy Niflheim or fogland." Niflheim is the dark, cold realm of the dead in Norse mythology, and his severance from Grace seems to Winterborne more "like a burial" than a rupture. He is not only trapped by circumstances; he traps circumstance in himself, and the metaphors that give poetic texture to the curve of his extinction are emblems of the actual process by which his decay and death will take place.

But our subject is the poetics of Hardy's novels, not the meaning of *The Woodlanders* as such. The crucial point is that its myth, like its painterliness, is also transformational. For all their historical fixity in place and time, the characters and incidents that together constitute the novel's total action have their correspondences, even when not obviously so, in the mythic legacy of man—Greek, Roman, or Northern European—not because in each case Hardy shaped them by analogy with a particular myth, but because his poetic imagination knew that what happens to oneself happens, has happened, and will happen to another, and that "the more perfectly [it] is reproduced, the more truly poetic the picture" of it will be if the poet, in prose or verse, has in fact seen "'into *the heart of* [*the*] *thing*.'" It will then be a fictive configuration of representative human experience just as surely as any myth delineated by a pagan, Christian, or heathen scop.

As the novel exhibits numerous genre-like paintings, it glances against numerous genre-like motifs. Though it often hovers on the brink of farce, no one in it is frankly absurd; no one has the statuesque grandeur of tragedy though tragic possibilities are carefully planted and just as carefully left unharvested. Besides tragedy and farce, there are echoes of the pastoral tale, the gothic tale, the sentimental romance, the comedy of manners, even of the detective novel. But the novel is none of these. Even *tragicomic* is an unsuitable term, reducing its ambiguous, skeptical, anti-sentimental but sympathetic relentlessness to a stereotype. By analogy with its technique of painterliness internalized and transformed, it simultaneously suggests and resists genres, both recognizing and transcending formulations that would make it merely conventional and derivative. It sees reality simultaneously in several ways—in "the mirror" and "from the bank and from the river," as the Lady of Shalott sees Sir Lancelot. But it does not allow for the Lady's terrible Idealist crisis because it registers no mighty Romantic collision between Art and Reality. Instead, it uses the poetic imagination in a quieter, more modest, more stoical way—"'to intensify the expression of things . . . so that the heart and inner meaning is made vividly visible'" (177) and to offer the reader "'an imaginative solace in the lack of any substantial solace to be found in life'"(310).

NOTES

1. These are the phrases Walter Pater uses in his "Wordsworth" essay to characterize the influence of Wordsworth on those who underwent his *"disciplina arcani,"* or secret discipline.
2. Jonathan Culler, Foreword to T. Todorov's *The Poetics of Prose* (Ithaca, N. Y.: Cornell University Press, 1977).
3. Florence Emily Hardy, *The Life of Thomas Hardy 1840–1928* (New York: Macmillan, 1962). Specific references are hereafter given in parentheses in the text.
4. Thomas Hardy, Preface to *The Dynasts* (New York: St. Martin's Press, 1965), p. xxvii.
5. Preface to *Lyrical Ballads* (1800).
6. Preface to *Poems* (1853).
7. "Afterword" to *Jude the Obscure* (New York: New American Library, 1961).
8. Preface to *Lyrical Ballads*.
9. Ibid.
10. Preface to *The Dynasts*, pp. xxvi–xxvii.
11. Arnold, Preface to *Poems*.
12. See Hardy's "Apology" to *Late Lyrics and Earlier* (1922).
13. Philip Mayerson, *Classical Mythology in Literature, Art, and Music* (Waltham, Mass.: Xerox College Publishing, 1971), p. 153.
14. Hillis Miller uses the same text in *The Woodlanders* to make a similar but different point. See *Thomas Hardy: Distance and Desire* (Cambridge, Mass.: Harvard University Press, 1970).

New Work in the Study
of Literature and Society:
Applications for the Analysis of
Nineteenth-Century British Fiction

Roger B. Henkle

Two recent books by prominent critical theorists, Terry Eagleton and Edward
Said, have argued the case for a "new" emphasis in literary criticism—upon
the political implications of textual presentation, and upon the relationship
between fiction and ideology and culture. Said contends, in *The World, The
Text, and the Critic*, that "the inevitable trajectory of critical consciousness
is to arrive at some acute sense of what political, social, and human values are
entailed in the reading, production, and transmission of every text."[1]
Eagleton's *Literary Theory: An Introduction* seeks in his characteristically
lucid (and, perhaps characteristically, tendentious) way to indicate to the
student of literature the political and ideological context and content of all
critical approaches in vogue during the past thirty years (new critical, phe-
nomenological, structural, semiotic, post-structural, psychoanalytic) and to
argue for political criticism in the form of "discourse theory" or "cultural
studies."[2] These books reflect the rise to critical prominence in the past decade
of a field that some call more generally "literature and society."

In a certain sense, the study of literature and society, or at least of literature
in relation to its social "context," is as old as the hills. In the analysis of
nineteenth-century English fiction, it has almost seemed to be an imperative,
so sensitive is that literature to the great social changes of the time, so
referential and even topical, so beset by its various concepts of realism. But
a new convergence has taken place in the past ten or fifteen years that has
altered the nature of such study. One element has been the effort by a growing

number of historians to analyze history in ways that bring them closer to literary study or into more literarily sophisticated use of literary texts. In the hands of Hayden White, this has meant reading histories through the use of "literary" techniques for the study of narrative, and finding within them patterns of emplotment and significant recurring tropes.[3] For Dominick LaCapra, it has entailed the "rethinking" of intellectual history, premised on the assumption that the very (re)construction of "historical reality" takes place on the basis of "textualized" articulations, in which literature plays a primary role. As LaCapra points out, too often historians used literary works as a kind of second rate "evidence" of attitudes or ways of life or as subjective responses to a past event or situation. But because almost all textual discourse transforms its material, the distinction between fictive and nonfictive representation becomes much more problematic.[4] And all kinds of texts, but especially literary ones, demand more than a synoptic reading of content. For Michel Foucault, this requires consideration of a much broader field of discourse between social relationships, institutions, and literary expression. Correspondingly, the division between objects of study has broken down among historians and literary critics, enabling Said, in his definition of "orientalism" to posit a *distribution* of a special kind of consciousness throughout a range of textual expressions, "aesthetic, scholarly, economic, sociological, and historical."[5]

The other element in the convergence is the influence of literary critics such as Raymond Williams, Terry Eagleton, and Fredric Jameson, who have greatly sophisticated the practice of analyzing literature in relation to ideology and society. Williams's *The Country and the City* is a central text here— perhaps the most accessible of such studies to the general reader and student— and it stands in a body of work that has revolved the issues of social "context," of the representation of ideology, and the definition of culture in a seminal way.[6] Much of the work done in the area has been by scholars who have a Marxist orientation, and it has been furthered (and sometimes obfuscated) by the existence of an ongoing ideological dialogue in journals such as *The New Left Review*. Although Jameson has contended that only Marxism can provide a philosophically coherent and adequate account of the cultural process, the "school" of critics has expanded, in England and the United States, to include a broad spectrum of intellectual dispositions. The question remains whether it is possible to develop a coherent analysis of ideological change and its representation without a conceptual position such as Marxism, but it still *is* an unresolved question and it has not inhibited the growing interest in "literature and society." For the convergence of historians looking in new ways at literary texts and employing literary methods to interpret traditional historical discourses, and of literary critics treating social phenomena and cultural expressions as something more the context for literary works, has opened up the possibilities of new interdisciplinary analyses that will invigorate both disciplines.

As I noted, such an approach is particularly compelling for those of us who work with the nineteenth-century English novel, and the aim of this essay is to look at several recent books, including Jameson's *The Political Unconscious*, that focus the assumptions and methodological problems of a "literature and society" approach to such fiction. These particular works can, I believe, help define the field of study itself and demonstrate the possibilities it offers for a richer interpretation of the English novel. The vexing critical issues of contradictions within texts, of unsatisfying endings or false resolutions, of the ways of representing "reality," of suppressions and obscurities, can be considered from new perspectives and understandings, and our critical and pedagogical operations will have a cultural density they did not have before. This is not a summary of all recent work that turns to social material in interpreting English novels, or that seeks to link the social to the literary; rather, it is a selection of a few books that frame the issues in particularly revelatory ways. Nor is this a review of those books per se, for I treat them as presenting the problematics of a particular critical approach. I have chosen books that I admire, and that are unusually sophisticated and provocative in their insights. Consequently, this is more in the nature of a dialogue with these texts than a review of them, with the objective in mind of using this dialogue to try to sharpen and refine the literature and society study of nineteenth-century English fiction.

Terry Eagleton, echoing in a sense what historical theorists have urged, invites us in literature to widen our field to inquiry beyond fictive works to study "discourses, sign-systems and signifying practices of all kinds, from film and television to fiction and the languages of natural science, [for they] produce effects, shape forms of consciousness and unconsciousness, which are closely related to the maintenance or transformation of our existing systems of power."[7] Jonathan Arac's *Commissioned Spirits* endeavors to do just that, by cross-connecting a variety of discourses in an investigation of a moment of possibility in the development of the English novel, roughly 1835 to 1865.[8] He argues that the ferment and change in the early part of this period caused creative writers to open up to discourses of the social sciences: to borrow ways of observing actuality, for instance, from the concept of Bentham's panopticon: adopting an elevated, crow's nest position in the hub of human activity, as it were, in order to see life arranged around one in a removed, compartmentalized manner. This mode of observation influences the way writers such as Dickens ask us to look at character. On another level, writers of this generation borrow from the social sciences the language and imagery of contagious disease and plague, associating its prevalence in urban slums with the "disease" of overcrowding and social desperation itself, and thus dramatically conflating concrete social analysis with metaphor. Still another set of factors in the composition of the novels of the period are those of opening literary possibilities. The Gothic provides a language and sign system for connecting character with environment in a quasi-scientific way, giving writers physical correlatives (broken down, haunted, tortured houses) for psychological states for which there is as yet no adequate separate terminology. Carlyle, Arac points out, breaks with the visionary mode of presentation of history that was characteristic of Romantic discourse, and in *The French Revolution* develops a new mode that incorporates description of action, while still retaining a bardic overview. The irony created by a gap between the disillusioning dramatization of social reality in the troubled times of abuse of power and mob rule, and Carlyle's visionary means of presentation, generates striking power, for one can sustain the intensity of the possibilities of individual action and yet master the trauma of beholding it. It allows Carlyle to follow Scott in showing how history is made by living men, and yet keep a "philosophical" vantage point. Arac then shows us how Dickens adopted this strategy of presentation in *Bleak House*.

Although he does not use this terminology, Arac is analyzing modes of production, a concept that clearly has Marxian origins. He is interested in what writers in this period have to work with and how they respond to the productions of discourse in other spheres of activity: historical writing, journalism, popular fiction, science, industry. Indeed, he sees the writer in a particularly heady, even "heroic" relationship to his time: "the institution of literature itself seems one of the transforming forces of the age, along with the city, railroad, epidemic, and revolution." The role of journalism in newspapers and cultural journals was seminal in both representing the new society and in commenting upon its values. Arac's study does, however, highlight two of the critical issues of such an investigation of the mode of production. First of all, one realizes that the translation of a way of seeing or depicting something from one mode of discourse to another requires a highly discriminating methodology. One must initially map the former discourse, show its patterns, its characteristic imagery, its rhetorical strategies, in order to discern how meaning is established. The critic must make the same kind of analysis of the borrowing discourse, and in the process show how meaning is sustained or altered when it enters into another sphere and another rhetorical context. This does not always happen in Arac's book, sometimes because discourses are used in different and perplexing ways: as figural representations (the plague), or as presentational strategic techniques (Carlyle's new mode), or as a point of view or narrative perspective (the panopticon overview); and at other times because a generative insight is not quite worked through to all its implications. For example, Arac notes that the advent of the railroad produced a sense of its destructive transforming force, as it obliterated not only the old measures of time but also whole sections of the city, and that the compression in time of travel and in space as districts were condensed shrunk England and also increased the "knowability" of the city. One might take the discourse of the railroad further, and indeed Dickens does it in *Dombey and Son*, when in chapter 20 he describes the trajectory of the railroad train that carries Dombey:

> Away, with a shriek, and a roar, and a rattle from the town, burrowing among the dwellings of men and making the streets hum, flashing out into the meadows for a moment, mining in through the damp earth, booming on in darkness and heavy air, bursting out again into the sunny day so bright and wide . . . (etc.)

Such description continues for four more paragraphs, and then we are brought down into the mind of Mr. Dombey, "'so, pursuing the one course of thought, he had the one relentless monster still before him. All things looked black, and cold, and deadly upon him, and he on them. He found a likeness to his misfortune everywhere. There was a remorseless triumph going on about him, and it galled and stung him in his pride and jealousy . . . "[9] The connection between the manner of Dombey's thought and what we can call the discourse of the railroad train, forward moving, heedless, oblivious to surroundings that speed by, tracked toward a set destination, makes a valuable connection for us between the new, projective thinking of the group of industrialists/ mercantile figures that Dombey represents and its great machine. Dickens reveals that projection as the characteristic mental mode of the new middle class, and it is contrasted with the imaginative, transformative mental mode that Florence Dombey and others represent.

The comparative analysis of the two modes of discourse takes us one step beyond "ways of seeing" or traits of vision toward the representation of an aspect of ideology, for projection mentality is a powerful attribute of English middle class cultural and self definition, and it is one that Dickens wants to explore. This underscores the second critical issue that Arac's study raises, which is that the elements in production may have to be discussed and diagnosed as processes fraught with ideological implications, and not as relatively neutral techniques or modes of vision. Arac does this effectively with the panopticon and social observation, and his work seems to suggest that this must be done with the Gothic, the journalistic enterprise, etc. They come laden with values that affect how they shape meaning in the borrowing text.

Igor Webb's *From Custom to Capital: The English Novel and the Industrial Revolution*[10] takes perhaps the most openly "literature and society" approach of any of our books dealing exclusively with the English novel. It concentrates specifically on Jane Austen and Charlotte Bronte, and to a lesser extent on Dickens, and raises the connection between the consciousness that is recorded in the novel, and the social order. In illuminating readings of Austen's *Pride and Prejudice* and *Mansfield Park*, Webb poses a crux of literature and society criticism: what is the relationship between social circumstances and the fictional recording of them? He notes how effectively Austen was able to maintain her balance in *Pride and Prejudice* between the values of the old landed gentry and the new mercantile, individualistic order. A resolution could be achieved in that novel by integrating Elizabeth Bennet and Charles Darcy, who reflect the new blood of individually self-defined social value, back into the sources of value of the gentry, specifically through their assumption of the direction of the Pemberley estate. They supersede the devitalized older generation and yet reinvigorate those sources of power and social precedence. Austen is unable to pull that trick off in the later novel, *Mansfield Park*, for we never see Fanny Price's development—she comes to the scene "full-blown"—and although the estate, Mansfield Park, seems to be the scene of jaded, dispirited privilege, it is nonetheless mystified and hallowed as a source of value. This, Webb contends, signals a failed connection between the representation of consciousness in the novel and the social actuality—the values adhered to in the former do not correspond with what is dramatized (or what we can see from extrinsic social "evidence" is actually the case) of the latter.

A critical judgment (in this instance a somewhat negative one) of a novel based on the unfaithfulness of that novel to the social "reality" will always present difficulties. We create the impression that fiction is or should be a reflection of actuality, that it should at least be "true" to the conditions of social life of the time. This oversimplifies interpretation of the novel, and causes us to start making value judgments on the basis of historical accounts of the actuality which are themselves only recreations of it. I do not think that Webb falls into this tendency, but the position he is in underscores the need to define the nature of that actuality upon which a novel draws. Here, as in many instances, Jameson's book, *The Political Unconscious*, helps immensely.

Jameson premises his critical inquiry on the understanding that literature is not simply an imaginary reflection of a social context. The literary text must "itself be seen as the rewriting or restructuration of a prior historical or ideological *subtext*, it being always understood that that 'subtext' is not immediately present as such, not some common-sense external reality, nor even the conventional narratives of history manuals, but rather must itself always be (re)constructed after the fact." One of the most difficult concepts to ask students to sustain is that events or situations do not go into historical being until they are recorded. Their enduring existence depends upon their being represented. Thus, the French Revolution exists for historians as well as for literary critics only in terms of its written and graphic representations. But the literary work, as one of many texts drawing upon, say, the French Revolution, sets up a special relation to the "Real" that it incorporates, a relation that actualizes that Real as a subtext of that work itself. As Jameson says, "the symbolic act therefore begins by generating and producing its own context in the same moment of emergence in which it steps back from it, taking its measure with a view toward its own projects of transformation. . . . It articulates its own situation and textualizes it. . . ."[11] The Real does exist for Jameson—hard Necessity tells us that; we suffer and die—but it is not a text itself; it is non-narrative and non-representational, accessible only in textual form, through the representations of it. He distinguishes his approach from that of structuralism and semiotics, which generally insist that the referent or subtext does not exist, and from earlier social criticism, which is disposed to abstract or reify the subtext as something that the text passively reflects.

The implication of such a definition of the relationship between the literary text and its social subtext is not to deny the significance of examination of nonfictive materials such as historical accounts and documents in analyzing a work such as *Mansfield Park*. Rather, it is to reformulate the analysis, so that we are not proceeding as if we were comparing two bodies of representation (the historical/documentary and the fictive) but rather thinking more in terms of how the fictive actualizes its subtext. This inevitably privileges the aesthetic representation as containing its unique formulation of the social subtext and not just a mimetic rendition of a consensus of representations. Such a perspective tends to cast us into a different sphere of interpretation, so that we are more inclined to consider a literary rendition of its subtext as an indicator of characteristic representations of ways of seeing, thinking, or of ideology.

Thus, the particularly mystified exaltation of the estate Mansfield Park in the novel is more likely to be interpreted symbolically as an ideological expression, a class fantasy. Indeed, when Jameson analyzes Balzac's *La Vieille Fille* he evaluates the power of a particularly fine town house in terms of the ideological elements it enacts—its awakening of the longing for possession of aristocratic spaciousness, its evocation of peace from Parisian struggles, its meaning in the social consciousness of a world that savors images of domestic order, regularity, and privilege. While not all novelistic subtexts carry such resonances—some of them will purport to represent only particularized moments of scene or action—they all should invite this kind of interpretive move.

Webb's book frames yet another interpretive crux of the literature and society approach. As he takes his inquiry beyond Austen into Bronte and Dickens, he notes advances and failures in the novelistic formulations of the social and ideological contradictions that inhabit their subtexts. *Jane Eyre* encapsulates a more competitive aspect of self-definition, corresponding with the social climate that we attribute to the 1840s, and individualism is expressed in a more intense and concrete form than in Austen, producing for Jane a measure of independence and scope of power. But Webb notes that these gains on the personal level cannot be effectively translated into social change, and Jane and Rochester significantly retire to a kind of overgrown paradise or retreat. As he puts it, "the transformations of self once achieved, the full transformation of society seems daunting . . . "[12] Similarly, while Dickens effectively critiques Coketown in *Hard Times*, the alternatives to its world of stultifying Fact are not apparent to him within the Coketown world. Dickens opposes Fancy, embodied in Sissy Jupe and the circus, to Gradgrindism, but circumstance retains a powerful grip on individual expression, and, Webb argues, while Fact pervades all modes of production, Fancy does not seem to be an equivalent source of value. Webb concludes that the comprehensiveness in Dickens' novel of the sense of the quality of urban life does not yield a corresponding comprehensiveness of response, analysis, or understanding.[13]

Webb wrestles with one of the persistent critical concerns of the criticism of nineteenth-century English fiction: the felt inadequacy of endings, especially in novels that powerfully represent the disorder and alienation of industrial society. The instances of such "failed" endings are legend—*Vanity Fair*, *Bleak House*, *Little Dorrit*, *Mary Barton*, *Sybil*, *Middlemarch*—and we are beyond the point where we are satisfied with the explanation that the happy marriage or arbitrary disposal of the bodies is simply a novelistic convention.

Here, again, the work of critics such as Jameson and Williams can allow us to reframe the inquiry, at least, and perhaps to consider such endings in other than formalistic terms. Jameson, in *The Political Unconscious*, establishes for himself a matrix of interpretive concepts that inevitably direct the nature of our analysis. There are three frameworks—or "levels," or horizons. The first framework for analysis of a text is in terms of its representation of the subtext of a particular moment in time and social composition—the industrial world of the 1840s, for example. Jameson differentiates his analysis from an *explication de texte* because, following Lévi-Straus, he considers the individual work a symbolic act, and specifically an imaginary resolution of a real contradiction. To a certain extent these contradictions may be simply situational and the novel only represents them as such. Josiah Bounderby's character in *Hard Times*, and Stephen Blackpool's, can be ascribed to the conflict between management and labor in a particular phase of their relationship. But that conflict does not entirely account for the fraudulence in Bounderby's self-presentation, nor does it explain the presence, in Dickens' composition, of characters such as Louisa and Tom Gradgrind who embody certain kinds of malaise, nor does it account for the reasons why Blackpool is put in his frustrating relationship with Rachel. As has been remarked often, Dickens deploys a range of characters who represent aspects of the anxieties and desires of the times, and this in itself is a significant characteristic of his art. To deal with this interpretively, Jameson says we must think in terms not only of socially specific contradictions, but in terms of ideology. Here he uses devices to separate out facets of what is a self-contradictory (or at least self-vexing) ideological state, and to attribute them to various characters. The ideology in Dickens' case contains his own attraction to competitive activity, his distrust of labor unions and the various causes of it, his highly ambivalent attitude toward the imaginative ideal (which he often represents in terms of death and passivity), his inability to work out social and psychological drives through women but his determination to do so, his ambivalent attitude toward the middle class, and more factors. Aspects of his ideological position are represented through characters in the plot, and enacted by them, and it is possible, Jameson suggests, to map them out. What the mapping will reveal is that Dickens at this moment in time simply cannot transcend the ideological positions he is in, that the novel's attempt to achieve a "resolution" of inconsistencies or contradictions will fall short, largely because a society and its members cannot get beyond their own social consciousness.

Thus a novel like *Hard Times* will always be turning about these oppositions and attempted syntheses, will always be presenting the antinomies of the ideology within a closed frame, will always be caught in the bind of its own ideological position. Resolutions will always be attempted—that is the objective of the symbolic act of writing the novel—but they cannot be fully achieved. For Jameson, the next step as an interpreter is to move on to another framework of inquiry, where we see things in terms of the confrontation of social classes. Here we can begin to discover those modes of procedure a novelist takes and those strategies that are characteristic of the hegemonic class. We can observe, from the perspective of a dominant class addressing and co-opting its subordinate groups, the ways in which a variety of materials and schemes of presentation have been absorbed and put to use in the dominant cultural tradition—how folk culture is absorbed into high culture, how melodrama, romance, and adventure modes are appropriated and reworked. In this framework, Dickens' use of the circus as a nodal point of value can perhaps be given a more elaborative reading, and Fancy can perhaps be seen in terms of hegemonic cultural assumptions of considerable latent power, as Martin J. Weiner suggests in his *English Culture and the Decline of the Industrial Spirit: 1850–1980*.[14] To a certain extent, Jameson's interpretive procedure is to move from the sphere of characterological presentation (and also of what we used to call specific "content") to that of formal strategies of presentation (which can only be understood historically through analysis of their implications in longer-term class confrontation) and then—his third framework—to a sphere in which we can address the rise of genres and of cultural modes of production and their relation to various human social formations.

Jameson's method of approach yields its own richnesses, among them, of course, a disposition to consider literary artifacts as ideological and cultural expressions in a moment (now) when we should be doing that. It also allows us to move among texts armed with new sets of questions and new understandings. As an example, Jameson's analysis of the characters and of the aspects of ideology that they embody in Balzac's *La Vieille Fille* isolates two figures who are competing for the favors of the woman who owns the desirable townhouse I described earlier. One of them embodies the New Order of the rising middle class, and he is "abrupt, energetic, with loud and demonstrative manners, brusque and rude of speech . . . terrible in appearance . . . " The other, a Chevalier, is "mild and polished, elegant, carefully dressed, reaching his ends by the slow but infallible methods of diplomacy, and upholding good taste to the end, [offering] the very image of the old court aristocracy."[15] Yet for all his apparent vigor and aggressiveness, the former is sexually impotent, a curious anomaly. Jameson's analysis makes clear that the impotence is symbolic, in those who have newly risen to social ascendancy, of their integral self-doubt, their sense of themselves as imposters, and of their repressed impression that the aristocracy do and will still control the ultimate power. Such an insight, which is not a salient one but is grounded in the ideological conflicts of the early nineteenth century, transfers across the Channel to figures like Mr. Dombey, who as a representative of new commercial power lives in fear of sexual humiliation, and of course to Merdle in *Little Dorrit*, who comes to represent that class dread of being an imposter.

Another consequence of such an approach is that it liberates us as critics from a fixation on the failure of novelistic endings. If we see the novel as a presentation of contradictions, and then work out and back to the cultural and ideological implications of characterological representations and of strategies, we open ourselves up to another kind of inquiry. We need not forsake our reading response to *Hard Times*, but the sensed inadequacy of its attempted resolutions can be ascribed to other, complex factors at work, can be a key to a different sort of reading, and can extract us from that age-old debate that is premised on some concept of artistic unity and totality. It also frees us from prescriptive readings of socially involved texts. I sense, perhaps unfairly, such a prescriptive impulse at times behind Webb's criticism of *Hard Times* and *Jane Eyre*—the implication that these authors are evading the real social critique, and ducking the issue of revolution and radical change. (If that is the case, he is engaging in what Eagleton calls for in *Literary Theory*: a programmatic approach to literary criticism. "It is not a matter of starting from certain theoretical and methodological problems;" Eagleton says, "it is a matter of starting from what we want to *do*, and then seeing which methods and theories will best help us achieve these ends."[16] Eagleton makes clear that the "liberal" purpose of understanding a text is not quite enough, there must be goals for the use of the critical act—in constituting an alternative culture, for instance, for those who have been excluded from the dominant culture.) In one of his earliest attempts to articulate his concept of "structures of feeling," Raymond Williams began by lamenting the effect of essentially prescriptive criticisms of Dickens. "Nothing is clearer" when an analysis of Dickens' treatment of social issues is undertaken, he acknowledges, "than that Dickens is often contradictory, often confused, and indeed often, to use fashionable terms, unenlightened and unintelligent. I do not mean that any of these observations is negligible, but it is only a critical response when it is part of a whole response."[17] That whole response requires that we understand Dickens' relation to the general condition of his culture and situation, and that we appreciate that he is essentially rendering his experience—not only of the events, but of living through the times leading up to them, and of the ideological qualities of his apprehension of society.

Thus Williams's critical approach is also primarily descriptive, whatever larger view of historical development and cultural formation he undeniably has. His approach to the relation between literary expression and social forces has been one of describing "structures of feeling" that are represented in significant novels. In *Marxism and Literature* he amplifies on what he means by "structures of feeling":

> [W]e are concerned with meanings and values as they are actively lived and felt. . . . We are talking about characteristic elements of impulse, restraint, and tone; specifically affective elements of consciousness and relationships: not feeling against thought, but thought as felt and feeling as thought; practical consciousness of a present kind, in a living and interrelating continuity. We are then defining these elements as a 'structure': as a set, with specific internal relations, at once interlocking and in tension. Yet we are also defining a social experience which is still in *process*, often indeed not recognized as social but taken to be private, idiosyncratic, and even isolating, but which in analysis . . . has its emergent, connecting, and dominant characteristics, indeed its specific hierarchies. These are often more recognizable at a later stage, when they have been (as often happens) formalized, classified, and in many cases built into institutions and formations. By that time the case is different; a new structure of feeling will usually already have begun to form, in the true social present.[18]

Williams's concept has been rather elusive to apply, but its main elements are provocatively suggested: the private, often idiosyncratic way in which artists register emerging structures of feeling, the later "institutionalization" of them, the constant dialectic of emerging, dominating, and rigidifying structures of feeling. When one considers how idiosyncratically Dickens or Hardy presented cultural concepts such as alienation, privatization, commodification, hysterical transference, as symptoms of the modern social order, one is aware how generative Williams's way of interpretation may be. As with Jameson's approach (which also, by the way, assumes the presence in any time of older, disintegrating ideologies along with dominant ones and nascent ones) the possibilities are great for reconsidering the meaning and form of nineteenth-century texts.

The next book that I want to examine, Allon White's *The Uses of Obscurity: The Fiction of Early Modernism*,[19] provides us with its own highly provocative means of reconsidering nineteenth-century texts—in this case the often obscure works of Meredith, James, and Conrad. His book demonstrates how a textual practice arises out of what he calls a convergence of different ideological transformations in the nineteenth century. The growing sense of alienation of the artist/intellectual is one such transformation, of course, but White warns us not to consider this in isolation. For at the same time, there is an increase in what White defines as "symptomatic reading"—reading that is disposed to look at aspects of literary expression as symptoms of the writer's psychological concerns. Meredith's *The Egoist* would thus be presumably read in part as an elaborated encounter with Meredith's own failed first marriage, his treatment of his first wife, his shame, his narcissism. Often the text invites us to engage in symptomatic reading; James's fiction is populated by characters who insist upon observing the actions or analyzing the words of other characters in an effort to discern what they are *really* saying, what really motivates them. Symptomatic reading is itself the product of growing awareness and interest in psychology, of a change in the attitude toward "truth" (and its rhetorical correlative, lucidity), and of the final division of the reading public into the so-called mass market and a sophisticated elite.

In this cultural context, opaqueness is adopted by early modernist writers as a "key protocol" of their writing. Rather than signifying a failure to articulate meaning, obscurity is a major means of its representation. Nor can we assume that we need only decipher the mystery, penetrate beyond the obscure expression to some underlying explanation, for obscurity is itself the object of the discourse. "Modes of obscurity are important signifying structures in literature and carry distinct and distinctive kinds of meaning which are not secondary to an anterior obscured content. . . . It is because certain things are opaque to the novelists themselves that the novels were written. . . . They are . . . moments when knowledge threatens to destroy something so fundamentally constitutive of the fiction-making that its clear and direct revelation would silence the discourse."[20] In the chapters dealing specifically with the three novelists, nonetheless, White takes us a long way toward defining the nature of these obscured anxieties or desires. In Meredith, the partially obscured concern is the mortification associated with his notorious cuckolding by Mary Ellen Peacock and Henry Wallis; in James it is his prurient interest in assignations and sexual encounters that he finds it vulgar to reveal.

It is intriguing that although White attributes the phenomenon of symptomatic reading and obscurity in representation in part to the rise in interest in psychology, he will not engage in psychological readings of the practice of repeated textual play with obscuration. White contends that we can distinguish psychically critical instances of obscurity from what might be simply bad writing by their recurrence over the body of the writer's work. Again and again, at crucial points, the prose will become opaque, and will resist any kind of demystifying paraphrase or explanation. Such a pattern would seem ripe for the psychological mode of analysis that a critic such as Peter Brooks uses on Dickens and other writers, in which he sees in the novels a process of return to deep-seated anxieties, a persistent reworking of troubling psychic material in repetitions and new figural elaborations of them, seeking all the while the appropriate "discharge" and, on the narrative level, the appropriate ending.[21] Similarly, in his analysis of Balzac, Jameson deems it essential to introduce elements of psychological interpretation into his methodology.

The absence of such a psychological dimension in White's analyses of these texts may be attributable to nothing more than his own program of explication, but it does shift the emphasis of his interpretive approach. The positional relationship between the writer and his audience and his time is given more emphasis as the cause of the phenomenon of obscurity than is underlying psychological patterning. Such a shift in emphasis may denote one conception of a "literature and society" approach: the primary factors in affecting a mode of production are cultural ones, such as the change in the relationship to the reading public and in manners of reading. Again, such an emphasis may privilege one line of inquiry over another. In the case of Meredith, it would appear to invite us to look at the topic of cultural coding. This would prove to be an especially fertile ground in his fiction, for in works such as *The Egoist* the frequently obscure, often involuted discourse seems to reveal the inability of a character to define himself except in modes of signification that have been detached from what they once signified. This is particularly the case with Willoughby Patterne, whose self-definition is confounded by the emptiness of the codes for gender and class that he haplessly tries to enact. Similarly, the darkness "at the heart" of Willoughby may be more attributable to the failure of these codes than to any deep-seated psychological characteristic. Meredith's insistence on foregrounding obscurity in matrices of social interchange and conversation, and in elliptical dialogues among his multiple narrative personae, casts the issue of obscurity into the sphere of the cultural and ideological, rather than into the subjective and psychological. A pure separation of those spheres is impossible, of course, but the emphasis can still be noted—we can see *where* we are invited to engage in interpretation.

On such a level of interpretation, we would also seem to be induced to consider the role of the new media consciousness in self-definition and communication. Indeed, many of Meredith's novels, such as *Diana of the Crossways*, engage us directly with the effect of media. White alludes to changes in the media, but does not treat it as a major factor. Patrick Brantlinger, in *Bread and Circuses: Theories of Mass Culture as Social*

Decay,[22] shows us that we must integrate our interpretation of the great works of nineteenth-century English literature with studies of mass culture, if we are to approach anything like a full understanding of them. Brantlinger's study of a central operating mythology of Western civilization—"the 'negative classicism,' according to which the more a society comes to depend on 'mass culture,' the more it falls into a pattern of 'decline and fall' once traced by Rome and perhaps by other extinct civilizations"—generates a rich variety of implications. With respect to White's findings about the growth of symptomatic reading, Brantlinger's discussion of Jürgen Habermas's suggestion that the mass media tends to privatize public concerns adds an ominous dimension. The inclination in mass media—as part of its program of lowering the level of discourse, and, of course, of selling consumer goods—to transform politics into items of social psychology or individual "style" or impulse, serves the purpose of depoliticizing events. This process potentially trivializes issues such as cultural development, or social conflicts between the classes, or failures of institutions, by absorbing them into categories of personal response—deviant behavior, private struggles, even sexuality. Think back to Dickens' inclination to transpose many larger social problems into personal, even familial ones; in this perspective, literature acquires a potency we may not have gauged. Similarly, the reflexiveness of the media consciousness—always adapting, playing with its own material, parodying itself—finds an analogue in Meredith's method of representation, suggesting a further connection between his complexly involuted prose and changes in middle-class cultural consciousness. And the arbitrary shifting of meaning, characteristic of a media expression that celebrates the "new" and the fashionable, and that inflates the value of products and ways of living, generates a highly unstable and arbitrary cultural milieu, one that is susceptible to devious misrepresentations and manipulations of power.

Bread and Circuses traces the mythology and critiques of mass culture through a long historical course to the present, but its chapter on nineteenth century themes of decadence, masses, and imperialism reveals a complex of interacting motifs. Brantlinger describes how bohemian and then decadent artists, in their effort to shock the bourgeoisie into an awareness of its materialism and soullessness, incorporated reified bourgeois representational techniques—lapidary imagery, overly determined description, nerveless narration. He stresses the importance of Malthus's notion of a redundant population of the unemployed poor as a central image in nineteenth-century social thought. He traces the patterns of imperialist thought and propaganda in its volatile sensationalizing of barbarianism and its cynical exciting of lower- and middle-class audiences. He analyzes the crucial significance of work on crowd psychology by Gustave Le Bon and Sigmund Freud. The interaction of all these factors expands the cultural and psychological implications not only of decadence, but of concepts such as Nietzsche's *ressentiment*, a pattern of thinking and behavior that Jameson considers to be of great significance. Nietzsche believed that this "slave mentality" infected modern bourgeois consciousness, and Jameson argues that it has an enervating effect on declassé intellectuals such as George Gissing, even as they use a variation of it— philanthropy—as an organizing representational strategy in dealing with the urban poor. In Brantlinger's hands the concept, tied as it is to Christian mythology, forms part of a pervasive manner of regarding culture in Western Europe—one that is difficult to disengage from his other elements.

The broad perspective that Brantlinger employs has the benefit of highlighting grand cultural assumptions, specifically one that is central to Marxist and post-Marxist thought: the belief in a "fall" from a more harmonious community of the pre-industrial past. So fundamental is this to the thinking of Georg Lukacs and also of Jameson that it situates much of their interpretation of individual literary works. Brantlinger's book does not necessarily "invalidate" that reading of modern cultural change, but it allows us to approach the study of literature and society from a different angle, from consideration of patterns of belief and social myth that have a long heritage. Finally, *Bread and Circuses* serves another salutory purpose in social/literary criticism by reengaging the theorists of the Frankfurt School (Theodor Adorno, Herbert Marcuse, Max Horkheimer, and Walter Benjamin) in our investigations. They were never far away, for Williams, Eagleton, Jameson, and John Berger all reflect indebtedness to them,[23] but it is clear that their writing will play a major role in literature and society criticism. The critical approach that we have been dealing with has the virtue of particular relevance to contemporary life, as Brantlinger's observations on the 1960s and '70s and on television make clear. Nothing is more important to teach than an awareness of culture and its representations when one is in the midst of a society that manipulates vestigial ideological traces through media, political propaganda, and social pressure as our society does. The Frankfurt School theorists provide us with methodological and theoretical bridges back to re-examinations of the development of those ideologies in the nineteenth century.

Another such bridge, obviously, is feminist studies. The convergence that I described—of new historiographical formulations and of increasing literary interest in symbolic representations of ideology—corresponds with the growth of interest in the social position of women and their modes of expression within a dominantly masculine social order. If we are to recuperate a women's subculture of the nineteenth century, then we must devise a critical approach that provides for the comprehension and analysis of ideology and that allows us to register the inhibited, repressed, or deflected expression. Mary Poovey, in *The Proper Lady and the Woman Writer: Ideology as Style in the Works of Mary Wollstonecraft, Mary Shelley, and Jane Austen*, observes that ideological readings are necessary because gender roles are part of familial, political, social, and economic relationships, and that the values formed in women by these relationships are internalized so as to delimit the very way in which one conceptualizes feminity and self. Ideology, she contends, is inescapable, "for simply by living together, men and women establish priorities among their needs and desires and generate explanations that ratify these priorities by making them seem 'natural.' In this respect, despite its inevitable kinship with power, ideology *enables* ideas and actions; it *delimits* responses, not just in the sense of establishing boundaries but in terms of defining territories."[24] Like Jameson, she treats literature as a symbolic representation, and believes that social and self-determining contradictions are reproduced in literary texts, which represent their authors' attempts to resolve them imaginatively.

Poovey reconstructs the matrix of beliefs and codes of behavior that constituted propriety in women at the end of the eighteenth and the beginning of the nineteenth centuries. It is an evolving construct that is fraught with inconsistencies and accommodations. Thus even innocence of behavior might be characterized as a lure to men, even modesty of demeanor might be a misrepresentation, so that all modes of surface behavior were subject to ambiguous readings and had to be reinterpreted through conduct and through reputation. At the very time of the rise in individualism in England, women were expected to use their force of individual character to exercise self-control. The changes in economic configurations in the eighteenth century made daughters more important—they were the means by which a wealthy capitalist or merchant might achieve social status, and by which a financially straitened aristocrat or member of the gentry might refinance his estates—but it also put them under stricter constraints as to chastity and choice of partner. The social flux engendered by the French Revolution appeared to have produced less rather than more freedom for women, as a backlash of alarm opened the way for nineteenth-century repression. Such a web of conflicts and ironic reversals produced a female subculture of highly ambiguous coding, which could often express itself only through indirection or a process of assertion and denial.

Poovey analyzes Mary Shelley's *Frankenstein* as such an expression. Constantly having to modulate what she deemed an assertive and often self-dramatizing persona, Mary Shelley found herself creating, in a sense, her own projective monsters, and then having to disengage herself from them. Poovey interprets Frankenstein's story as an expression of Shelley's own projection of herself imaginatively as a writer. But instead of adhering to the Romantic belief that one defines oneself through imaginative projections that are responded to by a benevolent natural world, Mary Shelley saw imagination as an egoistic assertion, received by a natural environment that she paints in forbiddingly bleak, arctic scenes. Consequently, in the revisions to the novel in 1831, Shelley looks back in uneasiness if not dismay at the dimensions of this impropriety, and mystifies the process in language of determinism and indirection, as well as remarking with wonder in the 1831 Preface how she "then a young girl, came to think of and dilate upon so very hideous an idea." Perhaps dimly conscious that Frankenstein's creation of the monster acted out a desire figuratively to murder his family, and certainly uncomfortable over the role of a female public artist in a culture that disapproves of such a thing, Shelley began processes of dissembling that account for the restrained nature of her later writing.

My brief summary of Poovey's more complex analysis allows us to see how well certain lines of feminist criticism fit in with "literature and society" approaches. It can, indeed, be argued that the potential for the kind of ideological interpretation that I have been describing is attributable in part to the contributions that women's studies have made. Feminist readings of eighteenth- and nineteenth-century English novels have attuned us to ambivalences and nuances that we could not otherwise have detected, they have opened up strategies for the understanding of ideological expression, and they have given us perspectives on dominant-subservient relationships that would otherwise have eluded us. But as Poovey's study indicates, their greatest contribution may be the angle of subjectivity that they have defined. Her sensitivity to the deflection of subjective desires and fears in Shelley's writing establishes a set of overlapping lenses that permit us to shift subtly between associated interpretations. Her essentially symptomatic reading of Shelley's complex attitude toward imaginative projection and self-assertion relates in a psychologically illuminating manner to the more familiar reading of the novel as a tale of arrogation of scientific knowledge when science is ambivalently regarded and imperfectly understood. It relates to Ellen Moers's reading of *Frankenstein* as birth trauma. It relates to a reading that argues that there never was a monster, that Frankenstein has repressed his perverse past of incestuous desires, oedipal conflict, and murder, through a pathological lie. It probably relates to a reading that stresses the issues of education and nurturing that are, as Poovey notes, so crucial to female self-definition in this time. The relationships occur because the desires and anxieties that such readings reflect are all interconnected in a woman in Shelley's position: ambivalence about self-assertion attunes her in such a particularly sensitive way that she alone is able to create the great prototypical work of scientific arrogation; as a woman, the imagery of birth and the anxieties about self-cultivation are integral to any expressive composition; as a denied and repressed daughter and wife, she is conscious of the fantasms of incest, the oedipal, the sadomasochistic. By centralizing subjectivity, feminist criticism causes us to move through this series of closely calibrated lenses.

Poovey's reading of *Frankenstein* may also point up the limitations of such a subjective orientation in interpretation, for it does not seem to account for the phenomenon of the book itself—its particular cultural power. Few books have caught the imagination, have become so much a part of our language, as *Frankenstein*. Its impact suggests that it touches broad cultural concerns, not only about science, but about the "sublime" (there is a highly overdetermined treatment of the aesthetic in the novel), about civilization and primitivism, and about male self-definition (Frankenstein is, after all, a man, and the evocation of manly adventure and exploration resounds through the tale). In order to accommodate such dimensions we may have to pitch our interpretation into those other, broader spheres that Jameson elaborates, although Poovey has tried to incorporate aspects of ideology, and the introduction of the element of class conflict does not seem to be immediately generative. These are, I suspect, methodological questions in literature and society criticism that still have to be addressed.

Such methodological sophistication remains as the primary business of literature and society criticism. Oddly enough, though, the first order of business may be to reorient our teaching and writing. Too often in class we all revert to talking about history and politics and social materials as "background" to reading the literary text, and this is a habit difficult to shed. Similarly, there is an inclination to divide up books of literature and society analysis into an introductory chapter setting out "the social milieu" and then a series of intensive readings of individual texts, creating a division and abstraction of the "subtext" from its representation. But assuming we can gradually overcome these bad habits and procedures, then the way is open for a critical practice that will redetermine our reading of nineteenth-century fiction, align our study with exciting new research and theory in history and the social sciences, give the study of English culture a new "relevance" for our students, and "keep the faith" that most of us have had in socially situated interpretation of the nineteenth-century English novel.

NOTES

I want to acknowledge the important contributions that have been made to this review essay by two members of Brown University's Program in Modern Literature and Society, Sara Holbrook, to whom I am greatly indebted for reviewing and analyzing these and other recent books in the field, and Katharine McCullough, who identified most of the texts under consideration. I also wish to thank David Cody for his helpful analyses.

1. (Cambridge, Mass.: Harvard University Press, 1983), p. 26.
2. (Oxford: Basil Blackwell Publisher Limited, 1983). See also his *Criticism and Ideology* (London: New Left Books, 1976).
3. *Metahistory: The Historical Imagination in Nineteenth-Century Europe* (Baltimore, Md.: The Johns Hopkins University Press, 1973). See also his *Tropics of Discourse* (Baltimore, Md.: The Johns Hopkins University Press, 1978).
4. *Rethinking Intellectual History: Texts, Contexts, Language* (Ithaca, N. Y.: Cornell University Press, 1983). See also Dominick LaCapra and Steven L. Kaplan, eds., *Modern European Intellectual History: Reappraisals and New Perspectives* (Ithaca, N. Y.: Cornell University Press, 1982).
5. *Orientalism* (New York: Pantheon Books, 1978).
6. *The Country and the City* (New York: Oxford University Press, 1973). See also Williams's *The Long Revolution* (London: Chatto & Windus, 1961); *Marxism and Literature* (Oxford: Oxford University Press, 1977); and *The Sociology of Culture* (New York: Schocken Books, 1982). For further reflections on his works, see *Raymond Williams, Politics and Letters: Interviews with New Left Review* (London: New Left Books, 1979).
7. *Literary Theory*, p. 210.
8. Full Title: *Commissioned Spirits: The Shaping of Social Motion in Dickens, Carlyle, Melville, and Hawthorne* (New Brunswick, N. J.: Rutgers University Press, 1979).
9. *Dombey and Son* (1848), ed. Alan Horsman (Oxford: The Clarendon Press, 1974), pp. 275–277.
10. (Ithaca, N. Y.: Cornell University Press, 1981).
11. *The Political Unconscious: Narrative as a Socially Symbolic Act* (Ithaca, N. Y.: Cornell University Press, 1981), pp. 81–82.
12. Webb, p. 86.
13. Webb, p. 99.
14. (Cambridge: Cambridge University Press, 1981).
15. Jameson, p. 162.

16. *Literary Theory*, p. 210.
17. "Social Criticism in Dickens: Some Problems of Method and Approach," *Critical Quarterly*, 6 (1964), 221.
18. P. 132.
19. (London: Routledge & Kegan Paul, 1981).
20. White, pp. 18 and 24.
21. See Peter Brooks, *Reading for the Plot* (New York: Knopf, 1984).
22. (Ithaca, N. Y.: Cornell University Press, 1983).
23. The Berger book is *Ways of Seeing* (London: British Broadcasting Corporation and Penguin Books, 1972). The Jameson work that most extensively discusses Frankfurt School figures is *Marxism and Form: Twentieth-Century Dialectical Theories of Literature* (Princeton, N. J.: Princeton University Press, 1971), and the Eagleton book I have in mind is *Walter Benjamin or Towards a Revolutionary Criticism* (London: Verso Editions and New Left Books, 1981). For an introduction to the Frankfurt School, see Martin Jay, *The Dialectical Imagination: A History of the Frankfurt School and the Institute of Social Research, 1923–1950* (Boston: Little, Brown and Company, 1973).
24. (Chicago, Ill.: University of Chicago Press, 1984), pp. xi–xiv.

Recent Dickens Studies: 1983

Richard J. Dunn

Commentary and scholarship on Dickens during 1983 continued at a rapid pace, with important new editions, new biographical study, consideration of Dickens within more general examination of Victorian literature and of the novel, several collections of essays on Dickens, and a concentration on *Bleak House*, *A Tale of Two Cities*, and *Great Expectations*. Three books particularly focus on a long-neglected topic, Dickens and women, and I give these studies detailed attention in my final pages. Because it is necessary to make comparisons and to consider some of the 1983 work in different contexts, I am providing at the end of this essay a list of the full titles for all the studies I mention.

EDITIONS

For new Dickens editions, Cohn's and Collins's *Dickens Studies Newsletter* checklists provide a full listing; I shall comment only on the World's Classics editions Robert Patten was unable to include in his 1982 review, on Irving Howe's preface to *Oliver Twist*, and on Angus Wilson's edition, *The Portable Dickens*.

The World's Classics *Oliver Twist* (ed. Kathleen Tillotson), *Dombey* (ed. Alan Horsman), *Little Dorrit* (ed. H. P. Sucksmith), and *Edwin Drood* (ed. Margaret Cardwell) adapt the Clarendon editions to inexpensive paperback texts. Each offers a new and exceptionally informative introduction and a Dickens chronology, and each provides explanatory notes that were not in the Clarendon editions. Number plans are appended where available, and Tillotson's *Oliver Twist* reprints her useful glossary of thieves' cant. Absent from the paperback editions are the Clarendon textual apparatus, some of the appendices, and the bulk of the illustrations (each has only eight). The one objection I have to these editions is that their print seems cramped because the forty-four line page of the larger Clarendon is reproduced on the smaller page with its darker paper (*Little Dorrit*, for example, runs some 190 fewer pages than in the Penguin paperback). Compared with the Penguin editions with which they will surely be competitive, the World's Classics have more concise introductions, less expansive but often more lucid notes, but fewer illustrations. Each of the introductions attends particularly to the inception, contemporary context, and reception of the work, reminding us of the uncommon achievements of Dickens even as he attended to such contemporary matters as the Poor Law, the coming of the railroad, the Crimea.

Irving Howe's "*Oliver Twist*: The Spell of Fagin" in *The New Republic* is announced as the introduction to a Bantam paperback, but no such edition appeared in 1983. Howe sees Dickens the entertainer and Dickens the social critic as shadowing each other, and he mentions "a deep split between what Dickens the writer shows and what his mind imposes on his concluding pages." But in the portrayal of the forceful Fagin and of a London with a "distinct tone of diffuse anxiety," Howe sees signs of the later Dickens. *Oliver Twist* is for him a story of "moral rage."

For his edition of *The Portable Dickens*, Angus Wilson has written a lengthy introduction which stresses the importance of Dickens' childhood experiences, reminding us "that biography must play a central part in Dickensian criticism." Because *The Portable Dickens* includes the whole of *Great Expectations* Wilson has much to say about that novel in his introduction, and he regards it foremost in "power to persuade the reader to accept a mixture of exact social observation and wild fantasy as a credible world." In passing mention of other works he makes two observations I do not recall him making in his many previous writings about Dickens. He suggests that the concept of Steerforth as David Copperfield's "bad angel" originated in Dickens' memory of James Lamert, who introduced the child Dickens to the blacking factory. And despite the general absence of the sensuous in Dickens' fiction, Wilson notes the exceptional scene in *Bleak House* when Bucket arrests the murderess. Wilson's is the novelist's Dickens, and he respects him as the genius for whom "any academic idea of an artistic ideal" makes little sense. Wilson's otherwise excellent chronology of Dickens' career inadvertently omits mention of *Little Dorrit* but combines an outline of the life with a listing of the works. The front matter and *Great Expectations* occupy all but 234 of this book's 772 pages, and Wilson's brief excerpts from novels, stories, speeches, and letters cover fifteen topics, such as London, Prisons, Childhood, Theater, Dickens the Traveler, and The Black Side of the Imagination.

A student coming to Dickens first through *The Portable Dickens* not only will find Wilson a reverent guide but will gain an immediate sense of the magnitude of Dickens' interests and talents.

ADAPTATIONS

"Nicholas Nickleby," an adaptation from London stage to television, appeared in 1983, and the *DSN* checklist traces responses to its reception. As a further commentary on the London stage version, Robert Giddings's collection of Dickens essays includes David Edgar's "Adapting *Nickleby*," especially useful as a complement to Leon Rubin's *The Nicholas Nickleby Story* (1981). As Edgar says, Dickens in *Nickleby* was not merely distressed over the current state of things but was "also expressing not just a hope but a conviction that things could be different." Edgar's impression that the adaptation was as much about Dickens as about his novel may help explain the phenomenal success of the Royal Shakespeare production.

For consideration of Dickens' own adaptations as public reader, David Ponting's essay, mentioned under "Biography," is useful.

Mike Poole's "Dickens and Film: 101 Uses of a Dead Author," in the Giddings collection, is a brief discussion of the treatment of Dickens by film and television, which in Poole's opinion too frequently avoid social and historical matters most central to the novels.

In *Dickens Studies Annual*, volume 12, H. Philip Bolton makes a hand list of *Bleak House* stage adaptations, and I again mention Bolton's work among separate Dickens studies.

BIOGRAPHICAL DICTIONARY ENTRIES

Philip Collins's entry on Dickens in *Makers of Nineteenth Century Culture* (ed. Justin Wintle) merits mention because, besides the basic information essential for a biographical dictionary, it provides a brief definition of the relation of Dickens' fiction to his time. Collins stresses the literary quality of Dickens' work and mentions Dickens' peripheral place in the Benthamite tradition but reminds us that Dickens' significance was not primarily political. Nonetheless, Collins grants that in most of the novels contemporary political or social issues are prominent subjects. Although reformist in much of his thinking, Dickens remained, in Collins's view, "conservative or retrograde"

on "the Woman Question," a view generally compatible with Michael
Slater's in *Dickens and Women*.

It is good to see biographical dictionary articles by such eminent Dickens
scholars as Philip Collins. In this respect 1983 was a banner year, because
George Ford's "Charles Dickens" also appeared in Ira B. Nadel's and
William E. Fredeman's *Victorian Novelists Before 1885*. In the generous
twenty-five page entry Ford outlines the "success story" of Dickens' life,
including such specific information as a comparison of his earnings with those
of Thackeray (Dickens received £11,000 for a novel in the 1850s; Thackeray
only £600), but he is careful to locate among childhood and adolescent sources
the "specter of insecurity that was never to disappear" from Dickens' life.
Ford comments on each of the major works, includes quotations from some
reviews, mentions the major modern Dickens criticism. The one omission I
regret from Ford's selective bibliography is notice of the *DSN*, *DSA*, and
Dickensian. Ford's excellently written and illustrated article is simply the best
brief overview of Dickens' life and writing I have encountered. The entire
volume is useful for information about Dickens' contemporaries, and its
appendices include a number of contemporary documents pertaining to fiction—of interest to Dickensians will be Anthony Trollope's article, "The
Works of Charles Dickens."

BIOGRAPHY

The year's major contribution to Dickens biography is Slater's *Dickens and
Women*, which with Phyllis Rose's *Parallel Lives* I shall discuss in more detail
at the end of this essay. David Paroissien well documents Dickens' ideas about
his own and other art to show that his view of literature corresponds closely
with his more general social and political ideas. Paroissien's is the first essay
in Robert Giddings's *The Changing World of Charles Dickens* and is one of
the better parts of an uneven collection. In the same collection, David Ponting
comments upon Dickens as public reader, suggesting that the reading career
was less destructive, even less distracting, than it has been regarded by many
biographers. In *Convivial Dickens: The Drinks of Dickens and His Time*,
Edward W. Hewett and W. F. Axton provide the libatory formulas to assure
continuing conviviality of Dickensians but they also note several volatile
ingredients of Dickens biography. Their Dickens, unlike the writer sometimes
denounced by the nineteenth-century Americans whose cocktails so amused
him, was a temperate man for whom the punch bowl was a theatrical occasion.

But as Hewett and Axton note in "Pickwick, Principle, and Punch," this was "a Man's World unabashed." They may, especially when we take into account the more serious considerations of Dickens and women, overstate the situation by further declaring that male world's punch bowl as "the Female Principle, Source and symbol of life."

Dickens biography often may be illuminated by studies of Dickens' friends and associates, and I looked forward to learning more about the Dickens-Forster relationship from James A. Davies's critical biography of John Forster. Although Davies gives us ready reference to the amazing range of Forster's literary activities and friendships (especially with Hunt, Lamb, Bulwer, Macready, and Carlyle, as well as Dickens), there is no new view of the Dickens-Forster connection. In a year which brought forth several discussions of Dickens and his wife, I had hoped the Davies book would have something to say about Forster's role at the time of the separation, but (perhaps because Davies focuses on the literary Forster or because he has no new information) there is no mention of Forster's representation of Dickens in negotiations with Catherine. Davies is helpful in detailing the basis for Dickens' well known caricature of his friend as Podsnap, and he reminds us of the ultimate irony, Forster's apparently unknowing praise of Podsnap as one of the few successes in *Our Mutual Friend*.

The obvious biographical importance of psychologically oriented criticism and of studies interested in Dickens' autobiographical fictions should be apparent in my subsequent consideration of work by Albert D. Hutter, Jack Rawlins, and Avrom Fleishman.

DICKENS IN HIS TIME

The focus of considerable scholarly interest on Dickens and women and on such works as *Bleak House*, *A Tale of Two Cities*, *Great Expectations*, and *Our Mutual Friend* implicitly concerns many questions of Dickens and society, but 1983 studies which turn more explicitly to these matters are disappointing even though two titles—Laurence Lerner's *The Literary Imagination: Essays on Literature and Society*, and Giddings's *The Changing World of Charles Dickens*—seem to promise a focus on Dickens and his times.

Lerner's book is a collection of his lectures, and his attention to Dickens is slight. His chapter on the bourgeois imagination mentions Dickens as a writer with the opinions of a reformer "but the imagination of despair," and he acknowledges a conflict between novelistic convention and social awareness.

Lerner's preference for what he calls "human content" and an inexcusable number of typographical errors tax the patience of anyone looking for a cleanly expressed and commanding argument.

In the introduction to his collection, Robert Giddings realizes Dickens was greatly affected by the changing social structure, and he insists "the point is not so much Dickens's effect on history as history's effect on Dickens." Fair enough; here would seem a germ for a more substantial introductory argument and a more unified collection of essays than Giddings supplies. Neither he nor his contributors systematically pursues the question of Dickens and the changing times, although Thomas J. Rice's essay "The Politics of *Barnaby Rudge*" does directly examine Dickens' view of some particular contemporary events. Rice shows the analogues between events of the 1840s and details of the Gordon Riots. His point is that *Barnaby Rudge* was a response to the possible alliance between the extremist factions of militant chartists and anti-Catholic ultra-Tories.

In "Blackmail Studies in *Martin Chuzzlewit* and *Bleak House*" (*DSA*, 11), Alexander Welsh draws upon legal history to show blackmail to be a nineteenth-century creation, and shows that Dickens' use of the idea of blackmail in these works was in advance of most treatments of the subject in English fiction. Welsh notes "one very real reason for blackmail and the fear of blackmail, real or imagined, in Victorian times: namely, the mobility of the population, particularly upward mobility, and the sensitivity to class origins." Welsh shows Dickens using "the symbiosis of blackmailer and blackmailed to evidence psychological guilt," and he points out that Lady Dedlock's "guilt with respect to her feeling about Tulkinghorn is strictly psychological." This assessment makes a great deal more sense to me than Baruch Hochman's analysis of Lady Dedlock's "subterranean" relationship with her past (see below).

DICKENS AND THE NOVEL

Robert Patten last year observed that it is no longer possible to exclude Dickens from The Great Tradition even as we find his enormously varied work essential for testing any proposition about the novel as a genre. One of the major 1983 studies of the novel is Martin Price's *Forms of Life*, whose subtitle *Character and Moral Imagination in the Novel* identifies its Great Tradition viewpoint. After three more general chapters on fiction, Price's chapter "Dickens: Selves and Systems" accompanies separate considerations of

Austen, Stendhal, George Eliot, Tolstoy, James, Conrad, Lawrence, and Forster, and a concluding examination of "The Beauty of Mortal Conditions: Joyce, Woolf, Mann." In an era of many slight books and of irritatingly occasional collections and reprints, Price's is a welcome big book. Price finds in Dickens "the confident artifice of a writer who trusts his readers to make the appropriate response." In the line of Leavis and Trilling, Price regards the novel as the vehicle for the moral imagination, shaping, condensing, clarifying, and intensifying experience "so that meaning or its absence or its ambiguity is not only more easily attained, but its attainment is the end of the experience the novel provides." Price, like many other current readers of Dickens, comments on the women characters of the later novels, whom he sees particularly imprisoned in an inauthentic social system. Unsurprisingly, *Little Dorrit* is a primary text for Price, and he differs from Trilling's reading of Amy Dorrit as symbolic child by arguing for her psychological reality, because for him she remains faithful in memory to the past.

Price examines forms of passive assent by a number of Dickens characters who find ambitions and fantasies realized and cultivated by the social system. He notes that characters who seem most Dickensian "are those who are at once most free and most compulsive"—Pecksniff exists solely for the occasion to produce anew his fictional self, but Dickens himself, in Price's view, differs from Pecksniff because he is the master of his fictions. Price thus insists that Dickens had something of Bentham's "scorn for the fictions by which men enslave themselves, but he has sympathy for the needs, whether real or imaginary, which they fulfill." This is a reasonable position to maintain when examining various characters who as creatures of the dehumanized society sacrifice "fullness and balance to dominant passions and prepossessions." Energies of self in the Dickens character are both expressive and repressive, calculated and instinctive, although I suspect the energies of Dickens himself were less free than Price argues; to the end of his writing Dickens remained compulsive. The difference between him and a Pecksniff or Sairey Gamp was that his ambitions and motives remained more masked. To this extent Dickens was free of the social structures he so thoroughly castigates, but, as Price well shows, the question remains of just what his moral imagination puts in place of that society. According to Price, the moral imagination may be gauged by the degree to which the novelist "recognizes the complexities of decision or action or inaction and the effort or release involved in solving or ignoring or evading problems." So far as that recognition serves as a function of Dickens' presentation of character, his is indeed a moral imagination we can measure with some precision; so far as it is similarly easy to describe the ambiguities of Dickens himself as independent of these creations, the case seems less clear.

Coincidence of publication date occasions some arbitrary comparative review essay groupings, and my linking of George Anastaplo's discussion of Dickens with that by Martin Price therefore could imply a trend back through Trilling toward rediscovery of the Dickens Leavis at first so grudgingly appended to the Great Tradition. In *The Artist as Thinker: From Shakespeare to Joyce*, Anastaplo declares his major interest to be in the relationship between literature and moral judgment. His Dickens chapter centers on *A Christmas Carol*, and although it argues that the sin of avarice is the effort to fence oneself off from death and also from the offsetting virtue of liberality, the essay (published earlier in *Interpretation*) does little more than remind us of the very obvious moral focus in Dickens' most famous Christmas book.

Two other more general studies of the English novel—Baruch Hochman's and Elizabeth Ermarth's—give Dickens considerable attention. Hochman's *The Test of Character: From the Victorian Novel to the Modern* examines the Victorian novel as the victim of its own impulses, dispersing "energies that might have inhabited and informed the characters . . . into the organizing literary fabric of the novel." Therefore the chapter on Dickens bears the apt title "Deadlocked Maternity: The Subtext of *Bleak House* and the Problem of Dickens's Last Novels." Hochman stresses the "vital though subterranean" relationship between Lady Dedlock and her past and thinks the book does not satisfactorily explain the persisting vitality of her suppressed love. And this is the point he carries forward to later Dickens: "until his very last novels, Dickens does not even try to build an action around characters who are either naturalistically motivated or capable of grasping the nature of their experience." As a number of other studies of Esther Summerson, Arthur Clennam, even of Pip, indicate, Hochman's point is arguable. When he declares that "questions of how and why people emerge into fullness of being, feeling, consciousness, or relationship do not seem to concern him," Hochman is more concerned with the directness of such questions as expressed through characters' self-consciousness than with granting such questions as those which *are* central to *David Copperfield* and *Great Expectations* especially. Hochman holds that *Great Expectations* and *Our Mutual Friend* were marred by their "protagonists who approximate the patterns of confrontation and growth that were more or less normative for the realistic novel." That Dickens is not George Eliot (the subject of Hochman's following chapter) we may grant, and also that the Dickens world is one largely impermeable to human will, one where the hero's will and consciousness cannot be mobilized for effect. But we need not therefore come to the conclusion that Dickens' novels are seriously flawed.

Elizabeth Ermarth's *Realism and Consensus in the English Novel* is an important study which relates particular attention to Dickens well to her larger study of English fiction. She ranges farther than Hochman and writes more persuasively, recognizing as does he the importance of such repressed characters as Lady Dedlock. Earlier I regretted the absence of much direct commentary on Dickens and his times, but one of the effects of Ermarth's achievement is that it turns my attention to the more problematic matter of realistic representation (a principal accomplishment also of David Miller in a *Bleak House* essay I will treat separately). Ermarth, as do numerous Dickens critics, finds not simply individual characters but the entire fictional world unintelligible. Thus Dickens characters tend either to incorporate or rebel against their society. As she remarks, the self-splitting between private and public character fosters not only idiosyncracy but self-multiplication through role playing by the character and self-duplication by the novelist's analogical and duplicative characterization. Ermarth defines the Dickens narrator as a "mediating Nobody of realism" and praises the narration of *Little Dorrit* and *Our Mutual Friend*, where narrative distancing permits Dickens to present the values of history and memory as the basis for social and personal definition. The "consensus" for Ermarth is "agreement between various viewpoints made available by a text," and she points out that because it calls attention to the act of rationalization, "this realistic consensus is . . . a profoundly self-reflexive device." Dickens, by this reading, frequently experiments with the problems of consensus and community; *Bleak House* "brings to the forefront the problem of consensus in time, separating the two functions that ordinarily work together in realism, overview and recollection."

Although Ermarth rightly credits the effective Dickens narrator with assuming identities of various characters and leaving the reader the task of coordinating a variety of roles, and although I think she is correct in defining tensions between centripetal and centrifugal energies, I am bothered by her assertion that "Dickens understood intuitively and from the beginning . . . the systematic nature of his own realism." Whether we find it as systematic or Dickens as self-aware as she suggests, Ermarth's application of ideas about realism and consensus to *Our Mutual Friend* remains effective. The problem she finds the novel most persistently addressing is one of maintaining an independent consciousness as various characters—Harmon, Wrayburn, the Boffins, Lizzie—function as the narrator alone had functioned in earlier novels. This results in a more affirmative reading than usual for *Our*

Mutual Friend because Ermarth regards the novel as a demonstration of individual identity salvaged from circumstance. Cautious in most of her claims about Dickens' realistic self-consciousness, excellent in demonstrating the relationship between realistic narration and characterization, Ermarth like Martin Price connects form with life, and in her opening three chapters makes many analogies with painting, geometry, and history. While we may wonder just how self-reflexive or how intuitively realistic Dickens may have been, as critics we certainly may accept Ermarth's argument that realistic art is systematic:

> The realist does not imply that the object *has* no reality apart from its aspects; the squares of the parquet floor are square regardless of viewpoint, and the existence of the invariant form is what makes possible the rational perception of identity through difference in the first place. The realist says that the object can be grasped in any one instance only in aspect, and that fuller apprehension depends on the reductive comparisons made from a series of instances. What the spectator perceives, then, are not discrete objects "like" objects in experience, but a system of relationships. By showing sight rationalized in painting, or consciousness rationalized in the novel, the realistic work mimes the act of system-making. What is represented is the act of representation itself.

So based for her extensive study of Defoe and Richardson, Austen, George Eliot, and Henry James as well as of Dickens, Ermarth can look keenly at the common activities of Dickens narrators and characters who share the search for continuity and meaning in the face of social and moral fragmentation. She concludes that an overview independent of particular cases was an impossible goal because of Dickens' "insistent holism." Therefore, if we follow Ermarth's logic a step further, we may accept *Our Mutual Friend* as a powerful statement but may wonder just where Dickens actually stood in his postscriptural assurance that he was well aware of what he had been doing in this novel.

SEPARATE STUDIES

Although it was published late in 1982, *Charles Dickens: New Perspectives*, edited by Wendell Stacy Johnson, did not appear in time for Robert Patten to include it in his review of that year's work, but because so few of its reprinted works present genuinely new perspectives, I do not have a great deal to say about the collection. Except for Gerald Coniff's "The Prison of This Lower World" and Richard Barickman's "The Subversive Methods of

Dickens' Early Fiction: *Martin Chuzzlewit*,'' all the essays are reprints (even Barickman's appeared later in 1983 as part of *Corrupt Relations*). Coniff's short article is a thematic study tracing images of the prison forward in Dickens from *Little Dorrit* and interpreting the prison as evidence "of the human lapse from true humanity in a world where society makes prisons for its people and individuals imprison themselves."

Professor Johnson remarks in his short introduction that "Myth, self-revelation, and reflection upon kinship in the human family" as well as "the very idea of language as mythic expression" are central to criticism of Dickens. This editorial comment suggests Johnson's favoring of far more new or at least of more exploratory work than he in fact includes. Several essays—Robert Colby on Oliver Twist as an unfortunate foundling, Harry Stone on *Dombey and Son* as a Dickens fairy tale, and complementary work by Ruth Vande Kieft and George Levine on communication in *Great Expectations*—appeared first between 1961 and 1967, and the collection's final item is from Edgar Johnson's 1952 biography. That leaves principally Barickman and Coniff as the more recent work, although Johnson does reprint Gordon Hirsch's 1980 psychoanalytic reading of *David Copperfield* as well as Dianne F. Sadoff's "Storytelling and the Figure of the Father in *Little Dorrit*" (1980).

Even a cursory examination of recent work on Dickens or a close reading of Robert Newsom, Sylvia Manning, Sylvère Monod, and Robert Patten on the state of Dickens studies over the past few years (*DSA*, vols. 9, 10, 11, 12) should bring a chorus of protest to Johnson's collection as falling short of the Prentice-Hall Twentieth Century Views commitment "to present the best in contemporary critical opinion on major authors, providing a twentieth century perspective on their changing status in an era of profound reevaluation." As Patten remarked of 1982 Dickens studies, many critics "synthesize in different mixtures post-war European theory and apply those perspectives thoroughly and unflinchingly to Dickens' texts." But apart from Sadoff and Hirsch, and to a lesser extent Barickman, those perspectives are not among Professor Johnson's selections.

"Self-reflexivity" (a term that to me seems inherently redundant) is one of those contemporary critical preoccupations we either share or deplore, but is one we cannot ignore when considering the forms of autobiographical fiction. As are Price's and Ermarth's, Avrom Fleishman's book is a major study of the novel. *Figures of Autobiography: The Language of Self-Writing in Victorian and Modern England* begins with more than a hundred introductory pages discussing earlier autobiographical writing and also structuring a critical theory of it, even as Fleishman grants the absence of "agreed norms for a genre of autobiography.'' The chapter on Dickens, ''*David Copperfield*: Experiments in Autobiography,'' appeared earlier in George P. Landow's *Approaches to Victorian Autobiography* (Ohio University Press, 1979) but merits reconsideration in the context of Fleishman's extensive study. He treats David as the synthetic image of Dickens the ultimate autobiographer, and recognizes the composite formed by David's ''self-indulgent sense of his past and interwoven awareness of himself as an accomplished author who has outstripped his dreary origins.''

The majority of essays on individual works in 1983 concerned the later novels, but Juliet McMaster's ''Visual Design in *Pickwick Papers*'' is a welcome exception. She reminds us that Dickens is a highly visual writer and she finds him ''particularly generous to the eye'' in his first novel. As have Robert Patten and Michael Steig, McMaster stresses visual contrast as Dickens' icon for ''a moral and physical complementarity,'' and she details especially the novel's repeated attention to fat and thin forms.

Besides the new introductions by Kathleen Tillotson and Irving Howe, and another note on Fagin's name by Robert Fleissner (*Explicator*, Spring), 1983 brought one longer commentary on *Oliver Twist*—Burton M. Wheeler's ''The Text and Plan of *Oliver Twist*'' (*DSA*, 12). Unable to support Tillotson's contention that *Oliver* may have had its beginnings as early as 1833, Wheeler traces the origins and compositional history, paying particular attention to deletions Dickens made for the 1838 edition. Wheeler thinks the deletions contain evidence that Dickens did not think of this work as a novel until sometime after May, 1837 (the month of Mary Hogarth's death) and did not work out his basic plot before October of that year.

David A. Miller's ''Discipline in Different Voices: Bureaucracy, Police, Family, and *Bleak House*'' has my vote as the most stimulating essay on Dickens published in 1983. Appearing in the new journal *Representations*, Miller's study centers on the Court as one of Dickens' carceral institutions in *Bleak House* set in opposition to the domestic institution. Miller shows how ''the novel subtly identifies the reader's demand for closure with a general social need for the police,'' and he finds the book affirming the inadequacy of its closure as it attempts to differentiate ''its own narrative procedures from those of the institutions it portrays.'' Just as did Robert Newsom in *Dickens on the Romantic Side of Familiar Things* (1977), so does Miller respect the reader's uneasiness with this novel. For Newsom that uneasiness had its source in Dickens' sense of the uncanny; for Miller there is the unsettling context of institutions, cultural needs, the book's own work ethic—an ''imposing refusal of rest and enjoyment.''

In one of his many expansive, often enlightening notes, Miller calls *Bleak House* one of the first texts adumbrating the Modernist commonplace "that a literature worthy of the name will respect mystery by keeping it inviolate." Throughout, Miller keeps his critical perspective lucid; against Marxism, he stresses "the positivity of contradiction," and against Deconstruction he urges "that undecidability must always be the undecidability of *something in particular.*" Surely, therefore, although I am hesitant to speak for Jerome Meckier, Miller would not be one of the critics Meckier denounces as "gangsters of literature." In his two-part article "Double Vision Versus Double Logic" Meckier mentions *Bleak House,* especially, as a subject "for the deconstructionist who breaks novels down to irresolvable tensions."

I find John Kucich's "Repression and Representation in Dickens" less lucid than Miller's longer essay, but like Miller he is interested in the oppositions at play in Dickens. Kucich's point is that rather than being a symptom of unresolved conflict, "Dickens's apparent dualism . . . can be recognized as a coherent strategy of representation." In the Dickens hero, violence and repression are congruent parts of the same psychic system. Aware of the abstractness of much of his argument, Kucich examines *Our Mutual Friend* as the most evident demonstration of this "economy." Like David Miller, Kucich attempts new perspective on Dickens, and his work is more provocative than most included in anthologies collecting recent Dickens criticism. Kucich gives us much to think about, sometimes to argue over, but his criticism demands time and work by the reader. At times he is concise and extraordinarily lucid: "Dickens's heroes exemplify the passion of repression, not the repression of passion," he observes, and he well supports this argument. But elsewhere, admitting that this is a subject demanding far more space than his original talk or this paper provided, he restates his complex overview: "What often appears to the modern sensibility as a neurotic deviation from psychic norms is actually a method of representing and recovering, in a general, nonrestrictive economy, the self-transcending consummation we have come to associate conventionally with violent passion."

I have noted Jerome Meckier's impatience with deconstructions of Victorian literature, and in another essay, "Hidden Rivalries in Victorian Fiction: The Case of the Two Esthers" (published in Giddings), Meckier contrasts Esther Summerson with *Felix Holt*'s Esther Lyon. Meckier finds rivalries between—rather than within—Victorian novels providing "a counterpoint that is genre-wide," and he argues that *Felix Holt* is a complete redoing of *Bleak House.* To the consideration of Dickens and George Eliot as realists, Meckier adds the opinion that their "competing realisms are . . . simultaneously competing idealisms.'' The Giddings collection contains one other essay on *Bleak House*, Bert Hornback's ''The Other Portion of *Bleak House*.'' Sportively and incisively, Hornback too has little use for criticism that takes itself too seriously, but his own serious speculation comes in recognitions he shares with all those commentators preoccupied with the repressed life in and of Dickens. The ''other portion'' is the story neither Esther herself nor the narrator has written; her narrative incompetency for Hornback, then, is an incompetency of omission. At issue is not simply the characterization or narrative authority of Esther but the meaning of the novel; as Hornback says, Dickens loads ''the novel with knowings and not knowings, pushing us to make a decision about what it means to know—to know anything—in this world, and the value of such knowledge.''

Unlike Hornback, who speculates about the unwritten story in *Bleak House*, Patrick J. Creevy in ''In Time and Out: The Tempo of Life in *Bleak House*'' (*DSA*, 12) considers the implications of some five hundred references to time. He examines the situations of a number of characters who do not engage themselves in the living present, but is interested primarily in Esther's growing ability ''to live gracefully, in time, and out . . . as she triumphs over her orphan's history.''

The good sense and critical modesty of both Meckier and Hornback make me more wary than perhaps I should be of Christine van Boheemen-Saff's reading of *Bleak House*, '' 'The Universe Makes an Indifferent Parent': *Bleak House* and the Victorian Family Romance.'' Ambitiously she attempts to apply a Darwinistic ''dislodgement of God the Father by Mother Nature . . . to a novel embodying abstractions in the situations and roles of everyday life.'' She treats *Bleak House* not merely as a ''personal nightmare'' of Dickens but as a work seriously and compassionately addressing mid-century human problems. She insists that the form of the Victorian novel represses consciousness of ''a purely biological, nonphallic, nontranscendental notion of human origin.'' In other words, it represses precisely what Esther's illegitimacy represents. And contrary to any suggestion that Bucket is an anomalous or threatening figure of male assertion, van Boheemen-Saff regards him as an embodiment of the nineteenth-century confidence in scientific investigation (in contrast, particularly, to the outmoded masculinity of Tulkinghorn). This essay is most interesting for its psychoanalytic theory of the detective story, a ''least prestigious stepsister of a scientific treatise.'' But the conclusion that in his psychological statement of his age Dickens' ''narrative magic wipes the cobwebs of doubt from the Victorian sky, giving his audience on an unconscious level what it needs to pull through, *the reassuring message of the familiar myth,''* remains for me un-convincing.

Another index to what Dickens in fact gave his audience comes by way of *Bleak House* stage adaptations in its own day and since. In *"Bleak House* and the Playhouse'' (*DSA*, 12), H. Philip Bolton discusses various stage versions and makes a hand list of them. Bolton mentions the uneasiness in the theater over such secularization as Jo's death makes of sacred words. And Janet L. Larson's excellent study, ''The Battle of Biblical Books in Esther's Narra-tive,'' looks closely at *Bleak House* for ''antithetical allusions'' suggestive of the ''broken Scripture'' Larson finds behind much of Dickens' later fiction. Meckier mentions the relevance of the Book of Esther to both Dickens and George Eliot; Larson carefully traces a number of parallels between Dickens' novel and the books of Esther and Job. Citing Victorian biblical commentary, she shows Dickens' interest in the Book of Esther as a subtext for the fairy-tale part of Esther Summerson's story and in Job as a subtext for the tale of her suffering. Larson is persuasive in documenting that for Dickens ''the Bible becomes a paradoxical book: it is at once a source of stability, with its familiar conventions of order, and a loss of hermeneutical instability reflecting the times of religious anxiety in which Dickens wrote.''

No year's work, and few anthologies of criticism today seem to lack a study of dialogic form, and Roger Fowler's ''Polyphony and Problematic in *Hard Times*'' appears in the Giddings collection. Granted, *Hard Times* is a ''poly-phonic'' novel—what Dickens work is not, I wonder—and certainly the story and the language present the ideology in an unsettling way. But as I read Fowler on *Hard Times* I find myself wanting to apply his critical interests to the much larger, more cacophonic *Bleak House* or *Little Dorrit*. The cramping Dickens felt from *Hard Times*'s weekly format limited the range for his voices more than Fowler seems to realize.

Publication of volumes 11 and 12 of the *Dickens Studies Annual* came in 1983, the first of these beginning incorporation of papers from the summer conferences of the Dickens Project at the University of California, Santa Cruz. The topic for 1981 was secrecy in Dickens, and the focal text was *Great Expectations*. I have reviewed these essays more fully for the *Dickens Quarterly* (September, 1984) and shall here avoid repetition. A number of the essays examine personal secrets of Dickens' childhood, and several theoret-ically treat language itself as secretive (see Robert Tracy, ''Reading Dickens' Writing''; Murray Baumgarten, ''Calligraphy and Code: Writing in *Great Expectations*''; John O. Jordan, ''The Medium of *Great Expectations*''; Elliot L. Gilbert, ''In Primal Sympathy: *Great Expectations* and the Secret Life'').

Ranging more widely through Dickens, Robert Newsom distinguishes shame (as distinct from guilt) as a motive force in Dickens' portrayal of heroes from Oliver to Pip. And in a very original study, Albert Hutter examines "Dismemberment and Articulation in *Our Mutual Friend*." At issue is Dickens' and his age's fascinations with both order and disorder, and although he hesitates to regard Dickens as a prototypic connoisseur of chaos, Hutter points out the novelist's uneasiness with plot resolutions that signaled enduring order. More problematically, Garrett Stewart writes at length on "The Secret Life of Death in Dickens," claiming that for Dickens "the drowning mind is the perfect model for agnostic ephiphany."

Whether we regard Pip's story as nightmare or dream vision, bourgeois *Bildungsroman* or love story, Jack P. Rawlins in *SEL* makes a fresh reading in "Great Expiations: Dickens and the Betrayal of the Child." Even without the pun the title is somewhat misleading, because Rawlins is pointing out the fate of the poetic spirit within Dickensian society. That such spirit springs forth in childhood is evident in Dickens, as Angus Wilson once more notes in his introduction to *The Portable Dickens*. The "betrayal" for Rawlins is of the Pip who "is perfectly, selfishly intact at the novel's beginning." Noting the sad fact that the poetic Pip "is survived by a clerk," Rawlins argues that Dickens the dreamer, tormented by demons of his own childhood, must deny Pip the peace of dreaming. Although I think Rawlins makes great sense of the novel by seeing how Pip's pursuit of goodness compromises his opportunity "to love grandly . . . to aspire, . . . to dream," I am hesitant to agree that when Pip looks over the rubble of his life and concludes that he should have been a Joe *we* necessarily "know better" and assume "Pip is destined to be Dickens." That Dickens was to be, even for a time, Pip is evident; that the partiality, the "pip," if we will, was the totality we know as Dickens is less certain.

In his article surveying Dickens' career and reputation, George Ford remarks that despite its popularity *A Tale of Two Cities* has never received much serious critical attention. With focus on Dickens and Carlyle and using *A Tale of Two Cities* as its book for study, the 1982 Santa Cruz Dickens Project produced a series of papers that appear in the twelfth volume of the *Dickens Studies Annual*. Several of the essays are of exceptional quality.

Albert Hutter, with nods both to Derrida and his California colleagues, leads off the volume with "The Novelist as Resurrectionist: Dickens and the Dilemma of Death." Hutter thoroughly documents the nineteenth-century cultural fascination both with death and its simultaneous denial, and following Derrida he argues that novelists, like historians and archeologists, "disinter, unlock, and decode what has deliberately been buried and enclosed." Obviously, as we know from the stress on secrecy in the eleventh volume of the *Annual*, the novelist frequently interred, locked, and coded even as he resurrected. This is, by definition, grim business, and through recognition of Jerry Cruncher as a more disturbing than comic figure, Hutter shows Dickens developing a dark vision. Such an image opposes the more obviously religious one of Carton; we have him as resurrection and life, but we also have the resurrection man as nihilistic.

The question of Dickens' self-consciousness is a frequent concern of contemporary criticism; does he subtly incorporate analogues for novelistic narration? Catherine Gallagher, in "The Duplicity of Doubling in *A Tale of Two Cities*," sees the doubling as more deceptive than revelatory, but she tries to go beyond text "to investigate the separate but competing social functions of the novel and the phenomena it takes as its dark doubles." As do Hutter and several other writers on *A Tale of Two Cities*, she therefore considers the phenomena of English public executions, the crime of resurrectionism, and the French Revolution itself. The fiction, and subsequently the further remove of Dickens' readings, becomes an act of appropriation and displacement of actual events, and this process for Gallagher is an ultimate triumph of the novelistic. Michael Goldberg more precisely ties the novel to actual history in an essay arguing the importance of the Revolution of 1848 to Dickens' thinking, and Elliot Gilbert in " 'To Awake from History': Carlyle, Thackeray, and *A Tale of Two Cities*" contextualizes Dickens amid the interest of his contemporaries in history, a recognition at once historical and anti-historical because it grants an instructive ideal but also fears the dry-as-dust imprisonment of history. Complementing but more theoretically, Chris R. Vanden Bossche's "Prophetic Closure and Disclosing Narrative: *The French Revolution* and *A Tale of Two Cities*" acknowledges the problematic nature of prophecy in both works.

Rounding out the *DSA* essays on *A Tale of Two Cities* are several which in differing ways examine Dickens' (and frequently Carlyle's) use of the picturesque, the theoretical, and dramatic. Richard Dunn's "A Tale For Two Dramatists" describes the writers' distinctions between drama as artifice and as heroic spectacle; Murray Baumgarten's "Writing the Revolution" points to "a dreamlike ambience, [in which] narrator and reader find themselves sympathizing with the revolutionary actors at the same time that they are revolted by their excesses." Michael Timko's "Splendid Impressions and Picturesque Means: Dickens, Carlyle, and the French Revolution," picks up on Dickens' stated desire to add to Carlyle's account an accomplishment, says

Timko, that clearly stresses the positive sides of the Carlylean message. One way in which this happens is through rhetorical transcendence of the revolution's chaos, as Carol MacKay argues in "The Rhetoric of Soliloquy in *The French Revolution* and *A Tale of Two Cities*."

In addition to the attention given *A Tale of Two Cities* in volume 12 of the *Annual*, James E. Marlow focuses on that novel in "English Cannibalism: Dickens After 1859." Marlow shows that for Dickens in 1859 cannibalism was not simply a metaphor for the savagery of the French Revolution but a sign of contemporary spiritual emptiness which had complex causes. Marlow therefore sees *A Tale of Two Cities* presenting "physical and public forms of hunger and aggression," *Great Expectations* portraying "their spiritual and private forms," and *Our Mutual Friend* and *Edwin Drood* concentrating "on the psychological divisions which generate forms of cannibalistic behavior." Whether, as Marlow suggests, Dickens was in 1859 exploring cannibalism *per se* (an interest stimulated by the writing of Douglas Jerrold and by public attention given to cannibalism during the doomed Franklin Expedition), Marlow is persuasive in demonstrating Dickens' dread of cannibalism as the symbol of a self-serving society. As Marlow says, "against the psychological and social forces which combined to create English cannibalism, Dickens opposed all the comedy, satire, sentiment, and rhetorical mastery that his great imagination and experience could muster."

A Tale of Two Cities is also the focal point for a short section of Harry E. Shaw's *The Forms of Historical Fiction*. Describing the various forms which often coexist in historical fictions, Shaw finds Dickens using the historical material to enforce a pacifying pastoral through the Manette story. This seems most evident in the "prophetic" final passage, and Stone's is one of the more complete accounts of the novel's ending. The contrary force of the drama— the vivifying energy of the revolution's violence—adds the necessary formal counterbalance for the book to function "as an incantation that raises the specter of revolution and then dispels it."

Although the bulk of the Dickens studies in *DSA* volume 12 come from the California conference, several others concern different topics, and one, Robert Kiely's "Plotting and Scheming: The Design of Design in *Our Mutual Friend*," is particularly noteworthy. Edwin Eigner, in "Charles Darnay and Revolutionary Identity" (to a considerable extent a continuation of his volume 11 study "The Absent Clown in *Great Expectations*"), argues the connection between the fictional structures and Victorian pantomime. Readers intrigued by Hutter's volume 11 discussion of fragmentation and dismemberment should be interested in the attention Kiely gives to the incessant plotting by characters and novelist. Rather than refute Hutter's recognition of the nearness of chaos, Kiely substantiates it by reminding us that "the need to author one's own designs is associated with the most universal and fundamental human instinct, the urge to live."

DICKENS AND WOMEN

Michael Slater's long awaited book, *Dickens and Women*, Phyllis Rose's chapter on the Dickenses in *Parallel Lives*, and the feminist reading of Dickens by Barickman, MacDonald, and Stark in *Corrupt Relations* do much to fill a great gap of serious attention to these subjects. The Dickens we find in all three works is more similar than are their estimations of his achievement, and reassessment of what Dickens presented through his women characters and what positions he held on the woman question are certain to continue.

Slater begins with study of Dickens' experience with women, tracing origins for and complexities of his attitudes and beliefs concerning them. The second part of Slater's book surveys women in the fiction, and the final section summarizes Dickens' comments on women, connecting his with the Victorian womanly idea. Throughout Slater writes with grace and moves easily, perhaps too easily for some, between Dickens' life and work. But he takes care to separate his own and other people's speculations from the facts.

The first two-thirds of Slater's book concerns the various women in Dickens' life—his mother, sister, early loves, sisters-in-law, wife, daughters, and Ellen Ternan. Here meticulous research is evident, and in telling stories familiar to many Dickensians Slater weighs the available evidence, makes a number of reassessments, and recognizes developing threads of emotional experience that not only connect various and often multiple prototypes to women characters but also form a mosaic of Dickens' conception of women and of male-female relationships. For example, most readers have followed the Dickens biographers in associating features of Mrs. Nickleby and Mrs. Micawber with Dickens' mother, Elizabeth. Slater reminds us that Mrs. Nickleby is a particularly harsh caricature and Mrs. Micawber is a more complicated and more distanced view by the child David "re-enacting his author's childhood sufferings"—by Dickens rewriting the role his mother played during the blacking-factory time.

Just as in his fiction concepts of mother-wife-sister-child interrelate in characterizations of women, so did various simultaneous relationships complicate Dickens' emotional life. The cumulative experience, well documented and powerfully described by Slater, is of Dickens confirming his views more than changing them, except in the confused self-justifications at the time of his separation from Catherine. But even then we see Dickens transferring to his wife many of the inalterable views he had held about his mother. Here the deftness of Slater's writing and the extensiveness of his research serve well. Describing the absence of confidences in Dickens' letters to Catherine, Slater cites as an exception a letter admonishing Catherine to read Dr. Johnson's *Life of Savage* attentively. Whether he expected her to receive Savage's as a version of his own story or as maternal conduct to avoid is less the point than, as Slater realizes, Dickens' response to Johnson's account of "an unnatural mother and also debtors' prisons." As Slater points out earlier, Dickens' interest in Savage pertains also to his feelings about his mother.

Slater gives chapters to often neglected relationships in Dickens' life (such as with his sister Fanny and his childhood sweetheart Lucy Stroughill), and in presenting the account of Dickens' frustrated courtship of Maria Beadnell Slater sets straight various details. But his extensive discussions of Mary Hogarth and Catherine Dickens necessarily pertain to nearly all of Dickens' other relationships with women. Mary, Slater observes, was an ideal sister figure, especially in memory after he had lost his actual sister. Recently discovered letters of Mary's substantiate Dickens' estimation of her as an exceptional person. The fictional representation most like her, says Slater, was not the often-cited Little Nell but Rose Maylie, and Agnes Wickfield was the novelist's subsequent attempt to base a heroine on the idealized Mary.

Slater's two chapters on Catherine Dickens document his opinion that modern biographers, through sympathy to Dickens and the lack of much concrete information about Catherine, have been too hard on Mrs. Dickens. Slater can find no seeds of later trouble during Dickens' courtship and early years with Catherine, although he notes an egocentric Quilpishness in some of Dickens' conduct. But, before Dickens' mid-1850s charge concerning Catherine's "lassitude of character," there is no documentary evidence of his holding an ill opinion of her. Slater hesitates to accept the tradition of Catherine's domestic incompetence, for he reminds us that she has little opportunity to stand forward as competent or incompetent in the face of Dickens' "domestic masterfulness." Slater goes so far as to suggest that Dickens' conception of Agnes came as a tribute to the actual Catherine as well as to the idealized Mary Hogarth. Catherine, then, was neither a childish Dora unrelieved by early death nor the dolt Dickens declared her in the anger surrounding the separation.

Slater presents a fuller account than most who comment on the separation.

Much occurred in the mid-1850s to darken Dickens' optimism, and Slater thinks the marital unhappiness may have been as much symptom as cause of his "basically disturbed state." There is no doubt, however, that as a much disturbed man he severely misrepresented Catherine's character. Although Slater does not attempt much psychological analysis he suggests that Dickens had to regard his wife as an inadequate mother "so that he could the more freely pity himself in the eyes of his own children," thus re-enacting in them "his own childhood loss of mother-love." This seems to be a reasonable observation, for certainly Dickens' revulsion to Catherine builds upon his earlier revulsion for his mother; both women in his view had betrayed him emotionally. Slater stands with Katey Dickens' mixed regard for her father, and given his defense of Catherine it is surprising to find him as protective of her husband as he is when he speaks of Dickens' "curious, almost objective appreciation of his own uniqueness." Such self-congratulation by Dickens under the proper circumstances might have led him to some generosity toward Catherine, but clearly he remained blind to anything he had had in common with her before the break in their relationship.

In discussing Catherine, Slater downplays the often repeated story of the separation precipitated by her receipt of a gift intended for Ellen Ternan, and Slater's chapter on Ellen reminds us of the lack of evidence concerning her relationship with Dickens. (Interestingly, Ford in his survey of Dickens' life and Wilson in his biographical introduction both accept the likelihood of Ellen as Dickens' mistress, and both acknowledge Slater's assistance with their work.) But I think the point is not arguments over the precise nature of the relationship, or even over the possibility of progeny. What matters now is the impact of Ellen on Dickens' work. Slater notes that characters in the novels that we most readily associate with her are actually "developments or modifications" of types Dickens had begun to explore long before she entered his life. The genuine impact Slater grants is that from 1858 she became a major focus of his emotional life, and that we should recognize her influence on Dickens' portrayal of love-passions in later *male* protagonists.

Part II, "The Women of the Novels," well complements and does not unnecessarily duplicate the more biographical Slater's Part I. The discussion of women in the key period from *Dombey and Son* through *Little Dorrit* is one of Slater's best. Three Dickens novels of this period center on heroines, and in all of them Dickens presents passionate and suffering women who reflect on their predicaments. Contrasted with the earlier novels in which, with few exceptions such as Nancy, the view of women is that of traditional masculine attitudes, Dickens in the 1840s engaged his imagination more deeply with the nature and social role of women. This development coincides with his changing actual relationships as son, brother, brother-in-law, father, and husband during this time, but Slater points out that although Dickens was preoccupied with women who often were injured or frustrated, he ventured no real condemnation of the prevailing patriarchy. Women as heroic rather than as long suffering or insufferable seldom stand forth in Dickens, but Slater cites Betsey Trotwood (to me a most mannish woman) as his finest example of the former. As in his earlier discussion of the emotional impact of Ellen Ternan on Dickens, Slater concludes Part II with attention to Dickens' shifting interest in men as passionate lovers in his final four novels.

The third part of this book covers, in *Bleak House* phrase, "a multitude of sins" in Dickens' and his age's views of women. Though often criticized for his particular varieties of patronizing (those little women, darling Doras, shrews and termagants, dawdling Mrs. Micawbers, melodramatic lost souls), Dickens for Slater was more conventional than idiosyncratic in his views. He upheld notions of essential differences between the sexes, glorified woman as a potential angel-savior, but saw women's as a primarily domestic role. He did have high regard for some women writers—Martineau, George Eliot, Mrs. Gaskell (he did not read or take seriously the Brontës)—but he portrayed very few women capable of effective inspiration and guidance either through professional activity or through personal relationships. (Here it is helpful to supplement Slater with Beverly B. Cook's "Mrs. Jellyby," an account of and excerpts from an 1854 American lecture which appropriated Dickens' satire as total opposition to ideas of women's movement.)

Slater has a fine discussion of Dickens' views of prostitutes and of his practical efforts to reclaim them, itself remarkable to me in light of what Slater shows to have been Dickens' nervousness over any manifestations of aggressive female passions. But throughout his life and fiction, Dickens held most firmly the idea of natural sisterhood, epitomized by Dora-Agnes. Unapologetically, Slater ends "for better or worse" with Agnes expressing "not everything he knew or felt or understood about women but everything he believed female nature, at its finest and purest, to be."

In *Parallel Lives* (her Dickens chapter also appeared in *Yale Review*) Phyllis Rose has little new to say about the Catherine Hogarth-Charles Dickens relationship, but her consideration of it with four other well-known Victorian domestic histories provides a number of opportunities to consider not only the literary and political dimensions of these lives. The political interest arises from Rose's regard for marriage as the "primary political experience in which most of us engage as adults." Compared with the fullness of Slater's study,

Rose's presentation of the Catherine-Charles relationship remains sketchy. Granted, without having the primary materials about Catherine that she had about Jane Carlyle and other wives in her study, Rose has to speculate about Catherine's feelings as both she and her family increased in size. While we can grant that Dickens' disgust with Catherine may seem "unjustified by anything she was," we surely cannot so readily agree with Rose's assumptions that Catherine thought herself the same person Dickens had fallen in love with and "did not know why that no longer satisfied him."

Rose stresses Dickens' efforts in *The Frozen Deep* (1857) to project his marital difficulties. Here, as in *A Tale of Two Cities* and *Our Mutual Friend*, she finds Dickens "providing a structure for emotions and impulses obscurely felt." By the time he came to his final and unfinished work, Dickens had become able to yoke the contrary instincts of self-sacrifice and self-indulgence in a single character. Impressive as she finds this artistic development, Rose finds nothing inspirational in Dickens' emotional development, which she regards as a story of survival.

To read Rose on the Dickenses should encourage readers to turn to Slater for fuller discussions of the literary consequences of Dickens' domestic turmoil. Rose notes that Dickens had little inkling that his dissatisfactions might have been normal, or at least shared by others to some extent. As Rose acutely remarks, "it is partly the source of his greatness as a writer—though the source, too, of whatever smallness one may see in him as a moral being—that he could feel his own life so intensely and project his imagination so powerfully onto the rest of life that he seemed to be living in a world with only one real person in it, himself. He could be kind and genial to the rest, but they remained supporting players." This does much to complement Slater's mention of Dickens' awareness of his uniqueness.

Rose's book is refreshing in its view of the Dickenses, Carlyles, Mills, Ruskins, and Leweses precisely because Rose resists the scholar's argumentative urgency and yet does not often settle for the superficiality of popular biographers. Granted, the feminist perspective leads her to speculate about the unstated views of Catherine Dickens, but it does not keep her from understanding the evident paradoxes of Dickens' own parallel lives. Manipulative mesmerist, paterfamilias, dissatisfied melodramatist—these are the headings under which Rose puts Dickens as his marriage becomes the critical event of his creative years. That event, like most in his life, was one he both suffered and created, a failure inseparable from his many successes.

Compared to the readability of both Slater and Rose, Richard Barickman, Susan MacDonald, and Myra Stark produce a book that could be improved by relaxing the urgency of its tri-authored thesis that major male writers persisted extensively in the conflicts of sexual values pervading their culture. *Corrupt Relations* is an ambitious work, challenging familiar dismissals of these male writers as uninvolved in the woman question except as reactionary satirists. The authors contend that the male novelists presented sexuality as "a complex of desires, attitudes, roles, and norms that is virtually coextensive with all social life." But as members of the prevailing patriarchy, these novelists participated in the conflict of sexual values and therefore present the tensions with more intensity than we might suppose. Barickman, MacDonald, and Stark do not argue that these writers reached many resolutions or transcendences of divided impulses concerning sexual relations, but they find a number of ways by which they think the novelists transformed their culture's contradictions into principles of fictional creation. The intriguing final chapter, "Toward Better Relations," summarizes their readings of the male novelists and calls for more methodical "radical comparativism" between men's and women's writing. Concentrating on four male novelists, they find a corruption in the Victorian "sexual system": the dialectic of the novels reveals deforming dependency of female roles and deforming authority of male roles (a not surprising finding). To define this as a centrist feminist perspective rather than to castigate the novelists for shortsightedness allows these critics to credit Dickens, Thackeray, Collins, and Trollope with exploring "the interiority of the whole system, the precondition and constant modifier of conscious life."

The chapter on Dickens combines general observations about his presentation of women and closer readings of several major characters and of *Martin Chuzzlewit* as "an assault on the patriarchal sexual system." The authors argue that "Dickens's special preoccupation, his most profound insight, concerns the multitude of ways in which corrupt patriarchal values have infiltrated family relations," and it is their sense that institutional corruption in Dickens' novels "always cloaks itself in some version of paternalism." (Arthur A. Adrian's *Dickens and the Parent-Child Relationship*, 1984, complements this argument by stressing parent-child relationships as socio-political metaphors.)

Much that the authors point to in support of their reading is familiar. Whatever our conclusions, most of us recognize the restrictive roles of Dickens' women, the absence of many happy families, the many surrogate parents, the comic and not-so-comic patriarchs. The father's tyranny looms large in Dickens' fictional world, but as Michael Slater shows, so too did the particular sense Dickens had of the mother profoundly affect his view of male-female relationships. But in discussing Mrs. Joe Gargery as grotesquely fusing traditional features of mothers and fathers, these critics recognize " a credible psychological portrait of an enraged and resentful woman." As they remark, "she is the Victorian angel-idea turned inside out." The angel-idea to which they give sustained attention is Esther Summerson, a character they regard as Dickens' rather reluctant probing of "what underlay the ideal of Right Womanhood." We may well agree that in *Bleak House* the heroine-narrator reveals the crippling strain of living up to stereotypes, but the idealization of Esther the character (and for that matter of Agnes before her) remains troublesome.

Esther, like sympathetic women in later novels, counterbalances a number of female types, joined in what this study sees as "an analogical pattern," made psychologically complex because Esther internalizes "the standards of society." This development of the more complex heroine, accompanied by repeated instances of abusive patriarchy (both self-victimizing as in William Dorrit and vicious as in Bounderby), obviously may subvert "the narrator's moral and sentimental pronouncements." But I wonder if this necessarily means that the later Dickens, taken together, "presses, instantly, though only implicitly, for a remaking of the whole sexual system."

The reading of *Martin Chuzzlewit*, on the other hand, as an indictment of the "crippling distortions of sexual and familial roles by the oppressive patriarchy," is wholly convincing. The authors find many parodic figures and argue persuasively for Sairey Gamp as a satirist, "a creator who rivals her author and opposes the sexual values of his overt narrative structure—the only woman in Dickens' novels who has this double distinction.

At this point in review essays it is customary to summarize the year's work, trample again what has been necessary to step on and sing again the glories of the praiseworthy achievements, hoping to have sufficient energy and intelligence to make prophetic statements about what should now follow. I am disinclined to summarize, prophesy, or even grumble very much, and conclude simply by remarking that 1983 saw continuing fine work on Dickens by both established and less-well-known people, brought long-needed examination of Dickens and women, and (unsurprisingly, considering its contexts and volume) saw work of varied quality and usefulness. Obviously, Dickens remains before us an intriguing subject, a figure to be reckoned with when examining Victorian literature, and a major element in histories and theories of the novel. I would be remiss to close without mention of activities that now annually precipitate any year's published Dickens studies—the meetings of the Dickens Society at the MLA convention and the University of California programs. More than ever, Dickensians are talking as well as writing to one another. The Dickens Society has long encouraged fresh perspectives and work by younger scholars, awarding the Robert B. Partlow, Jr. prize each year for the best essay by someone who has not previously published work on Dickens. And by its unique format the California Dickens project brings together distinguished senior faculty, advanced graduate students, and a cross-section of other teachers and the general public. These gatherings, along with the continuing research and publication, well assure continuing scholarly interest in Dickens, and I say this as reporter, not prophet.

Works Mentioned

Because of frequency of appearance, the following journals are listed by abbreviation: *Dickens Studies Annual: Essays on Victorian Fiction (DSA)*; *Dickens Studies Newsletter (DSN)*; *Nineteenth-Century Fiction (NCF)*; *SEL: Studies in English Literature (SEL)*.

Anastaplo, George. "Charles Dickens." In *The Artist as Thinker from Shakespeare to Joyce*. Athens, Ohio: Swallow/ Ohio University Press, 1983.

Barickman, Richard, Susan McDonald, and Myra Stark. *Corrupt Relations: Dickens, Thackeray, Trollope, Collins and the Victorian Sexual System*. New York: Columbia University Press, 1982.

Boheemen-Saff, Christine van. "'The Universe Makes An Indifferent Parent': *Bleak House* and the Victorian Family Romance." In *Interpreting Lucan*. Joseph H. Smith and William Kerrigan, eds. New Haven, Conn.: Yale University Press, 1983. 225–258.

Cohn, Alan M., and K. K. Collins. "The Dickens Checklist." *DSN*, 14 (March-December, 1983), 28–32, 75–79, 123–127, 162–164.

Collins, Philip. "Charles Dickens." In *Makers of Nineteenth Century Culture 1800–1914*. Justin Wintle, ed. London: Routledge & Kegan Paul, 1983. 163–166.

Cook, Beverly B. "Lecturing on Woman's Place: 'Mrs. Jellyby' in Wisconsin." *Signs*, 9 (Winter, 1983), 361–376.

Davies, James A. *John Forster*. Totowa, N. J.: Barnes and Noble, 1983.

Dickens, Charles. *Oliver Twist*. Kathleen Tillotson, ed. New York: Oxford University Press, 1982.

———. *Dombey and Son*. Alan Horsman, ed. New York: Oxford University Press, 1982.

———. *Little Dorrit*. Harvey Peter Sucksmith, ed. New York: Oxford University Press, 1982.

————. *The Mystery of Edwin Drood*. Margaret Cardwell, ed. New York: Oxford University Press, 1982.

————. *The Portable Dickens*. Angus Wilson, ed. New York: Viking Penguin, 1983.

Ermarth, Elizabeth Deeds. "Mutual Friendship and the Identity of Things in Dickens." In *Realism and Consensus in the English Novel*. Princeton, N. J.: Princeton University Press, 1983.

Fleishman, Avrom. "*David Copperfield*: Experiments in Autobiography." In *Figures of Autobiography: The Language of Self-Writing in Victorian and Modern England*. Berkeley: University of California Press, 1983.

Ford, George. "Charles Dickens." In *English Novelists Before 1885*. Ira B. Nadel and William F. Fredeman, eds. Detroit: Bruccoli Clark/ Gale Research, 1983. 89–124.

Giddings, Robert, ed. *The Changing World of Charles Dickens*. New York: Barnes and Noble, 1983. (Includes: Robert Giddings, "Introduction"; David Paroissien, "Literature's 'Eternal Duties': Dickens's Professional Creed"; Thomas J. Rice, "The Politics of *Barnaby Rudge*"; David Craig, "The Crowd in Dickens"; Roger Fowler, "Polyphony and Problematic in *Hard Times*"; David Ponting, "Charles Dickens: The Solo Performer"; David Edgar, "Adapting *Nickleby*"; Mike Poole, "Dickens and Film: 101 Uses of a Dead Author"; David Trotter, "Circulation, Interchange, Stoppage: Dickens and Social Progress"; Bert G. Hornback, "The Other Portion of *Bleak House*"; Loralee MacPike, "Dickens and Dostoyevsky: The Technique of Reverse Influence"; Jerome Meckier, "Hidden Rivalries in Victorian Fiction: The Case of the Two Esthers.")

Hewett, Edward W., and W. F. Axton. *Convivial Dickens: The Drinks of Dickens and His Times*. Athens, Ohio: Ohio University Press, 1983.

Hotchman, Baruch. "Deadlocked Maternity: The Subtext of *Bleak House* and Dickens's Last Novels." *The Test of Character: From the Victorian Novel to the Modern*. Rutherford, N. J.: Fairleigh Dickinson University Press, 1983.

Howe, Irving. "*Oliver Twist*: The Spell of Fagin." *New Republic* (June 20, 1983), 27–32.

Johnson, Wendell Stacy, ed. *Charles Dickens: New Perspectives*. Englewood Cliffs: Prentice-Hall, 1982. (Includes: Wendell Stacy Johnson, "Introduction"; Robert A. Colby, "*Oliver Twist*: The Fortunate Foundling"; Richard Barickman, "The Subversive Methods of Dickens' Early Fiction: *Martin Chuzzlewit*"; Harry Stone, "The Novel as Fairy Tale: Dickens' *Dombey and Son*"; Gordon D. Hirsch, "A Psychoanalytic Rereading of *David Copperfield*"; Alex Zwerdling, "Esther Summerson Rehabilitated"; Gerald Coniff, " 'The Prison of This Lower World' "; Dianne F. Sadoff, "Storytelling and the Figure of the Father in *Little Dorrit*"; Ruth M. Vande Kieft, "Patterns of Communication in *Great Expectations*"; George Levine, "Communication in *Great Expectations*"; John M. Robson, "*Our Mutual Friend*: A Rhetorical Approach to the first Number"; Edgar Johnson, "The Dying and Undying Voice.")

Kucich, John. "Repression and Representation: Dickens's General Economy." *NCF*, 38 (June, 1983), 62–77.

Larson, Janet L. "The Battle of Biblical Books in Esther's Narrative." *NCF*, 38 (September, 1983), 131–160.

Lerner, Laurence. *The Literary Imagination: Essays on Literature and Society.* New York: Barnes and Noble, 1983.

Marlow, James E. "English Cannibalism: Dickens After 1859." *SEL*, 23 (Autumn, 1983), 647–666.

McMaster, Juliet. "Visual Design in *Pickwick Papers.*" *SEL*, 23 (Autumn, 1983), 595–614.

Meckier, Jerome. "Double Vision Versus Double Logic." *DSN*, 14 (March, June, 1983), 14–21, 41–47.

Miller, David A. "Discipline in Different Voices: Bureaucracy, Police, Family, and *Bleak House.*" *Representations*, 1 (February, 1983), 59–89.

Price, Martin. "Dickens: Selves and Systems." *Forms of Life: Character and Moral Imagination in the Novel.* New Haven, Conn.: Yale University Press, 1983.

Rawlins, Jack P. "Great Expiations: Dickens and the Betrayal of the Child." *SEL*, 23 (Autumn, 1983), 667–684.

Rose, Phyllis. *Parallel Lives: Five Victorian Marriages.* New York: Alfred A. Knopf, 1983.

Shaw, Harry E. "*A Tale of Two Cities.*" In *The Forms of Historical Fiction: Sir Walter Scott and His Successors.* Ithaca, N. Y.: Cornell University Press, 1983.

Slater, Michael. *Dickens and Women.* Stanford, Calif.: Stanford University Press, 1983.

Timko, Michael, Fred Kaplan, Edward Guiliano, eds. *Dickens Studies Annual: Essays on Victorian Fiction.* Vol. 11. New York: AMS Press, 1983. (Includes: Robert Newsom, "The Hero's Shame"; Alexander Welsh, "Blackmail Studies in *Martin Chuzzlewit* and *Bleak House*"; Robert Tracy, "Reading Dickens' Writing"; Murray Baumgarten, "Calligraphy and Code: Writing in *Great Expectations*"; John O. Jordan, "The Medium of *Great Expectations*"; Elliot L. Gilbert, "'In Primal Sympathy': *Great Expectations* and the Secret Life"; Edwin M. Eigner, "The Absent Clown in *Great Expectations*"; Albert D. Hutter, "Dismemberment and Articulation in *Our Mutual Friend*"; Garrett Stewart, "The Secret Life of Death in Dickens"; Leonard F. Manheim, "Dickens and Psychoanalysis: A Memoir.")

Timko, Michael, Fred Kaplan, Edward Guiliano, eds. *Dickens Studies Annual: Essays on Victorian Fiction.* Vol. 12. New York: AMS Press, 1983. (Includes: Albert D. Hutter, "The Novelist as Resurrectionist: Dickens and the Dilemma of Death"; Burton M. Wheeler, "The Text and Plan of *Oliver Twist*"; Patrick J. Creevy, "In Time and Out: The Tempo of Life in *Bleak House*"; H. Philip Bolton, "*Bleak House* and the Playhouse"; Richard J. Dunn, "A Tale for Two Dramatists"; Catherine Gallagher, "The Duplicity of Doubling in *A Tale of Two Cities*"; Edwin M. Eigner, "Charles Darnay and Revolutionary Identity"; Murray Baumgarten, "Writing the Revolution"; Michael Timko, "Splendid Impressions and Picturesque Means: Dickens, Carlyle, and *The French Revolution*"; Carol

Hanbery Mackay, "The Rhetoric of Soliloquy in *The French Revolution* and *A Tale of Two Cities*"; Chris R. Vanden Bossche, "Prophetic Closure and Disclosing Narrative: *The French Revolution* and *A Tale of Two Cities*"; Michael Goldberg, "Carlyle, Dickens, and the Revolution of 1848"; Branwen Bailey Pratt, "Carlyle and Dickens: Heroes and Hero-Worshippers"; Elliot L. Gilbert, "'To Awake from History': Carlyle, Thackeray, and *A Tale of Two Cities*"; Robert Kiely, "Plotting and Scheming: The Design of Design in *Our Mutual Friend*.")

Index

Contents of Previous Volumes

Volume 4 (1975)

Volume 5 (1976)

The Intelligibility of Madness in *Our Mutual Friend* and
   The Mystery of Edwin Drood
   LAWRENCE FRANK

Volume 8 (1980)

Volume 9 (1981)

Volume 13 (1984)